United States Oil Policy, 1890–1964

United States Oil Policy 1890-1964

Business and Government in Twentieth Century America

Gerald D. Nash

University of Pittsburgh Press

Preface

FUTURE HISTORIANS seeking to record salient changes in twentieth-century America may well wish to focus on significant shifts in the kind of problems with which Americans were confronted during this period. For almost a century after the Civil War one of the central issues of public policy was the question of the government's relation to the economy. The New Nationalism, the New Freedom, the New Deal, the Fair Deal, John F. Kennedy's New Frontier, and even the Great Society were all concerned with this great theme. Yet, as the United States entered the last half of the twentieth century, this once momentous problem seemed to retreat into the background, although politicians as late as 1964 still engaged in abstract debates about government intervention as opposed to laissez-faire. The younger generation of Americans, however, became increasingly concerned with crises in international relations and nuclear warfare, with urban development, and with Negro rights. After 1964 these problems appeared to be moving to the center of the stage in public discussion. As far as the government's relation to the economy was concerned, a growing consensus on this issue seemed to take it out of the realm of the bitter controversy that had surrounded it during the previous generation.

With this changing emphasis perhaps the time is peculiarly apt for a backward glance at the road that Americans have traveled during the last seventy-five years in delimiting the relationships between their political institutions and the economy. That this question no longer aroused such heated passionate debates in 1964 as in 1890 was largely due to the growth of a gradual consensus on the need for business-government cooperation. Although formulated by scores of individuals and groups, many of the major themes of that growing consensus were first articulated by Theodore Roosevelt in his doctrine of the New Nationalism during the Progressive Era. Roosevelt's catchy phrasing clearly delineated the outstanding features of the government's functions in American economic life over the next sixty years. If Roosevelt's vision of the New Nationalism was vague, succeeding generations filled in the details for the broad outlines that he sketched. In their efforts to provide institutional mechanisms to facilitate business-government cooperation envisaged by the New Nationalism, Roosevelt's successors frequently made substantive changes in the doctrine themselves. Yet, the relationship of the government to the economy under Wilson's New Freedom, in the Age of Normalcy of Harding-Coolidge-Hoover, during Franklin D. Roosevelt's New Deal and Harry Truman's Fair Deal, under Dwight Eisenhower's Modern Republicanism and John F. Kennedy's New Frontier, and in Lyndon B. Johnson's Great Society followed the paths broadly hewn out by Theodore Roosevelt.

A central theme of this consensus as emphasized by Roosevelt was the need for government to cooperate with business and to assume the function of an arbiter in the new, highly industrialized society that was emerging in America. Until the opening of the century the national government had confined itself to a relatively passive role as the promoter or regulator of economic life. In the years thereafter its responsibilities came to include active direction of many phases in the conduct of private economic enterprise. This shift in the scope of governmental action did not occur suddenly, but was developed slowly over the course of at least sixty years. By the end of that period it became clear that the United States had undergone a silent revolution in adjusting its eighteenth-century political institutions to the exigencies of twentieth-century industrialism. The consensus that was so developed proved sufficiently resilient to withstand the challenges of socialism, fascism, and communism. Ideological struggles that accompanied the adjustment of political institutions to industrialism in other portions of the world were not to be duplicated in the United States. Americans had developed a unique, intricate structure of cooperative relationships between the government and an economy characterized by a mixture of private and public enterprise. Within a framework of inherited values, they fashioned a role for the government as the arbiter of the national economy.

The prime purpose of this study is to analyze and describe the growth of cooperation as a prime characteristic of public policy in the petroleum industry. A focus on one particular industry is desirable, if only because of the vast dimensions of the changes affecting the government's role in the economy. Moreover, since petroleum ranked consistently as one of the nation's five leading industries between 1890 and 1960, it provides a convenient looking glass through which to view shifting conceptions of the government's responsibilities regarding business. It is hoped that an investigation of the factors that shaped American oil policies during this era will illuminate similar trends in other industries.

I would not maintain by any means that cooperation is the only significant development in business-government relations during the twentieth century. But I do consider it sufficiently important to merit special consideration. Cooperation provides a useful perspective from which to appraise many public policies and public figures of this period. The Chief Executives during these years cannot be properly characterized as having been for or against business; rather, they were responding to particular problems emanating from structural changes in the American economy. Woodrow Wilson's prime contribution to business-government cooperation was the creation of an institutional framework to facilitate mutual collaboration. Calvin Coolidge was not a slavish servant of Big Business, but revealed much flexibility in experimenting with various ways to further cooperation between federal agencies and the oil industry. Herbert Hoover, on the other hand, despite his advocacy of cooperation in theory, failed to implement it in practice. The era of Franklin D. Roosevelt was significant not for bold innovation in U. S. oil policies but for the crystallization of compromise among competing groups. The postwar presidents—Truman, Eisenhower, and Kennedy—played a role as consolidators, for they added little in thought or deed to U. S. oil policy as it had developed between the wars. Cooperation in public policy thus arose out of far-reaching technological and economic changes that frequently overrode political considerations. The consequent consensus between government and business reflected an increasing bureaucratization of both private and public institutions, of corporations as well as federal and state agencies.

A word concerning the scope of this book is necessary. I have not sought to write an exhaustive history of American oil policies and to provide a detailed examination of its manifold aspects in great detail. My purpose is more modest. I have made a conscious effort to combine breadth and concentration in order to provide a balanced survey of American oil policies during the past seventy-five years. Unlike a previous fine study by John Ise, *The United States Oil Policy* (New Haven, 1926), I have avoided concentration on detailed incidents. Instead, I have attempted to provide an overview and to place specific problems within a broad context rather than to analyze them in depth. For example, the reader will not find an extended discussion of pipelines and pipeline problems, a subject on which Professor Arthur M. Johnson, an authority on this subject, has prepared detailed studies *(The Development of American Petroleum Pipelines: A Study in Private Enterprise and Public Policy, 1862–1906,* Ithaca, 1956, and *Petroleum Pipelines and Public Policy, 1906–1959,* Cambridge, 1967). Nor have I provided detailed, intensive analyses of specific economic problems plaguing the petroleum industry, for these have received the attention of many specialized monographs in recent years. My omissions will, I hope, raise questions and will point to problems that will encourage others to examine specific aspects of U. S. oil policy more fully and more deeply than I have been able to do in this broad sketch. My main objective has been to place in historical perspective the many changes that affected the developing consensus concerning needed cooperation between the government and the industry.

Since the major portions of this book are based on archival and manuscript materials I have incurred many debts and obligations. My thanks go to the courteous and efficient staff of the National Archives in Washington, D. C., and especially to Miss Jane F. Smith, who, as head of the Social and Economic Branch, made a great variety of materials available. Dr. Elizabeth Drewry, director of the Franklin D. Roosevelt Library in Hyde Park, New York, and her entire staff made special efforts to locate a great variety of relevant records. Dr. Philip C. Brooks, director of the Harry S. Truman Library in Independence, Missouri, provided material assistance not only in making available the Presidential papers but also in enabling me to secure access to restricted collections under his supervision. Dr. William D. Aeschbacher, former director of the Dwight D. Eisenhower Library in Abilene, Kansas, was kind to inform me of relevant materials in that depository before they were opened to the public. Dr. Rita R. Campbell of the Hoover Institution at Stanford University allowed me freedom to search that great institution's rich collection of hitherto unexploited manuscripts relating to Herbert Hoover. Rear Admiral Onnie Lattur, director of the Office of Oil and Gas in 1965, along with his staff, took time from his own busy schedule to peruse classified records pertaining to World War II, for the examination of which he then graciously gave me permission. Other institutions that made their resources available include the Manuscripts Division of the Library of Congress in Washington, D.C., the Library of the American Petroleum Institute in New York City, the Manuscripts Division of the University of Oklahoma Library, the Universities of Wyoming and New Mexico, the New York Public Library, and the Columbia University Libraries. The University of New Mexico granted aid to facilitate completion of the manuscript. To all of these individuals and institutions I express gratitude. For errors and imperfections I alone assume responsibility.

G.D.N.

Albuquerque, New Mexico
November 1, 1967

Contents

United States Oil Policy, 1890–1964

1 / Emergence of a New Industry and Public Policy, 1890–1917

THE ERA between 1890 and 1917 was one of the most crucial in the development of the government's relation to business in America. It was significant in witnessing the birth of a consensus that endowed the government with a major role as the arbiter or supervisor of major industries. Such a shift from more passive roles was directly related to important changes in the very structure of industry itself. In 1890 the oil business was still characterized by monopoly—starkly symbolized by Standard Oil. By 1917 Standard had lost its dominant position, however, and was beset by a host of new competitors. The structure of the industry was no longer primarily monopolistic but instead displayed tendencies toward oligopoly. The transformation was wrought by new petroleum discoveries, often made possible by striking new technological innovations, by the growth of additional great markets, and by bold business leadership.

Americans sought to accommodate public policy to these far-reaching changes. Until 1911 the prime thrust of federal and state laws on oil was negative—to prevent undue concentration of economic power. But thereafter the fervor of the antitrust movement subsided, as government officials became increasingly concerned with the regulation and supervision of a wide array of practices in the industry. Their interest was based on the fear of oil depletion, on the increasingly important function of petroleum in the nation's economy, and on the needs of the Navy. They turned public policy to problems with which industry representatives also were preoccupied. Instead of conflict between the government and the oil industry they tended to develop an increasing number of cooperative relationships that created a consensus concerning their respective roles.

This far-reaching transformation in the relationships between business and the government was caused in part by the changing structure of the petroleum industry at the opening of the twentieth century. The period witnessed a veritable Energy Revolution. If the years between 1815 and 1890 had been largely an age of steam, succeeding decades saw an important shift to electricity and to oil and gas as new major sources of the nation's power. Discovery of new sources of petroleum prompted this change and created new demands. To be sure, the oil industry had been expanding since the post–Civil War era. But after 1890 it was virtually transformed, as producers and refiners no longer concentrated largely on markets for kerosene but on meeting new demands for gasoline, fuel oil, and lubricants.[1]

Technological innovations and new markets, then, wrought far-reaching changes in the industry and created problems that led oilmen to seek a modification of their relationships with state and national governments. The maintenance of competition, stabilization of oil production, the rapid depletion of oil by waste, its imminent exhaustion, and the needs of national defense all seemed to spring full-blown from the tremendous increase in oil production after 1900. As individuals in the oil industry increasingly turned to state and federal officials for aid or guidance, they collaborated in the development of public policies to meet challenges posed by the new conditions. Reflecting the rise of a new, major industry beset by growing pains, U.S. oil policy between 1890 and 1917 came to embody maintenance of competition, conservation of oil resources, and safeguarding of military needs.

1. Changes in the oil industry are traced to Harold F. Williamson *et al.*, *The American Petroleum Industry* (2 vols., Evanston, 1959–1963), II *(Age of Energy)*, 167–205; Ralph W. Hidy and Muriel Hidy, *Pioneering in Big Business, 1882–1911* (New York, 1955), 372–493; Arthur M. Johnson, *The Development of American Petroleum Pipelines: A Study in Private Enterprise and Public Policy, 1862–1906* (Ithaca, 1956).

EXPANSION OF THE INDUSTRY

Improvements in petroleum technology exercised a profound influence on the industry. After 1859 engineers tapped hitherto hidden resources. Most of these major new discoveries were in the West. Thus, from their earlier oil center in the Appalachian region, oil producers after 1890 moved westward to the midcontinent field, the Gulf area, and to California. As late as 1899 the Appalachian oil fields supplied 93 percent of the nation's total oil production; by 1919 they accounted for less than 10 percent. Increasingly advanced technology also boosted the total amount of crude oil production, as did the growth of new markets. Development of internal combustion and diesel engines, in particular, led to an unprecedented demand for oil products. In less than a generation these changes transformed the petroleum industry.

Although explorations for oil had begun in the midcontinent area as early as 1858, the great surge of production did not come until the late nineteenth century. In 1894, the Standard Oil Company started serious exploration in Kansas, and also built a large refinery there at Neodesha. During the following decade prospectors undertook intensive drilling so that by 1905 the state's total annual production reached 6 million barrels. Oil finds in Kansas were sporadic and resulted in violent fluctuations in production from year to year.[2]

Oklahoma witnessed a similar pattern of ups and downs, although its most productive areas were not discovered until after 1904. Within the next ten years, developers found some of the state's richest fields, including Bartlesville, Glenn, Cushing, and Healdton. Together these made the midcontinent fields a major producing region. The Glenn Pool, discovered near Tulsa in December, 1905, proved to be one of the most prolific oil bonanzas of the century. Its crude products were especially well suited for emerging new markets for fuel oil and gasoline. Intensive explorations also led to strikes at Cushing (1912) and Healdton (1913), both major producing fields.[3]

2. Williamson *et al., American Petroleum Industry,* II, 21, 90–91; Hidy and Hidy, *Pioneering,* 393–402.

3. Carl Coke Rister, *Oil: Titan of the Southwest* (Norman, 1949), 80–94, 119–142, 231–269; John Ise, *The United States Oil Policy* (New Haven, 1926), 77–84; L. C. Snyder, *Petroleum and Natural Gas in Oklahoma* (Oklahoma City, 1913).

While the black wealth of the midcontinent field was being uncovered, other energetic oil prospectors moved into Texas and the Gulf region. In 1901 Anthony Lucas and Patillo Higgins struck Spindletop, one of the richest oil gushers in the world. Within half a year after its first discovery this well yielded more than 6 million barrels and whetted the expectations of other prospective investors. Spindletop inaugurated large-scale petroleum exploration throughout Texas and marked the beginning of an unprecendented boom. Rich oil bonanzas at Sour Lake, at Saratoga, at Humble, and elsewhere laid the basis for one of the state's major industries during the twentieth century. During this period oilmen in Louisiana uncovered the rich Jennings gusher, which added to the growing petroleum production of the Gulf region.[4]

Concurrently, the spurt in oil production of the midcontinent and Gulf regions was augmented by new oil discoveries in California. One of the founding fathers of the petroleum industry there, E. L. Doheny, drilled important wells in the Los Angeles area as early as 1892, and the state's total production grew steadily thereafter. By 1899, big strikes in the Bakersfield and Kern County area and in the Santa Barbara and Coalinga regions made California a leading oil-producing state. By 1919 it contributed 26.7 percent of the nation's total output.[5]

INCREASED DEMAND FOR OIL

As petroleum producers more than doubled their output between 1890 and 1917 they were fortunate, indeed, that technological advances were creating new markets for them. The percentage of the output of U.S. refineries absorbed by domestic consumers increased from 60 percent in 1899 to 85 percent twenty years later. This was due partly to increases of population (from 75 million in 1899 to 105 million in 1919) and to the accompanying rise in national income. But mainly the sevenfold rise in demand for oil products during this period resulted

4. Williamson *et al., American Petroleum Industry,* II, 19–20, 74–75; Ise, *United States Oil Policy,* 62–70; J. S. Spratt, *The Road to Spindletop: Economic Change in Texas, 1875–1901* (Dallas, 1955); Rister, *Oil: Titan of the Southwest,* 50–65, 219–230, 270–343.

5. Joe S. Bain, *The Economics of the Pacific Coast Petroleum Industry* (3 vols., Berkeley, 1944–1945), II, 2–60; Ise, *United States Oil Policy,* 85–92; Gerald D. Nash, *State Government and Economic Development* (Berkeley, 1964), 304, 308, 318–323.

from the perfection of diesel-powered ships and locomotives, automobiles, and oil heating equipment. Suddenly, oil was supplanting coal as one of the nation's leading energy resources.[6]

Especially striking was the great increase in the consumption of fuel oil. In 1899, only 12 million barrels were sold in the United States, but twenty years later demand had grown to 224 million barrels. Some of this supply was used for home heating, some was utilized to enrich gas produced from coal, and some was adapted to industrial operations such as smelting, iron and steel manufacture, and cement and brick production. Most fuel oil was used in rail and marine transportation, however. Few railroads powered their engines with fuel oil in 1899, but within two decades their conversion to diesel-burning locomotives increased fuel oil consumption more than tenfold. For railroads, oil had many advantages over coal. Not only did mechanical feeding eliminate the heavy labor of firing, but it allowed more complete combustion. Western railroads especially—far removed from coal mines—were among the first to switch to diesel fuel.

Marine Transportation

The magnitude of the shift was greatest in marine transportation, however. Greater convenience and lower cost were important factors in prompting shipping officials to make the change from coal to petroleum. By 1914 they had converted about 5 percent of the world's merchant fleet. The United States Navy Fuel Oil Board had recommended as early as 1904 that American war vessels convert to oil. Only ten years later Secretary of the Navy Josephus Daniels reported that all American battleships and destroyers were burning fuel; fuel oil consumption of the United States Navy rose from 360,000 barrels in 1912 to almost 6 million barrels in 1919. Together with about 44 million barrels consumed by the American merchant marine, these requirements accounted for about one-fifth of total fuel oil sales.

Automobiles

A large amount of crude petroleum eventually found its way into new automobiles as gasoline. In 1900 there were perhaps no more than 3,723 cars in the country. Within another decade annual auto produc-

6. U.S. Bureau of the Census, *Statistical Abstract* 1910 (Washington, 1913), 545–547; *Mines and Quarries* 1909 (Washington, 1913), 263–269, 279–286.

tion rose to 127,000 units and by 1919 it had increased tenfold. By the end of World War I improvements in self-starters, tires, and interchangeable parts made the automobile a family vehicle for the many rather than a luxury for a few. The tremendous change was reflected in vehicle registrations. From 8,000 in 1899 they rose to 7.6 million two decades later. This revolution had a profound impact upon the petroleum industry. Only about 6 million barrels of gasoline were sold in 1899 but almost 75 million barrels were sold in 1919.

Increasing use of automobiles and trucks also created an important new market for lubricants. Domestic demand for such products more than quintupled during the first two decades of the twentieth century. Furthermore, the purchase of large numbers of cars also generated a widespread demand for more and better roads. At the turn of the century there were only 125,000 miles of surfaced highways in the United States, but the pressures of motorists led to the construction of 225,000 additional miles within the next twenty years. This accelerated construction program increased the demand for asphalt, a significant byproduct in the refining of crude petroleum; in fact, production of asphalt increased thirtyfold in this period.[7]

INDUSTRY PROBLEMS

The dramatic expansion of markets for petroleum products between 1890 and 1917, together with important new discoveries of oil in Oklahoma, Texas, and California, virtually transformed the petroleum industry and gave it a major role in the new twentieth-century industrial complex that American businessmen were then creating. But great changes in business or politics are rarely wrought without some stress or strain. This is also true of the petroleum industry. As striking as its achievements were during these years, the transformation brought many new and difficult problems.

Monopoly

One problem that was frequently on the public's mind—and in newspaper headlines—was the alleged monopoly of the Standard Oil Com-

7. The above paragraphs are based on Williamson *et al.*, *American Petroleum Industry*, II, 167–170, 174–203; U.S. Bureau of the Census, *Statistical Abstract 1910* (Washington, 1913), 500–501, and *Mines and Quarries* 1909 (Washington, 1913), 263–269, 273–287, 301–316.

pany, and its supposed unfair business practices. While this problem preoccupied readers of Henry Demarest Lloyd and Ida Tarbell, industry spokesmen themselves after 1901 became increasingly concerned with growing competition in the oil trade and expressed a desire for stability. Indeed, overproduction and cutthroat competition created the specter of exhaustion and pointed to the need for conserving a precious natural resource. At a time when the United States was expanding overseas and was placing great reliance on its Navy for defense, the problem of maintaining sufficient oil reserves to satisfy military requirements attracted increasing attention from President Theodore Roosevelt, from military leaders, and from Congress. At the opening of this century, therefore, monopoly, conservation, and defense were becoming important issues in the formulation of national oil policy.

Seemingly the most pressing oil problem in 1900 was the domination of the industry by the Standard Oil Company. The charges against the combination were widely aired in the works of Henry Demarest Lloyd, Ida Tarbell, and (after 1903) in the more sober reports of the United States Bureau of Corporations.[8] Despite variations in emphasis, their collective criticism contained at least four complaints. Most vulnerable perhaps was Standard's practice of receiving rebates from railroads and other carriers. Indeed, Tarbell and many independent producers believed that this was a major factor in explaining Standard's monopolistic position. Later historians have found some substance in this charge. The Standard combination's discriminatory pricing policies, frequently used to secure competitive advantages, also came in for criticism. In addition, Standard's policy of suppressing competitors by use of bribery, mergers, or secretive means aroused anger.

Instability

Although it was not apparent to contemporaries, increasing instability, not monopoly, was becoming the major problem in the oil industry during this era. Standard was the major company in the field between 1890 and 1917, but it was, in fact, losing its dominant marketing position to important new competitors. Even before the United States Supreme Court issued the famous dissolution decree of 1911, Standard's

8. Hidy and Hidy, *Pioneering,* 642–663; Ida Tarbell, *History of the Standard Oil Company* (New York, 1904).

alleged monopoly was rapidly disintegrating as a result of fierce competition. Between 1900 and 1911 at least half a dozen new integrated oil firms entered the field, including the Pure Oil Company and corporations like Texas, Gulf, Sun, Union, and Shell. Capturing old markets and new, by 1910 they had reduced Standard's share of domestic production to only 60 percent of the total national output, compared to the 90 percent it had enjoyed just thirty years earlier. Perhaps Standard was still a symbol of monopoly but it was certainly not one in fact. Its decline was especially pronounced in the newer markets. In 1911 Standard's competitors were supplying 70 percent of the nation's fuel oil, 45 percent of its lubricants, and about 35 percent of needed gasoline. Indeed, on the eve of World War I, increasing competitiveness between major and minor producers and refiners replaced monopoly as a major characteristic of the oil industry's structure.

Why did Standard's influence decline so rapidly? The decline was partly due to the failure of Standard executives to take advantage of new opportunities. As the Hidys have noted, Standard's leaders did not seize new market opportunities nor did they expand into the rich new mid-continent and Gulf oil regions. In Texas the strict antitrust laws also dissuaded the Standard combination from embarking on large-scale operations there. A relatively old company, Standard was slow to take advantage of new markets, to undertake aggressive promotion of new oil products, and to court new consumers.[9]

Waste

Excessive waste of oil was also causing much concern during the first decade of the twentieth century, as production outstripped demand. Moreover, discovery of the great new western fields was often characterized by careless drilling and refining methods that aroused serious fears of exhaustion. Scientists and technicians especially deplored the waste and forecast future shortages. In 1908 David T. Day, director of the Petroleum Division of the United States Geological Survey, warned that recoverable crude oil reserves in the United States might constitute no more than 10 to 25 billion barrels. A few years later, in 1915, Ralph

9. Harold W. Williamson and Ralph Andreano, "Competitive Structure of the American Petroleum Industry, 1880–1911, A Reappraisal," in *Oil's First Century* (Cambridge, 1960), 71–84; Hidy and Hidy, *Pioneering*, 573–579; Gabriel Kolko, *The Triumph of Conservatism* (New York, 1963), 39–42.

Arnold, one of California's outstanding petroleum engineers, forecast reserves of 8 billion barrels, an estimate with which the United States Geological Survey agreed. Based on prevailing consumption, such predictions presaged exhaustion of the nation's oil reserves in about twenty years. All of these estimates revealed a growing fear among oil experts over the wasteful depletion of a valuable resource.[10]

Later studies showed such calculations to be unduly pessimistic, but between 1890 and 1917 they set the tone for conservation efforts by the industry and by state and federal governments. Many industry leaders also welcomed restrictions on production as a means of stabilizing oil markets and prices. State and federal conservationists, on the other hand, favored the preservation of reserves for national defense and other needs. Conservation of petroleum and stabilization of the industry were closely related, and the relationship served to focus the attention of government and businessmen on a common problem.

Defense Needs

Although historians have not included the military establishment as a prime interest group in the conservation movement, it did play a significant role. For Army and Navy strategists, uncertainty over the nation's future oil supply created a major dilemma. Perhaps Navy men worried most over future oil sources, occupied as they were between 1890 and 1917 with converting their ships from coal to fuel oil. But the Army was also affected, since many of its new weapons, including tanks, trucks, and airplanes, were directly dependent on petroleum products. By the time of World War I a diversified group of U.S. military leaders had become directly concerned with petroleum problems.

Navy planners took the initiative in safeguarding their needs. Their pleas to Congress first received recognition during the Spanish-American War, when the legislators appropriated $15,000 for the Navy to conduct inquiries into the practicability of petroleum-powered vessels. Four years later the investigation was broadened when Congress granted the Navy Department another $20,000 to ascertain the value of crude petroleum for naval uses. The Navy thereupon created a Fuel Board to conduct relevant experiments. At the same time, private inter-

10. Williamson *et al., American Petroleum Industry,* II, 44–49; Ise, *United States Oil Policy,* 416–420.

ests, such as the Standard Oil Company and various steamship companies, spent much larger sums in cooperative experiments with the Fuel Board to learn more about the practicability of petroleum-burning ships. Results of these tests did not yet fully convince Navy officials of the wisdom of large-scale conversion, for, as Secretary of the Navy Paul Morton noted in 1904, this was "a question that cannot by any means be regarded as settled." A leading trade publication, the *Oil Investor's Journal,* between 1906 and 1911 criticized naval planners for such timidity and for not taking more decisive action in converting all war vessels from coal to oil.[11]

Much of the hesitancy shown by United States Navy officials over conversion stemmed from their uncertainty about available oil supplies in the future. Already in 1909 Secretary of the Interior Richard A. Ballinger warned President William Howard Taft about the dire effects of a potential oil shortage and especially about its impact on the Navy. As a remedy he suggested a determined federal program to decrease waste, to include, first, a Presidential order to restrict private entry on publicly owned petroleum lands. "The time appears opportune for legislative action that will assure the conservation of an adequate supply of petroleum for the Government's own needs," he wrote. "The legislation should give authority to fix the terms of disposition of public oil lands so as to provide for future demands of the Navy."[12]

Prices

Military men also evinced concern over oil procurement and rising prices. The increasing domestic and international demand for oil between 1890 and 1917 resulted in a steadily upward spiraling of oil prices. After 1912 the rising cost of oil aroused great fears among Navy officials. Rear Admiral Thomas J. Cowie, chief of the Bureau of Supplies and Accounts, told the House Naval Affairs Committee in 1913 that the Navy's fuel oil bill had increased 50 percent over the preceding year. Secretary of the Navy Josephus Daniels was more blunt. He casti-

11. John A. De Novo, "Petroleum and the United States Navy Before World War I," *Mississippi Valley Historical Review* [hereafter cited as *MVHR*], XLI (March 1955), 641–644.

12. Richard A. Ballinger to William Howard Taft, September 17, 1909, William Howard Taft Papers, Library of Congress, quoted in *ibid.,* 646.

gated the "exorbitant and ever-increasing prices [of] private companies that now completely control the supply," fattening "the pockets of a few oil companies."[13] Shortly thereafter he advocated a partial nationalization of American oil supplies in the interests of defense. The increasing consumption of oil products thus confronted the federal government with important problems of national security, as fuelburning vessels led to a growing dependence on adequate supplies secured at reasonable prices.

PUBLIC POLICIES

All of these issues—defense requirements, conservation, monopoly, price—presented as many problems to representatives of the oil industry as to officials in state and federal governments. In groping for solutions on matters of common interest or joint concern, neither group followed any well-defined policy patterns; both were guilty of much floundering.

How were these various difficulties to be met? The formulation of public policies was worked out pragmatically by a wide array of interest groups affected by the energy revolution. Disagreements among these interests were considerable. Yet they found sufficient consensus to formulate a series of compromises. U.S. oil policy from 1890 to 1917 emerged out of such conflict and consensus, as private entrepreneurs sought governmental sanctions and restraints to cope with problems of their rapidly changing industry.

Anti-Trust

The problem of monopoly was one of the first to be subjected to direct public action. Concentration of economic power in the hands of a giant corporation such as Standard Oil posed a direct threat to thousands of smaller competitors and understandably provoked loud cries of protest. State and federal antitrust policies developed as a direct response to aggrieved groups of oil producers, shippers, and consumers and to the sensationalism of muckrakers, especially Ida Tarbell, whose *History of the Standard Oil Company* was brought out in book form late in 1904. With much public concern over the general merger move-

13. Secretary of the Navy, *Annual Report* 1913 (Washington, 1914), 14–15.

ment in American industry between 1899 and 1904, the time for an attack on Standard's alleged monopoly appeared propitious.

Some of the first efforts to deal with monopoly were made by the states. In the new oil-producing areas feelings ran high against real—or sometimes imagined—abuses by the Standard combination. This was true in Kansas, where in 1895 Standard built a refinery. Resentment against the company flared up in 1904 as about 500 independent producers embarked on a production spree in the state that led to a drastic decline in prices. Meanwhile, Standard's refinery, the only one in Kansas, was unable to process the unexpected flood of oil with which it was suddenly confronted. Standard was also unable to provide adequate storage facilities for which producers were now clamoring to hold the vast quantities of crude oil.

Despite a publicity campaign by Standard in Kansas during the early months of 1905 to explain the limitations of its refining facilities, many producers there became hostile to the company. When the Kansas legislature met in April, 1905, many of its members were in favor of punitive legislation. Under the urging of Governor Ed Hoch, himself an independent oil producer, it enacted a law to establish a state-owned refinery at Peru, Kansas, which would compete with Standard's plant at Neodesha. A $200,000 public bond issue was to finance the project. In addition, the Kansas lawmakers enacted a law declaring pipelines to be common carriers and another to prohibit price discrimination so as to assure fairness in the marketing of petroleum products.[14] Since the state Supreme Court declared the statute establishing the state refinery to be unconstitutional, this enterprise was never placed in operation. But the legislative program of 1905 was clearly designed to thwart the alleged monopolistic practices of the Standard Oil Company in Kansas.

Two years later Texas also struck at the monopoly of Standard Oil. In May, 1907, after a report on Standard's practices by the United States Bureau of Corporations, the Attorney General of Texas secured an indictment of the Waters-Pierce Oil Company (affiliated with Standard Oil [N.J.]) for violation of the Texas antitrust laws. The district court of Travis County ordered the company to cease operations in the

14. The Kansas episode is discussed in Hidy and Hidy, *Pioneering*, 671–676, and Ise, *United States Oil Policy*, 241–245, which also contain bibliographical references to the vast literature on the subject.

state, and within the next two years other state court decisions forced all of Standard's affiliates to end their operations in Texas.[15]

The strong reaction against Standard's alleged monopoly in Kansas had a direct impact on national oil policies. On February 15, 1905, Representative Philip W. Campbell (Kansas) sought to allay the fears of his constituents by introducing a House Resolution calling for a Congressional investigation of the petroleum situation in his home state. Congress approved the suggestion and ordered the United States Bureau of Corporations to undertake the task. Commissioner James R. Garfield of the Bureau of Corporations decided, however, that his inquiry would have to embrace the petroleum business in the entire country, not merely within a single state. During the next fifteen months his staff conducted the inquiry. On May 2, 1906, they published their first report, which received far-flung publicity. This report charged Standard with domination of the industry, largely through receipt of secret rebates from the railroads.[16]

Publication of this report had immediate repercussions in Washington. On May 4, 1906, two days after it was issued, President Theodore Roosevelt made special reference to it while addressing Congress on the need for passage of the Hepburn Bill to control railroads. When Congress enacted the Hepburn Act in June, 1906, it also included a provision—offered by Senator Henry Cabot Lodge—authorizing the Interstate Commerce Commission to extend its jurisdiction over pipelines.[17]

The report of the Bureau of Corporations on Standard's control over transportation facilities also led President Roosevelt and the Department of Justice to initiate dissolution proceedings against the company under the Sherman Anti-Trust Act. Between May and December, 1906,

15. Williamson *et al.*, *American Petroleum Industry*, II, 76–86; Hidy and Hidy, *Pioneering*, 688–689, 696.

16. U.S. Bureau of Corporations, *Report on the Transportation of Petroleum*, May 2, 1906 (Washington, 1906); *Congressional Record* [hereafter cited as *CR*], 58 Cong., 3 sess. (February 15, 1905), 2666.

17. 59 Cong., 1 sess., *Senate Document* No. 428 (Washington, 1906), *CR*, 59 Cong., 1 sess. (May 4, 1906), 6358, *ibid.* (May 17, 1906), 6998–7008; for Lodge, see *ibid.*, (June 25, 1906), 15438, 9104–9112; Williamson *et al.*, *American Petroleum Industry*, II, 104–107; Arthur M. Johnson, "Theodore Roosevelt and the Bureau of Corporations," *MVHR*, XLV (March 1959), 571–590; a good summary can be found in Johnson, *The Development of American Petroleum Pipelines*, 219–242, and Gabriel Kolko, *Railroads, Rates and Regulation* (Princeton, 1965), 127–154.

federal grand juries collected data that served as a basis for indictments against Standard Oil companies in California, Louisiana, Missouri, Tennessee, Illinois, and New York. But the main attack was made on November 15, 1906, in the United States Circuit Court for the eastern district of Missouri, when the United States Attorney General filed a bill in equity against Standard and its affiliates for violation of Sections 1 and 2 of the Sherman Anti-Trust Act. The evidence in the report of the United States Bureau of Corporations was used to buttress the federal complaint. It charged local price-cutting, secret rebates, discrimination, and bribery of competitors. During the next five years this suit made its way through the federal courts.[18]

While this case was pending, the Standard monopoly came under further federal attack. In January, 1907, the Interstate Commerce Commission issued a report on the investigation of Standard's relations with the railroads, which it had started in February, 1906. It charged that the company was defying the provisions of the Hepburn Act and was continuing to receive secret rebates from various carriers. A few months after the Interstate Commerce Commission issued this report, the new Commissioner of Corporations, Norbert K. Smith, published a second installment of his agency's conclusions concerning the oil industry. This report stressed Standard's monopolistic position in the industry, which was largely due to its control over pipelines and its unfair marketing practices.[19]

The United States Supreme Court's decision of 1911 in the Standard case further dramatized the federal effort to prevent monopoly in the oil industry. As noted, changes in the oil industry itself were already diminishing Standard's power and influence. But the court found the company guilty of restraining competition in interstate commerce. Its ability to do so had come about largely because the parent corporation held the stock of its subsidiaries; the judges therefore issued a dissolution decree ordering Jersey Standard to dispose of the voting stock of its

18. Williamson *et al., American Petroleum Industry,* II, 8–14; Hidy and Hidy, *Pioneering,* 682–687.

19. Interstate Commerce Commission, *Report of Investigation of Railroad Discriminations and Monopolies of Oil,* January 28, 1907, in 59 Cong., 2 sess., *House Document* No. 606 (Washington, 1907); U.S. Bureau of Corporations, *Report of the Commissioner of Corporations on the Petroleum Industry,* Part I (Washington, 1907).

thirty-seven guilty affiliates and to surrender control over their operations. Whether this decision to break up an integrated company was wise from an economic point of view has been widely debated.[20] Since the aim of federal policy was to prevent dominance of the industry by a single company, the court tried to implement this principle in its ruling.

Conservation

At the same time state and federal governments were seeking remedies for impending problems of oil depletion. The tremendous rise in crude-oil production between 1890 and 1917 aroused fears of an oil shortage and produced a rash of state conservation measures. "The time will come," warned W. S. Blatchley, State Geologist of Indiana in 1896, "when the stored reserves . . . will have been drained," and his views were seconded by many of his fellow scientists. Such warnings by technical men were partly responsible for the enactment of state conservation laws. New York in 1879 and Pennsylvania in 1881 had already made regulations for plugging of oil wells to cut down waste. Blatchley's influence on Indiana lawmakers led them in 1889 to create a Department of Geology and Natural Resources for the state and in 1893 to prohibit oil wastage. In 1903 the Indiana legislature made regulation of waste more effective by creating the office of State Natural Gas Supervisor. Kansas in 1891 and West Virginia in 1892 also regulated the drilling and operation of oil wells.[21]

As new western oil fields were developed after 1890 the states there followed the pattern of the eastern regions. In Texas, waste attending increasing oil exploration was appalling, and in 1899 the legislature began to regulate drilling practices. California adopted a law to regulate the casing and plugging of wells in 1903 but the legislature waited until 1915 to establish a State Oil and Gas Supervisor to administer state regulations.[22]

Oklahoma inaugurated the most comprehensive program of oil conservation. Its legislature first adopted drilling regulations in 1905 and four years later empowered a state inspector to execute them. With the

---

20. *United States* vs. *Standard Oil Company of New Jersey,* 173 Fed. Rep. 183.
21. Quoted in Ise, *United States Oil Policy,* 279; 1879 N.Y. Stats. 295; 1881 Pa. Stats. 110; 1889 Indiana Stats. 23; 1893 Indiana Stats. 300; 1903 Indiana Stats. 110, 213.
22. 1899 Texas Stats. 68; 1915 Cal. Stats. 1404.

development of the Glenn Pool (1907)—and resultant overproduction —crude-oil producers there petitioned the legislature to intervene on their behalf to prevent unmarketable surpluses and excessive waste. They also charged pipelines with discrimination in transporting oil. The lawmakers responded to this appeal by enacting an antitrust bill classifying pipelines as common carriers. Meanwhile, the Oklahoma Corporation Commission held hearings concerning problems of flush production, particularly the ruinous decline of prices. The commission then issued an administrative order fixing the minimum price of Glenn Pool crude oil at 65 cents a barrel. This order was largely ignored by most purchasers of petroleum, but was significant in foreshadowing state control over prices and production during the next fifty years.

By World War I problems of petroleum overproduction in Oklahoma were worsening rapidly. In 1915 wasteful production in the rich Cushing field created a real crisis. Oil prices plummeted, and many producers indulged in wasteful and excessive production. This posed a dilemma for the state, since the conservation of one of its most valuable natural resources as well as the stability of its economy, were at stake. The legislators were so alarmed that they enacted the first state law in the nation to prorate oil production. The measure provided for state restriction of petroleum production by private operators whenever excessive waste was evident in a particular field, when market demand for existing oil was insufficient, or when prices fell below production costs.[23] Administration of this remarkable statute—which provided for closer state control over the oil business than for any other industry in the United States—was placed in the hands of the Oklahoma Corporation Commission.

Defense

The growing alarm over the rapid depletion of the nation's oil resources was also reflected in national policies. When Theodore Roosevelt requested Congressional action in May, 1906, to control Standard's business practices, he also asked for authorization to prevent the sale or lease of federal oil lands. Several bills and resolutions to implement his suggestion were introduced in the United States Senate, but without

23. Oklahoma Corporation Commission, *Report* 1915 (Oklahoma City, 1916), 4–6, 151–169; 1907 Okla. Stats. 54; 1915 Okla. Stats. 35, 149, 398, 549; Ise, *United States Oil Policy*, 283–284.

tangible results. A similar plea was made in February, 1908, by George Otis Smith, director of the United States Geological Survey. He wrote to Secretary of the Interior Garfield to request withdrawal of all remaining federal oil lands in order to preserve a supply for the United States Navy. His suggestion had no imediate effect, however. But it did lead Secretary of the Interior Richard A. Ballinger to write President Taft about the urgent necessity for oil conservation, and the desirability of withdrawing federal oil lands from sale in California. This strong plea led the Chief Executive in September, 1909, to issue an executive order reserving three million acres of oil lands on the public domain in California and Wyoming for the national government.[24]

By his action President Taft unwittingly sharpened the demands of various interest groups concerned with oil conservation. Navy men, scientists, and others concerned with rapid depletion of the oil reserves applauded the President's withdrawal order and urged reservation of all public oil lands and the creation of naval oil reserves. Opposed were many western oil producers, especially Californians, who advocated the removal of federal restrictions on private entry upon public lands. Thus the issue was clearly crystallized: should federal policy stress conservation or unrestricted exploitation?

For the next ten years, from Taft's withdrawal order in 1909 to the enactment of the Mineral Leasing Act of 1920, oil conservation became embroiled in the struggle over disposition of oil-bearing public lands. Federal mining laws had been framed with regard to gold and coal but not petroleum. Moreover, by encouraging rapid development such national legislation tended to foster waste. President Taft's order thus gave impetus to a movement for amendment of the federal mineral land laws, especially since his directive was virtually ignored by the California operators for a decade after 1910. During this period new mining bills were introduced at every session of Congress, and its committees held lengthy hearings on the problem.[25]

Within the Wilson Cabinet the two diverging views also created con-

24. Max W. Ball, *Petroleum Withdrawals and Restorations Affecting the Public Domain*, U.S. Geological Survey, *Bulletin* No. 623 (Washington, 1917), 104; Ise, *United States Oil Policy*, 312–313; J. Leonard Bates, *The Origins of Teapot Dome: Progressives, Parties, and Petroleum, 1909–1921* (Urbana, 1963), 21–22.

25. The lengthy controversy is discussed in detail by Bates, *Origins of Teapot Dome*, 33–53, 97–199 and Ise, *United States Oil Policy*, 313–322.

flict. Secretary of the Navy Josephus Daniels was greatly concerned over the Navy's oil supplies, present and future. Along with Gifford Pinchot and Commander G. Richardson, he came to be a spokesman for groups desiring the withdrawal of federal oil lands from public sale. Just as vehement in opposition was Secretary of the Interior Franklin K. Lane, himself a former California oil operator, who provided leadership for those who believed that leasing of federal petroleum properties should be made less restrictive.[26]

Faced with these difficulties, Navy planners between 1909 and 1917 offered at least two solutions. One was the establishment of naval oil reserves by executive order of the President; the other was for federal operation of petroleum-producing and refining facilities. Secretary of the Navy G. von L. Meyer urged the former course and prevailed upon President Taft in 1911 to create the Elk Hills and Buena Vista Hills naval oil reserves in California. Three years later Woodrow Wilson yielded to the pleas of Secretary of the Navy Josephus Daniels and added the Teapot Dome reservoirs in Wyoming.[27]

But Daniels felt that the program did not go far enough and that the Navy should develop and manufacture its own petroleum products. Some consumer groups also favored partial nationalization of the oil industry. A resolution of the Minnesota State Legislature addressed to Congress in 1913 openly urged such action. In November of that year Daniels wrote to Senator Benjamin Tillman (S.C.), chairman of the Senate Committee on Naval Affairs, requesting consideration of his plan by the committee. Then, in his annual report the following month, Daniels noted bluntly: "The only possible relief from . . . a staggering item in the expense account of the Navy in the future is in the control of oil wells and the refining of its own oil." In January, 1914, Daniels, together with Admiral Robert S. Griffin, chief of the Navy's Bureau of Steam Engineering, also went before the House Committee on Naval Affairs to plead for creation of a government refinery. At the same time Senator Thomas P. Gore secured passage of a resolution in the United States Senate directing the Departments of the Navy and the Interior to

26. Bates, *Origins of Teapot Dome,* 54–78.

27. *Oil Land Leasing Act of 1920 with Amendments and other Laws Relating to Mineral Lands,* compiled by Elmer A. Lewis (Washington, 1952); Bates, *Origins of Teapot Dome,* 200–218.

investigate the feasibility of a federal pipeline from the midcontinent fields to the Gulf.[28]

The suggestions of Daniels were based on some of the best advice of naval officers, especially the recommendations of Admiral George Dewey and the Navy General Board. In a comprehensive report in 1914 the board pointed to the increasing shortage of fuel oil on the one hand and the Navy's increasing reliance on oil on the other. In 1913 only one bidder had sought a contract to supply oil to the Atlantic fleet, a possible harbinger of a future shortage. Dewey therefore urged federal ownership of oil lands and possible production and refining of oil by the Navy Department itself. The Bureau of Steam Engineering in the Department of the Navy urged an immediate Congressional appropriation to establish a federal refinery, a recommendation approved by the Navy General Board, and also by the Interior Department.[29]

These proposals generated much discussion. The suggestion that the national government enter the oil business brought a mixed reaction. Obviously, large private integrated companies could not be overjoyed by such potential competition. Numerous independents looked upon the plan with favor, however, for a publicly owned pipeline might diminish the effectiveness of Standard's extensive control over existing pipelines.

But the issue was not crystallized in legislation. While the matter was under consideration, on June 22, 1914,• the United States Supreme Court handed down a decision upholding the Interstate Commerce Commission's authority (under the Hepburn Act) to regulate the rates charged by pipelines, now legally declared to be common carriers in interstate commerce. This decision apparently persuaded a sufficient number of lawmakers that federal regulation would be adequate to control the oil industry and that federal production and refining were not necessary. The decline of oil prices in 1914 and 1915, partly be-

28. De Novo, "Petroleum and the United States Navy," *MVHR*, XLI (March 1955), 647–648; Ise, *United States Oil Policy*, 324, 356; Bates, *Origins of Teapot Dome*, 22–24, 115–119; CR, 63 Cong., 1 sess. (June 13, 1913), 1988, for the Minnesota Legislature's Resolution for government ownership; the letter to Tillman is in *Oil and Gas Journal* [hereafter cited as *O&G Jl.*] (November 27, 1913); Secretary of the Navy, *Annual Report* 1913 (Washington, 1914), 15; New York *Times* [hereafter cited as *NYT*], January 31, 1914; CR, 63 Cong., 2 sess. (January 15, 1914), 1561.

29. De Novo, "Petroleum and the United States Navy," 649–653.

cause of increased production, strengthened this belief. To be sure, Daniels himself continued to press his proposal for government ownership, but for a time Congress seemed content to rely on regulation.[30]

Federal Research Projects

Although the federal government did not itself directly enter the business of oil production, it did seek to avert possible shortages by encouraging private operators through its diversified research functions. Because of the demands of producers, both federal and state governments enlarged their research activities in this period. They collected and published statistics and other relevant data and experimented with new processes for oil exploration. The United States Geological Survey conducted advanced theoretical research, while the United States Bureau of Mines dealt with practical problems. By World War I many states had created similar agencies, and most large integrated oil companies were establishing geological departments. In government and in industry the professional scientist and engineer were assuming more important roles. They were establishing a common ground, creating a community of interest in mutual problems, and undertaking a large number of cooperative projects involving public agencies and private business.

A good example was the United States Geological Survey, which had a great influence on the oil industry. Its leaders during this period included some of the most prominent petroleum geologists in the nation. George Otis Smith, director of the Survey in 1908, was generally regarded as an outstanding scientific authority. David T. Day, director of the Survey's Petroleum Division, pioneered with the first efforts to estimate oil reserves in the United States and the development of methods for such analysis. David White, chief geologist of the Survey, was a prime influence in demonstration of improved mapping and discovery methods. This able staff of scientists gave the Survey an enviable reputation.[31] Indeed, many young geologists hired by large oil companies received their first training in the United States Geological Survey, and their fine performance won grudging respect from the industry.

The Survey's research work had a direct impact on the industry. To

30. *Ibid.*, 651–654.
31. Brookings Institution, *The United States Geological Survey* (New York, 1918), 45–47, 64–68, 106.

be sure, until about 1909 practical oilmen were generally skeptical about the value of the Survey's scientific findings. But in that year the Survey effected a great change in the industry's attitude when it published a report that popularized the anticlinal theory. In this technical paper the Survey's scientists revealed what was already known to geologists—that most large oil finds had been made on anticlines. The study provided guidance for discovery of potential oil fields and led producers to realize the close relationship between accurate scientific information and economical exploration and drilling. By World War I, the importance of the Survey's work for the industry was rarely questioned.

The Survey also stimulated the conservation movement. In 1907 David T. Day made the first effort to estimate crude-oil reserves in the United States. If his figures, forecasting a potential supply of from 8 to 25 billion barrels, were incorrect, his effort nonetheless resulted in an increased awareness by many oilmen and military leaders that the wasteful depletion of a valuable natural resource was rapidly taking place, and that its exhaustion was not far off, perhaps within a decade.[32]

Although originally created in 1884 to serve the needs of the coal industry, the United States Bureau of Mines came to shift more of its attention to oil problems as the industry grew in importance after the turn of the century. This emphasis became clear by 1915, when the bureau created a special Petroleum Division. Much of its work dealt with practical scientific and technical matters attending the elimination of waste and the attempted increase of recoverable crude petroleum from oil-bearing sands. In 1917 the bureau established its first petroleum experiment station in the midcontinent field at Bartlesville, Oklahoma, where it could concentrate directly on problems of producers.[33]

State Research Projects

Between 1890 and 1917 many of the states greatly expanded their existing research services to aid the industry in increasing production. In most cases these services were rendered by mining bureaus or geological surveys created by lawmakers in the middle of the nineteenth century to aid farmers and miners. By 1882 Edward Orton, Ohio's State Geologist, concerned himself with the discovery of new sources for petroleum. Better known was William E. Blatchley, who was largely

32. Williamson *et al., American Petroleum Industry,* II, 44–48.
33. Fred Wilbur Powell, *The Bureau of Mines* (Baltimore, 1922), 25–29, 48–49.

responsible for the creation in 1889, of the Indiana Department of Geology and Natural History, which was to work on problems faced by oil producers. In 1906 Louisiana created a State Board of Engineers, which was concerned with problems of gas waste attending the production of oil. Texas undertook a survey of its minerals in 1905, and four years later established a Bureau of Economic Geology, which provided much aid for oilmen through its important map-making activities. Oklahoma established a Geological Survey while still a Territory. Its prime focus was on methods of oil discovery. California's legislature heeded requests of oilmen by creating, in 1915, a Gas and Oil Supervisor, who published production statistics and introduced new drilling methods that vitally affected the industry.[34]

Increasingly, therefore, the growing importance of oil was creating problems for the industry and for government—problems in which they had a mutual interest. As long as monopoly was a major issue, public policy focused largely on antitrust action. As the structure of the oil industry gradually came to be characterized by oligopoly, state and federal policies came to embrace a much wider sphere of industrial regulation and to emphasize cooperation. Cutthroat competition not only demoralized the industry but was beginning to pose a threat to the economic stability of the national economy. Oil depletion affected not merely the future expansion of the industry but also the increasingly important military needs of the U.S. government. Consequently, public policy witnessed a significant shift during this period. Passive regulation, characteristic of the nineteenth century, was being transformed as governments came to assume a supervisory role. Between 1890 and 1917 these changes were slowly gathering momentum. But in the latter year they were swiftly accelerated by U.S. entrance into World War I. Under the impress of the wartime mobilization experience, the newly emerging relationships between government and industry crystallized rapidly and formed a pattern that was to become characteristic during the twentieth century.

34. Ise, *United States Oil Policy,* 274–288; Nash, *State Government,* 318–323, 340–342; National Research Council, *Bulletin* No. 88 (November 1932) (Washington, 1932), 93–108.

2 / The Wilson War Program

WORLD WAR I had a profound impact on the pattern of the government's relations with the oil industry as it brought Theodore Roosevelt's New Nationalism squarely within the mainstream of public policy. Wartime exigencies no longer made the dissolution of monopoly and antitrust actions an immediate problem. Instead, the increase in demand for petroleum products necessitated maximum production for the war effort. Thus, federal and state policies now focused on the regulation of business practices within the industry, on the maintenance of prices and economic stability, and on oil conservation. Suddenly trust-busting seemed remote, indeed. But the New Nationalism was vague about specific agencies or methods through which business and the government could achieve closer cooperation. Under the stress of war, however, businessmen and government officials created institutional mechanisms to implement the new emphasis on cooperation.

By the summer of 1917 both American and Allied demands for petroleum placed great pressures on available oil supplies. World War I was unique in the annals of warfare as the first conflict in which the belligerents were largely dependent on motorized equipment, whether on land or sea. As Lord Curzon remarked late in 1918: "The Allies floated to victory on a sea of oil."[1] After April, 1917, the heavy buying of the Allied purchasing commissions in Washington contributed much to a growing shortage of petroleum products within the United States itself. The demands of the United States Navy and a fledgling United States Air Corps, and the building of a large American Army placed further strains on domestic petroleum resources and on prevailing price levels.[2] This shortage led the Wilson Administration to emphasize maximum oil production in pursuit of its broader aim of victory.

OIL INDUSTRY ADVISORY COMMITTEE

Along with many advocates of preparedness, President Wilson sought to anticipate industrial war needs. At his suggestion, in April, 1916, Congress created the Council of National Defense. Although largely an adjunct of the Cabinet, the council established an Advisory Committee composed of leading businessmen.[3] One of its dominant figures was Bernard Baruch, who organized a large number of special advisory committees composed of representatives from particular industries. As President Wilson extended the scope of naval operations in March, 1917, and American entrance into the war seemed imminent, Baruch got in touch with leaders of the petroleum industry. He approached A. C. Bedford, chairman of the board of directors of the Standard Oil Company of New Jersey, and asked him to form an advisory committee to represent the oil industry. Bedford agreed, and also served as chairman of the group.[4]

Like other businessmen, those engaged in some phase of petroleum processing saw the government-industry committees as a means of securing greater cooperation. Some representatives of the industry immediately rose to the occasion by offering their help in solving crucial supply problems. "Suggest a board of experienced and loyal oilmen," declared the *National Petroleum News* in April, 1917, ". . . to aid

1. See his speech, New York *Times* [hereafter cited as *NYT*], November 23, 1918.

2. *Ibid.*, February 20, March 6, August 4, 1917.

3. Council of National Defense, *Report* 1917 (Washington, 1917), 110–111.

4. On Bedford, see George Gibb and Evelyn H. Knowlton, *The Resurgent Years, 1911–1927* (New York, 1956), 237–242; Bernard Baruch, *American Industry in the War: A Report of the War Industries Board, 1921* (New York, 1941), 3, 17–28, 78–81.

department heads, who know nothing of the oil industry. Tell them how much better this great problem can be solved with the intelligent and well planned aid of the industry than by the inefficiency and mismanagement of government employees going it alone."[5] The journal proposed A. C. Bedford, H. F. Sinclair, E. L. Doheny, and others whom Baruch later actually appointed to deal with petroleum procurement. Such a group, it was hoped, could facilitate coordination between the industry and federal agencies. To implement his plans, Bedford selected key figures such as E. L. Doheny, president of the Mexican Petroleum Company, G. S. Davidson of the Gulf Oil Company, J. W. Van Dyke of the Atlantic Refining Company, Harry F. Sinclair, and C. F. Lufkin, president of the Texas Company. In order to make the committee more representative, he also chose individuals from three trade associations to speak for smaller, independent petroleum producers and refiners.[6]

The advisory functions of this committee were broad in nature. One of its immediate tasks was to ensure the delivery of adequate oil supplies for the Navy and for other branches of the armed forces. At the same time it was to make recommendations concerning allocation of available production to meet demands of the Allies, particularly the British, French, and Italians. These foreign needs were to be balanced with the petroleum requirements of domestic war industries, however. It was also the committee's task to work out the details of a specific plan of distribution. Coordination of petroleum production and distribution was to be attained without creating shortages in any sector of the economy and without any significant advance in oil prices.[6] During the spring of 1917 the advisory group busied itself with working out specific plans to implement these functions. When President Wilson dissolved the Council of National Defense to create the War Industries Board in July, 1917, the petroleum industry advisory committee continued its existence under the aegis of this new agency as the National Petroleum War Service Committee.[7]

5. *National Petroleum News* [hereafter cited as *NPN*] (April 1917); see also *ibid.* (May 1917).

6. For Bedford's speech outlining his committee's work, see *ibid.* (October 1917), 46.

7. *NYT,* October 10, November 5, December 3, 1917; *NPN* (October 1917), 43; Bernard Baruch, *The Public Years* (New York, 1960), 40.

NATIONAL PETROLEUM WAR SERVICE COMMITTEE

Many business leaders became increasingly enthusiastic about their new cooperative relationship with the federal government. Citing Herbert Hoover, A. C. Bedford told the Western Petroleum Refiners Association in October, 1917: "We must keep our eyes on the goal of a still more complete and wholehearted cooperation, of a more perfect coordinated unity of aims and methods." The possibility of stabilizing competition within an industry through consultation represented an unusual opportunity. What pools, trusts, and mergers had been unable to accomplish because of the antitrust laws could be achieved under this new device for intraindustry cooperation. At the same time these committees facilitated greater cooperation between an industry and the federal government, and thus allowed public officials a greater measure of control in regulating business practices. The ultimate aim of such a coordination effort was greater efficiency, a goal highly prized by a generation of managers under the impress of Frederick W. Taylor's ideas of scientific management. These hopes were clearly voiced by Harry A. Wheeler, president of the United States Chamber of Commerce (1917), and a prime mover in the organization of war service committees:

Organization for war service is giving business the foundation for the kind of cooperative effort that alone can make the United States economically efficient enough to take its place with the nations in world trade. . . . Creation of war service committees promises to furnish the basis for a truly national organization. . . .

And, unabashedly, he added: "The integration of business, the expressed aim of the national chamber, is in sight."[8]

During the summer and fall of 1917, however, critics in Congress and elsewhere pointed to certain weaknesses of industry committees. First, their purely advisory functions prevented them from carrying out their recommendations and limited their effectiveness. When Congress conferred virtually plenary powers upon the President in the Lever Act of August, 1917, many hoped that President Wilson would strengthen the advisory committees by delegating some of his broad authority to them. Another weakness of the existing committee structure was the selection and appointment of individual members. Wilson did not pro-

8. *Nation's Business* (August 1918); Bedford's speech, *NPN* (October 1917), 44.

vide for any systematic procedure to ensure adequate representation for diverse segments of a particular industry. Moreover, committee members performed two incompatible functions, a condition that led to a conflict of interests. On the one hand, they advised the federal government on purchases and allocations. On the other, they represented the very companies from which the federal government secured its supplies. Consequently, the suspicion that they could not serve God and Mammon, or two masters concurrently, had some foundation. Nor did most committees have adequate representation for smaller elements of a particular industry—or for government officials.[9]

The course of the war during the second half of 1917 also prompted President Wilson to reorganize his domestic mobilization program. Abroad, the Italians were still reeling from the defeat at Caporetto; the bloodshed at Gallipoli was a reminder that final victory would be dear; and German submarines were stepping up their attacks in the Atlantic. At home the nation's railroad system was near breakdown. In such circumstances the President deemed a reorganization of war agencies imperative, and Congress granted him sweeping wartime powers when it enacted the Lever Act in August, 1917.[10]

As part of the general reorganization in July, 1917, the President requested the Chamber of Commerce of the United States to help him in developing an organizational framework. He was perhaps thinking of a trade conference, which would facilitate closer working relations between federal agencies and important industrial interests. In response to this suggestion the Chamber called a War Conference of American Industry to meet in Atlantic City, New Jersey, from December 12 to December 14, 1917, to formulate specific plans. Two hundred delegates, representing 160 industries, gathered there to reorganize the committees that had originally been formed under the auspices of the now defunct Council of National Defense. Their prime aim was to make them more representative and, in addition, to require members to cut

9. Chamber of Commerce of the United States, *National War Service Committees, Their Scope and Duties* (Washington, n.d.), 1–5; *NYT,* December 13, 1917; Baruch, *American Industry,* 22–23; see *NPN* (December 19, 1917), 8, for a list of members.

10. For domestic difficulties, see Grosvenor Clarkson, *Industrial American in the World War* (Boston, 1923), 10–64; Walker D. Hines, *War History of American Railroads* (New Haven, 1928), 15–22.

formal ties with their respective companies so as to eliminate conflict of interest.[11]

The petroleum trade committee headed by A. C. Bedford was also affected by these changes. Even after the dissolution of the Council of National Defense it had continued its existence. Now, at Atlantic City, the Chamber's Executive Committee for the War Industries Committee reconstituted it to allow for better representation of diverse elements within the petroleum industry. Officially designated as the National Petroleum War Service Committee, it continued to function under the chairmanship of Bedford.

This new group was designed to develop a closer cooperative relationship between oilmen and federal agencies. While the members of the old advisory group had been appointed by the President, now national trade associations were asked to select representatives to the War Service Committee in the hope that all important segments of the industry would be represented. Since the petroleum industry as yet had no trade association, the National War Service Committee of the Chamber of Commerce of the United States made the formal appointments. In addition to Chairman Bedford it selected E. L. Doheny, Harry F. Sinclair, W. F. Teagle (president of Standard Oil [N.J.]) and W. S. Farish. Except for three new men to represent trade associations, this personnel was the same as that on the earlier committee of the Council of National Defense. The continuity was due in large part to Bernard Baruch, who feared an oil shortage if the experienced advisory committee were disbanded.[12]

However, the members of the committee were not sure whether the thousands of producers and refiners who comprised the industry actually endorsed either themselves or their projected policies. Consequently, early in 1918 the committee embarked on a publicity campaign to secure the support of a wide spectrum of oilmen. It sent letters to many oil companies, asking for specific statements of approval from

11. *Nation's Business* (December 27, 1917); Chamber of Commerce of the United States, War Service Executive Committee, *War Service Committees of the Nation's Industries as an Aid to the War Program* (Washington, 1918), 1–9.

12. For list of members, and letter of Waddell Catchings, Chairman of War Service Executive Committee, to A. C. Bedford, December 27, 1917, see *Oil and Gas Journal* [hereafter cited as *O&G Jl.*] (December 28, 1917); see also *NPN* (January 2, 1918).

their executive officers. It also used the pages of the leading trade journals for such appeals. If such support were not forthcoming, the committee warned, complete government control such as had just over-taken the railroads might be the result. "But the oil industry has a chance to avoid this unhappy issue," the *National Petroleum News* noted. "It can respond with every energy at its command . . . organizing itself into a complete unit."[13] Self-integration was coming to be a major goal.

UNITED STATES FUEL ADMINISTRATION

But believers in the New Nationalism envisaged not only responsible self-regulation by industry; they also stressed the need for federal business regulation. Late in 1917, however, there was still little national control of the oil industry. Yet the creation of the National Petroleum War Service Committee necessitated some federal agency to observe, or even to supervise, its operations. Thus, within a month after the organization of the new industry group, Wilson enlarged his wartime machinery for petroleum. Already in August, 1917, he had appointed Harry Garfield to direct a new United States Fuel Administration to deal with problems in the production and marketing of coal and the regulation of coal prices. Now, at Garfield's urging, on January 11, 1918, Wilson also issued an executive order to establish an Oil Division within the Fuel Administration to impose similar controls on petroleum products. All manufacturers and distributors with an output of more than 100,000 barrels of fuel oil yearly were required to secure licenses from the Fuel Administration. The administrator was also empowered to allocate oil to the industries with the greatest needs, and to institute a system of priorities.[14]

The appointment of an Oil Division, together with the organization of the industry's War Service Committee, created a set of working institutions to facilitate cooperation between the government and oilmen. The War Service Committee played an important role in the self-regulation of the petroleum industry and in securing cooperation among its various elements. The Oil Administrator, on the other hand, found it

13. *NPN* (January 2, 9, 1918).
14. *Ibid.* (January 16, February 6, 23, 1918); for text of Wilson's proclamation, see *O&G Jl.* (February 7, 1918).

a convenient agency for channeling his orders to implement federal regulation of the oil business. Thus, the wartime demand for maximum oil production, in addition to changes in the structure of the oil industry after 1911, forced the Wilson Administration to reorient federal petroleum policies. Wilson took the initiative in shifting the emphasis of public policy from antitrust measures to cooperation, from efforts to dissolve large integrated corporations toward attempts at their more effective regulation. Such a change did not emanate primarily from ideological considerations. Rather, it was worked out pragmatically by various interest groups in response to specific problems, and reflected petroleum's new role in the economy and in national defense.

To direct the operations of the United States Fuel Administration's Oil Division, Garfield chose Mark Requa, a protégé of Herbert Hoover. A well-known California petroleum engineer, Requa began his career in Nevada mining enterprises at the turn of the century. During the oil boom in California in the decade before World War I he formed his own oil company in the Coalinga field. Meanwhile he gained diversified experience as the general manager of the Nevada Consolidated Copper Company, and as president of the Eureka and Palisades Railroad. When the United States entered World War I, Herbert Hoover called him to Washington to serve as his assistant in the United States Food Administration. It was from this post that Requa went to direct federal oil policies in the United States Fuel Administration and to assume a role not unlike that of Harold Ickes during World War II. A passionate advocate of cooperation among businessmen, and of cooperation between them and the government, Requa was a convert to Theodore Roosevelt's doctrine of regulated competition. During the war years and for a decade thereafter, he was to exercise an important influence on the transformation of public policies toward the petroleum industry.[15]

Requa's appointment was regarded with much satisfaction by important spokesmen for the industry. Most of them pledged him their immediate and wholehearted support. In fact, A. C. Bedford, chairman of the Petroleum War Service Committee, met with Requa just a day after his appointment to discuss detailed plans for an effective working relationship. Meanwhile, numerous other oil company executives hurried to

15. A good concise account of his background is in *NPN* (January 16, 1918).

Washington to confer with the new oil czar and to sound him out on his projected policies.[16]

Soon after assuming the new position Requa announced his plans. One of his immediate concerns was to broaden representation of various interests on the War Service Committee. Thus, he asked Bedford to appoint additional representatives from diverse segments of the industry, and also to include important federal officials, such as Dr. Van Manning, director of the United States Bureau of Mines. In expanding his committee structure, Bedford now agreed to establish sixteen subcommittees to represent regional and functional groups to ensure closer collaboration between oilmen and the new federal agency. By March, 1918, when Bedford completed the reorganization, he had established subcommittees dealing with problems involving tank cars, shipping, tankers, pipelines, oil well supplies, natural gas, and allied industries. The chairmen of these subcommittees were given a place on the National War Service Committee, which throughout 1918 conferred with Requa on issues of mutual interest.[17]

Requa also expressed the hope that federal controls over production would not be necessary—a not-too-subtle hint to oilmen that it would be well for them to meet wartime needs through voluntary action. He noted that he expected to issue directives for the pooling of oil supplies and to supervise their distribution, largely through a system of priorities and licenses. Although Requa did not envision immediate national control over petroleum prices, the possibility remained. While the Fuel Administration would encourage maximum production to meet war needs, Requa emphasized that his agency would at the same time insist on the practice of efficient, sound conservation methods and the prevention of waste. Requa expected to enforce this policy by issuing or withholding priorities for materials needed by producers. Conservation would also be promoted, he believed, by the development of industry-wide, uniform standards. These were to apply not only to the machinery used by producers and refiners, but also to a wide range of their products. At the same time the Oil Division was ready to aid any kind of

16. *Ibid.* (January 23, 1918); Gibb & Knowlton, *The Resurgent Years,* 240–241.
17. *NPN* (January 16, 1918); *O&G Jl.* (February 14, 1918), 32–34; see also U.S. Fuel Administration, *Proclamation by the President of the United States,* Publication No. 28 (Washington, 1918).

voluntary, cooperative policies that promised to further the national war effort.[18] In short, the Fuel Administration was anxious to further integration of the oil industry. The new emphasis on cooperation was ironic only because the United States Supreme Court, just seven years earlier, had sought to prevent this kind of cooperation or "collusion."

Production Control

Perhaps the most important action taken by Requa in the early months of 1918 was his development of a plan to control production. This scheme had a pronounced impact in fostering greater cooperation within the industry and in strengthening federal control. In a proclamation of February 11, Requa announced that producers in each oil-producing region of the country were to form committees to develop proposals for increasing production. The chairmen of these local committees were to meet as a state board that was to provide direct contact with the Fuel Administration in Washington. Requa appointed another California oil producer, Thomas O'Donnell, to organize oil producers in the fields and to supervise the organization of this new administrative framework designed to facilitate closer cooperation between the industry and government.[19]

Pooling

In the ensuing months Requa also furthered cooperation within the industry by asking it to pool fuel oil. The Fuel Administration decided to draw upon supplies as circumstances warranted and to cancel private contracts of fuel oil companies with their customers, when necessary. In effect, this step resulted in pooling of all fuel oil supplies. In consultation with the War Service Committee, Requa announced in March, 1918, that he would direct deliveries to those whose needs in his estimation warranted highest priority, and at "a fair market price." This was a threat only, however, for Requa was willing to suspend his plan if the industry itself could supply all necessary needs.[20]

18. For organizational framework, see U.S. Fuel Administration, *Final Report, 1917–1919* (Washington, 1921), 261–271; see also *NPN* (April 3, 1918) for a list of committees, and *ibid.* (April 24, 1918); *O&G Jl.* (April 4, May 30, 1918).

19. *NPN* (February 20, 1918), 13; *O&G Jl.* (February 14, 1918); A. C. Bedford to E. C. Lufkin, May 17, 1918, in Correspondence, U.S. Fuel Administration Records, National Archives [hereafter cited as FA Records], Washington, D.C.

20. *NPN* (March 6, 13, 27, April 3, 1918).

The Fuel Administration also sought to secure lower transportation costs for the oil industry. Responding to the pleas of producers and refiners who complained that an anticipated rate rise of 25 percent by the Railroad Administration would seriously curtail supply of petroleum products, the Oil Division and the War Service Committee together persuaded William McAdoo to refrain from authorizing such an increase. Their joint appeal proved to be enormously effective.[21]

Price Stabilization

Increasing demands for petroleum inevitably provoked rising prices. Price stabilization was therefore one of Requa's prime concerns, since inflation made it difficult for federal agencies to meet pressing needs. In June, 1918, he asked the committee to prohibit the payment of premiums above market prices for scarce crude oil, a practice prevalent among many refiners.[22] Since some of the smaller operators feared that such regulations would drive them out of business, the Mid-Continent Producer's Association raised objections to the Fuel Administration's plan. Only a personal appearance by both Requa and Bedford at a meeting of the midcontinent producers led them to compromise on a limited premium schedule in late July, 1918.[23] By August, Requa approved a final price plan worked out by the National War Service Committee. The significance of such action transcended the immediate issue, for it reflected the industry's ability to govern itself. As Bedford said: "The plan is unusual and unique in that it is wholly a voluntary action of the industry."[24]

Both the Fuel Administration and the War Service Committee furthered standardization procedures to raise efficiency in most phases of petroleum production. For example, the first American specifications

---

21. *Ibid.* (June 12, 1918).

22. *Ibid.* (June 26, July 10, 17, 1918); *O&G Jl.* (June 28, July 12, 26, 1918).

23. *O&G Jl.* (July 26, 1918), 40–51; Requa's and Bedford's speeches, *ibid.* (August 2, 1918); *NPN* (June 20, July 24, 31, 1918); Walter Teagle to Mark Requa, July 18, 1918, in FA Records; A. C. Bedford to Mark Requa, July 17, 1918, in War Industries Board Records, National Archives, Washington, D.C.; see also Bernard Baruch to E. N. Hurley, May 3, 1918, in War Industries Board Records.

24. *NPN* (August 21, 1918); *O&G Jl.* (August 16, 1918); for Requa-Bedford correspondence concerning stabilization plan for industry which both men developed, see *O&G Jl.* (August 23, 1918).

for aviation gasoline were formulated at Requa's behest in May, 1918. The War Service Committee had also gathered the most complete set of statistics relating to the industry.[25]

Conservation

Increased production led to a renewed emphasis on conservation. Scientists in the Bureau of Mines, such as Dr. Van Manning, constantly urged oilmen to improve the technical efficiency of their methods in drilling, producing, and refining. Meanwhile, Requa threatened to close refineries that in his opinion were inefficient. The Fuel Administration also encouraged scientific research activities designed to improve oil recovery.[26]

Requa used his influence to promote tax reductions for oil producers by favoring a depletion allowance. The urgings of various oil producers had led Congress to provide special privileges for them in the Revenue Act of 1913, which allowed oil producers to deduct 5 percent of the gross value of their annual oil and gas production. The Revenue Act of 1916 removed the percentage deduction, and instead allowed a "reasonable" allowance for depletion, which was not to exceed the actual cost of discovery, however.[27]

As the wartime mobilization program increased its tempo in 1917, oil producers urged Congress to liberalize the depletion allowance. The United States Senate Finance Committee held lengthy hearings on the problem in April, 1918, at which Requa, Bedford, Sinclair, and other leading industry representatives testified. The gist of their argument was that in most cases deduction of the cost of discovery did not allow producers to replace their exhausted properties. The senators were sympathetic, especially since they were desirous of encouraging maximum production of oil now that it was becoming a strategic mineral resource. The report of the committee reflected this aim quite openly. It recommended a reduction of surtaxes and excess profits "to stimulate prospecting and exploration." Meanwhile, several congressmen introduced

25. *O&G Jl.* (July 26, 1918); *NPN* (January 15, 1919), 477; see also Mark Requa to Walter Teagle, November 27, 1918, and Walter Teagle to Mark Requa, December 18, 1918, in FA Records.

26. *NPN* (July 31, 1918) provides an example.

27. 1916 Stats. at Large 759; a brief survey is in John H. Lichtblau, *The Oil Depletion Issue* (New York, 1959), 30–34.

bills in the House to increase the depletion allowance for oil in view of its important wartime role.[28]

The Senate accepted these recommendations by increasing the depletion allowance in the War Revenue Act of 1918. The specific provisions that applied to petroleum producers now allowed them to base their "reasonable" deduction either on discovery cost, or on the "fair market value" of their properties. This granted them a greater flexibility than earlier laws had provided. In most cases the market value of mineral properties greatly exceeded direct discovery costs, and thus Congress provided oil producers with a vastly improved basis for securing tax benefits. Since this privilege was designed to increase production—in the interests of national defense—the depletion allowance reflected a consensus among government and businessmen in wartime.[29]

How far the emphasis on cooperation had moved public policy away from trust-busting was illustrated by Requa's controversy with the Federal Trade Commission. Understandably, the members of the recently (1914) created Federal Trade Commission, established to enforce antitrust legislation, had not as yet caught the new drift in public policy. Since their prime function was to maintain competition in American industry and to prevent concentration and consolidation of business corporations—within the conceptual framework of the New Freedom— the version of the New Nationalism espoused by Requa seemed strange, indeed. Thus, in April, 1918, the Federal Trade Commission issued a much publicized report accusing oil producers and refiners of profiteering. In addition, it charged Standard Oil of Indiana with violation of the Federal Trade Commission and Clayton Acts in its marketing practices. If the federal government was to meet its oil requirements, the report noted, nationalization of the industry might well be necessary.[30]

28. 64 Cong., 2 sess., Senate, Committee on Finance, *Hearings on Revenue Act* (H.R. 12863), 1918 (Washington, 1918); 65 Cong., 3 sess., Senate Committee on Finance, *Senate Report* No. 617 (Washington, 1919); Internal Revenue Commissioner, *Manual for Oil and Gas Industry under Revenue Act of 1918* (Washington, 1919).

29. 1918 Stats. at Large 1067–1068; a later appraisal is in *Legislative History of Depletion Allowance* (Staff Data Prepared by the Staff of the Joint Committee on Internal Revenue Taxation for Use of the Committee on Ways and Means) (Washington, 1950), 1–4.

30. *NPN* (May 1, 8, 1918); U.S. Federal Trade Commission, *Investigation of the Price of Gasoline, April, 1916* (Washington, 1916); *Report on the Price of Gasoline in 1915* (Washington, 1917; not released till 1918); *NYT*, May 1, 25. 1918.

It should be noted, however, that these charges were based on inquiries made in 1915, three years before publication. If outdated, they nevertheless revealed an effort by the Federal Trade Commissioners to challenge Requa's policies.

But the New Nationalism prevailed. Requa and his Oil Division immediately sprang into action to prevent formal proceedings by the Federal Trade Commission. Requa argued that the Lever Act, under which he exercised authority, took precedence over the Federal Trade Commission Act. Still, he was willing to discuss a compromise. Under an agreement made between the Federal Trade Commission and the Fuel Administration, the Federal Trade Commissioners could proceed to charge Standard of Indiana with false advertising and with making exclusive agency contracts to restrain trade. In turn, the Federal Trade Commission would do nothing to interfere with industry pooling agreements for the allocation of supplies under the Oil Division's direction. The Federal Trade Commission also agreed to abide by all future decisions of the Fuel Administration, although the latter was to keep the commission informed of any actions that infringed upon the antitrust laws in peacetime. Although the matter was not noted officially, apparently Requa also promised the Federal Trade Commission that he would use his powers to prevent an anticipated rise in crude oil prices. In a letter to Bedford he stated publicly that he would look most unfavorably upon such an increase.[31]

The first year of American participation in World War I had thus wrought a silent revolution in the federal government's relation to industry. From emphasis on competition and the dissolution of monopoly, public policy now stressed cooperation and regulation of business practices. That cooperation and stabilization of the oil industry should be a common goal of government and business was a theme emphasized repeatedly by A. C. Bedford, the acknowledged leader of the oil industry. "Such cooperation and mutual forebearance may not be in strict accord with the law of competition," he told the convention of the Western Petroleum Refiners, "but it is not contrary to the laws of . . . fair dealing."[32]

---

31. *NPN* (May 15, 29, June 12, 1918); Federal Trade Commission, *Annual Report* 1918 (Washington, 1918), 69–70.
32. The speech is reproduced in its entirety in *O&G Jl.* (April 4, 1918).

Cooperation, and not competition, would lead to greater efficiency. Not only would it increase profits, but it would aid in conserving the visibly exhaustible supply of oil. "Government control does not necessarily signify disaster to an industry," Bedford admonished. "If zonal distribution of petroleum products is necessary to supply national needs, zonal distribution will be accomplished. If pooling of tank cars and ships will more efficiently meet national demands, those facilities will be pooled. If well drilling supplies must be allocated . . . if licensing of jobbers and others is necessary . . . everything that is necessary will be done."[33] Thus, the thinking of business leaders such as Bedford was leading to a changed conception of cooperation within the industry and its relationships with the federal and state governments.

The pressure of wartime demands for petroleum led to the development of very similar attitudes within government. As head of the Oil Division, Requa urged, above all, the need for cooperation—not competition—in the industry. The ends such a policy could achieve Requa held to be beneficial for both. Like Bedford, he argued that greater efficiency and, thus, increased profits would be immediate results of the diminution of competition. Moreover, he, too, was concerned with the depletion of the nation's oil supply and the necessity for adoption of conservation measures.[34] The cult of efficiency, growing out of the scientific management movement at the turn of the century, had made as deep an impression on managers in business as it had on those in government.

World War I thus wrought rapid changes in public policy as industry self-regulation became the desired goal of businessmen and government. As the *National Petroleum News* noted, the spirit of cooperation heralded a new era for the oil industry. The erstwhile conflict between independent oil producers and a monopolistic Standard Oil Company had abated. When the National Petroleum Association, a leading spokesman for independent oilmen, met in 1918, it supported resolutions endorsing cooperation rather than competition within the oil industry. Perhaps the change was well dramatized by the association when it tendered a dinner to honor A. C. Bedford, chairman of the Petroleum War Service Committee and president of the Standard Oil Company

33. *Ibid.* (April 4, 1918).
34. Requa's speech is reprinted in *NPN* (May 29, 1918).

(N.J.), the same company that less than a decade before had been its archenemy and foe.[35] An industry rent asunder by bitter competition now worked toward cooperation in many spheres to achieve stabilization. Public policy recognized the change by encouraging voluntary self-regulation among oilmen under the aegis of federal supervision.

POSTWAR RECONVERSION

With the end of the war, in November, 1918, both business leaders and federal officials faced the immediate future with much uncertainty. Would the Wilson Administration continue to foster the new trend of public policy, or would it revert to the antimonopoly emphasis of the New Freedom? No one seemed to know. In contrast to his strong executive leadership before the fall elections in 1918, President Wilson now seemed so preoccupied with foreign affairs that domestic policies were left to drift. The Administration provided little guidance for businessmen on the course of demobilization. Would it be immediate or gradual?

During the difficult months of postwar reconversion, from November, 1918, to the summer of 1919, the Administration provided little guidance for businessmen seeking to adjust to peacetime problems. Maximum production was no longer a central problem. Now oil industry leaders focused primarily on stabilizing their industry, since supply suddenly outdistanced demand. Added to this central concern was their gnawing uncertainty over the immediate course of federal policies. Would government-industry cooperation and supervised competition be continued, or would the antitrust laws be restored? In the absence of clear direction from President or Congress, oilmen—like other business leaders—remained apprehensive and uncertain.

The Fuel Administration and its leaders—Garfield and Requa—planned a gradual dismantlement of controls over the oil industry. They began the dissolution slowly in December by closing the Pacific Coast section, the Bureau of Oil Well Supplies, the Bureau of Export Licenses, and the Bureau of Lubricants. Requa also abolished voluntary restrictions and ended priorities on all petroleum products except aviation gasoline. On the other hand, the War Service Committee continued its operations, while Requa announced that he was retaining price con-

35. *Ibid.* (November 13, 20, 1918); New York *Sun,* October 10, 1918.

trol under the Lever Act. In case of a price rise he was ready to reinvoke his powers.

Within the industry there was no strong desire for immediate abolition of the new regime of cooperation established during the war. In fact, the *Oil and Gas Journal* reported that much sentiment existed for continuation of the National War Service Committee's functions, especially among men like Bedford. The members of the oil industry's War Service Committee themselves expressed "unqualified approval" for a permanent industry organization based on the wartime model. Indeed, they appointed a temporary committee to draw up appropriate plans. Requa attended their meeting and added his support to the movement for a permanent oil industry trade organization. The American Iron and Steel Institute (formed in 1908) provided a precedent for the oilmen. Their spirit of cooperation was expressed in a formal resolution in which the committee recommended organizing a petroleum institute.[36]

The entire problem of postwar industrial policy was the prime topic of discussion at a Reconstruction Conference of Industrial War Service Committees in Atlantic City, New Jersey, December 4–6, 1918, which the Chamber of Commerce of the United States sponsored. This meeting attracted about four thousand executives, including the members of the 381 war service committees in operation. Their sentiment was well voiced by W. H. Manns, director of the Executive Committee of the War Service Committees (and a vice-president of the Baltimore and Ohio Railroad). He urged repeal or amendment of the Sherman Anti-Trust Act and of the Clayton and Federal Trade Commission Acts. In their place he urged federal endorsement of cooperation among businessmen to stabilize competition. This new emphasis on cooperation by businessmen was forcefully expressed by John D. Rockefeller, Jr., one of the main speakers at the convention.[37]

At this meeting Requa also reiterated his hope that the ideals of the New Nationalism would dominate public policy in the postwar period. The advantages of cooperation, he noted, had been proved during the war. "In place of the doctrine of unrestricted competition," he told the

36. *NPN* (November 27, 1918); *O&G Jl.* (November 15, 22, December 13, 20, 1918); *NYT*, November 22, 1918.

37. *NPN* (December 4, 1918); *NYT*, December 4, 5, 1918; for J. D. Rockefeller Jr.'s speech, see *NYT*, December 6, 1918; a full account of the oilmen's activities at the Atlantic City conference is in *NPN* (December 11, 1918), 1 ff.

assembled industry leaders at Atlantic City on December 5, 1918, "we must substitute the doctrine of cooperation." If competition had ruled during the war, it would "have proven fatal to our success." Indeed, he formulated a proposal for a National Board of Trade, to be made up of eminent business executives, to counsel, advise, and regulate industries. A bill embodying this proposal was introduced in Congress, where it died.[38] It is noteworthy that the New Deal embraced just such a plan when, in 1933, it created the National Recovery Administration.

In Atlantic City, Bedford, Requa, and other oil industry leaders made tentative plans for the organization of a permanent trade organization. They deferred further discussion until March, 1919. The National Petroleum War Service Committee meanwhile called a meeting of all of its subcommittees in New York City for March 14, 1919, to draft a constitution and by-laws for the new association, which would encompass existing trade groups. Bedford himself, a leading figure in the movement for a new organization, preferred to let others take credit for it. Much of the detailed work was performed by Henry L. Doherty of Cities Service and by E. C. Lufkin, president of the Texas Company. They arranged the New York conference, at which the principal speaker was Mark Requa. His topic, as one might expect, was "Cooperation." The institute would not be following the trend of the times, Requa said, unless it practiced cooperation. "If there is any one thing the war has demonstrated," he proclaimed, "it is the success of cooperation. . . . Because of it things are going to be accomplished that could not be accomplished before. I see no other way for the petroleum industry to cooperate among its own members and with the government as it will have to cooperate unless it takes some form to perpetuate the Petroleum committee."[39]

The final organization was effected ten days later in Chicago at the annual meeting of the American Petroleum League. This assemblage followed Requa's advice. It voted for the dissolution of the National War Service Committee on March 26. But the committee's members and Mark Requa were to serve as directors of the new American Petroleum Institute. Although the group wanted A. C. Bedford as first president of the institute, he declined, largely because he felt that it would

38. *NPN* (December 11, 18, 1918); for this type of proposal, see *Congressional Record* [hereafter cited as *CR*], 66 Cong., 1 sess., 1538 (H.R. 6426).
39. *NPN* (December 18, 1918, January 15, February 19, 1919).

not be desirable to have Standard Oil Company's chairman of the board as head of the new trade association. The committee then chose Thomas O'Donnell, Requa's director of production in the Fuel Administration and a former California oilman affiliated with the E. L. Doheny interests. H. F. Sinclair was elected treasurer and R. L. Welch, general counsel of the Western Petroleum Refiner's Association, took a similar position with the new American Petroleum Institute (API).[40]

At its inception, the founders of the API sought to delimit the purposes and functions of the organization. Its aims were essentially to facilitate cooperation within the industry and between the industry and the government, much as the Fuel Administration had done. It was to collect statistics and data on new processes and trends, to foster marketing of petroleum products, to represent its members in dealing with the federal and foreign governments, and to promote the industry.

Requa in addition urged the institute to embrace the cause of conservation. He called upon it to raise levels of technical efficiency in the industry, not only for increased profits but also to conserve the national petroleum supply threatened with depletion in the face of increasing demand. "The producer of petroleum is after all a trustee administering a wasting asset in behalf of the population as a whole," he told the assembled oilmen, rephrasing Theodore Roosevelt's doctrine of stewardship. The new organization should also further standardization of business procedures and of accounts, lest the federal government impose its own requirements.[41]

A major share of the API's energies were to be devoted to furthering the development of foreign oil sources and markets. Cooperation would further this objective. As Bedford told the delegates: "You are aware that . . . during the war, there was brought about a different and entirely new spirit of understanding between the various elements of the petroleum industry, an understanding which none of us . . . would in our most optimistic moments, have dreamed possible some three or four years ago." This unity should now be applied to the exploitation of foreign trade.[42]

40. *Ibid.* (March 12, 19, 1919).
41. *Ibid.* (March 19, April 2, 1919); Mark Requa, *Cooperation in the Petroleum Industry* (Chicago, 1919), pamphlet in FA Records.
42. Text in *NPN* (April 2, 1919), 34–38, from which quotations have been taken.

By the spring of 1919, the API began its work in dealing with important industry-wide problems. The Federal Trade Commission, for example, was investigating the practice of some companies in giving away pumps with sales of gasoline. Should the industry await a law suit, or try to make a suitable settlement with the federal agency? Bills concerning leasing of public oil lands, pending in Congress and in state legislatures, required the API's attention. Tax laws were another sphere to attract the institute's immediate interest. Cooperation with other related industries was a virtual necessity, and within weeks the API was approached by automobile manufacturers concerning common problems and future output. The formulation of conservation policies provided another important phase of anticipated work. No less significant was collection and dissemination of statistics to facilitate future planning by oilmen. From the beginning, therefore, the API undertook a rationalization and integration of industry-wide functions and served as a vital instrument of coordination.[43]

Soon after the organization of the API, the United States Fuel Administration undertook its own final dissolution. After March, 1919, it confined itself to minor problems. Its prime energies were devoted to concluding pending legal suits in the courts, and to regulating the supply of natural gas in communities that had inadequate supplies. Requa left his office for New York in early April to write his final report. Representatives of the industry were virtually unanimous in praising him for his astute leadership of the Fuel Administration. Complete abrogation of all regulations came on May 15, 1919.[44] The great experiment in cooperation seemed to have come to an end.

The record of the Wilson Administration in guiding the nation back to peace in 1919 was not one to inspire confidence. The President's insistence on the immediate liquidation of all wartime agencies created much unnecessary confusion. It seemed as if he were afraid of the very organizations he had just recently created. In giving virtually all of his time and energies to foreign problems during the first half of 1919, Wilson sadly neglected his responsibilities in leading the country onto an orderly path of reconversion. His precipitate and arbitrary demobili-

43. *Ibid.* (May 28, 1919).
44. *Ibid.* (January 22, February 12, 26, March 19, May 21, 1919); *NYT,* June 5, 1919.

zation created many unnecessary hardships for both business and labor. That complete abandonment of wartime relationships was not universally desired was reflected in the efforts of groups like the American Petroleum Institute, which sought to continue many of the same functions of intraindustry cooperation that had so recently shown themselves to be highly effective. No general appraisal of Wilson's Presidency, therefore, can afford to ignore his lack of responsibility in dealing with the dismantlement of wartime agencies.

The suddenness with which the Wilson Administration abolished federal controls between 1918 and 1919 left the oil industry entirely to its own devices. The fruitful cooperative relationship that industry leaders had developed with the Fuel Administration in 1918 was now rudely disrupted, and with it the uniformity that had characterized federal oil policies during the wartime period. Yet, 1919 was a year of confusion, a year in which the joint energies of government and industry were most needed as the economy underwent violent fluctuations in a critical period of postwar readjustment.

For those engaged in the petroleum industry the most immediate peacetime problem was fear of an impending oil shortage. The reasons for such predictions were not wholly unrealistic. In the first place, the anticipated increase of motor cars and trucks pointed to an enormously expanded demand for gasoline. Nor had the wasteful practices accompanying the production of petroleum escaped the notice of the United States Fuel Administration. Especially during the war, when prime emphasis had been placed on maximum production, waste had taken on serious proportions. At the same time, the drain of increased consumption of petroleum products on limited and dwindling domestic supplies aroused fears of depletion, perhaps within a decade. Although scientific estimates were largely inaccurate during these years, G. O. Smith, the highly respected director of the United States Geological Survey, in 1919 predicted the exhaustion of American petroleum reserves within ten years.[45]

Such a shortage was expected to have a serious impact on at least three phases of U.S. oil policy. First, military men were much con-

45. *NYT*, January 5, 1920; see editorial in *ibid.*, January 7, 1920; see also George Otis Smith, "Planning for Tomorrow," *Independent*, CIII (September 25, 1920), 366–367 and George Otis Smith, "Where the World Gets Its Oil," *National Geographic Magazine*, XXXVII (February 1920), 181–202.

cerned with securing adequate oil supplies for the United States Navy. Secretary of the Navy Daniels and Secretary of the Interior Franklin K. Lane (1913–1921), especially, were alarmed about difficulties of oil procurement and rising prices.[46] Secondly, scientists like G. O. Smith were anxious to conserve available U.S. oil resources by fostering more efficient methods of extraction. Finally, a group of influential industry leaders believed that the federal government should protect American petroleum exploitation overseas. Arguing that exploitation of foreign fields would conserve the meager U.S. supplies, many oilmen felt that some form of "dollar diplomacy" would be desirable whereby the State Department would support their endeavors to secure favorable conditions in other countries. At the very least they hoped for concessions equal to those received by foreign businessmen.[47]

How could the expected catastrophe be averted? Improved conservation practices at home certainly provided one possible avenue to the amelioration of the problem. But these could not provide a long-range solution. That could come only from the discovery of vast, new oil reserves. And these were to be found primarily overseas, in South America, the Middle East, and the Dutch East Indies. Thus, at the close of World War I many American oilmen and government leaders became convinced that the answer to the replenishment of American oil supplies lay in new foreign sources. The task of U.S. oil policy consequently was to develop means whereby U.S. exploitation of foreign oil sources would be facilitated.

The petroleum shortage of 1919 aroused dire fears in the mind of Secretary of the Navy Josephus Daniels. He was concerned not only with safeguarding future supplies, but—more immediately—with obtain-

46. E. David Cronon (ed.), *The Cabinet Diaries of Josephus Daniels* (Lincoln, 1963), 500–501 (February 28, 1920); Secretary of the Navy, *Annual Report* 1919 (Washington, 1920), 140–142; Franklin K. Lane to Van H. Manning, September 24, 1919, in Anne W. Lane and Louise H. Wall (eds.), *The Letters of Franklin K. Lane* (New York, 1922), 315–316; Franklin K. Lane, "The Oil Age and Its Needs," *Independent,* CI (January 17, 1920), 89–90.

47. The contemporary literature concerning this U.S. search for oil is large. See J. K. Barnes, "America Scouring the World for Oil," *World's Work,* XL (September 1920), 453–464, "American Oil Argonauts," *ibid.,* XL (July 1920), 256–267; "American Oil Intervention," *Literary Digest,* LXIX (April 16, 1921), 17–18; "How Long the Oil Will Last," *Scientific American,* CXX (May 3, 1919), 459; Mark L. Requa, "The Petroleum Problem of the World," *Saturday Evening Post,* CXCIII (October 30, 1920), 18.

ing fuel oil at what he considered reasonable prices. To meet the crisis he ordered Navy officers to seize necessary fuel if, confronted by rapidly rising oil prices, they failed to receive reasonable bids from suppliers.

The Navy's efforts to commandeer privately owned petroleum products added to postwar tensions. By March, 1920, it was reported that Daniels was ready to seize oil under the broad powers granted the President under the Lever Act.[48] The situation was particularly critical on the West Coast, where the commander of the Pacific fleet was about to take forcible possession of fuel oil in the hands of the General Petroleum Company of Los Angeles. Although the company was able to secure an injunction from the Federal District Court of Los Angeles, this did not deter the Navy. When the Union Oil Company refused to deliver fuel at $1.60 a barrel, as the Navy desired, six destroyers drew up to the San Francisco plant of the Associated Oil Company in San Francisco a few weeks later with orders to seize as much oil as they required. This action had the desired effect, for in the month thereafter the Navy Department was able to sign contracts with suppliers.[49]

That fall another acute oil shortage developed. Amidst denunciations of the Navy's commandeering policies by Thomas O'Donnell, president of the American Petroleum Institute, Secretary Daniels urged even more drastic action. In a speech to the American Society of Naval Engineers he suggested the nationalization of all U.S. petroleum resources to protect future interests of the Navy. At the very least, he thought that the federal government should have the power to prohibit the use of fuel oil for industrial purposes whenever it was needed to supply the Navy.[50]

A similar concern was shared by the United States Shipping Board, now responsible for a greatly enlarged American merchant fleet. Chairman E. H. Hurley even suggested that the federal government collect the royalties it was receiving from its public lands in oil instead of money. Like the Navy, the Shipping Board experienced difficulties in securing private bids for its supply contracts, and urged the President to use his war powers to assure an adequate flow for its vessels.[51]

48. *NYT,* March 12, 1920.
49. *NYT,* June 20, July 8, 27, August 12, 1920; Secretary of the Navy, *Annual Report* 1920 (Washington, 1921), 1081–1082.
50. *NYT,* November 19, December 19, 29, 1920.
51. *Ibid.,* January 5, 7, February 15, March 5, 9, April 17, 1920.

At the same time many scientists and engineers viewed the impending exhaustion of American petroleum resources with dismay. In a careful analysis of the problem, G. O. Smith, director of the United States Geographical Survey (and a protégé of Herbert Hoover) underlined the need for drastic action.[52] W. C. Teagle, Standard Oil (N.J.) Company's chairman of the board, expressed himself in similar terms. The great problem of the future, he felt, was to meet the tremendous pressure of new demands as diverse uses for petroleum were raising U.S. consumption by about 9 percent each year. The president of the American Institute of Mining and Mechanical Engineers in 1920, Herbert Hoover, reflected the same attitude when he noted that the great need of the age was to apply scientific principles in the oil industry to eliminate waste.[53] His warnings were shortly reinforced by a report from the United States Bureau of Mines, which emphasized that the United States was rapidly using up its oil supplies, estimated to last no longer, perhaps, than twenty years. This prediction was reinforced by statements from Mark Requa, who pointed to the gap between increasing consumption and production.[54]

Scientists, business leaders, and federal officials believed that the solution to the threatened oil shortage was overseas exploitation. The dire predictions of exhaustion gave rise to a widespread demand for American exploration of oil resources in foreign countries. G. O. Smith added his influential voice to the chorus of those who pointed to this as the solution to the nation's critical oil problem. Walter Teagle of the Standard Oil Company (N.J.) also expressed the view of other oil industry leaders when he urged worldwide prospecting to meet the heavy anticipated demands for petroleum products.[55] At the annual meeting of the American Institute of Mining and Mechanical Engineers in 1920 various speakers advocated overseas oil development by Americans as a

52. *Ibid.*, January 5, 1920; see also George O. Smith, "Foreign Oil Supply for the United States," in American Institute of Mining and Metallurgical Engineers, *Transactions* 1921, LXV (New York, 1921), 91–92.

53. *NYT*, February 18, 19, 1920.

54. *Ibid.*, May 3, 17, 1920; Carl H. Beal, *The Decline and Ultimate Production of Oil Wells*, U.S. Bureau of Mines, Bulletin No. 177 (Washington, 1919), 5–7; for Requa, see *NYT*, October 6, 1920, *CR*, 66 Cong., 2 sess., *Senate Resolution No. 354*, 6220, 6259, asking for report of Secretary of the Navy on necessity for acquisition of oil lands in foreign countries for naval purposes.

55. *NYT*, January 5, 30, 1920.

prime means of supplying U.S. military and domestic requirements in the coming decade.[56] Clearly, the search for oil by American companies must extend to all portions of the world. As early as June, 1919, the Department of State was instructing its representatives overseas to be alert to new sources of petroleum.[57]

But if American investors and oil prospectors were to venture abroad they must have the support and protection of the government. Thus, the Departments of State and Commerce early became involved with American oil activities overseas. Congress too, became concerned. In May, 1920, in fact, Senator John Phelan of California proposed that the U.S. government itself should bear the responsibility of finding oil overseas and that Congress should create a United States Oil Corporation, on the model of the Shipping Board, to stimulate American oil development in foreign countries.[58] At the same time Senator Henry Cabot Lodge secured the passage of a resolution calling for a report by the State Department on the discriminations imposed by foreign nations on American oil interests.[59] The Democratic Party platform in July, 1920, also gave explicit recognition to the importance of securing overseas oil sources and urged that the President and his Cabinet departments as well as Congress give full encouragement to private American interests in this endeavor. The policy statement also reiterated American support for the policy of the "open door," under which the United States should insist on the same rights being granted to its nationals doing business in foreign countries as those extended to others.[60]

As businessmen looked to the future in the middle of 1920, they

56. *Ibid.*, February 17, 18, 1920; American Institute of Mining and Metallurgical Engineers, *Transactions* 1920, LXIII (New York, 1920), xv ff.

57. Wilbur J. Carr [Acting Secretary of State] to Certain Consular Officers, May 31, 1919, in U.S. Department of State, *Foreign Relations of the United States* [hereafter cited as *FR*], I (1919), 163–165; A. A. Adee to Diplomatic and Consular Officers, August 16, 1919, *FR*, I (1919), 167–168.

58. *NYT*, May 18, 1920; *CR*, 66 Cong., 2 sess. (May 17, 1920), 7144; *ibid.*, 66 Cong., 3 sess. (January 17, 1921), 1491.

59. *CR*, 66 Cong. 3 sess., *Senate Resolution* No. 423, 1421; see also *ibid.*, 66 Cong., 2 sess., *House Joint Resolution* No. 374 (June 2, 1920), 8303. The State Department was already sending protests to Great Britain; see Earl Grey to Robert Lansing, November 6, 1919, *FR*, I (1919), 168–170, and Robert Lansing to Earl Grey, December 20, 1919, *ibid.*, 171.

60. *NYT*, July 3, 1920; Kirk Porter and Donald B. Johnson (eds.), *American Party Platforms, 1840–1960* (New York, 1961), 221.

could reflect on the preceding two years with satisfaction. America's oil production record had been little short of amazing. It had been brought about by the integration of industry operations, integration made possible by voluntary cooperation within the industry as well as by rules enforced by the Fuel Administration. Many oilmen hoped that the advantages of wartime cooperation could be maintained, for the problems of price stabilization and conservation were bound to recur in the immediate postwar period. Amid expectations that domestic U.S. oil reserves might be exhausted in another decade, cooperation within the industry and with the federal government also promised to assure attainment of one of the industry's main objectives in 1919—the exploitation of foreign and overseas oil resources.

3 / U. S. Oil Policy Overseas: the Middle East, the Pacific, and Latin America, 1919–1924

A FEAR that domestic petroleum reserves would soon be exhausted strongly gripped American businessmen and government leaders in the immediate post-World-War-I era. Amounting almost to an obsession, it led them into a worldwide search for petroleum overseas, particularly in Mesopotamia, the Dutch East Indies, Mexico, Venezuela, Colombia, and Peru. In view of intense international rivalry for oil, U.S. companies were eager for the diplomatic support of their government, concerned as it was with meeting the fuel needs of national defense, and increasing domestic consumption. Consequently, the years between 1919 and 1924 witnessed a renewed emphasis on the principle of the Open Door in U.S. foreign affairs. But the diplomatic skills of both the later Wilson and the Harding Administrations were meager. The policies of Robert Lansing, Bainbridge Colby, and Charles Evans Hughes revealed many weaknesses and vacillations. As a result, American efforts to secure foreign oil concessions in the Middle East and Sumatra met only minimal success. Largely for economic reasons American oil companies found a much wider field for exploitation in South America. This post-war period of intense foreign oil exploration closed in 1924 as vast new petroleum discoveries in Oklahoma, Texas, Louisiana, and California made overseas ventures less urgent. In fact, the new fields not only removed the threat of oil scarcity but actually created a surplus.

49

THE MIDDLE EAST

At the Versailles Peace Conference the U.S. delegation made little effort to promote American oil interests. Within weeks after the end of the war the British government was seeking to exclude all foreign oil companies from Palestine and Mesopotamia. Since the British army in 1919 occupied a goodly share of the former Ottoman dominions, English businessmen obviously had a clear advantage. Even while Allied peace negotiations were getting under way at Versailles early in 1919, the Standard Oil Company (N.Y.) sent a complaint to the State Department concerning a British officer in Palestine who had forcibly inspected the company's oil-prospecting maps there.[1] Moreover, at Mark Requa's behest, the State Department on May 21, 1919, informed the U.S. mission in Versailles that American oil interests were seriously considering acquisition of petroleum territories in Mesopotamia and Palestine. Consequently it urged the U.S. delegation to consider the possibility of future investments and to secure inclusion of provisions in the peace treaty that would allow U.S. companies concessions on a basis of equality with other nations. Requa thought it important to have such a prospective policy clearly delineated before the Allies apportioned territories. But the American Peace Commission testily replied that it could not consider such questions since bargaining about the disposition of the Ottoman Empire was still in progress.[2] Later events were to cast doubt on the wisdom of their decision.

Palestine

Such a negative attitude led the Standard Oil Company (N.Y.) to ask the State Department for protection of its interests in Palestine. On September 18, 1919, the State Department notified the American Peace Mission in Paris that the British government prohibited geographical surveys in Palestine and refused to grant new concessions there until it

1. For text, see U.S. Department of State, *Foreign Relations of the United States* [hereafter cited as *FR*], II (1920), 655–658; H. C. Cole to Acting Secretary of State, March 15, 1919, *ibid.*, II (1919), 250–252.

2. Frank L. Polk [Acting Secretary of State] to the Commission to Negotiate the Peace, May 21, 1919, *FR*, II (1919), 252–253, and the Commission to Negotiate the Peace to Acting Secretary of State, June 5, 1919, *ibid.*; J. B. Wright [U.S. Chargé in Great Britain] to Acting Secretary of State, June 5, 1919, *ibid.*, 253.

had formally established a mandate system. Faced with the necessity of choice, the Peace Commissioners sought to pass the buck. They believed that these were matters for a projected commission on Turkish mandates or perhaps for the American ambassador in London. British agreement to administer an "A" mandate, they pointed out, required assurances to maintain equal economic opportunities. Moreover, in Big Four meetings, Wilson himself had insisted that mandatory nations should not give priority to their own nationals in awarding commercial concessions.[3]

Mesopotamia

Despite disclaimers, the British continued their policy of exclusion during the remainder of 1919. When Standard of New Jersey sent a representative to Mesopotamia in October, 1919, to prospect for oil he was turned back by British army officers. On the other hand, a geologist for Shell, a Dutch-British firm, was allowed to proceed with his work. The British Foreign Office maintained that, since it had created a temporary military government for Mesopotamia, it seemed best for the moment to ban all prospecting as well as applications for permits.[4]

But the State Department kept up its pressure on the British, even after the United States Senate had decisively rejected the Treaty of Versailles. In May, 1920, Secretary Lansing embarked on another diplomatic campaign to secure a modification of British restrictive policies. In a long series of notes Lansing upheld American rights to equal opportunity in newly mandated areas. These the British violated when they refused the Standard Oil Company (N.J.) prospecting rights in Mesopotamia, at the same time that the Royal Dutch Shell Company enjoyed unlimited exploration privileges in the United States. Many Americans had the unfortunate impression, Lansing declared, that the British were using their mandates largely to further their own oil interests. Consequently the United States insisted on its prewar policy of the Open Door and looked askance at any grants of exclusive business concessions. Unfortunately, the British ignored the American demand

3. The Standard Oil Company of New York to Acting Secretary of State, March 15, 1919, *FR*, II (1919), 250–252.
4. Lansing to Davis, October 30, 1919, *ibid.*, 259–260; Davis to Lansing, November 22, 1919, *ibid.*, 260–261.

and busied themselves in consolidating their influence in Mesopotamia.[5]

Both the British and the French showed their contempt for the American position by concluding the San Remo Agreement in April, 1920. In an outright repudiation of Wilsonian principle—and the Open Door —the two powers sought to divide up the most desirable oil prospecting areas of Mesopotamia among themselves. Their understanding covered the Balkans and the Near East, including Mesopotamia. It stipulated that the British would grant the French 25 percent of the oil production there, to be exploited by a British company. Above all, both parties pledged themselves to keep out nationals of other countries.

The State Department refused to recognize the San Remo Agreement, however. Lansing, and Colby after him, questioned the legality of the pre-World-War-I agreements under which the British government claimed special rights to Mesopotamian oil concessions. These claims centered on a supposed concession by the Grand Vizier of the Ottoman Empire to the Turkish Petroleum Company, a British firm, in June, 1914. The American consul in Berlin charged in August, 1920, that the supposed concession had never been explicit, that it was surrounded by fraud, and that it had not received any legal sanction.[6] The United States could therefore not consider it valid. But the British Foreign Minister, Lord Curzon, rejected American contentions. He felt that problems concerning mandates should be discussed only by League members, a position that left the United States nowhere. Moreover, he noted that British oil development in Mesopotamia was due to purely military considerations. As an Associated power, the United States could not challenge such activities. In despair, during the summer of 1920 Secretary of State Bainbridge Colby continued to press for the principle of the Open Door but without securing any concessions for American oil interests.[7]

5. J. W. Alexander to Secretary of State, February 25, 1920, Frank L. Polk to J. W. Alexander, March 18, 1920, in Records of the Bureau of Foreign and Domestic Commerce, National Archives [hereafter cited as BFDC Records], Washington, D.C.; Davis to Curzon, May 12, 1920, Colby to Davis, July 26, 1920, *FR,* II (1920), 651–655, 658–659.

6. New York *Times* [hereafter cited as *NYT*], May 18, 1920; text in *FR,* II (1920), 655–658.

7. Coffin to Colby, August 4, 1920, Davis to Colby, August 11, 1920, 667, Colby to Curzon, November 20, 1920, *FR,* II (1920), 660–673; Acting Secretary of Commerce to Secretary of State, August 14, 1920, Norman Dain to Secretary of Commerce, August 27, 1920, in BFDC Records.

Thus, the Wilson Administration's diplomatic attempt to secure privileges for American oil companies in the Middle East yielded no fruit. Some of the blame rested on Wilson himself. The failure of the U.S. delegation at the Versailles Conference to press for the recognition of American oil prospecting rights in the Middle East seriously weakened the State Department's position thereafter. During 1919 and 1920 both Lansing and Colby unsuccessfully strove to secure British acceptance of the Open Door policy, a principle that the British violated even before the ink was dry on the Treaty of Versailles. With the lack of White House leadership the path for American diplomats seeking American oil privileges was made much more difficult in succeeding years.

Warren G. Harding's new administration in March, 1921, reaffirmed the existing American position. Anti-British sentiment had crystallized during the political campaign of 1920 and was well reflected on the floor of the United States Senate, where Senator Henry Cabot Lodge made a bitter attack on the British for their activities in Mesopotamia. Over the next three years the prime architect of American foreign oil policies, however, was Secretary of State Charles Evans Hughes. While President Harding himself was not wholly unconcerned with the nation's petroleum problems, much of the detailed work was left to Hughes. In view of his long experience, the ineffectiveness and amateurism with which he conducted American oil diplomacy was indeed surprising. His avowed goal was to support the efforts of Americans to secure overseas concessions, an objective he was rarely able to achieve, despite his loud protestations in favor of the Open Door policy.

Soon after Harding assumed the Presidency he threw his support behind the foreign oil exploration attempts of U.S. companies. The issue first arose in April, 1921, when independent producers sought to persuade Congress to enact a tariff on foreign oil imports into the United States. To this Harding was resolutely opposed, and his Administration was able to defeat the measure.

By 1921 independent oil producers were becoming increasingly anxious about the effort of major integrated corporations to import foreign oil. "The current demoralization of the oil industry is due to the great companies," Omer Benedict of the Mid-Continent Oil and Gas Association declared bluntly.[8] Their large purchases of cheap Mexican oil, for example, were already reducing the profits of smaller, domestic pro-

8. *NYT*, July 3, 1921.

ducers. Thus, Benedict urged an increase in American tariff duties on foreign oil to be included in the new Fordney-McCumber Tariff bill then being considered in Congress. However, in this demand the independents encountered the opposition of major producers, who were spearheading a drive in Congress to abolish all oil duties as a necessary prelude to large-scale overseas investment and exploration. The majors also argued that a tariff would only hasten the exhaustion of domestic oil reserves and weaken the conservation movement. For a while, the cause of the independents seemed certain of success. In the House debate on the Fordney-McCumber bill, Congressman Chandler of Oklahoma at the last minute inserted a provision for an oil levy, largely directed against cheap Mexican oil.[9]

But hopes for success were squashed by President Harding. As the Fordney Bill made its tortuous way through the House, Harding wrote a strong letter of disapproval to its author, the chairman of the House Ways and Means Committee. The President opposed a tariff on oil because he believed that future military and domestic needs made it desirable for the United States to exploit overseas petroleum resources. Like Josephus Daniels before him, he feared that the United States Navy would continue to be short on fuel. Consequently, he felt it necessary for the federal government to protect American investors. An oil tariff would not be in harmony with the broad goals of such a national policy. As further support for his views he pointed to Bainbridge Colby's efforts to secure entry for American interests in Mesopotamia, to Hughes's current attempts to open Dutch concessions in the East Indies, and to the recent signing of the U.S. treaty with Colombia, largely to stimulate American oil interests there.[10]

Other members of his Administration reiterated President Harding's views. Chairman E. H. Hurley of the United States Shipping Board also wrote to Fordney to point out that his agency used at least 40 billion barrels of foreign crude oil annually. Moreover, railroads in the Southwest depended heavily on Mexican supplies. New England manufacturers and ship powers added their voice to this protest, for they feared that a tariff on foreign petroleum would result in a general rise in crude

9. *Ibid.*, July 2, 7, 1921; see also *Congressional Record* [hereafter cited as *CR*], 67 Cong. 1 sess. (July 14, 1921), 3819–3823.
10. *NYT*, July 12, 13, 1921.

oil prices.[11] The Administration's opposition to new duties prevailed; the proposed oil tariff could not attract sufficient votes in Congress to secure passage.

Harding's stand was of undoubted benefit to integrated oil corporations seeking new overseas fields, yet it was also consistent with the larger perspectives of national interest. Certainly the military needs of the Navy—in view of existing geological knowledge concerning the availability of domestic reserves—required prime consideration. Overseas exploitation was also closely tied to domestic conservation policy, a policy that Republican administrations of Benjamin Harrison, Theodore Roosevelt, and Taft had done much to develop and that Harding sought to continue. Moreover, at a time when the United States was changing from an importer to an exporter of capital, it seemed highly desirable to lend federal support to private American investments abroad. Such a course of action was also closely tied to certain basic assumptions of U.S. foreign policy as developed under McKinley and Theodore Roosevelt—namely, the maintenance of the Open Door and the implementation of equal commercial privileges for Americans throughout the world. Any retreat on these principles could impair America's international prestige. Thus, while Harding's opposition to an oil tariff was injurious to the smaller independent oil producers, it was in accord with some of the major considerations of national resource policy.

During this same period, in the early months of the Harding Administration, Secretary of State Hughes was seeking to support the entry of Americans into Middle Eastern oil fields. Over the next three years he laid down three principles in regard to this problem. First, he refused to recognize the San Remo Agreement, under which the British and the French sought to divide oil-bearing territories in Mesopotamia. Secondly, the United States rejected the legality of a supposed oil concession agreement of June, 1914, between the Turkish Sultan's Vizier and the British-controlled Turkish Petroleum Company. Finally, the United States continued to uphold the Open Door principle, and to assert the rights of its nationals to equality of treatment in Mesopotamia.[12]

Unfortunately the strenuous efforts of Hughes were to be no more successful than those of his predecessors. In the spring of 1921, he

11. *Ibid.*, July 19, 1921.
12. Davis to Colby, March 1, 1921, *FR*, II (1921), 80–84.

pressed the first two contentions on the British without great success. The British simply argued that the concession of the Turkish Petroleum Company was no different from one granted by the Sultan to Standard Oil (N.Y.) in Palestine, or to American oil companies by the Mexican government.[13]

Nor did Secretary of Commerce Herbert Hoover provide constructive help. In November, 1921, Hoover called a conference of oil companies in Washington to urge them to participate in petroleum development of Mesopotamia. Present at the meeting were Walter Teagle of Standard (N.J.), E. L. Doheny, Amos Beaty of the Texas Company, G. S. Davison of Gulf Oil, Harry Sinclair, and others. Active discussions revealed, however, that not all of those present were interested in overseas exploitation. Moreover, Hughes noted that the British had not yet granted prospecting permits.[14] Hoover thus appeared to have jumped the gun in his anxiety to foster American overseas investments.

At first Hughes sought to appease the British. He informed them that the United States would continue to uphold the Open Door and would not recognize any move on their part to establish monopoly rights for British nationals in Mesopotamia. But he now agreed to subject the dubious claims of the Turkish Petroleum Company to arbitration, claims that Lansing and Colby had rejected outright.[15]

An important factor in Hughes's conciliatory attitude must have been his desire to secure British cooperation at the forthcoming Washington conference on disarmament. The British government in turn was anxious to retain the good will of the United States. It was hardly accidental, therefore, that in November and December, 1921, the British granted Standard Oil (N.J.) petroleum concessions in North Persia.[16] But they refused to yield on the broader issue of recognizing the Open Door policy.

13. *Ibid.;* Geddes to Hughes, April 20, 1921, *ibid.,* 71–80.

14. Hughes to W. Teagle, November 22, 1921, *FR,* II (1921), 87–88; Hughes to A. L. Beaty, November 22, 1921, in U.S. State Department Records in National Archives [hereafter cited as NA Records], Washington, D.C., Decimal File 80.6363 (Mesopotamia).

15. Harvey to Curzon, November 17, 1921, *FR,* II (1921), 89–93; see also A. C. Millspaugh [Foreign Trade Advisor in State Department] Memo, October 13, 1921, and A. C. Millspaugh Memo on Conversation with Standard Oil (N.Y.) officials, November 26, 1921, in NA Records (Mesopotamia).

16. *NYT,* November 28, 29, December 3, 1921; Hughes to U.S. Ambassador in London, January 30, 1922, in NA Records (Mesopotamia).

Spurred by Hoover, during the summer of 1922 American oil companies themselves took the initiative in securing access to Mesopotamian oil investments. Representing the interests of seven major U.S. oil companies in May, 1922, A. C. Bedford journeyed to London to talk with officials of the Anglo-Persian Petroleum Company and of the United States Embassy. Bedford sought American participation within the framework of the State Department's position. During August he was joined in London by Walter Teagle. But neither was able to secure an agreement on the basis of the Open Door.[17] Thus, on the eve of his departure from England in mid-August, Bedford inquired of the State Department whether it would object to American participation in the Turkish Petroleum Company. Hughes noted cautiously that this was entirely a decision for private individuals involved in the transaction, although the State Department would not alter its policy of refusing to recognize special privileges claimed by the Turkish Petroleum Company.[18] American businessmen were loath to take large risks, however, without the support of their government.

Turkey

The question of American oil rights in Mesopotamia was closely bound up with a peace settlement for the old Turkish Empire. The overthrow of the Sultan in 1922 and the rise of Kemal Ataturk, leader of the Young Turk movement, wrought a significant change in the British military and diplomatic position throughout the Middle East. Superbly organized by Kemal, Turkish armies began to drive out foreign occupation forces, largely British and French. Then, by the middle of 1922 they demanded revision of the humiliating Treaty of Sèvres, which they had been forced to accept three years earlier. The Turkish Revolution thus drastically affected the British policy of excluding American oil interests in the area.

The victories of Ataturk forced the British and French to accept his demands for a new peace conference to revise the Treaty of Sèvres. In

17. A. C. Bedford to Hughes, June 26, 1921, and A.C. Bedford to Sir Charles Greenway, June 27, 1921, *FR,* II (1922), 338–339; Harvey to Hughes, August 4, 1922, *ibid.,* 339–342; Herbert Hoover to Charles Evans Hughes, April 17, 1922, and Hughes to Hoover, May 2, 1922, in NA Records (Mesopotamia).

18. Hughes to Teagle, August 22, 1922, *FR,* II (1922), 342–344; *NYT,* October 24, 1922; Child and Grew to Department of State, November 20, 22, 1922, in NA Records (Lausanne).

October, 1922, this meeting opened in Lausanne, Switzerland. Unfortunately, the United States was not strongly represented there, since the State Department appeared satisfied with an ad hoc mission. This included the United States ambassador to Italy, Gordon Child, and the United States emissary to Turkey, Joseph C. Grew. Without specific instructions, or full briefings, their role at the conference was to be frustrating and ineffective.

Hughes's diplomacy in regard to this conference showed much vacillation and many weaknesses. Inexcusably, he neglected to send clear instructions to the American mission at Lausanne. On November 26, 1922, about a month after the start of the meeting, Child frantically cabled for instructions. He observed that the British and French were superbly prepared for the meeting and had a clear conception of their goals. In fact, Child complained, the Allies controlled and manipulated the agenda of the conference. If U.S. interests in Turkey and Mesopotamia were to be safeguarded, he needed precise guidance concerning U.S. policy toward the Middle East. But Hughes maintained an unrealistic stance. He urged Child and Grew to give their support to American companies desiring oil concessions in Mesopotamia if the conference decided to make it a British mandate. If the area reverted to Turkey, Hughes wrote, then the United States would oppose any effort to grant monopoly rights to a single government or private interest.[19] Instead of pursuing a positive policy of protecting American economic interests, therefore, Hughes was content to confine himself to weak protests in response to British moves.

At the same time, Standard (N.J.) representatives were seeking to take advantage of the weakening British position to secure access to investments in Mesopotamia. Montagu Piesse, London representative of Standard Oil Company (N.J.), wrote Hughes on December 12, 1922, that American oil companies would be granted a 24 percent interest in the Turkish Petroleum Company on the condition that the State Department reverse its refusal to recognize the rights of this British corporation.

19. Child and Grew to Hughes, November 26, 1922, Hughes to Child and Grew, November 27, 1922, *FR*, II (1922), 345–347; AM [American Mission] to Department of State, November 26, 1922, in NA Records (Lausanne). This interpretation of Hughes's diplomacy differs from the less critical account in Laurence Evans, *United States Policy and the Partition of Turkey, 1914–1924* (Baltimore, 1965), 236–268, 292–348.

Bedford asked Hughes to instruct the U.S. delegation at Lausanne to support this proposal. In addition, he had the audacity to urge the State Department to support the Standard Oil agreement only, and to exclude other interested American corporations or investors.[20] To this extraordinary proposal Hughes retorted quickly. He noted that he would continue to question the legitimacy of the Turkish Petroleum Company's claims. However, Bedford's proposal that the State Department cooperate with him in keeping other American companies out of the proposed arrangement was entirely unacceptable. The State Department sought the Open Door policy for all American business interests— not for the benefit of a single corporation.[21]

But Turkish successes—and extreme Turkish nationalism—led Hughes to modify his stand on nonrecognition of the Turkish Petroleum Company. In January, 1923, he instructed the American delegation at Lausanne to agree to arbitration of the claims. Nevertheless, his opposition to outright recognition led American oil companies to reject the British invitation to join the venture. Despite further negotiations between Teagle and the Anglo-Persian Petroleum Company in the spring of 1923, the two sides did not come to an agreement.[22]

One of the final results of the Lausanne Conference was British withdrawal of claims in Mesopotamia. Making a virtue of necessity, the British Foreign Minister repudiated the San Remo Agreement with France, and joined the United States in advocating the Open Door policy.

Such changing conditions in the old Turkish Empire eased entry for American oil interests there. Representatives of the American companies drafted a memorandum on April 12, 1923, in which they affirmed the Open Door policy of the State Department, and outlined a draft agreement concerning concessions from the new Iraqi government. Hughes supported this proposal since it embodied recognition of the Open Door. In addition, Teagle promised to uphold the State Depart-

20. Montagu Piesse to W. C. Teagle, December 12, 1922, *FR*, II (1922), 348.

21. Hughes to Teagle, December 15, 1922, *ibid.*, 348–349; Hughes to Teagle, December 30, 1922, *ibid.*, 351–352; Hughes to Teagle, December 2, 1922, and Teagle to Hughes, December 4, 1922, in NA Records (Lausanne).

22. Hughes to Child and Grew, January 30, 1923, *FR*, II (1923), 240–241; Child and Grew to Hughes, January 31, 1923, *ibid.*, 962–964; Teagle to Hughes, April 17, 1923, *ibid.*, 243–245; Child declaration of U.S. policy, January 23, 1923, in NA Records (Lausanne).

ment's policy of nonrecognition of rights claimed by the old Turkish Petroleum Company.[23]

But the United States missed an important chance to gain significant influence in the area. During the conference, representatives of the new Turkish government appealed to the United States to support their stand against English and French intervention in return for promised future oil concessions. The Turks believed that, unlike the British, the United States was unlikely to utilize economic concessions for purposes of political interference. Child eagerly asked Hughes for instructions concerning this proposal. Incomprehensibly, these were not forthcoming,[24] as Hughes showed himself to be singularly unreceptive to such offers and to a clear grasp of the rapid changes in the power structure of the region.

The Harding Administration's diplomacy in the Middle East was largely ineffective. To be sure, despite failure of the Lausanne Conference, Teagle and Standard Oil (N.J.) associates in succeeding years worked out a compromise with the Anglo-Persian Oil Company that allowed American interests certain rights in the Middle East. But the United States let slip a golden opportunity to secure formal recognition of its Open Door policy in this area of the world, and to provide support for American business interests.

If the avowed objective of American oil diplomacy between 1919 and 1924 was to extend government support to private investors seeking overseas concessions, Hughes showed himself to be largely inept in carrying out this policy. Inexperience, lingering isolationist sentiments, and the absence of clearly formulated diplomatic goals perhaps help to explain his course of action but do not condone the record of post-World-War-I American diplomacy in the Middle East.

THE PACIFIC

While Hughes was struggling with the British, he was engaged in an even more acrimonious dispute with the Dutch over entry of American

23. Text of agreement is in *FR,* II (1923), 243–245; Teagle to Hughes, October 25, 1923, and Hughes to Teagle, November 8, 1923, *ibid.,* 246–259.

24. Special U.S. Mission to Hughes, November 29, December 22, 1922, January 12, 13, 15, 28, April 23, 29, June 6, 9, 1923, *FR,* II (1923), 961–964, 989, 993, 1016, 1020, 1042–1043, 1045.

oil interests into the rich Djambi fields in the Dutch East Indies. More stubborn than the British, the Dutch repudiated Hughes's Open Door protestations and rigidly excluded American petroleum companies. Despite a long and drawn-out dispute, Hughes suffered an embarrassing diplomatic defeat in this episode. This was indeed surprising, not only because of the disparities of power between the United States and the Netherlands, but also because Hughes had at his disposal retaliatory means that he declined to use. American foreign policy toward the Dutch in the Pacific revealed some of the same weaknesses that were already apparent in regard to other areas.

American interest in the petroleum resources of Sumatra was aroused just before World War I. In 1910 the Standard Oil Company (N.J.) first secured a share in the Koloniale Petrol Company, a relatively unimportant Dutch firm seeking oil in the East Indies. As the war underlined the importance of petroleum, however, the Dutch government took steps to exclude foreigners. The Netherlands Parliament laid down its basic policy in the Mining Act of 1917, which virtually closed the door to foreign investments. The act reserved oil exploration rights for the Dutch government, and the Bataafsche, a government-controlled corporation. Partly, such a policy was motivated by nationalism; partly, it was also due to the influence of Dutch Socialists, who strove hopefully for a government monopoly over oil resources.[25]

The Wilson Administration took a strong stand against the Dutch position. In the midst of the postwar oil shortage, the United States minister in the Hague urged Lansing to persuade the Dutch to modify their policy since federal and state laws did not discriminate against foreign investors in the United States. His suggestions were accepted by that veteran diplomatist, Assistant Secretary of State, A. A. Adee. In April, 1920, Adee instructed him to protest the exclusion of Americans to the Dutch government and to demand a return to a more flexible policy as allowed by the Dutch Mining Law of 1912. He thought the time to be especially opportune, since in 1920 the Dutch were seeking a large export market in the United States. Their restrictive actions certainly belied their claims to reciprocity. The newly organized American

25. A good survey of U.S.-Dutch relations is lacking. But see George Gibb and Evelyn H. Knowlton, *The Resurgent Years, 1911–1927* (New York, 1956), 78–80, 91–94, and Leonard M. Fanning, *American Oil Operations Abroad* (New York, 1947), 49, 61–62; see also *FR*, III (1920), 260–263.

Petroleum Institute had similar views and, at its annual meeting in 1920, enacted a resolution calling for American diplomatic support for American oil companies in foreign countries. Unless the Dutch agreed to some compromise, Adee warned, the United States would be forced to retaliate by prohibiting foreign oil companies from exploiting American oil lands.[26]

Regrettably, American protests—without teeth—had little effect on the Dutch. Instead, they prepared to make their exclusion policy even more rigid. Soon after World War I, Dutch prospectors had come upon the valuable Djambi oil field in central Sumatra, one of the richest in the world. Determined to allow only Dutch interests to exploit these new discoveries, the Dutch government in April, 1920, fostered legislation in the Second Chamber of the Legislature to grant exclusive rights for the development of the Djambi fields to a government-controlled corporation. When queried by the American minister in the Hague about this proposal, however, the Dutch Foreign Minister feigned complete ignorance. At the very same time, working at cross purposes with the State Department, Congress extended very liberal privileges to foreign investors in the United States when it enacted the Mineral Leasing Act, in June, 1920.[27]

In fact, Secretary of State Colby sought to use this measure to court the good will of the Dutch, but without great success. In July, 1920, he pointed to the passage of the Mineral Leasing Act as an indication of the disparity between American and Dutch oil policies. While the Dutch confined all oil development to their own subjects or to corporations having a majority of Dutch nationals as directors, the new American law did not require corporate officers to be U.S. nationals. Once more he instructed the American minister at the Hague, W. W. Phillips, to warn the Dutch of possible retaliatory steps by Congress. But although Phillips conferred at length with Dutch Foreign Minister De

26. A. A. Adee to Gunther [U.S. Chargé at The Hague], April 13, 1920, *FR*, III (1920), 264–266; American Petroleum Institute, *Proceedings* 1920 (New York, 1921), 54, has Teagle's remarks; *NYT*, October 11, November 18, 1920.

27. A. A. Adee to Phillips [U.S. Minister in the Netherlands] April 24, 1920, *FR*, III (1920), 266–267; Phillips to Adee, June 5, 1920, *ibid.*, 267; *NYT*, May 18, 19, 1920; on U.S. Department of State, see *Restrictions on American Petroleum Prospectors in Certain Foreign Countries*, 66 Cong., 2 sess., *Senate Document No. 272* (Washington, 1920), 3–17.

Groot he secured no concessions. American capital was really highly desired, De Groot noted, but since Holland, unlike the United States, was a weak nation it had to be much more wary of foreign investments lest they lead to political intervention. In short, the Dutch refused to change their exclusive policy.[28]

Nevertheless, the prospective riches of the Djambi field tempted some American investors to seek out concessions in spite of the official Dutch attitude. Among the most enterprising were the Sinclair interests, which in August, 1920, sent a representative to the Hague. Although they were encouraged by the Dutch Foreign Office upon arrival, the Dutch were clearly stalling. After about a month Sinclair's request for concessions was rejected. The Foreign Office declared that it would soon foster introduction of a bill in the Dutch parliament to grant a monopoly for development of the Djambi fields to the Bataafsche, a subsidiary of the Royal Dutch Shell in which the Dutch government retained a large interest. Contrary to all evidence, the Dutch Foreign Minister maintained that his government had awarded the concession before Americans expressed any interest.[29]

Colby's response to this slap in the face was abject. The grant of a monopoly to the Royal Dutch Shell in Djambi was a clear violation of the Open Door. But instead of retaliation, Colby offered compromise. In a new State Department proposal of October, 1920, he declared that any change of Dutch policy whereby Americans would be assured of equal opportunity, or a division of the Djambi field, or perhaps a private agreement with American oil companies, would be satisfactory to the United States. The United States objected only to a policy of monopoly by the Royal Dutch Shell, which might lead the American government to withdraw privileges of reciprocity extended to the Dutch.[30]

The wearisome negotiations dragged on into 1921. The American minister in The Hague had further conferences with the Dutch Minister

28. Colby to Phillips, July 17, 1920, Phillips to Colby, July 22, 1920, *FR,* III (1920), 271–274.

29. Phillips to Colby, August 27, September 15, 1920, *ibid.,* 275–278; *NYT,* November 24, 25, December 12, 1920.

30. Colby to Phillips, September 4, 1920, *FR,* III (1920), 276–277; H. D. Butler to John P. Fowler, October 26, 1920, in NA Records (Dutch East Indies) Decimal File 856d.6363; Colby to Phillips, September 22, 1920, *FR,* III (1920), 278–279.

of Foreign Affairs in January, 1921, without any clear results. The State Department threatened to make its correspondence with the Dutch government public, but this in no way frightened the Dutch.[31]

Private American oil companies had no more success in gaining entry to the Dutch East Indies than the Department of State. P. D. Asche, a vice-president of the Standard Oil Company (N.J.), went to the Hague early in 1921 to confer with Dutch officials concerning a concession in Djambi. In discussions with the Colonial Minister, Standard officials offered to set up a company to exploit Djambi in cooperation with the Dutch government. To support their proposal Hughes urged the Dutch government to postpone action on the bill to grant a monopoly to Royal Dutch Shell. American capital was needed in virtually all segments of the Dutch economy except petroleum, Hughes argued, and refusal to grant oil concessions would lead the State Department to inform American businessmen that their investments were not desired in the Netherlands. But the discussions of Standard representatives with Dutch officials resulted in no agreement, largely because of the impossible conditions set by the Dutch.[32]

Meanwhile Congress became greatly aroused over Dutch and British exclusion policies. During 1920 the House Committee on Interstate and Foreign Commerce made a detailed study of restrictions placed upon American oil investors by various foreign nations. In April, 1921, the committee published its long-awaited report detailing foreign discriminations. The report urged retaliation by withdrawal of unrestricted rights extended to foreigners prospecting for oil on the public lands.[33]

The accession of the Harding Administration led to expectations that the State Department would adopt a more vigorous attitude toward Dutch policies in the East Indies. In the Presidential campaign Harding himself had promised to support the principle of the Open Door, and to oppose monopolization of oil resources.[34] Within a month after taking office, Secretary of State Hughes sent a vigorous note to the Dutch insisting on American rights to equal opportunity. Summarizing more

31. 67 Cong., 1 sess., *Senate Document* No. 11 (Washington, 1922).

32. Phillips to Colby, February 4, 1921, Henry Fletcher to De Beaufort [U.S. Chargé in the Netherlands], March 14, 1921, Phillips to Hughes, March 23, 1921, Hughes to Phillips, April 12, 1921, *FR*, II (1921), 531–535.

33. 68 Cong., 1 sess., *Senate Document* No. 39 (Washington, 1921); *CR*, 68 Cong., 1 sess. (February 13, 1924), 2352; *NYT*, April 28, 29, 1921.

34. NYT, October 10, 1920.

than a year of American diplomatic protests, Hughes noted that his government had few alternatives left other than to retaliate.[35] It seemed as if the weak diplomacy of drift that had characterized the last two years of the Wilson era had now come to an end.

Despite a good start Hughes was to be no more successful than his predecessor. Shortly after receipt of his first note the Dutch Second Chamber passed a bill to grant exclusive privileges for oil exploitation in Djambi to the Royal Dutch Shell Company. Dutch Foreign Minister Karnebeck noted that he had kept up negotiations with the State Department only to maintain its good will, but that such discussions had been academic for some time, since his government was determined to retain unilateral oil exploitation privileges in Djambi for itself.[36] Although approval of the Djambi bill by the First Chamber was no more than a formality, Standard Oil (N.J.) quickly sent another representative to Holland to inquire about a possible concession. But the Dutch press—egged on by the British—expressed resentment against alleged American interference, and on June 30, 1921, the upper house of the Dutch Parliament finally enacted the much-discussed measure.[37]

This exclusive policy precipitated a minor diplomatic crisis between the United States and the Netherlands. Amid demands for retaliation, Secretary Hughes recalled Phillips, the American minister to The Hague, for consultations with the President. Hughes also sent another strong note, which reviewed efforts of American companies to secure concessions in the East Indies.[38] But the Dutch government remained stubborn, and vaguely promised other concessions in the future. In late July, 1921, Phillips returned to the Netherlands, and the United States gave up further protest.[39] The Standard Oil Company (N.J.) made certain price reductions for its products, however, which were expected to cause serious losses to Royal Dutch Shell. A decline in the value of the Dutch company's shares bore out the expectation.[40]

It was indeed surprising that Hughes failed to take retaliatory meas-

35. Hughes to Phillips, April 22, 1921, *FR*, II (1921), 536; *NYT*, April 29, 1921.
36. *NYT*, May 1, 2, 4, 6, 1921; see *ibid.*, May 13, 1921, for Dutch rejection of U.S. protest, and *ibid.*, May 27, 1921, for text of Hughes note.
37. *Ibid.*, June 1, 2, 12, 24, July 2, 6, 1921.
38. *Ibid.*, June 26, 1921.
39. *Ibid.*, July 27, 1921; on British White Paper see *ibid.*, July 6, 20 (text), 1921.
40. *Ibid.*, June 23, 1921.

ures against the Dutch, French, and British as a means of implementing American demands. Among those who urged strong exclusive measures was Secretary of the Interior Albert B. Fall. Soon after assuming office in 1921 he wrote a long memorandum for Secretary of State Hughes, outlining the Interior Department's refusal to grant prospecting permits under the Minerals Leasing Act of 1920 to nationals of nations that were discriminating against the United States.[41] Fall further implemented his views in a widely publicized decision in which he refused to grant a permit to the Roxana Company, a subsidiary of Dutch Shell. Fall argued that the federal government, under the Mineral Leasing Act of 1920, could easily place restrictions on prospecting by Dutch oil interests in the United States. In 1923 he turned down their application for the assignment of Creek Indian leases to retaliate against Dutch exclusion of Americans in Djambi. This was his last decision before leaving the Cabinet. It was his belief that such resolute action would impede the Royal Dutch Shell Company's efforts to monopolize world oil reserves.[42] During this same period a group of American stockholders also fought successfully to prevent Royal Dutch Shell's effort to acquire majority control in the Union Oil Company of California.[43] Fall's position revealed considerable realism, but his advice was not followed. And in the aftermath of the Teapot Dome scandals he was so thoroughly discredited that many of his earlier constructive suggestions were widely disregarded. Perhaps Fall's course would have been more successful than the one Hughes followed.

Americans are perennial optimists, however, and so, for a few years after 1921, U.S. oil companies continued their interest in the Dutch East Indies. In 1922, Standard representatives approached the American minister in The Hague to discuss the possibility of investment in Sumatra oil fields other than Djambi.[44] The Commerce Department also alerted major U.S. oil companies in 1922 to the gradual opening of

---

41. 68 Cong,. 1 sess., *Senate Document* No. 97 (Washington, 1924), 9–24.

42. *NYT,* March 18, 20, 1923.

43. *Ibid.,* January 4, 1923; Federal Trade Commission, *Report of the Federal Trade Commission on Foreign Ownership in the Petroleum Industry* (Washington, 1923).

44. Assistant Secretary of State to Department of Commerce, January 17, 1922, in BFDC Records.

new concessions outside Djambi.[45] By late 1923 it had become evident, however, that no oil fields outside Djambi were worth developing.[46] Meanwhile, the Commerce Department was seeking to secure the appointment of an oil expert in the American embassy in Holland to keep a possible eye on shifts in Dutch policies, and perhaps to use persuasion.[47] But by late 1923 the Commerce Department expert on the Dutch East Indies reported that prospects for entry were less bright than in 1921 and that no change of Dutch policy had taken place or seemed likely.[48]

Throughout the 1920's rumors of Dutch willingness to allow the entry of foreign capital in the Dutch East Indies continued. In 1925 the United States commercial attache in Sumatra reported that Standard Oil (N.J.) would be welcomed. While the company received some concessions, these were not of major importance. But by this time the world oil situation had changed entirely, not only because of new oil discoveries in the United States, but largely because of the great glut of petroleum on the world markets. The Dutch government itself by 1932 had become hesitant about granting further concessions, as it was unwilling to add to the depressing overproduction that was plaguing the industry throughout the world.[49] By the time of the Great Depression, new oil concessions there had become an academic issue for Americans as well as Dutch.

In sum, Hughes was no more successful than his predecessors in opening opportunities for American oil investors in the Dutch East Indies. To be sure, he had inherited a difficult and knotty diplomatic problem, but he revealed no special skills or imagination in coping with

45. H. C. Morris to Standard Oil Co. (N.J.), August 18, 1922, H. C. Morris to Sinclair Petroleum Co., August 18, 1922, H. C. Morris to Walter C. Teagle, March 8, 1923, Chase National Bank to H. C. Morris, March 29, 1923, in BFDC Records.

46. H. C. Morris to Chase National Bank, December 16, 1923, in BFDC Records.

47. Under Secretary of State Henry Fowler to Herbert Hoover, April 21, 1923, Fowler to H. C. Morris, May 29, 1923, in BFDC records.

48. A. T. Coumbe to Fox, December 13, 1923, in BFDC Records.

49. U.S. Commercial Attaché [Dutch East Indies] to H. C. Morris [Director, Bureau of Foreign and Domestic Commerce], June 12, 1925, in BFDC Records; New York *Journal of Commerce*, September 18, 1928; John Frey [Bureau of Foreign and Domestic Commerce] to Lamont, July 5, 1932, in BFDC Records.

it. As a result, the principle of the Open Door was openly flaunted by the Dutch in the face of weak protestations from one of the strongest powers in the world. The amateurism characteristic of American diplomacy at various stages was never more evident than in the oil negotiations conducted by the Wilson and Harding Administrations during the immediate post-World-War-I era.

LATIN AMERICA

The failure of American diplomats to secure exploitative rights for U.S. oil companies in the Dutch East Indies and the Middle East led them to a more intensive search nearer home—in Mexico and South America. This was not so much an isolated reflection of Yankee Imperialism as a part of the broader worldwide American effort to secure oil in the face of expected domestic depletion. Mexican petroleum had been exploited since the turn of the century by Americans like E. L. Doheny and the Standard Oil (N.J.) Company, and by Royal Dutch Shell as well. After World War I, American companies also expanded their operations in Argentina, Bolivia, Colombia, Ecuador, and Peru. Most important were the new discoveries in Venezuela, which rapidly became the major Latin American oil producer after 1919, taking the place of Mexico, whose governments were seeking to eliminate foreign investors in the process of nationalizing the entire industry.

Mexico

The State Department sought to support activities of U.S. companies in Mexico during the Carranza era (1917–1920). When the United States first recognized the Carranza regime in 1917, the Mexican president assured American Ambassador Henry P. Fletcher that U.S. oil interests would not be disturbed under the terms of the 1917 constitution, especially Article 27, which prohibited exploitation of natural resources by foreigners. But in 1918 the Carranza government levied a 5 percent tax on all oil produced, prompting American companies to urge the State Department to issue a series of diplomatic protests.[50]

50. Summerlin [U.S. Chargé in Mexico] to Colby, January 21, 1920, *FR*, II (1920), 204; 66 Cong., 2 sess., *Senate Document* No. 272 (Washington, 1921), 15; Association of Mexican Oil Producers to Colby, August 3, *FR*, II (1920), 217–219; Colby to Summerlin [Chargé], August 13, 1920, *ibid.*, 219–221. For background, see Howard F. Cline, *The United States and Mexico* (Cambridge, 1953), 229–231, and Roscoe B. Gaither, *Expropriation in Mexico: The Facts and the Law* (New York, 1940), 2–19.

With the Obregon era (1921–1923) American relations with Mexico became seriously strained over oil. Indeed, the United States deferred recognition of the new regime in the hope of inducing moderation in its oil policies. In 1921 the government levied a tax of 25 percent on the export of petroleum, which appreciably increased the cost of production by American companies.[51] When they failed to persuade the State Department to protest, a group of executives, including Teagle, Doheny, Sinclair, and others, conferred directly with Finance Minister Adolfo de la Huerta in Mexico City during April, 1922—without visible results.[52] The problems continued to mount until 1925, when the Mexican Congress enacted a drastic mining law designed to accomplish the eventual nationalization of the oil industry. American oil companies persuaded the State Department to make strong protests against the policy, but the Mexicans persisted. Political and military considerations led President Coolidge to avoid direct American intervention, however, and in 1927 he dispatched Dwight Morrow as ambassador to Mexico, largely to work out a compromise agreement between the Mexican government and U.S. oil interests. Although Morrow established a close personal relationship with President Calles, and improved the tenor of American-Mexican relations, few could guess at the time that arriving at a mutually agreeable settlement would take another fourteen years.[53]

Colombia

The expansion of overseas oil operations was also reflected in American policy toward Colombia. In 1916 several American oil prospectors, including M. L. Benedum and J. C. Trees, secured a part in the De Mares oil concession in Colombia. During the next three years they infiltrated wild jungles and braved hostile natives to uncover some of the richest oil wells in Latin America. Organized as the Tropical Oil Company in 1919, this group also triggered a tremendous oil boom in Colombia, which aroused the interest of many American companies.[54]

51. Henry P. Fletcher to Summerlin [Chargé], November 19, 1921, *FR*, II (1921), 444; C. J. Wrightsman to C. E. Hughes, June 19, 1921, *ibid.*, 448; C. E. Hughes to Summerlin, August 6, 1921, and Walter Teagle to C. E. Hughes, August 18, 1921, *ibid.*, 452–455, 458–459.
52. Summerlin to C. E. Hughes, April 29, 1922, *FR*, II (1922), 693; Walter Teagle to C. E. Hughes, May 11, 1922, *ibid.*, 693–695.
53. Cline, *United States and Mexico*, 186–187, 205–212; Gaither, *Expropriation in Mexico*, 21 ff.
54. Gibb and Knowlton, *The Resurgent Years*, 369–372.

New Jersey Standard bought the Tropical Oil Company in August, 1920, and soon undertook large-scale operations. The permission of the Colombian government was needed to approve the transfer. At the same time Walter Teagle urged Secretary of State Hughes to improve American relations with Colombia by approving a new treaty in April, 1921, under which the United States was to pay 25 million dollars for injuries sustained by Colombia during the Panama Revolt of 1903. The approval of this treaty was greatly facilitated in July and August, 1920, by James W. Flanagan, operating manager of the International Petroleum Company—a New Jersey Standard pipeline affiliate in Colombia. Returning to Washington, D.C., he brought together the Colombian minister to the United States—Carlos Urueta, and Senator Albert Fall of the Senate Foreign Relations Committee. He also approached Senators Lodge, Hitchcock, and Underwood, and enlisted the support of President-elect Warren Harding for approval of the treaty.[55]

Venezuela

The most important new oil discoveries between 1921 and 1928 were made in Venezuela, and there, too, State Department policy was designed to encourage American oil companies. Europeans took the first initiative in Venezuela. Royal Dutch Shell secured its first concession in 1912 and started large-scale exploration. Geologists from Jersey Standard toured the country in 1915 and 1916. But it was only in the midst of the postwar fear of an impending oil shortage during 1919–1924 that Walter Teagle decided to expand his company's operations to Venezuela.[56]

Quite early American diplomats helped U.S. companies to secure oil concessions. Juan Vicente Gomez, the dictator of Venezuela, was inclined to be friendly toward the United States in 1919, since his pro-German sympathies during World War I were now something of a liability. Accordingly, the United States minister to Venezuela, Preston McGoodwin, in December, 1919, arranged an audience for T. R. Armstrong, New Jersey Standard's representative, who was then seeking a Venezuelan oil concession. Armstrong's clumsiness in initial negotiations with the Minister of Development resulted in the award of the concession to the Sun Oil Company instead. Between 1920 and 1922,

55. *Ibid.,* 374–380.
56. *Ibid.,* 384–391.

however, New Jersey Standard was able to secure extensive land holdings. Meanwhile Minister McGoodwin urged that U.S. oil companies and the Venezuelan government work out a partnership agreement so that exploitation of the nation's oil would be of benefit to both. Partially as a result of his prodding the Venezuelan Congress enacted a broad petroleum law in July, 1922, which designated oil companies as public utilities and explicitly regulated their rights and duties.[57]

American diplomats were far more successful in promoting the entry of U.S. oil companies into South America than into the Middle East or the Pacific. Competition was less keen south of the border and, above all, the United States was not challenged by old and experienced diplomatic powers like Great Britain and the Netherlands. Much of the impetus behind American efforts to expand oil explorations in Latin America stemmed directly from the obstacles placed in the path of American businessmen in other portions of the world.

U.S. oil policies in the foreign sphere were very closely related to considerations of domestic policy. American expansion overseas was initially dictated largely by the unwarranted fear that the depletion of domestic petroleum resources within the United States was close at hand. Requirements of national defense and the expanding technological economy, which were increasingly dependent on petroleum, were responsible for the burst of energy revealed by U.S. oil companies seeking overseas expansion between 1919 and 1924. The strenuous, if ineffective, efforts of the Wilson and Harding Administrations to support their endeavors were dictated by their desire to maintain oil supplies for the Navy, and to conserve what was believed to be rapidly diminishing reserves at home. By 1924 the world oil situation changed completely, however, as the threat of shortage and exhaustion was transformed by new oil discoveries into glut and overproduction. Thus, American domestic and foreign oil policies were to undergo drastic changes as the prime goal came to be stabilization of what was emerging as one of the nation's major industries.

57. This subject is fully discussed in Edwin Lieuwen, *Petroleum in Venezuela* (Berkeley, 1953).

4 / After Teapot Dome: Calvin Coolidge and the Management of Petroleum Resources, 1924–1929

THEODORE ROOSEVELT'S New Nationalism did not die in the 1920's. During these years the Coolidge Administration provided implementation for many of Roosevelt's doctrines as they affected federal business supervision. In the oil industry Coolidge sought not only the further development of cooperative relations between businessmen and government officials, but also the extension of federal and state controls for the regulation of competition. The goals of the Administration included oil conservation, stabilization of production, and maintenance of competition, aims that many segments of the industry accepted before the end of the Coolidge era. To achieve these objectives the President created a new agency in 1924, the Federal Oil Conservation Board. This was a cabinet group headed by Secretary of the Interior Hubert Work, and it included, in addition, Secretary of Commerce Herbert Hoover and the Secretaries of the Army and the Navy. The work of these men between 1924 and 1929 made an important contribution to the formulation of American oil policies. Their investigations, reports, and recommendations crystallized major problems and policy alternatives for both industry and government. The Coolidge era was not a period of reaction in U.S. oil policy. Rather, it was one of ferment in public policy, prompted by the transformation of what had been a nearly monopolistic industry into one more aptly characterized as an oligopoly. In historical perspective, the most significant development in American oil policies during the 1920's was not Teapot Dome. Rather, it was the gradual adjustment of oilmen and government officials to federal and state regulation of the industry, necessitated by changes in its economic structure.

Why did the oil industry and the federal government move toward closer cooperation? From Coolidge's point of view, impelling considerations of national policy required action. Conservation of petroleum was very much on his mind as he contemplated rising domestic needs, prompted by the great expansion of auto and truck traffic. He was also greatly concerned with military requirements, with the procurement of oil supplies for the Navy and the nascent air force. Moreover, oil already constituted one of the nation's leading industries in terms of the value of its products, and thus made a major contribution to the stability of the national economy. In addition, the political scandals that resulted from the Teapot Dome affair only emphasized the importance of a more clearly defined federal oil policy to delimit private and public interest.

THE TEAPOT DOME SCANDAL

Any analysis of Calvin Coolidge's oil program requires some examination of the relationship between the Teapot Dome affair and national oil policies. Certainly the main outlines of this episode are well known. Soon after he became Secretary of the Interior in Harding's Cabinet Albert Fall prevailed upon the President to issue an executive order to transfer jurisdiction over three naval oil reserves from the Navy Department to his own. Under an amendment to the Mineral Lands Act of 1920 (ironically drafted by former Secretary of the Navy Josephus Daniels), the Secretary of the Interior was authorized to lease, sell, or otherwise dispose of these properties to assure the Navy an adequate supply of oil. President Harding issued the necessary directive on June 1, 1921. Within a year, in an atmosphere of relative secrecy, Fall had issued leases to the two most lucrative reserves. One he awarded to his close friend, oil tycoon E. L. Doheny, who sought to develop the Elk Hills reservoir in California (July 12, 1921). The other he granted to Harry F. Sinclair for the valuable properties in Teapot Dome, Wyoming (April 7, 1922). At the time these concessions did not arouse any unusual criticism or comment.[1] Indeed, the New York *Times* announced with some enthusiasm that Fall's actions heralded a new policy of protecting naval oil reserves against severe drainage. The Wilson Administration, Fall charged, had failed to drill sufficient protective wells to conserve naval oil reserves in the ground.[2] Under the new policy, lessees would not only drill for oil. They were also to store crude oil reserves in tank facilities strategically located to meet the Navy's requirements. The contract with Doheny, for example, required him to construct oil storage bins for the Navy at Pearl Harbor in Hawaii.[3] In effect, Fall was reversing Josephus Daniels' plans in the Wilson Administration to secure direct Navy control over petroleum reserves. Instead, he was seeking to delegate this prime responsibility to private enterprise, and to continue the policies of his predecessor under Wilson, Franklin K. Lane. The dispute had already aroused bitter hostility between opposing groups during the preceding decade, however, and could be expected to arouse further controversy, since Congress provided no guidance on naval reserves policy.

Not surprisingly, therefore, those who had supported the Daniels policies rushed to attack Fall's program. Among them, Gifford Pinchot and Senator Robert La Follette were prominent. Indeed, one of Pinchot's good friends, journalist Harry Slattery, embarked on a series of newspaper and magazine articles that probed Fall's conservation policies critically. In addition, Slattery was able to persuade Senator Robert La Follette to begin a congressional investigation of the naval oil reserves. La Follette introduced a resolution to that effect in the Senate, where, on April 29, 1922, it received unanimous approval.[4]

1. Albert B. Fall to Edwin Denby, November 8, 1921, Albert B. Fall Papers, University of New Mexico Library, Albuquerque; Burl Noggle, *Teapot Dome: Oil and Politics in the 1920's* (Baton Rouge, 1962), 1–42, discusses the scandals; see also M. R. Werner and John Starr, *Teapot Dome* (New York, 1959), *passim;* David H. Stratton, "Albert B. Fall and the Teapot Dome Affair" (unpublished Ph.D. dissertation, University of Colorado, 1955); J. Leonard Bates, "Senator Walsh of Montana" (unpublished Ph.D. dissertation, University of North Carolina, 1952); background is well treated in J. Leonard Bates, *The Origins of Teapot Dome* (Urbana, 1963).

2. *New York Times* [hereafter cited as *NYT*], April 8, 15, 1922.

3. Contracts are reprinted in U.S. Senate, Public Lands and Surveys Committee, 68 Cong., 1 sess., *Leases Upon Naval Oil Reserves, Senate Report* No. 794 (3 vols., Washington, 1924), I, 6–21, 177–178, 296 ff.

4. Pinchot's general views are clearly explained in Gifford Pinchot, *The Fight*

Hearings in pursuance of this inquiry did not begin until October 22, 1923, however, after Fall had left his Cabinet position. Head of the special investigating committee was the ambitious and aggressive Democrat from Montana, Thomas J. Walsh. Testimony by various witnesses in early 1924 revealed suspicious activities by important politicians in both major parties. It appeared that E. L. Doheny had kept several prominent Democrats in his employ, among them Wilson's Secretary of the Interior, Franklin K. Lane, and also William G. McAdoo, Wilson's son-in-law and former Secretary of the Treasury, George Creel, and others. These revelations caused irreparable harm to McAdoo, until then a leading contender for the Democratic Presidential nomination in 1924. But the most damaging disclosures concerned Albert Fall who, it was revealed, had received $404,000 in loans from Doheny and Sinclair. Although both of the oilmen later were acquitted of attempted bribery, in 1929 Fall himself was convicted on the charge of receiving a bribe and sentenced to a one-year prison term. He died in 1944, an impoverished and broken man.[5]

If contemporaries and later observers tended to stress the political implications of the Teapot Dome affair, yet its significance for national oil policy was no less profound. Viewed in historical context, Teapot Dome revealed a continuation of the conflict between the opposing advocates of public and private exploitation of petroleum as the best means of providing for the Navy's military needs. Fall represented a common Western attitude, which favored rapid exploitation of natural resources by private enterprise to hasten the economic growth of underdeveloped areas. Such a conception was seriously questioned by many Easterners, some of whom viewed themselves as the nation's only true conservationists. Among them Gifford Pinchot was preeminent. Indeed, so pronounced was the moralism of Pinchot and his group that Harold Ickes—himself a devoted conservationist—once contemptuously called

---

for Conservation, introduction by Gerald D. Nash (Seattle, 1967); J. Leonard Bates, "Fulfilling American Democracy: The Conservation Movement, 1907 to 1921," *Mississippi Valley Historical Review,* XLI (June 1955), 46–54; Noggle, *Teapot Dome: Oil and Politics,* 13–42.

5. See Noggle, *Teapot Dome: Oil and Politics,* 64–215 for details and sources; David H. Stratton, "Behind Teapot Dome: Some Personal Insights," *Business History Review,* XXXI (Winter 1957), 385–402, and "New Mexican Machiavellian? The Story of Albert B. Fall," *Montana, The Magazine of Western History,* VII (Autumn 1957), 2–14.

Pinchot "the Sir Galahad of the Woodlands."[6] Between 1913 and 1921 the struggle between these contrasting conceptions was personified by Josephus Daniels and Franklin K. Lane. Although the Republican platform of 1920 espoused Pinchot's conservation views, the appointment of Fall presaged a continuation of the battle during Harding's Administration. Walsh, La Follette, and Daniels formed ranks behind Pinchot, while Fall upheld Lane's position.

In his Senate career (1913–1921) Fall had been consistent in his attitude toward natural resource policies. He believed in the rapid exploitation of natural resources by private entrepreneurs as the most effective means to facilitate the economic development of sparsely populated areas. "I stand for opening up every resource," he once noted. As a corollary, he favored federal aid to stimulate economic growth, and opposed government regulation that might interfere with private enterprise. Not that he was against conservation per se. On various occasions he introduced Senate bills to provide for the establishment of national parks and national monuments.[7] But his record revealed a decided predilection for rapid resource development. In regard to timber, for example, he opposed placing of restrictions on private operators in national forests, but urged federal road construction in these federal preserves to hasten their development.[8] He also expressed doubts about the inclusion of grazing lands in federal forest preserves when such lands might be made available to cattlemen.[9] That he criticized the Forest Service's administration of federal properties did not endear him to Pinchot, although he favored increased federal appropriations for the making of public land surveys.[10] On various occasions he urged the transfer of federal lands to private ownership and a liberaliza-

6. M. Nelson McGeary, *Gifford Pinchot* (Princeton, 1960), 408–413.

7. For Fall's denial that he was against conservation see Albert B. Fall to Ernest Hill, March 15, 1922, Fall Papers; *Congressional Record* [hereafter cited as *CR*], 62 Cong., 2 sess. (1912), 5729, 5995, 6355, 9372; *ibid.,* 63 Cong., 2 sess. (1914), 2290; *ibid.,* 64 Cong., 1 sess. (1916), 314; quotation in Robert Shankland, *Steve Mather of the National Parks* (New York, 1951), 220; see also David H. Stratton (ed.), *The Memoirs of Albert B. Fall,* University of Texas at El Paso Monograph No. 15 (El Paso, 1966), 7–8.

8. *CR,* 62 Cong., 2 sess. (1912), 4522; *ibid.,* 63 Cong., 3 sess. (1915), 4502; *ibid.,* 64 Cong., 1 sess. (1916), 7297, 7447–7450.

9. *Ibid.,* 64 Cong., 2 sess. (1917), 771.

10. *Ibid.,* 62 Cong., 2 sess. (1912), 6391–6398, 6487–6497, 6547–6554, 6561, 9356–9357.

tion of the 640-acre limitation.[11] As for minerals, he favored their rapid transfer into private hands. Accordingly, he came out in favor of the sale or lease of federal coal lands to private business, even when these were within Indian reservations. At the same time he was quick to charge government interference with the activities of private mineral producers.[12]

By 1921 Pinchot and his followers were probing for weaknesses in Fall's armor. Ever since the Ballinger-Pinchot Affair of 1910 Pinchot had viewed the Interior Department with hostility. Fall's appointment did not diminish his suspicions. When queried by an admirer in February, 1921, as to where he stood on Fall, Pinchot replied: "Want to go carefully over his record in the Senate. . . . He has been with exploitation gang, but not a leader. . . . Trouble ahead." And a little later he noted: "On the record, it would have been possible to pick a worse man for Secretary of the Interior, but not altogether easy." His friend, Harry Slattery, was similarly shocked. Within a few months both men became more perturbed over the Interior Department's plan to encourage private exploitation of Alaska's natural resources. Even more aggravating to Pinchot were Fall's efforts to bring the Forest Service into the Interior Department—a plan also proposed by his successors, including Ickes. Suspicion between the Departments of Agriculture and the Interior transcended personalities and was not unique to the Harding era.[13]

Pinchot's men soon opened their attack on Fall's administration. Pinchot himself went to see Fall in July, 1921, and came away convinced that the New Mexican was seeking to undermine the entire federal conservation program, of which Pinchot considered himself to be the sole architect. By September, 1921, Slattery had begun his publicity campaign against Fall, inaugurating it with a series of articles on

11. *Ibid.*, 64 Cong., 1 sess. (1916), 2207–2211; *ibid.*, 65 Cong., 1 sess. (1917), 7751.

12. *Ibid.*, 63 Cong., 2 sess. (1914), 5224–5225, 5294–5297, 5356–5359; *ibid.*, 65 Cong., 2 sess. (1918), 7480; *ibid.*, 66 Cong., 1 sess. (1919), 4161–4162, 4169–4171.

13. Noggle, *Teapot Dome: Oil and Politics,* 20–24; Gifford Pinchot to Walter Darlington, February 24, 1921, and G. Pinchot to Samuel M. Lindsay, March 6, 1921, Pinchot Papers as quoted in *ibid.*, 13; Circular, American Forestry Association, "Shall Alaska Become the Promised Land of Bilk and Honey for the Interests?" in Fall Papers; E. C. Finney to Albert B. Fall, December 27, 1921, in Fall Papers; Department of the Interior Memorandum, December 31, 1921, Fall Papers, has a reply.

Alaska forestry in the *Christian Science Monitor*. Pinchot also alerted the various state forestry associations and the national Society of American Foresters against Fall's proposals. In 1922 Secretary of Agriculture Henry C. Wallace was won to the cause and gave his full support to the crusade by questioning Fall's resource policies in the Cabinet.[14]

This dispute also extended to the oil policies of Secretary Fall. Urged on by Pinchot and La Follette, former Secretary of the Navy Josephus Daniels entered the fray. Back in 1917 Daniels had wanted the naval oil reserves entirely closed to private lessees and had sought their development under exclusive federal control. In the midst of the very pressing oil shortage that the Navy faced throughout 1920 he modified his views. In that year he drafted an amendment to the Mineral Land Act allowing the Secretary of the Interior to grant leases on existing reserves in the hopes of making additional oil supplies available to the Navy. But he distrusted Fall's execution of this provision. Alerted by Slattery, in April, 1922, Senator La Follette wrote to Daniels, soliciting his opinion on the transfer of the naval oil reserves from the Navy Department to the Department of the Interior. Daniels replied by urging La Follette to engage in close consultation with high naval officers. A week later he wrote to Senator La Follette again to defend his policy of establishing oil reserves during the Wilson era, but urging Congress to be firm against the Fall policies.[15]

Fall himself believed the leasing of the naval oil reserves to be in the best interests of a long-range policy to secure the Navy all of the oil it needed. His plan envisioned primary, if not exclusive, reliance on private oil operators for drilling in naval oil reserves. In addition, he felt that they could best provide storage facilities in diverse geographic locations where the Navy's needs were greatest. Such a policy was in the interest of conservation, since drainage from these wells and drilling by private operators in neighboring tracts were rapidly depleting the underground store of the Navy's oil. To hold, as Pinchot did, that

14. Noggle, *Teapot Dome: Oil and Politics,* 25–31.
15. J. Leonard Bates, "Josephus Daniels and the Naval Oil Reserves," *Proceedings of the United States Naval Institute,* LXXXIX (February 1953), 171–179; Reginald Ragland, *A History of the Naval Petroleum Reserves and of the Present National Policy Respecting Them* (Washington, 1944), 37–53; *CR,* 66 Cong., 2 sess. (April 8, 1920), 6214–6215; *ibid.,* 68 Cong., 1 sess. (January 29, 1924), 1639; Belle C. La Follette and Fola La Follette, *Robert M. La Follette* (2 vols., New York, 1953), II, 1045–1049; *NYT,* April 22, 1922.

merely leaving the oil underground would accomplish conservation was illusory.[16] Some scientific support for Fall's views came late in 1923 when technicians in the Interior and Navy Departments reported results of their investigations, which found increasingly rapid drainage in the Teapot Dome naval oil reserves.[17] Fall envisaged preservation of oil for future use in above-ground storage tanks, where it would be available for immediate use in emergencies. An important group of officers in the Navy Department favored such a "stand-by" policy, for they ardently desired large ready reserves in case of a Pacific war with the Japanese. Under Fall's scheme the Navy could also exchange its crude oil in underground reserves for refined oil provided by private suppliers in Pacific ports. The Elk Hills lease required Doheny to construct oil storage facilities at Pearl Harbor in Hawaii. After the Japanese attack in December, 1941, Fall felt that the wisdom of his judgment twenty years earlier had been vindicated.[18]

Fall's plan secured support among various interest groups. The prestigious *Oil and Gas Journal* commended him for his policy of "constructive development," which contrasted favorably with the more shortsighted approach of Josephus Daniels. Small oil producers in Wyoming welcomed the planned large-scale exploitation of Teapot Dome, which they hoped would result in the building of a pipeline to the Gulf Coast. This would enable them to reach new markets. F. B. Tough, supervisor of oil and gas operations for the United States Bureau of Mines, also appraised the policy approvingly.[19]

Subsequent changes in naval oil reserve policies between 1924 and 1939 provided some justification for Fall's proposals. Within a decade after Teapot Dome, Naval planners realized that their Reserves Numbers 2 and 3 were nonexistent as reserves because of drainage. More-

16. Perhaps the clearest defense is in an unpublished manuscript dictated by Albert Fall in 1925 entitled: "A History of the Naval Oil Reserves," in Albert B. Fall Papers, 1–30; see also Fall's letter to Harding in *Leases Upon Naval Oil Reserves, Senate Report* No. 794, I, 27–68.

17. *NYT*, October 18, 1923; Washington *Post*, October 19, 1923.

18. Albert B. Fall to Edwin Denby, October 30, 1921, Fall to Denby, November 18, 1921, E. C. Finney to Edwin Denby, December 14, 1921, in Fall Papers; Stratton (ed.), *Memoirs of Albert B. Fall*, 5.

19. *Oil and Gas Journal* [hereafter cited as *O&G Jl.*] (April 27, 1922); an intensive examination of press reaction to Teapot Dome is in Robert A. Waller, "Business and the Initiation of the Teapot Dome Investigation," *Business History Review*, XXXVI (Autumn 1962) 334–353.

over, drilling by private operators near Naval Reserve No. 1 compelled the Navy to engage in offset operations there and made it impossible to maintain petroleum in the ground for future use. Consequently, the Navy Department in 1938 asked Congress to enact a special law governing Reserve No. 1, which permitted the Secretary of the Navy to enter into oil conservation agreements with private owners of adjoining wells. Under this statute the Secretary of the Navy was empowered to exchange government lands for private properties in the Reserve.[20]

Unfortunately, in 1924 the taint of political corruption overshadowed the real merits of two divergent viewpoints concerning national petroleum policies. More than ever, Pinchot's position on conservation became tinged with a fervid moralism. On the other hand, the advocates of the "Western" view were thoroughly discredited. The debate over federal naval oil policy came to a grinding halt. An important effect of the Teapot Dome scandals, easily overlooked amid an emphasis on their political implications, was to retard development of federal oil policy in relation to defense requirements.

As for Fall, if he was not completely innocent of creating a situation in which his integrity could be questioned, yet it appears evident that both Democrats and Republicans made him a convenient scapegoat. The Teapot Dome investigations uncovered close relationships between oilmen and important politicians, including Harding, Coolidge, Hoover, Charles Evans Hughes, William McAdoo, George Creel, A. Mitchell Palmer, Lindley Garrison, and others. Fall "took the heat off" the others. He himself always insisted that the moneys he received from Doheny and Sinclair were legitimate loans, quite unrelated to his leasing of the naval oil reserves. His views on conservation before 1921 gave much credence to his assertion, for he had consistently favored rapid resource exploitation by private enterprise. Probably he would have issued the oil leases without securing financial favors since the contracts were in accord with his conception of efficient resource policies. If he had really sought bribes, his biographer, David Stratton, has noted, in view of the value of the naval oil properties he could have demanded a much greater sum—possible $2 million.[21] Rather, he displayed extra-

20. Ragland, *History of Naval Petroleum Reserves,* 84–157.
21. J. Leonard Bates, "The Teapot Dome Scandal and the Election of 1924," *American Historical Review,* XL (January 1955), 303–322; Stratton, "Behind Teapot Dome," 392–394.

ordinary bad judgment in embroiling himself with Sinclair and Doheny at this point in his career. Teapot Dome therefore involved a brazen and inexcusable conflict of interest rather than bribery, pure and simple. In the sensationalism surrounding the disclosures, however, problems of public policy were subordinated to political expediency.

PRESIDENT COOLIDGE'S OIL POLICY

Teapot Dome led President Coolidge to reverse U.S. naval oil policies by returning to the Josephus Daniels–Pinchot approach. The scandals placed Coolidge on the defensive. Throughout the summer of 1924 the Democrats sought to taint him with Teapot Dome although they did not succeed. He emerged unscathed from the attack by maintaining a discreet silence.

But conscious of his vulnerable position, Coolidge took a number of steps designed to remove the blemish of the disclosures. In March, 1924, he appointed a special naval oil reserves commission to study efficient management of the naval oil reserves. He also chose Curtis D. Wilbur as Secretary of the Navy. Wilbur appointed Commander Nathan W. Wright—a known conservationist of the Pinchot school—as his oil advisor. Then he established a Naval Petroleum Reserve office in the Department for consulting purposes. He also selected naval officers to inspect the reserves periodically.[22] By the middle of 1924, therefore, Coolidge had quietly but effectively switched the emphasis of U.S. naval oil policies from exploitation to conservation. In ridding himself of the political stigma attached to Fall, however, Coolidge also closed the door to a serious consideration of the possible merits of Fall's proposals for the Navy's petroleum policies. It seemed that the President threw out the baby with the bath.

But nonpolitical factors—other than Teapot Dome—were also leading Coolidge to reappraise federal oil policies. In one way or another changes within the industry itself had an enormous impact on the stance of government. During the post-World-War-I decade competition in the petroleum trade increased greatly as new integrated companies sought to profit from a rapidly expanding market for oil and oil products.

22. Secretary of the Navy, *Annual Report* 1924 (Washington, 1925), 55; *NYT*, March 14, 15, April 1, 11, 18, 1924; *Literary Digest*, LXXX (February 9, 1924), 7–10.

The accelerated pace of the energy revolution increased the demand for petroleum just as steadily as that for coal decreased. The enormous rise in the number of automobiles between 1924 and 1929, the widespread shift of home owners to fuel oil, and the expansion of chemical and synthetic industries requiring petroleum products created unprecedented demands. Even so, the pace of new oil discoveries in the midcontinent region, in the Gulf area, and in California often exceeeded the growth rates of new markets. Technological advances in the industry further boosted its productive capacities, with the result that maladjustments between supply and demand occurred with increasing frequency. Overproduction, in terms of existing markets, was very real in the petroleum industry after 1925, several years before other industries were beset with similar problems.[23]

By the fall of 1924, as the excitement of Teapot Dome faded, erstwhile fears of oil depletion were giving way to a widespread concern about overproduction. The glut of oil then on the American market and the consequent declining prices led business leaders to pause and reflect on the need for stabilization in the industry. Excessive production was leading to cutthroat competition and increasing rivalry between various segments in the industry. At the same time it resulted in such reckless waste that conservationists became alarmed. Oil geologists of the United States Geological Survey were aghast at overproduction and worried about complete exhaustion of the nation's petroleum resources within a decade. Engineers in the United States Bureau of Mines were more optimistic, for they viewed the scientists in the Survey as doctrinaire theorists. But they too were concerned.[24]

Some leaders of the oil industry were also planning to avert a potential petroleum shortage. Among them Henry L. Doherty was prominent. A keen, independent thinker, he was a former consulting engineer, but after World War I he enjoyed his role as the intellectual of the petroleum industry. He was preeminently practical as well, and directed a

23. Harold F. Williamson *et al., The American Petroleum Industry* (2 vols., Evanston, 1959–1963), II, *Age of Energy,* 299–338; Henrietta M. Larson and Kenneth W. Porter, *History of Humble Oil and Refining Company* (New York, 1959), 110–142, 171–192, 219–263; Kendall Beaton, *Enterprise in Oil* (New York, 1957), 117–352; Paul H. Giddens, *Standard Oil Company (Indiana)* (New York, 1955), 210–435.

24. *National Petroleum News* [hereafter cited as *NPN*] (December 24, 1924).

vast oil empire in Mexico and the Cities Service Company in the United States.

During World War I, Doherty served as a member of the National War Service Petroleum Committee. Deeply influenced by the positive benefits of cooperation within the industry, he became a firm believer in unit development of petroleum fields. Such a plan envisioned an orderly planned development of new oil reserves instead of the prevailing mode of haphazard exploitation. Under a unit agreement, prospectors agreed, prior to actual operations, to apportion respective fields and their production according to a rational, coherent, and scientific plan. This was designed to prevent not only wildcat drilling, responsible for much surplus production; it would also eliminate waste, and so would lead to conservation. Doherty's unit plan synthesized fundamentals of scientific management with the latest technological information to achieve maximum productive efficiency.[25]

In the fall of 1924 Doherty visited the White House in order to press his conservation views on Coolidge personally. A lifelong Republican, and a friend of the President, he conveyed his fears of oil depletion to the frugal Chief Executive and pointed to the effects that this would have on national defense. Writing to Coolidge, he asserted:

For a long time I have viewed with great alarm the rapidity with which we are depleting the petroleum oil reserves of this country. . . . Under our present system we are bound to become a pauper nation so far as oil is concerned. . . . I have been forced to the conclusion that only through the efforts of our federal government, can the oil problem be solved, for time is of the essence. . . . It has gotten beyond a more departmental problem and has become a real administrative problem of the first magnitude.[26]

Doherty found Coolidge in a receptive mood. His inherent frugality made him sympathetic to ideas of resource conservation. During the storm following the disclosures of Teapot Dome he had been urged by

25. The literature on Doherty is extensive, and he has not yet found a biographer. Informative contemporary accounts include *Literary Digest,* LXXVII (June 2, 1923), 56–58; *World's Work,* XLIII (March 1922), 505–512; *Magazine of Business,* LIV (October 1928), 387, has a portrait; his ideas on conservation were expounded in *NYT,* November 20, 1924, *NPN* (November 26, 1924).

26. *NPN* (December 24, 1924); H. L. Doherty to Calvin Coolidge, August 24, 1924, Federal Oil Conservation Board Records (Correspondence File), National Archives, [hereafter cited as FOCB Records], Washington, D.C.; *Oil Trade* (February 1925).

his Secretary of the Interior, Hubert Work, to take forceful steps to safeguard petroleum resouces. Work, a Colorado physician, was attempting to return to the policy of Josephus Daniels by creating special naval oil reserves. In the confusion that followed Secretary of the Navy Denby's resignation on February 18, 1924, Work created a Naval Conservation Board in his department to develop plans for assuring the Navy an adequate supply. During 1924 this board performed useful work in estimating anticipated needs and available supplies. The experience convinced Work that a similar group might be created to deal with oil supply problems on a national scale. In his annual report for 1924 he urged the President to create a federal oil commission composed of the Secretaries of War, Navy, Commerce, and Interior to study and analyze the conservation of the nation's oil deposits. In view of Coolidge's parsimony, a committee composed of cabinet members appeared especially desirable, since it entailed little additional expense.[27] And it would further dim lingering memories of Teapot Dome.

The Federal Oil Conservation Board

Prodded by Work and Doherty, on December 18, 1924, Coolidge created the Federal Oil Conservation Board (FOCB). In a letter to Work he clearly enunciated the federal government's motives in stimulating the conservation of petroleum. Needs of national security were very much on his mind. Coolidge noted that "present methods of capturing our oil deposits is [sic] wasteful to an alarming degree. Developing aircrafts indicate that our national defense must be supplemented, if not dominated, by aviation." Hardly less compelling was his concern for economic stability. "I am advised," he continued,

that . . . the failure to bring in producing wells for a two year period would slow down the wheels of industry and bring about serious industrial depression. The problem of a future shortage in . . . oil . . . must be avoided, or our manufacturing productivity will be curtailed. Oil . . . is largely taking the place of coal. I would express the desire that . . . the oil industry itself might be permitted to determine its own future. . . . but for the patent fact that the oil industry welfare is so intimately linked with the industrial prosperity and safety of the whole people, that Government and business can well join forces to work out . . . practical conservation.[28]

27. *NYT*, March 26, 27, April 13, December 2, 1924; *NPN* (December 31, 1924); Secretary of the Interior, *Annual Report* 1924 (Washington, 1924), 8.
28. Text of Coolidge statement can be found in *Christian Science Monitor*, December 19, 1924, and *NYT*, December 20, 1924.

Composed of the Secretaries of the Interior, Commerce, War, and Navy, the new board had primarily investigative functions. It would hold conferences and hearings and would undertake various studies as a prelude to recommendations concerning needed federal and state legislation as well as measures to be taken by the industry itself.

Reaction to Coolidge's establishment of the FOCB was generally positive. Senator Thomas Walsh, who had unearthed the Teapot Dome scandals, complimented the President. Representatives from oil states, such as Senator John Harrald (Okla.), saw creation of the FOCB as an opportunity to secure stabilization in the industry. The Naval Affairs Committee of the House approved enthusiastically. Industry associations such as the American Petroleum Institute were also favorably impressed. President J. Edgar Pew of the API promised to appoint a special committee to represent his organization in cooperative projects with the new federal board. Leading trade periodicals were hopeful that the new agency would help the industry to solve various problems, particularly overproduction. Some oilmen hoped that they could virtually write their own oil stabilization and conservation program, which the federal agency would enforce.[29]

Tax Policies

Fears of an oil shortage also led the Coolidge Administration to encourage Congressional efforts to revise the tax structure in favor of oil producers. These attempts began early in 1925 and grew partly out of a feud between Secretary of the Treasury Andrew W. Mellon and Senator James Couzens. In response to a Senate Resolution calling for an investigation of the Bureau of Internal Revenue advocated by Couzens, the Senate appointed a select committee, headed by Couzens, to look into the prevailing system of depletion deductions and allowances, among other matters. This group held extensive hearings during 1925, and at the close of the year issued a report. It found that during the previous four years numerous disputes had arisen between oil producers and the Internal Revenue Bureau over valuations which the bureau placed on each new oil well. The task of placing a discovery value on every new discovery became increasingly cumbersome as petroleum explorations rapidly increased during the first half of the

29. *Petroleum World* (January 1925); *NPN* (December 24, 1924, January 7, 14, 1925); *Oil Weekly* (January 9, 30, 1925).

1920's. The committee also recommended a revision and simplification of existing laws governing the appraisal of oil and gas properties. They urged adoption of a depletion allowance based on a percentage of gross sales.[30]

Early in 1926 the Senate Finance Committee considered these recommendations in detail. The members also held additional hearings of their own on the depletion issue. Two key problems still remained undecided. Should the percentage deduction be the same for all minerals? And how great an allowance should be granted? The committee believed that rates might vary with different industries. In the committee's report, Senator Reed (Pa.) also included a suggestion by the President of the Mid-Continent Oil Producers' Association that a deduction of 25 percent of gross income should constitute a minimum.

In the formal report, committee members recommended this 25 percent allowance. Senator Couzens argued on the Senate floor that only cost depletion should be allowed, but he was overridden. The Senate amended the bill to provide for a 30 percent deduction, as suggested by Senator Matthew Neely (W. Va.). When the bill was sent to a Conference Committee with the House, this group worked out a compromise that provided for a 27.5 percent depletion allowance. Congress adopted the proposal. It hoped not only that the change would distribute depletion more uniformly throughout the industry, but also expected it to lessen the administrative burden of the Internal Revenue Bureau. A uniform depletion allowance relieved that agency of the heavy responsibility involved in making individual valuations of oil properties.[31]

Conservation

Meanwhile, Work, Hoover, and the other two members of the FOCB devoted their energies to the development of plans and laws to promote

30. *CR,* 68 Cong., 1 sess. (March 12, 1924), 4014; 69 Cong., 1 sess., Select Committee on Investigation of the Bureau of Internal Revenue, *Report,* Part II in *Senate Report* No. 27 (Washington, 1926), based on its *Hearings on Senate Resolution 168,* 1924–1926 (Washington, 1926), II-VIII; *NYT,* February 20, 25, May 31, 1925.

31. 69 Cong., 1 sess., Senate, Committee on Finance, *Hearings on Revenue Act of 1926* (Washington, 1926); 69 Cong., 1 sess., Senate, Committee on Finance, *Senate Report* No. 52 (Washington, 1926), 16–18; *CR,* 69 Cong., 1 sess. (February 11, 1926), 3761–3778; Cong., 1 sess., *House Report* No. 356 (Washington, 1926), 22–32.

oil conservation. Their first project was to make a survey of prevailing production methods in the industry, and to suggest ways of improvement. After 1927 they concerned themselves with methods of limiting production, with petroleum substitutes, and with foreign oil imports, especially after the outbreak of the depression. Perhaps the most important function of the FOCB was to serve as forum for the formulation of national oil policy on the part of both government and business.

The inquiries and reports of the FOCB raised important questions concerning the future course of U.S. oil policy. How great were the oil reserves of the United States? Exactly what substitutes for oil were readily available in case of depletion? Should the industry restrict production? What improvements were desirable in production or refining techniques? And how should federal and state laws be brought to bear upon these problems? In at least four of its major inquiries the FOCB made an effort to make concrete policy recommendations on these issues. The first report in 1926 critically appraised the industry's production methods. The second probed the feasibility of oil shales and other petroleum substitutes. A third report dealt with foreign oil imports and their impact on domestic producers. And the recommendations published in 1932 discussed alternatives for restricting production. Altogether, the studies of the FOCB were an important factor in crystallizing opinion among public officials and business leaders about possible directions of petroleum policies.[32]

The honeymoon between the board and the industry was short-lived. When in 1925 the FOCB busied itself with gathering necessary information concerning production efficiency and waste, it prepared a series of questionnaires for producers, asking them to describe their methods. Succeeding inquiries solicited information about marketing techniques. But these queries notably cooled the initial ardor of Pew, the API, and many oilmen who objected to this "snooping" into their affairs. Instead, the taciturn Pew appointed a special API committee to investigate practices of the industry.[33] The API group became known as the Commit-

32. Federal Oil Conservation Board, *First Annual Report,* 1926 (Washintgon, 1926), *Second Annual Report,* 1928 (Washington, 1928), *Third Annual Report,* 1929 (Washington, 1929), *Fourth Annual Report,* 1930 (Washington, 1930), *Fifth Annual Report,* 1932 (Washington, 1933).

33. *Oil Weekly* (January 23, 30, 1925); *NPN* (February 11, 1925); *Oildom* (March 19, 1925); *O&G Jl.* (May 21, 1925).

tee of Eleven. It included leading executives like W. S. Farish (president of Humble Oil) and other important oil company executives. Most of them went about the country making speeches in which they deprecated Coolidge's view that an oil shortage in the United States was imminent. Meanwhile they refused to cooperate with the FOCB, and declined to return completed questionnaires.[34]

In a hasty effort to forestall Congressional legislation in support of the FOCB's possible recommendations for federal conservation laws, the API's Committee of Eleven issued its own findings in April, 1925. It emphasized, above all, that the United States was in no imminent danger of exhausting its oil reserves and that there was no reason for concern over supplies for national defense. Estimating available reserves to be more than 30 billion barrels, the Committee of Eleven believed that new production processes, such as deep drilling, increasing use of substitutes for oil, and exploitation of foreign sources, made shortages unlikely. With considerably less candor, the committee denied that prevailing production methods in the industry were accompanied by much needless—indeed, reckless—waste. The hastily drawn report was perhaps unduly optimistic about future oil reserves, yet new discoveries in Oklahoma and Texas during the following decade supported some of its predictions.[35]

The well-publicized report of the API did not go unchallenged. Numerous scientists expressed doubts about it. Thus, E. J. Fohs, a consulting engineer and member of the American Institute of Mining and Metallurgical Engineers, pointed to the great and excessive waste that he felt characterized the operations of the American oil industry. A similar opinion was expressed by John Hammond, a member of the United States Coal Commission.[36] The Rocky Mountain Association of Petroleum Geologists also unanimously questioned the API report. Similarly, D. N. Killeffer, secretary of the New York section of the American Chemical Society, predicted the exhaustion of gasoline supplies within 20 years. This prediction was close to the estimates of the

34. *Petroleum World* (April 1925); *O&G Jl.* (April 30, May 21, 1925).
35. American Petroleum Institute, Committee of Eleven, *American Petroleum Supply and Demand* (New York, 1925); *O&G Jl.* (July 2, 23, 1925); *Oildom* (April 15, August 7, 1925); *Petroleum World* (September 1925).
36. *O&G Jl.* (June 4, 1925); *Oildom* (April 15, 1925).

United States Geological Survey's scientists and of the American Association of Petroleum Geologists.[37]

But the most acid criticism of the API report came from one of the institute's own directors, the bête-noire of the industry, Henry L. Doherty. He charged his colleagues with making a conscious effort to forestall government controls. Not only did he think the API forecast of reserves erroneous. The failure of the Committee of Eleven to condemn reckless waste and inefficient production methods, Doherty charged, laid its members open to charges of deliberate distortion. Doherty's views were reinforced by Mark Requa, head of the Oil Division of the United States Fuel Administration during World War I.[38]

A minority of businessmen in the oil industry opposed federal conservation legislation. One of their most vocal representatives was G. S. Davison of the Gulf Oil Company, widely regarded as a spokesman for the Andrew W. Mellon interests. His position was endorsed by J. Howard Pew of the Sun Oil Company, a somewhat doctrinaire opponent of government restrictions on the industry. The API provided Pew with a platform from which to campaign for laissez-faire.[39]

Pew lost no time in acquainting the Coolidge Administration and the FOCB with his views. Early in 1926 the FOCB held public hearings, allowing various individuals within the oil industry to present their proposals for a national oil policy. These discussions also aired suggested conservation measures. To represent the API at the sessions Pew secured the services of Charles Evans Hughes, who had just recently resigned as Secretary of State. Unfortunately Hughes's deep knowledge of the law was offset by lack of experience with the oil industry's problems. Nevertheless, his great prestige publicized the opposition to federal oil regulation.

In his formal argument before the FOCB in May, 1926, Hughes urged a "hands off" policy and dwelt almost exclusively with constitutional issues. These bore little relevance to the real and acute problems then confronting the industry. His major argument revolved about the proposition that the oil industry could itself cope with its twin problems, waste—on the one hand—and overproduction—on the other. Volun-

37. *Oildom* (July 8, 1925).
38. *Ibid.* (October 15, 22, November 9, 1925); *O&G Jl.* (October 29, 1925).
39. *O&G Jl.* (October 8, 1925); *NYT,* January 20, 1926.

tary measures, aided by scientific research, he argued, would redound to the consumer's benefit. Any artificial restrictions of output would merely raise prices.

Even if Congress sought to place curbs on oil production, however, it could not do so, since it lacked constitutional powers. Although admitting that greater efforts to conserve petroleum might be desirable, Hughes noted that ultimately technological advances made by the industry itself would result in improved efficiency.[40] But, almost as if to mock Hughes's arguments, prospectors struck great new oil discoveries in the Seminole fields of Oklahoma in July, 1926. Accompanied by an orgy of waste, their drilling of new wells further demoralized oil markets. Such conditions underscored Hughes's formalism and endowed his abstract and theoretical legal arguments with an air of unreality. Except for a temporary flurry of attention, the case made by Hughes for a strict laissez-faire policy in the oil industry had little impact on the development of future oil policy.[41]

Hughes was directly challenged by Henry L. Doherty and a small but influential group of business leaders. They urged the adoption of unit plans by the industry and federal laws to provide legal sanctions for the execution of voluntary cooperative efforts. The FOCB lent its support to the movement in its first report on conservation problems in October, 1926. Reflecting Coolidge's position, it emphasized the need for industry leaders to initiate more effective conservation practices supported by federal sanctions. The unit plan was especially attractive as a conservation measure during these years. It embodied Herbert Hoover's almost passionate belief in voluntary cooperation, and combined the best elements of scientific management with technological and engineering knowledge. Unitization in the oil industry represented a practical application of Hoover's philosophy concerning the relation of government, science, and economic progress.[42]

The recommendations of the FOCB in 1926 provided the main topic of debate for API members at their annual meeting in December of that

40. Federal Oil Conservation Board, *Public Hearing,* May 27, 1926 (Washington, 1926), *passim* [Hughes testimony]; *NYT,* May 28, 29, 1926.

41. *NYT,* July 13, August 18, 1926; *O&G Jl.* (June 3, 1926).

42. Federal Oil Conservation Board, *First Annual Report,* 3 ff.; *NYT,* September 2, 3, 1926; for Work's views see *NYT,* September 6, 1926, and for Coolidge's reaction, *ibid.,* September 8, 1926.

year. The organization's board of directors was split on the government recommendations, reflecting fundamental cleavages within the industry. Some, like Doherty, agreed with the FOCB's predictions of an impending oil shortage and the immediate need for drastic conservation statutes; others, including Pew, followed the report of the API's Committee of Eleven and felt that American oil reserves were ample. Nevertheless, in seeking some semblance of unity, the API went on record in 1926 as endorsing the FOCB report. Albeit with some reluctance, the institute underscored the need for more effective conservation practices to be adopted by members of the industry themselves. As R. L. Welsh, general counsel of the API, argued shrewdly, this would allow producers to restrict their output. A few individuals, such as Mark Requa, urged the API to support federal enforcement of conservation practices, but his proposal received little support. The various segments of the industry were still widely divided over the most desirable course of oil policy in 1926. Nevertheless, the resolution urging greater efficiency and better conservation techniques reflected a significant shift of industry opinion. It revealed that an increasing number of oilmen had come to favor conservation, if only because it promised to curb overproduction.[43] Efficiency—from an economic and scientific standpoint—was a prime motivation in producing this new consensus in the industry, just as increasing military needs and the unsettling effects of business fluctuations were leading to similar views on the part of government officials.

Antitrust Legislation

But the advocates of voluntary cooperation were always beset by a nagging question. How would their efforts be regarded by the Justice Department in its enforcement of the antitrust laws? Thus, a sizeable group of executives from large, integrated corporations, and some members of the Coolidge Administration as well, favored amendment of antitrust legislation as the best means of allowing the industry to solve its own problems. Their main source of support in Washington was Secretary of Commerce Herbert Hoover, who felt that cooperation among businessmen was the solution to most difficulties besetting mod-

43. Tulsa *World,* December 10, 14, 1926; *NYT,* December 10, 1926; Washington *Herald,* December 15, 1926; *NPN* (December 8, 15, 1926); *O&G Jl.* (December 16, 1926); American Petroleum Institute, *Proceedings* 1926, 1–2, 11–13, 15; *ibid.,* 1927, 1–13.

ern industry. Largely under his prodding, API officials early in 1927 sounded out other Republican leaders. At its annual meeting of December, 1926, the API had also appointed a committee to study needed revisions in the antitrust laws and to make recommendations for appropriate federal and state legislation. API President E. W. Clark declared early in 1927 that, while the industry did not desire wholesale exemption from the Sherman and Clayton Acts, it did desire legal approval of cooperative agreements to restrict production and to improve conservation.[44] To relay his views, in May, 1927, Clark sent Walter Teagle, president of Standard Oil (N.J.) and a powerful figure in the industry, to confer with Secretary of the Interior Hubert Work. Although Work expressed a cautious and qualified support for efforts to amend the antitrust acts, he attempted to straddle the issue. Instead, he referred Teagle, Clark, and the other oil leaders to Assistant Attorney General William J. Donovan, head of the Department of Justice's antitrust division.[45]

A supporter of Hoover's philosophy of self-help, Donovan was a leading advocate of antitrust revision. His version of the New Nationalism eschewed mere dissolution of cooperative agreements among businessmen. Rather, he envisaged federal supervision of business practices and regulation of those that appeared harmful to the national economy. He enunciated this approach to antitrust enforcement in what appeared to be an unauthorized policy statement during February, 1927. Businessmen should no longer fear antitrust laws, he announced, for the Department of Justice would seek to enforce the Sherman Act without disrupting economic stability. Any industry group desiring to engage in cooperative activities could confer with him prior to carrying out its intended programs to determine whether or not the proposed cooperation was legal under existing antitrust statutes. If, in his opinion, such agreements did not violate antitrust laws they could be executed without fear of federal prosecution. His role was to be that of a legal advisor, not a prosecutor. As Donovan stated:

44. Washington *Star,* January 6, 1927; *O&G Jl.* (January 13, February 3, 1927); Washington *Herald,* May 14, 1927.
45. Hoover's views on cooperation in oil industry were expressed in *O&G Jl.* (October 25, 1926), New York *World,* May 12, 1927, *Petroleum World* (January 1927); see also *O&G Jl.* (November 3, 1927).

The function of the Department of Justice in the prosecution of the Sherman Anti-Trust law is to meet these problems . . . at the very threshold of a commercial enterprise that is undertaking to put into effect legitimate business economies. Discussion of this act has frequently aided the Government, and promoted success in avoiding violations of the act. At the same time it has permitted business to go forward with the object of benefitting the public, both by economies of production and by providing employment.[46]

Since this declaration had not been cleared with his superiors, however, neither the President nor the Attorney General endorsed this new line of policy.

In fact, Coolidge was reluctant to espouse the New Nationalism without some qualification. Instead, he revealed a greater inclination toward Brandeisian views favoring the dissolution, and not the regulation, of Big Business. Moreover, he was too shrewd a politician to support major revisions in antitrust legislation, which could arouse acrid debate. Thus, when Mark Requa visited him in February, 1927, to discuss modification of antitrust laws as they applied to the petroleum industry, he was cool, if not outright negative. To be sure, he strongly favored petroleum conservation and industry efforts to improve efficiency. He was happy, too, about the increasing realization among oilmen that conservation was desirable, and he was willing to use federal powers to aid them in attaining this objective. But, he told Requa, if large, integrated oil companies secured legal authority to make voluntary agreements restricting production, they could easily manipulate prices. Tampering with the Sherman Act would very likely result in higher prices for consumers. And the political consequences of such action were difficult to predict. Could not the federal government be accused of furthering monopoly? While Coolidge did not go so far as to reject Assistant Attorney General Donovan's new policies outright he dampened the ardor of the API and other groups who hoped to secure the Administration's full support for amendment of the antitrust laws.[47]

Nevertheless, during the next few months Walter Teagle and API President Clark made further soundings. In the spring of 1927 the discovery of the rich Seminole fields in Oklahoma demoralized the in-

---

46. *O&G Jl.* (February 3, 1927); *U.S. Daily,* February 4, 1927; *O&G Jl.* (May 12, 1927); Washington *Herald,* April 29, 1927.

47. *U.S. Daily,* February 4, 1927.

dustry more than ever, as oil prices plummeted further. This crisis led Teagle along with W. S. Farish (a former president of the API) and other industry leaders to visit Secretary Work in May, 1927, to secure his approval of a voluntary plan developed by the major integrated companies to restrict production. Work not only refused to support this proposal; he also declined to endorse any revision of antitrust laws. The FOCB lacked powers to enforce production limitations, he told the oilmen, nor had the time come for federal execution of voluntary industry agreements. Reflecting the President's views, he noted that while the oil business clearly required stabilization, the Administration was greatly concerned about protecting the public against artificial price manipulation. He urged businessmen to cooperate in curbing production only when such collusion was not in violation of existing federal antitrust statutes.[48]

The Coolidge Administration's stand in opposing greater flexibility in antitrust policies greatly discouraged business leaders. After meeting with Work, the Teagle group issued a noncommital statement declaring that further conferences with the FOCB were needed to discuss future public policies. It went on record, however, in repudiating Secretary of the Treasury Mellon's recent statement that natural laws of supply and demand would solve problems related to the oil surplus. Indeed, two years before the Great Depression, Walter Teagle noted that: "The oil industry is faced with financial chaos unless the government can help to extricate it from overproduction." And Mellon himself was surprised at the violent objections to his laissez-faire views expressed by the oil industry executives who wrote him in protest. The only tangible result of the May 11 conference between Work and the industry leaders was an agreement by the industry representatives to appoint an oil dictator for the Seminole field, who was to apportion production quotas there.[49]

The movement for modification of the federal antitrust laws did not die, however. In Congress, numerous bills to this effect were introduced by representatives from oil regions. Moreover, during the summer of 1927 oil production soared further, prices fell, and divisions within the

48. Washington *Herald,* May 10, 1927; *Christian Science Monitor,* May 17, 1927; New York *Tribune,* May 24, 1927; *O&G Jl.* (May 12, 1927).

49. *NYT,* May 12, 1927; Washington *Herald,* May 12, 1927; New York *World,* May 13, 1927; Washington *Star,* May 13, 1927; New York *Tribune,* May 24, 1927.

oil industry deepened as the industry found itself in a crisis. Under these circumstances Secretary Work modified his previous opposition to antitrust law revision. In a widely discussed address before the Minerals Section of the American Bar Association in Buffalo, New York, on August 30, 1927, he urged the creation of a Committee of Nine to draft an appropriate statute to aid the oil industry through some form of federal action, perhaps even the limitation of production to market demands. Work promised that reasonable proposals would be forwarded by the FOCB to Congress for enactment. The committee was to be composed of three representatives from the oil industry, three federal officials, and three spokesmen for the American Bar Association.[50] Although Secretary Hoover declared that he favored voluntary action without government interference, yet in the fall of 1927 most trade journals were strongly in favor of Work's suggestion. The American Bar Association formally appointed a Committee of Nine composed of prominent individuals (including three former presidents of the API). After more than a year of study this group recommended revision of the antitrust laws so as to allow federal approval of industrywide agreements to restrict production.[51]

Federal and State Control Proposals

Meanwhile many oil executives late in 1927 were so discouraged by instability within the industry that they favored outright federal restriction of oil production. This sentiment was particularly strong at the API meeting in December, 1927. For some months Mark Requa had been holding conferences with important figures in the industry. Their discussions revolved about a bill that he was drafting to authorize federal regulation of production, just as in World War I. A majority of the API directors in December, 1927, approved of such federal legislation to encourage oil conservation—and at the same time to limit production. The API convention urged the enactment of federal and state laws to authorize producers to enter into unit agreements, and to exempt these

50. American Bar Association, *Report of the Fifty-First Annual Meeting* (Baltimore, 1928), 655–671; *NYT,* August 31, 1927. For Hoover's reaction see *NYT,* September 2, 1927; *O&G Jl.* (September 8, 29, 1927); *Oildom* (September 26, 1927); *NPN* (August 31, 1927).

51. *O&G Jl.* (November 16, 1927); *NPN* (November 23, 20, 1927); *Oildom* (December 12, 1927); American Bar Association, *Report of the Fifty-Second Annual Meeting* (Baltimore, 1929), 739–770.

from antitrust statutes. Although this was short of the comprehensive government controls advocated by Requa, these resolutions reflected a large measure of agreement among oil producers on the need for government regulation to achieve industrial stability.[52]

While the movement for revision of the antitrust laws was gathering momentum among business leaders between 1927 and 1929, another segment of the industry—including many independent operators—favored state regulation as the best means to meet existing problems. This group was led by E. W. Marland of Oklahoma, himself a leading producer of petroleum, and later governor of the state and a member of Congress. Marland, along with many independent producers, was afraid that government regulation under federal auspices would lead to the domination of public policy by the large, integrated oil companies. If such regulation were carried out at the state level, however, the influence of local groups (such as the independents) would still be strong. Marland secured initial hearing for this point of view in 1926, when the API directors appointed him chairman of a committee to draft state legislation designed to curb waste and perhaps to limit production. Through its Corporation Commission, Oklahoma had been experimenting with such laws for more than two decades, and Marland was thus especially well qualified to consider the extension of the Oklahoma system to other oil-producing areas.[53]

Early in 1927 Marland aired the first draft of his state conservation statute. It provided for rigid state regulation of oil producers by an Oil and Gas Conservation Board. This was to supervise production and refining techniques, to insure conservation, and to regulate production in relation to market demand. His prime purpose in presenting such a draft to the FOCB, Marland explained, was to stir up discussion concerning state regulation of the oil industry. Stir up discussion it did, especially in Oklahoma, where Marland had a version of his measure introduced in the state legislature. It aroused great furor there and revealed many divisions among oilmen concerning the proposed course of public policy. In testimony before the Joint Legislative Committee on Oil and Gas of the Oklahoma legislature, representatives of the Oklahoma-Kansas Division of the Mid-Continent Oil and Gas Association

52. *NPN* (December 7, 14, 1927); *O&G Jl.* (December 8, 1927); for Hoover's views see *O&G Jl.* (December 15, 1927).
53. *O&G Jl.* (January 20, 1927); *Inland Oil Index* (January 28, 1927).

were especially vociferous in opposition. They argued that conservation standards would increase production costs. Moreover, somewhat blindly, they opposed any restrictions on production. As the Executive Committee of this association noted: "The proper function of the state is to protect and aid industry. This bill reverses the established order . . . and compels the surrender of the industry to the state. It socializes the petroleum industry."[54] Marland's bill died in the Oklahoma legislature of 1927, but with the burgeoning production in succeeding years it was frequently revived. Gradually, an increasing majority of oil producers became New Nationalists on the state level—as they came to favor government regulation of competition to maintain stability within their industry. The FOCB was much impressed by Marland's proposal and gradually urged the states to enact conservation laws as a basis for settling the petroleum industry's problems.[55]

The Coolidge years saw the development of a slowly emerging consensus on national oil policies, both among leaders in the industry and in various branches of state and federal governments. To be sure, intra-industry and intragovernment conflicts were still rife, but between 1924 and 1929 the various interest groups narrowed their choices for alternate courses of action.

In 1924 most oilmen, and certainly the API, still failed to recognize the need for effective conservation policies. Five years later the API had reversed itself and officially endorsed a conservation program. During the same period the President and his Cabinet crystallized their own thinking on the oil problem. At first concerned only with investigation, they resolutely opposed relaxation of the antitrust laws but supported federal and state legislation designed to improve conservation practices on public and private lands. By 1929 both government and the industry clearly recognized that conservation and stabilization were two major and mutually related problems. The FOCB had done a great deal to bring about such an awareness, and now that Herbert Hoover, one of its most active members, had assumed the office of President, it was widely believed that he would take forceful action to put many of the FOCB's recommendations into practice.

54. *NPN* (February 2, 16, 1927); *O&G Jl.* (February 10, 1927); Tulsa *World,* February 9, 10, 1927.

55. *NPN* (March 2, 1927); *Inland Oil Index* (May 13, 1927); Washington *Herald,* May 23, 1927.

5 / Herbert Hoover's Oil Problems

THE ACCESSION of Herbert Hoover to the Presidency led many in the oil industry to hope that they would find a sympathetic and understanding Chief Executive in Washington. Himself a mining engineer, Hoover seemed peculiarly well suited to provide leadership in the formulation of viable natural resource policies. Well versed in political and technical problems relating to petroleum, and fresh from four years of service on the FOCB, Hoover aroused high expectations.

Yet, between 1929 and 1933 Hoover showed himself to be singularly inept in his conduct of national petroleum policy. To be sure, he was not responsible for the industry's predicament, nor could anyone be expected to perform miracles. But his lack of realism in approaching the industry's difficulties was extraordinary and compared most unfavorably with the insight of Harding and Coolidge. The goals and methods of the New Nationalism seemed to be submerged in political amateurism during the Hoover years as national oil policy floundered to an unprecedented extent.

Hoover's task was not an easy one. Not only did he inherit unresolved problems from his predecessors; these were greatly compounded by the Great Depression. The technological advances that had made the great increases in petroleum production possible were also leading to a great glut of oil in relation to existing demands and resulted in a continuing decline of prices. Overproduction had been the major problem of the oil industry since 1924, but conditions worsened in 1931, when prospectors exploited rich new finds in East Texas. At a time when available markets for oil were already shrinking, the discovery of one of the most productive petroleum fields anywhere came at an inopportune moment. A great boost in world petroleum production, from fields in Arabia, Rumania, the Soviet Union, and Venezuela, only added to a worldwide depression in the industry. Perhaps stabilization of production could have been achieved if the various producers in the United States had been able to cooperate on restricting production. But sharp divisions among producers and refiners and between independent and integrated companies created further confusion and demoralization, which deepened during the first four years of the Great Depression.

Amid such rapidly changing conditions Hoover's attitude was one of absolute rigidity. At a time when one of the nation's great industries was near collapse, the President concentrated on his own narrow goals of resource policy. He appeared oblivious to reality as he formulated objectives that included little more than conservation of petroleum on the public lands. Unlike Coolidge, Hoover lacked a broad concern for extending conservation practices to private enterprise on a national scale. Possibly because of his Quaker background, Hoover also revealed little inclination to safeguard petroleum reserves for the nation's armed forces. Deaf to the pleas of industry leaders for federal legislation to control overproduction, the President presented a program that bore little relation either to the acute oil problems of the industry or to the concerns of government.

Early in his Administration, Hoover outlined the elements of the national oil policy that he hoped to fashion. Reversing a position he had taken in 1926, he now openly opposed amendment of the antitrust laws to allow oilmen to make agreements restricting production. Such a step could easily result in monopoly and price-fixing, he feared. Instead, he focused much of his attention on persuading oilmen on the public domain to adopt more efficient practices so as to eliminate waste. Since the Secretary of the Interior controlled terms of leaseholders on federal lands, persuasion would be relatively easy. It was hoped that operators on private properties would voluntarily follow their example. Hoover made it quite clear, however, that he did not consider it the duty of the federal government to deal with production problems. This was a matter for the states. The President was willing to offer his good offices in promoting desirable state conservation legislation if it should prove absolutely necessary.[1]

Few could quarrel with Hoover's initial program. The trouble with it was that it hardly touched on the industry's major—and immediate— problem: overproduction. As during the next four years the Chief Executive stubbornly clung to the guidelines he had charted, the industry was largely left to its own devices in dealing with violent price fluctuations. No wonder, therefore, that oilmen who had expected to find sympathy in the White House became progressively disillusioned.

Aiding the President in his conduct of natural resource policies were three close associates. One was Dr. Ray Lyman Wilbur, a physician and former president of Stanford University. A good personal friend of Hoover's, he served as Secretary of the Interior in his Cabinet. Somewhat less of a novice with respect to petroleum policies was Mark Requa, another Californian, former director of the Oil Division of the United States Fuel Administration. Requa became increasingly disillusioned with the President's blind refusal to recognize the grave plight of the oil industry. After 1931 his influence with Hoover waned as Secretary of Commerce Robert P. Lamont came to have a greater voice in the direction of natural resource policies.

At the outset of his Administration the President had what he considered to be at least two solutions to the industry's ills. First, he argued that producers could accomplish much by voluntary action, by practicing greater efficiency, and by eliminating waste. This was also one of his major themes in dealing with national industrial problems. Secondly, he believed that conservation practices on federal lands would diminish the great flood of petroleum. But again and again he reiterated his belief that he did not consider it the duty of the federal government to deal with production problems; such responsibility rested primarily with the states. In this view he followed closely upon recommendations contained in the recent report of the Committee of Nine of the American

1. Washington *Post,* April 6, 1929; *National Petroleum News* [hereafter cited as *NPN*] (April 17, 1929); William D. Mitchell to Ray L. Wilbur, March 29, 1929, Ray L. Wilbur to R. C. Holmes, April 10, 1929, Ray Lyman Wilbur Papers, Hoover Institution [hereafter cited as Wilbur Mss.], Stanford University; Herbert Hoover Press Conference Statement, April 2, 1929, in Wilbur Mss.

Bar Association, which emphasized the need for state oil conservation laws and the undesirability of federal action in this sphere.[2]

Hoover lost little time in implementing these objectives. Just a few days after he entered the White House he issued an executive order to modify federal leasing policy. In his proclamation of March 13, 1929, he announced that the Secretary of the Interior would issue no further permits for the issuance of oil leases on public lands. Such action, it was hoped, would contribute to a decline of commercial production. Theodore Roosevelt's example in withdrawing coal lands during 1902 created a precedent for this step, and Hoover may well have thought of himself as following in the tradition of the New Nationalism. But the year was 1929, not 1902, and the fact that these lands yielded less than 10 percent of total U.S. oil production made his action far less significant than was immediately apparent.[3]

If the suspension of further leasing permits did little to solve the problem of overproduction, it had the unfortunate political effect of antagonizing many westerners and small independent oil producers. In states with large areas of public land, such as Colorado, Utah, and Wyoming, the order did indeed work hardship, however commendable in intent. In fact, the three governors of these Rocky Mountain states were so upset by Hoover's declaration that they met in Denver on March 22 to draw up a protest to the President.[4] And in the Senate, a special subcommittee began an investigation of Hoover's legal right to issue his directive under the Leasing Act of 1920, although the group ultimately did nothing.[5] Only three months after entering the White House, therefore, Hoover had managed to antagonize at least two important segments of the oil industry. In addition, he proved disappointing in failing to offer constructive, effective solutions to the problem of overproduction.

At the same time Hoover was firm in rejecting entreaties from industry leaders for some form of production limitation. His opposition sprang primarily from the fear that this would encourage monopolistic

2. New York *Sun,* April 3, 1929; Washington *Post,* April 3, 1929; *Oil and Gas Journal* [hereafter cited as *O&G Jl.*] (April 25, 1929).

3. Washington *Post,* March 13, 17, 1929.

4. Washington *Star,* March 24, 1929; *O&G Jl.* (April 18, 1929).

5. *U.S. Daily,* May 13, 1929; *Wall Street Journal,* May 20, 1929.

practices and price-fixing.[6] Consequently he rejected proposals for modification of the antitrust laws to allow oil producers greater freedom in cooperating for production restrictions. This represented a reversal of his 1926 views as Secretary of Commerce. Such limitations, he believed, would lead to price-fixing, either by the industry itself or, of necessity, by government. To both of these he was opposed.[7]

The issue came before him soon after he took office. In December, 1928, the API developed a plan for voluntary restriction of crude output. The Board of Directors adopted a resolution calling for a reduction in crude production during 1929 equal to that of the last nine months of 1928. Hopefully, the agreement was to continue in effect for several years. To administer this scheme the API proposed creation of five committees corresponding to geographical areas (Pacific Coast, Mid-continent, Gulf Coast, East Coast, Mexico, and northern South America). These were also to promote state regulation and to develop voluntary unit agreements. That the effort to limit the output of crude oil in the United States might be followed by worldwide curbs was possible. The idea of a global plan to restrict production was just then being endorsed by Sir Henry Deterding, head of the powerful Royal Dutch Shell Company.[8]

Shortly after the President's inauguration the API sent a delegation to the FOCB to discuss respective views on limitations of production. The API hoped for a revision of the antitrust laws that would make cooperation to restrict production legal. But in a press conference during early April, Hoover again publicly announced that he opposed price-fixing, whether by government or by private groups. He explained that his Administration's major objective in regard to oil policies would be to encourage scientific engineering, but this could be done only by the states, since the federal government had no such powers. Nor could he condone the API agreement to restrict production, for it violated the Sherman Anti-Trust Act. And he noted that any action by Congress to deal with the oil surplus would only lead to price manipulation.[9]

Hoover's fear that the API program was really aimed at price control

6. Washington *Post,* April 3, 6, 1929.

7. *Oildom* (April 8, 1929).

8. New York *Times* [hereafter cited as *NYT*], October 9, 20, 1928, February 26, 1929; Washington *Post,* March 28, 1929; *O&G Jl.* (April 25, 1929).

9. Washington *Post,* April 3, 1929.

was shared by others. Secretary Wilbur refused to give the plan his support and suggested that, instead, oilmen would do well to eliminate waste and to increase their efficiency in order to increase profits. Such a suggestion showed singular blindness in grasping the industry's problems, since Wilbur's advice was as likely to lead to further overproduction as to higher prices. But at least Wilbur warned Hoover that something must be done to avert a real catastrophe in the oil industry.[10] At Wilbur's request, however, Attorney General Mitchell rendered an opinion in which he declared the proposed API agreement unlawful. Thus, although on the one hand Hoover had encouraged business leaders to undertake voluntary cooperation, on the other he discouraged them from taking effective steps to implement their program. It was difficult to understand just what measures the President had in mind. Understandably, oil industry executives were very much disgruntled. The rebuff led the API to cease its campaign for modification of the antitrust laws, at least temporarily. With this avenue closed, the institute gave its support to state laws for the restriction of output.[11]

Apparently oblivious to the resentment that he had already stirred up in the first two months of his presidency, Hoover's next move was to foster voluntary cooperation for promoting conservation by individuals and among the states through an interstate oil compact. He hoped that conservation would cut down the rapidly increasing glut of oil. Upon the advice of Mark Requa in April, 1929, Hoover called a conference of leading petroleum experts in industry and government to frame an agreement toward this end. The President sounded out sentiment for such an idea in April, 1929, by sending George O. Smith, long-time director of the United States Geological Survey, to visit the governors of affected states and to discuss possible proposals with them.[12] Hoover's efforts received added support in late April when the API, despairing of its effort to secure Justice Department approval for a voluntary industry agreement to curtail production, also came out for the enactment of state regulatory laws and an interstate compact.[13]

10. Ray L. Wilbur to E. B. Reeser, March 28, 1929, and E. S. Rochester memo for Ray L. Wilbur, March 29, 1929, in Wilbur Mss.; *NPN* (April 17, 1929).
11. *Oildom* (April 22, 1929).
12. Ray L. Wilbur to William D. Mitchell, March 20, 1929, in Wilbur Mss.; Washington *Post,* March 28, April 3, 1929; *U.S. Daily,* April 3, 1929.
13. *O&G Jl.* (April 25, 1929); *Oildom* (April 29, 1929); Ray L. Wilbur to Herbert Hoover, April 25, 1929, in Wilbur Mss.

Hoover left the organization of this conference to Requa. The former Director of the Oil Division of the United States Fuel Administration on May 1 embarked for Oklahoma and the Pacific Coast to gather support from the industry, and to serve as an unofficial representative for Wilbur and the API.[14] In interviews along the way Requa noted cautiously that he was not advocating any specific program, but desired only an exchange of views among various segments of the industry in the hope that a cooperative endeavor would result.[15] Despite the fact that most independent Oklahoma producers were against any effort to restrict production, President Hoover on May 22, 1929, officially issued a call for an oil conference. He invited the governors of the western states as well as interested oil producers to a meeting on June 10 at Colorado Springs, which was to formulate an effective conservation policy.[16] The timing of this invitation was particularly poor, for westerners were still smarting under the President's recent land withdrawal order and were in a rebellious mood. At Wilbur's request, Requa was to preside at the meeting.

Amid much fanfare, including a coast-to-coast radio broadcast of the proceedings, the Colorado Springs Conference began on a hopeful note. In his opening address Requa urged those assembled, including governors of Wyoming, Colorado, Kansas, and Montana, representatives of the API, and scores of representatives from oilmen's organizations, to forget their differences and to cooperate in order to curb overproduction. Stabilization of the industry was bound to result, he noted, if producers would only use sound conservation practices. If, however, the industry did not itself curb the flow of excess oil, Requa warned, he would favor government coercion.[17] Although apt and timely, this speech hardly soothed the already wounded feelings of westerners.

The meeting soon revealed various rifts. In the first place, small operators were opposed to any restrictions of production and were against a compact—a position on which they diverged sharply from

14. *NPN* (May 1, 1929); Fort Worth *Star Telegram,* May 2, 1929.

15. Tulsa *World,* May 3, 1929; *California Oil World* (May 9, 1929).

16. Tulsa *Tribune,* May 15, 1929; Washington *Post,* May 23, 1929; *O&G Jl.* (June 6, 1929); *Oildom* (June 3, 1929); Mark Requa to Ray L. Wilbur, May 16, 1929, in Wilbur Mss.

17. *Oildom* (June 3, 10, 1929); *O&G Jl.* (June 6, 13, 1929); Washington *Star,* June 11, 1929; Ray L. Wilbur to Herbert Hoover, June 4, 1929, in Wilbur Mss.

that of the large integrated companies. Instead, the smaller producers favored a protective tariff to keep out foreign petroleum. On the other hand, the major oil companies relied on imports to a considerable extent and opposed duties.[18]

Even more disruptive was the smouldering resentment of the western governors. Still chafing under President Hoover's recent order prohibiting the issuance of new oil-drilling permits on the public lands, and eager to have it revoked, they were in no mood to cooperate with the Administration in the framing of a compact. Instead, they used the conference as a platform from which openly to condemn Hoover's new leasing policy. In fact, they virtually repudiated the President and questioned the wisdom of his proposed conservation policy.

No wonder, therefore, that the conference resulted in a deadlock and was forced to recess indefinitely. The poor timing of Hoover and Requa in arranging for the meeting, the anger of representatives of western states, and the conflict between the small and the integrated companies all contributed to the inconclusive results.[19] Requa himself became somewhat disenchanted with Hoover's failure to provide leadership, and in late July resigned as chairman of the conference. At the same time he hoped that Congress would take a more active role in restricting oil production. But Secretary Wilbur felt, in rebuttal, that such action was unnecessary. He also rejected Requa's suggestion that the President support a tariff on foreign oil imports.[20] The first year of Hoover's administration closed with his failure to deal effectively with the oil industry's problems. Indeed, it seemed that the fruit of his efforts was the hostility of most segments of the industry.

The beginning of the Great Depression only added to the already serious conditions prevailing in the oil industry. In 1930 production increased by at least 10 percent over the previous year, while markets shrank. By March, 1931, production in the United States was about 3 million barrels daily, while an additional 300,000 barrels were imported

18. Tulsa *World,* May 24, 1929; *U.S. Daily,* June 7, 1929; *Oildom* (June 10, 1929); New York *Sun,* June 7, 1929.

19. *NYT,* June 12, 13, 1929; *Oildom* (June 14, 1929); *Wall Street Journal,* June 20, 1929; Tulsa *Tribune,* June 22, 1929.

20. Ray L. Wilbur Memo for FOCB, July 29, 1929, in Wilbur Mss.; Mark Requa to Ray L. Wilbur, October 7, 1929, Ray L. Wilbur to Mark Requa, October 3, 1929, in Wilbur Mss.

daily. The inevitable result was a serious decline of prices. Crude oil sold for 75 cents a barrel and a pall of gloom fell over the oil fields.[21]

But the depths of economic crisis for the oil industry were not reached until early 1931, when the East Texas field was discovered. The site of one of the world's richest wells, it added to the existing glut of oil in the United States and also upset the international price structure.[22] More than any other new field, East Texas disorganized crude oil markets throughout the nation.

In the face of this unprecedented situation, Mr. Hoover's favorite remedy for industrial ills continued to be voluntary cooperation. In March, 1930, Secretary Wilbur suggested a six-day operating week to petroleum producers, with planned shutdowns on Sundays.[23] For a short while, this seemed to work, as some of the large integrated companies such as Humble, Shell, Union, Standard of California, and Standard of New Jersey agreed to the proposal. But many of the smaller refineries in Texas and Oklahoma rejected the plan as too costly and continued at full blast.[24]

As voluntary efforts to restrict production broke down, the independent producers sparked a concerted drive in Congress for an oil tariff. After their failure to secure Congressional passage of an oil tariff in the fall of 1929 they held a mass meeting in Tulsa late in January, 1930. This assemblage sent a delegation of 250 to Washington to lobby for a tariff. A committee of thirteen met with the President in the White House, and also with Secretary Wilbur, the FOCB, and members of Congress from oil states. In January, 1930, Congressional adoption of an oil tariff (one dollar per barrel of crude oil) had failed by only one vote.[25] Some members of the group also testified at hearings before the House Ways and Means Committee. Hoover was noncommittal concerning their pleas, however, and remained rather cool to endorsing a petroleum tariff. Perhaps it was partly his attitude that led the Senate, on March 5, 1930, to reject an oil tariff by a vote of 39 to 27. Whether

21. Washington *Post,* March 12, 1931; *O&G Jl.* (January 23, 1930).

22. *O&G Jl.* (February 13, 20, 1931); *NYT,* March 15, April 22, May 10, June 6, 7, 1931.

23. *O&G Jl.* (March 6, 1930).

24. *NPN* (March 12, 1930); *U.S. Daily,* March 3, 1930; Philadelphia *Public Ledger,* March 6, 1930; Los Angeles *Examiner,* March 5, 1930.

25. *NPN* (February 5, 12, 1930); the Wilbur Mss. contain voluminous correspondence from oil producers demanding a tariff.

the curtailment of the flow of foreign oil would have done much to alleviate the existing balance between supply and demand of petroleum in the United States is doubtful. As the Washington *Post* pointed out, it might not encourage producers to practice careful conservation.[26] But rightly or wrongly, many independents believed that it was likely to bring direct and immediate relief.

The worsening conditions in the industry during ensuing months led the independents to try once more to secure a tariff in the new session of Congress. Wirt Franklin, president of the Independent Petroleum Producer's Association of America, called a special conference of producers on January 15, 1931, to formulate specific demands. These were endorsed by the head of the oil workers union, Harvey Fremming. Although Secretary Wilbur openly expressed himself against any tariff, Secretary of War Patrick Hurley was more cautious and announced that the Administration took no position either for or against such a levy.[27] Nevertheless, Senator Gore of Oklahoma agreed to fight for the proposal in the United States Senate together with Senator Arthur Capper, the erstwhile leader of the Farm Bloc. Reflecting much of the contemporary disillusionment with World War I, they argued that competition for oil had been a major cause for wars in the past. The association also received the promise of Representative Harold McGugin, a Republican of Kansas, to vote with the Democrats in the organization of the House if Congress did not pass an oil tariff.[28] At the time, the House had 218 Republicans, 214 Democrats, 1 Farmer-Laborite, and 2 Democratic vacancies.

Once again the drama of the preceding spring was reenacted. With Senator Capper's backing, Wirt Franklin presented his case to Hoover in a personal interview. The President promised to lend his help, but spoke in general terms. And on January 18, 1931, Senators Capper and

---

26. *O&G Jl.* (February 13, 20, 27, 1930); *NPN* (March 5, 1931); *Congressional Record* [hereafter cited as *CR*], 71 Cong., 2 sess. (March 22, 1930), 5946; Harry Woodring to Herbert Hoover, January 28, 1931, in Wilbur Mss.

27. See Franklin's petition in *CR*, 72 Cong., 1 sess. (December 15, 1931), 497, and his testimony before House Ways and Means Committee, *ibid.*, 2988–2996. For Fremming see *ibid.*, 3844; Santa Fe *New Mexican*, January 15, 1931; Washington *Star*, January 5, 1931; 71 Cong., 3 sess., Senate, Committee on Interstate and Foreign Commerce, *Hearings on Regulating the Importation of Petroleum and Related Products* (Washington, 1931), Part I, 36–46, Part II, 71.

28. Kansas City *Star*, January 16, 1931.

Shortridge (Calif.) introduced a bill providing for a tariff of one dollar per barrel of oil.[29] One by one the representatives of independent producers appeared before the Senate Commerce Committee to present their case. Impressed by the force of the movement, Secretary Wilbur wavered, and announced in January, 1931, that he was ready to favor some limitation on oil imports.[30] But the opposition also made itself heard. Representatives from the East feared that fuel and gasoline prices would rise if the foreign inflow was restricted. Oil importers naturally were against a tariff, as were consumer groups like the powerful American Automobile Association.[31] The big integrated oil companies were divided on the question, since each looked primarily to its own interests. The Standard companies were neutral, while Gulf—with extensive production in Colombia—and Standard of Indiana—with vast producing wells in Venezuela—quite naturally opposed any effort to cut down the flow from their foreign sources.[32]

With tacit Administration support, foes of the oil tariff were able to impede its passage. Despite personal appeals to Hoover, the representatives of the Independent Oil Producers Association were unable to secure his support. To placate them, the House Ways and Means Committee passed a resolution calling for an investigation of conditions in the industry, and for a study of the effects of Soviet oil imports. The House group also instructed the United States Tariff Commission to investigate comparative costs of oil production.[33]

But domestic oil producers were angry. As an indication of their mood, the Independent Oilmen's Association of Oklahoma appealed to Governor Franklin D. Roosevelt of New York, already considered as a possible Presidential nominee, to back their efforts to secure protection.[34] Later in the summer of 1931, the independents expressed a

29. *NYT,* January 8, 16, 17, 18, 1931; New York *World,* January 16, 1931; *U.S. Daily,* January 17, 1931; *CR,* 71 Cong., 3 sess., (January 21, 30, 1931) 2861, 3567; Washington *Times,* January 18, 1931.

30. New York *Telegram,* January 29, 1931; New York *Evening Post,* January 30, 1931.

31. *U.S. Daily,* February 2, 3, 1931; New York *World,* February 4, 1931; Los Angeles *Examiner,* February 6, 1931.

32. *NYT,* February 15, 1931.

33. Washington *Post,* February 25, 1931; *Christian Science Monitor,* February 26, 1931; *NYT,* March 1, 1931.

34. *Christian Science Monitor,* March 2, 1931; *NYT,* June 4, 1931.

willingness to compromise and asked the President to impose at least an embargo on foreign oil. But Hoover informed them that he had no authority to take such action, despite a recommendation from the FOCB that imports be cut by 38 percent. By the fall of 1931 the situation in the oil industry had become so desperate, however, that producers were willing to try any possible remedy. At its annual meeting in November, 1931, even the API—in which large integrated companies had a strong voice—came out for a tariff. In his annual message to Congress just a few weeks later, however, Hoover neglected even to mention the subject.[35] At a time when one of the nation's major industries had collapsed, this inaction showed a marked lack of responsibility and an abdication of national leadership.

Instead of a tariff, President Hoover again urged voluntary cooperation—this time by large integrated oil companies—to secure voluntary curtailment of foreign oil imports.[36] In a letter to five governors of producing states (Texas, Oklahoma, New Mexico, Kansas, and California) Wilbur sought to assuage them by noting that Secretary of Commerce Lamont was negotiating voluntary import restrictions by the biggest oil importers. The date was no accident, for it came a day after the adjournment of Congress, which had refused to adopt an oil tariff and which failed to extend any other aid to independent oil producers. Meanwhile a conference of governors from oil-producing states was meeting in Oklahoma City where, again, they demanded a tariff.[37] They also warned large integrated companies who were importing oil from Venezuela and Arabia that state legislatures might prohibit operation of such corporations within their borders.[38] The FOCB and Wilbur thus secured pledges from the Big Four of the industry (Gulf, Standard of Indiana, Shell, and Sinclair) to cut down on their foreign imports. But Wilbur and Hoover refused to support any kind of federal action to enforce such an agreement once it was concluded. Some critics also wondered why the Administration had not encouraged such an agree-

35. Philadelphia *Ledger*, September 15, 1931; Denver *Post*, September 22, 1931; *Christian Science Monitor*, November 11, 1931; *NYT*, November 12, December 9, 1931.

36. San Francisco *Chronicle*, January 16, 1931; Arizona *Republican*, March 6, 1931.

37. *NYT*, March 9, 1931.

38. *Rocky Mountain News*, March 10, 1931.

ment earlier and whether, if secured, it would not violate the antitrust laws.[39] Amid these frantic efforts Hoover seemed vacillating and peculiarly ineffective.

Nevertheless, by April 1, 1931, the Big Four agreed to try the curtailment plan for a period of three months. By June the experiment in voluntary cooperation collapsed, however, as individual companies simply abandoned the program. As a result, it had only a slight impact on the overproduction problem. As one newspaper noted, Hoover's tepid effort in national economic planning turned out to be a colossal failure.[40] The President's course had been bewildering. Although on the one hand urging voluntary restriction, on the other he was unwilling to authorize federal enforcement; although against modification of the antitrust laws, he was encouraging an agreement to curtail distribution. No wonder that the industry was confused over the course of public policy.

Under the stimulus of increasing chaos, early in January, 1932, the independent oil producers redoubled their efforts to secure Congressional restriction of oil imports. Secretary Wilbur now came out in support of the measure, while the President was said to be willing to sign it if Congress presented it to him. By the middle of 1932, Congress enacted a tariff of one dollar on each barrel of foreign crude oil imported and the President accepted the inevitable and signed it.[41]

At the same time, throughout 1930 and 1931 the FOCB sought to aid stabilization of oil producers by inaugurating statistical forecasts that would aid producers in estimating market demand. In doing so the FOCB was responding to the urgings of industry leaders when, in 1930, it established a committee of five to forecast production trends.[42] This service had been rendered successfully by the Oil Administrator during World War I and was extremely useful in the midst of the Depression.

Demands for greater federal controls continued to be made by Henry L. Doherty, who was unceasing in his pleas for strong national action. Mark Requa, too, in 1931 urged creation of an oil czar and a reestab-

39. *Christian Science Monitor,* March 18, 1931; Washington *Post,* April 5, 1931; Ray L. Wilbur to A. W. Mellon, January 19, 1931, and January 23, 1931, Ray L. Wilbur to Herbert Hoover, January 19, 1931, in Wilbur Mss.

40. *NYT,* July 2, 1931; Denver *Post,* June 14, 1931.

41. Washington *Herald,* January 27, 1932; Fresno *Republican,* January 27, 1932; 1931–33 Stats. at Large 260 (June 6, 1932); *CR,* 72 Cong., 1 sess., (February 10, 25, March 14, 25, 1932) 3721, 4731–4734, 6044, 6825.

42. New York *Evening Post,* April 19, 1930.

lishment of the United States Fuel Administration, which had been so successful in stabilizing the industry during World War I. Since voluntary cooperation was not possible under the Sherman Act he advocated the appointment of a national umpire to supervise such action outside the framework of the antitrust laws.[43] In Congress, Senator Borah of Idaho, a long-time foe of "monopoly," urged legislation to make the petroleum industry a public utility, a proposal that was endorsed by Woodrow Wilson's Secretary of State, Bainbridge Colby.[44] And even Secretary of Commerce Lamont favored federal legislation in 1931 unless the oil industry and the oil states could put their own house in order.[45] But these efforts were neither coordinated nor given central guidance. They were merely suggestions amid the seemingly insoluble problems with which the oil industry was struggling without any guidance whatsoever from the President.

Thus, by November, 1932, the oil industry, as so many others, was in a state of utter demoralization. Its major problem was the failure to stabilize production and consumption. Despite high hopes, the experience of four years under President Hoover had been frustrating. To be sure, the President could not be blamed for existence of the industry's problems nor for not finding easy solutions to its troubles. But the record of the Administration in approaching these issues was not one to inspire confidence. It had emphasized voluntary cooperation and the elimination of waste, yet these remedies hardly affected a crisis of the magnitude in which the petroleum industry found itself. Hoover's policies were marked by a negation of leadership, by weakness and vacillation, by an unwillingness to confront prevailing problems, and by lack of realism and reluctance to experiment. Even close associates of the President sometimes found it difficult to understand him. Men like Requa, who had worked with him during World War I, had found him then to be a forceful leader. But from the very start of his Administration, even before the brunt of the Depression had made itself felt, he seemed to be overwhelmed by his responsibilities and showed an inflexibility that seriously hampered his effectiveness as the nation's Chief Executive.

43. Washington *Star,* January 15, 1931; *U.S. Daily,* February 4, 1931.
44. Seattle *Post Intelligencer,* April 18, 1931; Santa Fe *New Mexican,* April 13, 1931.
45. Los Angeles *Times,* November 12, 1931.

6 / State Policies During the Great Depression, 1929–1933

THE HOOVER policies cannot be assessed fairly without a closer analysis of their impact on the state and local level. Many oilmen could not forget that while the President resolutely refused to condone federal action to diminish the flow of oil during 1930, 1931, and 1932, the economies of major producing states like Texas and Oklahoma were totally disrupted. Chaos, violence, and anarchy prevailed there amid conditions that the drift of federal policies under President Hoover did little to remedy. In the absence of national leadership, state governments themselves, prompted by affected economic interest groups, undertook the task of maintaining a semblance of economic stability by establishing direct controls over the amount of oil produced by private enterprise. Long before the federal government assumed responsibility for maintaining economic stability—in the Employment Act of 1946—some of the states were already performing this function within the limits of their own narrower jurisdiction.

The problem of overproduction was especially severe in Texas and Oklahoma, where the petroleum industry represented a major segment of the regional economy. Unemployment and loss of revenues could not be ignored in state capitols in which oil interests wielded considerable influence. Moreover, state governments had a wide range of options with which to meet the crisis through exercise of their police power.

The states embarked on very close and regimented regulation of oil producers and refiners, a regimentation far more severe than under federal control. Indeed, they extended a measure of control virtually unprecedented in government's relation to the economy as it had unfolded in the American experience.

STATE CONTROL IN TEXAS

In Texas, for more than a decade before the Great Crash, the State Railroad Commission had sought to regulate oil production and to promote conservation. Extensive oil explorations during World War I had resulted in market surpluses that led the legislature to pass the Conservation Act of 1917, designed to eliminate waste in oil. Under the act the Railroad Commission of Texas was to enforce the law. Two years later a more comprehensive act enabled the commission to exercise broad powers to enforce the prohibition of waste.

The Texas Railroad Commission in 1919 began to regulate oil production by holding hearings and by conducting investigations of oil wastage in the state. By November, 1919, it had gathered sufficient information to issue conservation rules. Perhaps the most famous of these was No. 37, which ordered proper spacing of wells—at forty-foot intervals—in the interests of oil conservation. Yet, until 1929, the commission did not enforce its orders too strictly.[1]

By 1927 the commission already found overproduction to be its major problem. Even then major Texas oil producers were considering plans for restricting output, but their voluntary efforts to enforce curtailment programs broke down repeatedly. Many of these oilmen thus approached state legislators to seek state aid in limiting the amount of oil produced. In 1927, the operators in the Yates field made a prorationing agreement to limit production, which the Railroad Commission approved. In the following year the commission ordered operators in the Hendricks field in Winkler County to develop a similar plan for control of production, for the increasing glut was threatening to demoralize

1. Robert Hardwicke, *Legal History of Gas and Oil* (Chicago, 1938), 214–220; James P. Hart, "Oil, the Courts and the Railroad Commission," *Southwestern Historical Quarterly* XLIV (January 1941), 303–311; 1919 Texas Stats. 228, 285; [Robert W.] Conrod, "State Regulation of the Oil and Gas Industry in Texas," (unpublished MA thesis, University of Texas, 1931), 24–106.

the oil industry in the state and, indeed, to affect its entire economy.[2]

But voluntary efforts by individual groups of producers were increasingly less effective in dealing with the tremendous volume of unwanted oil that poured from the rich Texas earth during the Hoover years. Early in 1930 a group of influential Texas oil producers filed a petition with the Railroad Commissioners urging them to initiate direct statewide control of production. During the summer of that year the commission held hearings on the request and on the gravity of conditions in the industry. Testimony of the oilmen who appeared clearly revealed that they considered conservation programs as a means for limiting production and for raising prices.[3] But the crisis in the industry demanded immediate action, and guidance from Washington was not forthcoming. Paradoxically, conservation and stabilization were closely intertwined.

While Hoover was urging voluntary cooperation, on August 27, 1930, the Texas Railroad Commission issued its first mandatory statewide prorationing order, designed to enforce conservation rules and at the same time to limit production to market demand. The commission limited statewide production to 750,000 barrels daily, about 50,000 barrels less than the production of the preceding year. Governor Ross Sterling, himself a former president of the Humble Oil Company, as well as many legislators looked on this ruling with suspicion. They feared that it reflected an effort by the industry to manipulate prices. Yet the order was also specific in requiring adoption of conservation practices by producers. The commission allocated total production among Texas fields and then among individual operators. It determined monthly quotas through information secured at hearings and by reliance on the production forecasts of the United States Bureau of Mines.[4]

The Texas courts defended the Railroad Commission's power to regulate oil production. In a suit in which the Danciger Oil and Refin-

2. Kenneth C. Davis and York Willbern, "Administrative Control of Oil Production in Texas," *Texas Law Review,* XXII (1944), 149–153; Earl Oliver, "Stabilizing Influences," and H. C. Hardison, "Proration of Yates Pool, Pecos County, Texas," in American Institute of Mining and Metallurgical Engineers, *Transactions* 1931, Petroleum Division (New York, 1931), 9–10, 74–79; Ft. Worth *Star Telegram,* April 29, 1929. For Winkler pool, see Ft. Worth *Star Telegram,* May 5, 1929; *Wall Street Journal,* May 17, 1929.

3. Hardwicke, in *Legal History* (1938), 229; *NYT,* July 19, 1931.

4. *Legal History* (1938), 222–224.

ing Company challenged prorationing, the Texas Supreme Court clearly endorsed the commission's action. Danciger contended that the order was not designed to eliminate waste but to fix prices and that it violated the State Conservation Act of 1929. But the judges held that prorationing was mainly designed to eliminate physical waste and that any effects this policy might have on price levels was merely incidental.[5]

As the Texas Railroad Commission was just beginning its task of stabilizing conditions in the state's oil industry, most of its labors were rudely disrupted in the spring of 1931 by the discovery of the rich East Texas fields. Exploitation of these pools could not have come at a less propitious time, for they had disastrous effects. Their production of 800,000 barrels daily totaled more than that of all other Texas oil wells combined.[6]

To cope with this new development the commissioners tried to extend production control to the field. In April, 1931, they issued their first prorationing order for East Texas, now in the midst of a wild, frenzied boom. But many operators there simply refused to obey the commission's orders, and their large number made the commission's task of enforcement virtually impossible. Some oilmen even threatened the commission's agents with violence should they cut off the flow of the wells. Hundreds of others filed court suits praying for injunctions to stay the Railroad Commission's orders. Meanwhile, they continued maximum production accompanied by wanton waste and further demoralized the already weak price structure of crude oil. By the summer of 1931, in the depths of the general Depression, the East Texas oil situation created utter chaos as crude oil sold for 10 cents a barrel (compared to $3 a barrel in 1919).[7]

While the President and his advisers did little more than to take notice of the situation, Governor Ross Sterling called a special session of the legislature for July 14, 1931. He asked it to enact a new conservation law that would specifically empower the Railroad Commission to limit oil production to reasonable market demand. There was much sentiment for such legislation among oil producers, for Oklahoma's

---

5. *Ibid.,* 228; New York *Times* [hereafter cited as *NYT*], January 28, 1931.
6. Harold F. Williamson *et al., The American Petroleum Industry* (2 vols., Evanston, 1959–1963), II, *Age of Energy,* 543–545, 554–555; *NYT,* March 15, 31, April 13, 27, 1931.
7. Houston *Post,* April 4, 1931; *NYT,* April 4, 5, 12, 26, June 7, July 19, 1931.

pioneering regulations appeared to be reasonably effective. But the law-makers were split over a variety of other alternatives.[8] As the debate on the issue developed, suddenly, on July 28, 1931, a federal District Court in Texas declared the Texas Railroad Commission's prorating orders in East Texas invalid. Seriously divided, on August 12, 1931, the legislature enacted a weak conservation act that prohibited physical waste only but granted the Railroad Commission no power to limit production to market demand. As the press interpreted this law, it annulled all of the Railroad Commission's prorationing orders promulgated during 1930 and 1931.[9] Under the new conservation act the Railroad Commission was also restricted in issuing orders, for it was required to give operators ten days' notice and a hearing. As in Oklahoma, therefore, the federal courts were seriously interfering with the efforts of state authority to deal with immediate economic crisis.

At the same time, in July and August, 1931, oil operators and speculators in East Texas were indulging in unrestrained production. They turned the chaos that had characterized the Texas oil industry during the spring to anarchy by August. By then East Texas was producing about one million barrels of crude oil daily, enough to meet one-third of all the crude petroleum requirements in the United States. Crude oil at 10 cents a barrel became common—if there were takers. Much talk of violence was in the air, talk of dynamiting wells and pipelines to stop the production spree. The breakdown of the economy and of law enforcement in Texas seemed at hand, amid the general gloom and hopelessness of the Depression.[10]

What was to be done? Secretary of Commerce Lamont was in close touch with the situation but could offer no constructive suggestions. Similarly, Secretary of the Interior Wilbur kept himself informed, but

8. *NYT,* June 6, July 10, 15, 17, 1931; Dallas *Morning News,* July 15, 1931; Houston *Post,* July 15, 1931; Los Angeles *Times,* July 23, 1931; Oklahoma City *News,* July 22, 1931; the Texas newspapers in the period, July 15–28, 1931, carry extensive accounts of the debates; see also *Christian Science Monitor,* July 25, 1931.

9. 51F (2d) 400; Denver *Post,* July 25, 1931; Houston *Post,* August 13, 1931; Dallas *Morning News,* August 13, 1931; Baltimore *Sun,* August 13, 1931; Philadelphia *Public Ledger,* August 13, 1931; 1931 *General and Special Laws of the State of Texas, First Called Session* [Austin, 1931], 46–56.

10. *NYT,* July 5, 21, 1931; "East Texas Drowns Itself in Oil," *Review of Reviews,* LXXXIV (August 1931), 78–79.

took no action despite many frantic appeals from oil producers. The breakdown of law and order in the oil fields and the collapse of the industry evinced no energetic response from President Hoover, who maintained a sphinxlike pose. In fact, he even refused to make recommendations to Congress for exploration of ways and means to aid the oil industry. This responsibility lay solely with the legislators, he believed. As for the FOCB, he reiterated his conviction that it had no legal powers to control oil production, in East Texas or anywhere else in the United States. And he emphasized repeatedly the Administration's opposition to a tariff or an embargo against foreign oil.[11]

Martial Law

Thus, the state government of Texas itself had to take drastic steps to meet the unprecedented crisis within its borders. Governor Sterling, in a mood of desperation, on August 17, 1931, declared East Texas to be in a state of insurrection. Dramatically, he placed the area under martial law. In appointing General Jacob Wolters as head of the state militia he ordered him to enforce a temporary shutdown of all oil wells in the East Texas field. The governor then sent approximately 4,000 troops into the oil fields to police the closing of the wells, and to arrest all violators.[12]

Throughout the whole course of the Great Depression perhaps few episodes better illustrated the breakdown of the economy than the collapse of the oil industry in the Southwest. And few situations better revealed the ineptitude of the Hoover Administration in dealing with Depression problems. In late August, 1931, the great drills were silenced as militia poured into the region. A strange quiet settled over East Texas, a striking climax to the frantic production spree that had characterized the previous six months.

Meanwhile, late in August the Railroad Commission began hearings on the possible imposition of production controls under the terms of the

11. R. B. Brown to R. P. Lamont, July 24, 1931; R. W. Mercer to R. P. Lamont, July 29, 1931, Records of the Department of the Interior, Administrative Files, Correspondence of the Secretary, National Archives [hereafter cited as DI Records], Washington, D.C.; for Wilbur, see his letter to R. P. Lamont, April 10, 1931, to E. W. Sterling, June 1, 1931, and Herbert Hoover to R. P. Lamont, June 2, 1931, in DI Records.

12. Dallas *Morning News,* August 18, 1931; Houston *Post* August 18, 1931; *NYT,* August 16, 18, 1931; New York *Herald Tribune,* August 16, 18, 1931.

new conservation act. At these sessions most oil producers agreed that a total output of about 400,000 barrels daily in East Texas was compatible with good conservation practices. Thus, on September 2, 1931, the Railroad Commission issued an order limiting statewide production to this amount. In turn, Governor Sterling promised to supply the troops needed to enforce the quota. The state militia did not leave the oil fields, therefore.[13] In fact, during the next fourteen months the Railroad Commission issued monthly prorationing orders, which the governor enforced through martial law. Despite some violations, military control proved effective in limiting production. By July, 1932, the price of crude oil rose to 85 cents a barrel, which compared favorably with the low point of 10 cents a barrel in the preceding August.[14] The resolute action of the state had at least prevented total anarchy.

Once again, however, the federal courts intervened to thwart the efforts of the state to deal with the economic crisis. With a singular lack of realism, in May, 1932, the Federal District Court for East Texas issued injunctions against state martial law on the grounds that the governor had no authority to control oil production. Nevertheless, state troops remained in the oil fields in defiance of the injunction while the case was pending on appeal, and they succeeded in holding production down to 400,000 barrels daily. Meanwhile, the Texas state courts upheld the Railroad Commission's prorationing orders.[15] This conflict between state and federal jurisdiction did not ease what was already a highly critical situation. Tension heightened while the appeal slowly found its way from the federal District Court to the United States Supreme Court. What would the verdict of the nation's highest tribunal direct? The fate of the oil industry in Texas, and throughout the nation, was at stake.

On May 16, 1932, the United States Supreme Court handed down its long-awaited decision. The particular case, involving the Champlin Oil Company, concerned the legality of the Oklahoma prorationing statute. In a six-to-three decision the judges upheld the Oklahoma conservation

13. Dallas *Morning News,* September 3, 1931; *NYT,* August 11, 14, 17, 26, September 2, 5, 6, 12, October 26, November 14, 1932.

14. *Oil and Gas Journal* [hereafter cited as *O&G Jl.*] (July 14, 28, September 29, 1932); *NYT,* July 23, 1932.

15. *E. Constantin et al.,* vs. *Lon Smith et al.,* 57 F (2d) 227 (E. D. Texas, February 18, 1932); *NPN* (March 16, 1932); Dallas *Morning News,* February 19, 1932.

act. In reasoning that resembled that of the Texas Supreme Court they declared the limitation of production to reasonable market demand to be a proper method for preventing physical waste. If it had an effect on prices this was merely incidental. The ruling of the East Texas Federal District Court was reversed.[16]

Unfortunately, the United States Supreme Court's decision had little immediate effect in improving Texas conditions. Unlike Oklahoma's law, the Texas Conservation Act of 1931 specifically prohibited the commission from restricting production to market demand. Texas operators still filed suits against the Railroad Commission charging that under the act of 1931 it did not have the power to allocate production allowables in relation to market demand. While many of these suits were pending in the state courts a large number of oil producers again went ahead to indulge in an unrestrained production spree. They were encouraged by the Federal District Court for East Texas, which on October 24, 1932, in the People's Case, enjoined the Texas Railroad Commission from enforcing its limitation of production.[17] It seemed that unless the Texas legislature enacted a new law specifically authorizing the Railroad Commission to restrict oil production to market demand in Texas any control the state attempted to impose on the industry was destined for failure.

Consequently, in November, 1932, Governor Sterling called another special session of the legislature. The harrowing experiences of the past year had had a chastening effect. With a minimum of debate, on November 12, 1932, the lawmakers passed a Market Demand Act, which specifically allowed the Railroad Commission to limit production to available market demand. The act defined waste as any oil production in excess of what transportation or market facilities could absorb. Memories of the past year's chaos led Governor Sterling to abandon his earlier fears of possible price regulation by the industry. He signed the bill willingly.[18] Thus ended a dramatic episode in state government-business relations.

16. 287 U.S. 378, as Chief Justice Hughes for the U.S. Supreme Court affirmed the decree, December 12, 1932, which led to the withdrawal of Texas troops from the oil fields.

17. 60 F (2d) 1041.

18. 1932 *General and Special Laws of the State of Texas, Fourth Called Session* [Austin, 1932], 3; Dallas *Morning News,* November 13, 1932; *NYT,* November 3, 14, 1932.

Endowed with its new legal powers, in December, 1932, the Railroad Commission began to issue new orders for curbing the flow of Texas oil. The commission's engineers were able to show quite clearly at various hearings that scientific reasons alone dictated limitation of production, especially the conservation of reservoir energy and the prevention of premature encroachment of water into oil wells. Economic reasons— the need to maintain a measure of stability in the industry, and to prevent its collapse—were no less pressing.[19]

The failure of the Hoover Administration to provide guidance for stabilization of the oil industry left the problem squarely to producers themselves. With voluntary efforts increasingly ineffective, and with the White House's refusal to concern itself with oil problems, petroleum producers prevailed upon state government in Texas to undertake close regulation of the petroleum industry. In fact, the controls applied by the Texas Railroad Commission to restrict the amount of oil produced were far more rigorous than would have been possible under federal jurisdiction. Even in the depths of the Depression, public authorities rarely assumed the right to determine production quotas for private industries. The economic crisis called forth a revival of state mercantilism to maintain a semblance of economic and social order in the face of an obstinate lack of realism on the part of the President and the federal judiciary.

The big question in Texas during 1933 was: "How could government regulation of the oil industry—so vital to the welfare of the state—be made effective?" To many oilmen and lawmakers, the experience of the past four years pointed to at least three alternatives. One possible solution was rigid federal control, but this jarred the pride of many Texans. Another possibility was to continue exclusive reliance on individual state action. Because of the national interstate character of oil distribution as distinguished from production, this had led to difficulties that the state by itself could not remedy. A feasible remedy might be found through a compact among oil-producing states that faced similar problems. But the experiences of the oil fields between 1929 and 1934 indicated clearly that some form of governmental action was necessary.

19. *O&G Jl.* (January 5, 12, 19, 26, 1933), discusses the Texas Railroad Commission's hearings; see also *Legal History* (1938), 240–242.

STATE CONTROL IN OKLAHOMA

In Oklahoma, as in Texas, oil producers were encountering complex problems. Perhaps the impact of the Depression on the petroleum industry was even more disruptive there, since its economy was less diversified. Here, too, the collapse of oil prices by 1930 bred chaos, confusion, and violence. Yet Oklahoma had pioneered as early as 1907 with state regulation of oil production. If the prime aim of the Oklahoma Corporation Commission between 1907 and 1929 was to eliminate waste and to encourage conservation, the board was acutely aware of the added impact of its rules in limiting production and in affecting prices.

The development of conservation policies in Oklahoma was similar to that in neighboring states and was directed increasingly to restrict production. Heeding the entreaties of oil producers, the legislators on February 16, 1917, established an oil and gas department in the Corporation Commission to enforce oil and gas conservation statutes. The act also broadened the conservation responsibilities of this board and required the metering of all natural gas produced in Oklahoma. Moreover, it stipulated that all oil producers had to secure written permission from the Corporation Commission concerning the deepening, drilling, or plugging of their wells, and that they were to follow a list of approved conservation practices. Among these, pipeline companies were required to make monthly reports to the commission on their drilling operations and on their production. Companies that produced in excess of legal allowables were asked to file daily reports. Pipeline companies were not permitted to connect with any well until its owner had furnished a certificate to the commission showing that he had complied with state conservation laws. Each well owner had to keep a daily drilling record, which the commission had a right to inspect at any time. Oklahoma thus established a system of minute regulation of virtually every major operation in the oil-producing industry. Between 1917 and 1929 much of the commission's daily work lay in the enforcement of these rules.[20]

20. 1915 Okla. Stats. 35, 149, 549; for gas, see 1915 Okla. Stats. 398; Oklahoma Corporation Commission *Report* [hereafter cited as *OCC Report*], 1915 (Oklahoma City, 1916), 4–5, (Order No. 920), 261, (No. 846), 165; *Legal History* (1938), 125–127; 1917 Okla. Stats. 167; 1919 Okla. Stats. 276.

But stabilization of production proved to be a more difficult challenge than conservation. When, in 1921, the oil flowing from the Hewitt field in Carter County exceeded the capacity of available transportation and marketing facilities, the Corporation Commission on June 14, 1921, issued an order to prohibit the drilling of new wells in this pool. This action came in response to the demands of a meeting of producers at Ardmore, Oklahoma, who adopted a resolution urging the restriction of production until they could locate adequate markets. The Corporation Commission appointed a committee of five of these operators to act as advisers in the determination of reasonable production quotas. Any producer desiring to drill new wells could apply for exemption to this committee, which would then make a recommendation to the Corporation Commission urging approval or rejection.[21]

Overproduction became a serious problem in Oklahoma as early as 1926, when the great Seminole field was opened for production. Within a year the new flood of oil depressed petroleum prices and impressed many of the Seminole operators with the need for some way of limiting production. At first, in 1926, they agreed on a voluntary prorationing program to balance production with available demand. As in the case of so many of these voluntary agreements, however, in 1927 a minority of violators disrupted the entire industry. Thus, the producers petitioned the Corporation Commission to issue a prorationing order for the Seminole field to implement their voluntary plan. The commission held hearings on the request and then issued the requested order for official state enforcement of an oil restriction program. The commission also appointed an umpire for the Seminole field who, with the advice of a committee of producers appointed by the commission, worked out the details of allocation quotas for each individual.

During the next two years many new oil wells were discovered in Oklahoma, adding to the amount of unmarketable oil already there. In the face of plummeting crude oil prices, the Corporation Commission on September 9, 1928, issued its first statewide prorationing order. Estimating that the total demand for Oklahoma oil was about 700,000 barrels daily, it prohibited operators from producing more. It allowed

21. *OCC Order* No. 1884 (June 14, 1921) in *OCC Report* 1921 (Oklahoma City, 1922); see also *Legal History* (1938), 148–150.

the Seminole field about 425,000 barrels daily and apportioned the remainder to other Oklahoma fields.[22]

The fledgling efforts of the Oklahoma Commission to prevent oil wastage—and overproduction—were rudely upset by the discovery of the great Oklahoma City field in December, 1928. Suddenly oil surpluses took on truly alarming dimensions as an additional 400,000 barrels were added to daily oil production. The Seminole field operators were aghast and adopted a resolution urging further restriction of oil output by state authority. Meanwhile, the distance of the Oklahoma City wells from available pipelines and large markets created such a glut of oil there that in September, 1929, just before the Great Crash, the Corporation Commission ordered a 30-day shutdown of the field. At the same time it issued several orders to Oklahoma City producers designed to conserve gas pressures and to cut down output.[23]

The Oklahoma petroleum producers were so frightened that they demanded a new conservation law that would empower the Corporation Commission to exercise strong powers to control production. The Kansas-Oklahoma Division of the Mid-Continent Oil and Gas Association appointed a group of nine lawyers to study the Oklahoma statutes and to forward an appropriate measure to state legislatures for enactment.[24] In 1929 the Oklahoma lawmakers promptly enacted the recommended bill and in the following year the Oklahoma Supreme Court upheld it in all of its provisions.[25]

While the Hoover Administration extended no help to Oklahomans

22. Tulsa *World,* November 1, 2, 9, 10, 23, 30, 1926; *NYT,* August 18, 1926, November 2, 10, 23, 24, 30, 1926; a good discussion of early efforts to prorate petroleum production is in Leonard M. Logan, *The Stabilization of the Petroleum Industry* (Norman, 1930), 158–164, *Bulletin* No. 54 of Oklahoma Geological Survey; see also *OCC Report* 1929 (Oklahoma City, 1930), 709, 747, 752.
23. Tulsa *Daily World,* April 30, 1929, reporting E. B. Reeser's testimony before State Corporation Commission; *O&G Jl.* (May 9, 1929); Oklahoma City *Times,* May 3, 7, 10, 1929; Tulsa *World,* May 5, 10, 1929; Oklahoma City *News,* April 29, May 7, 1929; Tulsa *Tribune,* May 7, 9, 1929; Dallas *Morning News,* May 7, 1929; New York *Sun,* May 10, 1929; Logan, *Stabilization of the Petroleum Industry,* 107.
24. Oklahoma City *Times,* May 1, 1929; Tulsa *Daily World,* May 3, 1929; New York *American,* May 2, 1929; New York *Telegram,* May 2, 1929; *Legal History* (1938), 162–168.
25. 145 Oklahoma 237; *Legal History* (1938), 178–179.

in their efforts to stabilize the oil industry, the federal courts even obstructed their efforts. During April, 1931, a Federal District Court in the Champlin Case took testimony concerning the Corporation Commission's authority to restrict production. Before handing down a decision, however, the court adjourned until August 3, 1931. Just a week earlier, on July 28, 1931, the Federal District Court in Texas had struck down an oil prorationing order of the Texas Railroad Commission. This created great havoc in Oklahoma, too, and perhaps influenced the Federal District court there on August 3 to deny the Corporation Commission the power to limit oil production. It appeared that the oil industry in Oklahoma would be left to chaos such as already existed in neighboring Texas.[26]

In the absence of federal cooperation in this difficult situation, only resolute state action could maintain a semblance of order in the Oklahoma oil fields. Oklahoma's governor in 1931 was "Alfalfa Bill" Murray, one of the most colorful governors in the nation. Known for his flamboyancy, Murray was unlikely to shy away from the limelight. Savoring the drama, on August 4, 1931, only a day after the federal court decision, he declared martial law for every oil pool affected by the court decision. In ordering the closing of wells he sent the National Guard into the fields commanded by his nephew, Cicero I. Murray. His gesture seemed to have a marvelous effect on the federal judiciary in Oklahoma, because on the day following Murray's order two federal Circuit Court judges (Phillips and Cottrell) announced that they now considered the Oklahoma conservation statute to be valid, although they did not hand down their formal opinion until October 10, 1931.[27] But Governor Murray took no chances, and kept the Oklahoma City field closed until that date, while nephew Cicero closely policed his order. Thereafter, the Governor allowed limited operation under a prorationing order of the Corporation Commission. Meanwhile Cicero

26. 51 Fed. (2) 400; *NYT*, July 25, August 5, 1931; *U.S. Daily*, August 7, 1931.
27. The William H. Murray Papers in the Manuscripts Division of the University of Oklahoma Library contain little of value for historical researchers; see also William H. (Alfalfa Bill) Murray, *Memoirs of Governor Murray and True History of Oklahoma* (3 vols., Boston, 1945), III, *passim;* Gordon Hines, *Alfalfa Bill, An Intimate Biography* (Oklahoma City, 1932), *passim* and 294–296; Washington *Post*, August 4, 5, 6, 1931; *NYT*, August 5, 1931; New York *Herald Tribune*, August 6, 1931; *Daily Oklahoman*, August 6, 1931; Washington *Star*, August 6, 1931; 51 Fed (2) 823.

Murray continued to enforce production restrictions with the aid of the militia. Tensions did not really ease until March 23, 1932, when the United States Supreme Court in the Champlin Case unanimously upheld the Oklahoma Conservation Act.[28]

Governor Murray continued to keep soldiers in the fields, however, to execute the Corporation Commission's proration orders. On June 21, 1932, he also called out armed forces to enforce his executive order prohibiting hot oil—the sale or transport of oil produced in violation of the commission's quotas.[29] In his proclamation, Murray noted that he felt rigid enforcement of prorationing to be necessary in order to maintain a reasonable, stable market price for Oklahoma crude oil and for the collection of state revenues. He again established a military zone around wells and tanks to prorate Oklahoma City oil and to control its transportation, and he created a special ad hoc Prorationing Board to administer his order. This was in effect until late 1932, when the state Supreme Court denied the governor the power to take such measures.[30] Consequently, in 1933, the legislature strengthened the state's oil conservation laws to meet objections of state and federal courts and to expand the regulatory powers over oil of the Corporation Commission.[31]

INTERSTATE ACTION

During these dark years in Oklahoma and Texas the worsening overproduction of oil led their governors to think about coordination of their programs to limit oil production. Alfalfa Bill Murray of Oklahoma was especially interested in unified action. In late February, 1931, he called a meeting of nine governors from oil-producing states in Fort Worth, Texas. These representatives organized an Oil States Advisory Committee to coordinate the conservation and production curtailment activities of the states represented. They also agreed to make voluntary

---

28. Oklahoma City *News*, October 2, 10, 24, 1931; New York *Herald Tribune*, October 10, 1931; *U.S. Daily*, October 12, 1931; on Champlin case see 286 U.S. 210; Denver *Post*, September 12, 1931, Baltimore *Sun*, October 15, 1931; *U.S. Daily*, October 22, 1931.

29. *Daily Oklahoman*, June 22, 1932; *NYT*, June 22, August 25, 1932.

30. Governor Murray's proclamation is reprinted in 162 Oklahoma 216; *Daily Oklahoman*, December 14, 1932; *NYT*, August 25, December 14, 1932; *O&G Jl.* (December 15, 22, 1932).

31. 1933 Okla. Stats. 281, 312.

forecasts of production allowables for each state. At the same time the committee hoped to serve as a spokesman for the industry in discussions with federal officials, especially with President Hoover and his Secretaries of Commerce and Interior. Desirous also of securing a tariff against foreign oil, the group hoped to be able to influence Congress. Finally, the committee also suggested an interstate oil compact.[32]

This voluntary effort met with only partial success. During April, 1931, it is true, several states curtailed their oil production. President Hoover and Secretaries Robert P. Lamont and Ray Lyman Wilbur also talked with the committee. But they did little else. Hoover and Wilbur agreed to ask large oil importers to curtail imports by 25 percent in June, 1931, after Congress had failed to enact a tariff for foreign oil imports.[33] Yet the members of the committee concluded that only strong federal action could solve the dilemmas of the oil industry. Certainly this was the sentiment expressed at their conference in Amarillo on July 7, 1931, where they discussed the creation of a National Conciliation Board to enforce prorationing. No formal action was taken on this proposal, for events were moving too rapidly.[34] Within a month Governors Sterling and Murray had called out the National Guard to control oil production.

After the troops had occupied the oil fields in Oklahoma and Texas, the committee met again on September 11, 1931, in Oklahoma City. Soon thereafter the Legal Sub-Committee of the organization drafted a proposed federal bill, which was approved by the API and actively pressed in Congress after May, 1932. Known as the Thomas-McKeon Bill, it proposed creation of an interstate oil compact for the conservation of petroleum. It also provided for establishment of a Federal Interstate Oil Board to recommend production quotas, to approve private unitization agreements, and to promote uniform state conservation laws. After hearings on the measure, the House Judiciary Committee reported it favorably. But since the bill threatened to interfere with the impending passage of an oil tariff, the Oil States Advisory Committee reluctantly agreed to have it withdrawn temporarily. Lack of unity in the deepening economic crisis disrupted the committee. In December, 1932,

32. *NYT,* March 9, 10, 1931.
33. *Ibid.,* April 7, 8, 9, 10, 12, 16, 1931; Blakely M. Murphy (ed.), *Conservation of Oil and Gas: A Legal History, 1948* (Chicago, 1949), 545–548.
34. *NYT,* July 8, 9, 10, 1931.

however, the committee made arrangements for informal discussions with the new President-elect to acquaint him with the seriousness of the oil problem and to solicit his support for the Thomas-McKeon Bill. Roosevelt promised to give careful consideration to their requests, and to take some form of action. Soon thereafter, the committee went out of existence and eagerly awaited the action of the new Administration.[35]

In Oklahoma, as in Texas, the drift in federal policies left only the state governments to counter complete economic collapse of the oil industry and the breakdown of law and order in portions of the Southwest. There the states added another dimension to the complex arrangements that characterize government's relation to business in the United States. Even before the federal government assumed the responsibility for maintaining general economic stability, the states took on this task in a major industry threatened with breakdown. Their role in restricting oil production illustrated the viability of the federal system once again. Perhaps nowhere else in the United States during 1931 and 1932 was the American economic and political system as near total collapse as in the oil regions. Where else were military forces required for a prolonged period of supervision over the activities of a major industry? Amid the impending breakdown of the very framework of society, President Hoover's pronouncements on the need for oil conservation had a curiously unreal ring. Certainly, Hoover's refusal to acknowledge any federal responsibility for maintaining stability in the oil industry was not in keeping with the goals and methods of the New Nationalism, espoused in one way or another by every Chief Executive after Theodore Roosevelt. Was the President really unaware of the true nature of the crisis? Was there nothing that the federal government could do itself or aid the states to do to curb overproduction of petroleum? Few professed to know the precise answer to such questions during those dark critical days of 1932. But when Texans, Oklahomans, and others affiliated with the oil industry went to the polls that November, they unmistakably gave vent to their true feelings of protest.

35. *Ibid.*, September 12, 1931; 72 Cong., 1 sess., House, Committee on Judiciary, *Hearings on H.R. 10863* (Washington, 1932), 39–41 has text of bill; 72 Cong., 1 sess., *House Report* No. 1585 (Washington, 1932); Murphy (ed.), *Legal History, 1948,* 552–555. The correspondence of Senator Elmer Thomas (Oklahoma) in the Manuscripts Division of the University of Oklahoma Library contains dozens of letters from the producers in support of his measure.

7 / A New Deal For Oil

THE INAUGURATION of Franklin D. Roosevelt in 1933 did not usher in a revolution in oil policy. But it did bring a new leader into the White House who revealed an extraordinary political astuteness. Unlike Hoover, Roosevelt was able to formulate a consensus on a national oil program. An heir to the New Nationalism of Theodore Roosevelt and of Woodrow Wilson's New Freedom, Roosevelt did not shrink from using federal powers in experimenting with various efforts to solve the industry's major problems. Like Harding and Coolidge, he was keenly aware of the contributions of the petroleum industry to the economic stability of the nation as a whole. As a former assistant to Josephus Daniels and a special friend of the Navy, he was fully conscious of the vital importance of oil to national security. And as a country squire he had early become a passionate advocate of natural resource conservation. These were major aims of his oil policies as they had been of earlier Administrations. New Deal strategists were thus also beset with the twin problems of stabilization and conservation.

If Roosevelt made few contributions to the formulation of new policy goals regarding oil, he was more effective than other Chief Executives in developing administrative means to implement them. His efforts passed through at least two phases. In the first stage of the New Deal for oil that he developed in his crisis program between 1933 and 1935 he sought primarily to restrict production and to stabilize prices under the Oil Code of the National Recovery Administration (NRA).

Between 1935 and 1941, however, the Roosevelt Administration emphasized reform of various spheres of the industry. This included encouragement of production controls under state jurisdiction supplemented by federal prohibition of interstate oil shipments in violation of their quotas. Although Secretary of the Interior Ickes did not get his wish to have Congress declare the oil industry a public utility, yet the New Deal's ephemeral antitrust program during these years was designed to pinpoint alleged abuses of large integrated companies, particularly in the distribution of petroleum products. Roosevelt made no real effort to change the existing depletion allowance of 27½ percent or to tamper with the tariff on foreign oil, for these measures had strong support from many domestic producers. By the eve of World War II, Roosevelt had fashioned a consensus on national policy that incorporated many of the important proposals of the preceding two decades. Perhaps the major contribution of the New Deal in this realm of public policy was to select and crystallize the most feasible elements of a national oil policy as these emerged from two decades of discussion and deliberation, and to provide political and administrative means for their implementation.

Amid the deep despair of that dreary winter of 1932 many leaders of the oil industry could not help but wonder whether the new Administration would aid them in their plight. In the face of falling prices and further increases of total production, the immediate future of the industry looked bleak, indeed. Nor was there much in the new President's background to indicate that he had any special awareness of the petroleum industry's problems. But after the frustrations they had borne during the Hoover Administration many oilmen were hopeful that the President and his advisors would at least take some form of positive federal action. C. B. Ames, president of the API in 1933, spoke for many when he said that strong federal controls to curb production were an immediate need.[1] Between 1933 and 1935, therefore, most of the leading executives in the industry supported the Administration's oil policies.

1. *Oil and Gas Journal* [hereafter cited as *O&G Jl.*] (January 12, March 16, 1933).

To acquaint the new President with their views a delegation of oil-men visited him in December, 1932. They patiently explained the tribulations that the industry had gone through during the past four years and presented various alternative policy proposals as solutions. Roosevelt listened carefully and promised to give early attention to their problems—a promise that was fully kept. Prior to and during his first month in office, Roosevelt still clung cautiously to Herbert Hoover's method for meeting oil problems—voluntary cooperation to. restrict production. Just a few days after his inauguration on March 8, 1933, he instructed Secretary of the Interior Ickes to summon a conference of governors from oil-producing states to consider ways and means for stabilization of the industry. Ickes issued a call for such a meeting to be held in Washington, D.C., later that month and invited leaders of the industry and the API to attend.

On the same day, the API Executive Committee appointed a special board to negotiate an agreement to limit production with the governors of Oklahoma, Texas, and Kansas. The group included prominent men, such as C. B. Ames, J. Howard Pew, W. F. Teagle, and Harry F. Sinclair. If existing state laws to conserve oil were rigidly enforced, they believed, the glut of oil might be substantially reduced.[2]

As he felt his way during the First Hundred Days, Roosevelt frequently resorted to his experience as a World War I administrator in dealing with the economic crisis. Thus, he felt inclined to reestablish many of the emergency agencies that had served Woodrow Wilson so well during the mobilization crisis of 1917. This was also true in respect to the oil industry. Indeed, Mark Requa, the Director of the Oil Division of the old United States Fuel Administration, wrote an urgent letter to Roosevelt in May, 1933, urging him to revive Wilson's program. Similarly, Lewis Douglas, in discussing industrial mobilization before the House Ways and Means Committee that same month, suggested the reestablishment of the United States Food Administration and the Fuel Administration as models for Congressional action.[3] Thus, it was not surprising that the Petroleum Administration created under the National Industrial Recovery Act in September, 1933, bore consid-

2. New York *Times* [hereafter cited as *NYT*], March 8, 1933; Harold Ickes, *Secret Diary* (3 vols., New York, 1953–1954), I, 9–16; Ickes in API, *Proceedings, 14th Annual Meeting* 1933 (New York, 1933), 16–17.

erable resemblance, in organization and functions, to Requa's old Oil Division. During the eighteen months that it was in operation it developed various means to restrict oil production, while at the same time it encouraged conservation. Moreover, its ultimate impact upon national oil policies was profound. Not only did it help to crystallize a consensus among the industry and in Congress. Even after invalidation of the NRA by the United States Supreme Court many of its more successful features were continued in separate legislation. If the NRA was not as successful in stimulating economic recovery as contemporaries hoped, yet it served an important function in distilling essential elements of a national petroleum policy.

Amid much optimism, representatives of thirteen states met in the nation's capital on March 26, 1933, where Ickes welcomed them with a warning to put their own house in order. Roosevelt later received the delegates himself. To coordinate their discussions they appointed a Committee of Fifteen to work out a stabilization program.[4]

The various meetings of the delegates revealed more conflict than agreement. Spokesman for the governors was the aggressive Alfred Landon of Kansas, who strongly favored the appointment of a federal dictator to allocate and to enforce oil-production quotas. J. A. Moffett, one of the President's closest advisers on petroleum matters (a vice-president of Standard Oil [N.J.]) urged a similar course upon him. But most of the independent oil producers opposed any limitation of production. Face to face they pleaded with the President not to impose mandatory controls but instead to require integrated oil companies to divest themselves of pipelines.[5]

While the President was consciously seeking to probe public opinion on the oil problem before making specific recommendations, the legislative wheels in the states and in Congress began to turn. In Oklahoma,

3. *NYT,* March 16, 17, 19, 1933; FDR at Press Conference, March 22, 1933, in *Transcript of FDR Press Conferences,* I, 69, in Franklin D. Roosevelt Papers, Franklin D. Roosevelt Library [hereafter cited as FDR Mss.], Hyde Park, N.Y.; Mark Requa to FDR, May 9, 1933, in FDR Mss., Lewis Douglas in 73 Cong., 1 sess., House, Committee on Ways and Means, *Hearings on National Industrial Recovery* (Washington, 1933), 17–21.

4. *NYT,* March 27, 29, 1933; M. L. Benedum to FDR, March 24, 1933; a copy of Resolution, March 29, 1933, is in FDR Mss.

5. *NYT,* April 2, 3, 4, 5, 1933; George Otis Smith to FDR, May 4, 1933; Henry L. Doherty to FDR, May 12, 1933, in FDR Mss.

Governor Alfalfa Bill Murray signed a new proration law for his state and prepared to meet with other governors to discuss cooperation in Amarillo. Meanwhile, in Congress Senator Arthur Capper introduced a "hot oil" bill, to authorize federal enforcement of a prohibition of shipment of petroleum in violation of state regulatory laws. Capper also demanded that the Department of the Interior conduct an investigation into conditions in the industry. Capper's bill was written by the Solicitor of the Department of the Interior, Nathan Margold. In the House, Representative Marland of Oklahoma, himself an important oil producer, introduced identical legislation, which he drafted in consultation with Ickes at the President's suggestion. These measures were in line with Roosevelt's letter to the governors. Within ten days, hearings on the bill gave many leading oilmen an opportunity to express their support of the measure.[6] Important figures, including C. B. Ames, were enthusiastic about strict federal controls in 1933. R. C. Holmes, president of Texaco, declared that overproduction could be remedied only by effective federal enforcement of restrictions on output.[7]

Throughout April, 1933, midcontinent oil producers made an effort to secure at least a measure of unanimity. At a conference in Oklahoma City on May 4 they appointed a committee to convey their views to the President, while representatives of five states drafted a bill to give the Secretary of the Interior dictatorial powers over the industry. Although Governors Landon of Kansas and Murray of Oklahoma strongly favored federal enforcement of state oil-production quotas, and even greater restrictions on oil imports, Governor Allred of Texas demurred.[8] A few days later, on May 8, representatives of integrated companies at the API meeting showed themselves to be similarly divided. The directors deferred a decision on a specific course of policy, since some favored the centralization of authority in Ickes, while others were opposed. Thus, on May 12, 1933, they adopted a "wait and see" attitude at least until the Administration's general policy toward business became clearer. Meanwhile, during April and May, 1933, overpro-

---

6. *O&G Jl.* (April 20, 1933); *NYT,* April 7, 8, 11, 15, 1933; E. W. Marland to Louis Howe, April 22, 1933, in FDR Mss.

7. *NYT,* April 3, 5, 6, 22, 1933; R. C. Holmes to FDR, April 17, 1933, in FDR Mss.

8. *O&G Jl.* (May 4, 11, 1933); *NYT,* May 1, 2, 3, 4, 7, 1933.

duction of oil grew worse. The flush production of the East Texas field continued to demoralize the entire industry.[9]

In view of this continuing conflict within the industry Roosevelt shifted his position and came out for federal regulation. At his request, on May 30, 1933, Senator Arthur Capper and Congressman E. W. Marland introduced appropriate bills in Congress. In a letter to Vice-President Garner and Speaker Rainey, Roosevelt noted that the two-year emergency measures for federal limitation of oil production were immediately needed, although they could be incorporated in more general legislation if necessary.[10] Two days later Roosevelt urged Congress to abandon the two oil measures just introduced lest they delay Congressional action on the general industrial recovery measure, then being prepared by Raymond Moley.

Congress balked at the President's proposal and made a show of independence. In late May, 1933, the House Rules Committee held up action on the oil bills. The committee itself was deadlocked, five to five, over the Marland bill, and Chairman Doughton flatly refused to include it in the general recovery act under consideration. Despite the assurance of Ickes that Roosevelt urgently desired federal oil controls, Doughton refused to act until he received word directly from the President. Meanwhile, at hearings before the Senate Committee on Finance, Ickes urged adoption of the Capper bill, since he did not think that projected general recovery legislation would provide him with needed powers.[11] Possibly he was also reminded of Wilson's handling of the oil crisis in 1917, for Mark Requa was urging federal controls in 1933 like those he had administered in World War I.

But continuing pressure from the White House led Congress to yield. Roosevelt was confronted with two alternatives in extending the National Industrial Recovery Act to cover the special problems of the petroleum industry. Ickes suggested a lengthy amendment to spell out

9. *NYT,* May 4, 7, 9, 12, 15, 1933.

10. *O&G Jl.* (May 18, 25, 1933); M. L. Benedum to FDR, May 29, 1933, in FDR Mss. E. L. Doherty urged a special bill for the oil industry. See E. L. Doherty to FDR, May 21, 1933, in FDR Mss.; FDR at Press Conference, May 19, 1933, in *Transcript of FDR Press Conferences,* I, 284, FDR Mss.; *NYT,* May 19, 20, 21, 1933.

11. *NYT,* May 23, 24, 1933; FDR to Speaker Henry T. Rainey, May 20, 1933, in FDR Mss.

the powers he hoped to exercise in great detail. Roosevelt instead favored a brief general statement, and it was this that Congress adopted. But the President also accepted Senator Tom Connally's amendment to prohibit shipment of hot oil. This became Section 9(c) of the National Industrial Recovery Act, which delegated Congressional authority to the Chief Executive to prohibit the interstate shipment of hot oil (produced in violation of state quotas).[12] At Roosevelt's direction this became part of the National Industrial Recovery Act of June 16, 1933. Shortly after its passage, NRA Administrator Hugh S. Johnson told trade associations to begin the work of drafting codes of fair competition. Once he had approved their handiwork, the NRA would be on its way.[13]

The NRA crystallized important trends in government-business relations that had been gathering momentum for at least a decade. One was the movement to amend the antitrust laws and to allow greater voluntary cooperation among businessmen. Donald Richberg, who drafted the provisions of the National Industrial Recovery Act concerning industrial cooperation, indicated this clearly. The law was designed to remove the uncertainty in the minds of many businessmen about the legality of cooperative activities. He noted, in addition, that the Act was designed to achieve stabilization of competition by integration and rationalization of industry, an aim that was already explicit in Theodore Roosevelt's doctrine of the New Nationalism.[14]

This objective was clearly in the minds of many liberals in 1933. Perhaps Senator Robert Wagner expressed it most succinctly when he said, in speaking of the National Industrial Recovery bill: "I think this bill is important as the first step toward that which the Liberals of this country have been preparing for years. It was a part of the platform of the 1912 Progressive Party, namely the necessity of a national planned economy. Until we have that, I venture to say that we are not going to have an orderly organized economic system. A good deal of the chaos

12. *NYT,* June 2, 3, 6, 9, 1933; Ickes, *Secret Diary,* I, 36–47; Ickes Memo for Marvin MacIntire, June 1, 1933, in FDR Mss.
13. *NYT,* June 9, 16, 18, 1933; *O&G Jl.* (June 15, 22, 1933); George W. Stocking, "Chaos in the Oil Industry," *The Nation,* CXXXVI (June 7, 1933), 634–636.
14. See Richberg's comments in 73 Cong., 1 sess., House, Committee on Ways and Means, *Hearings on National Industrial Recovery* (Washington, 1933), 66–68, 80.

and disorganization from which we are suffering now is due to this lack of planning. . . . We have got plenty in the midst of all this starvation that we are witnessing. It is a paradox."

And he continued: "The purpose of the present bill is not to abolish competition, but to lift its standards and to raise its plane so as to eliminate destructive practices, unfair practices. In other words, efficiency, rather than the ability to sweat labor and undermine living standards, will be the determining factor in business success. Through the cooperative action made possible and lawful under this bill, industry may . . . provide for market research and analysis, cooperative marketing and sales promotion . . . simplification and standardization."[15]

In the oil industry the American Petroleum Institute took the lead in making preliminary preparations for the drafting of an industry-wide code. The institute sent out invitations to virtually all oil producer's organizations to attend a meeting in Chicago on June 17, 1933, to work out a national code of practices for the industry. But the institute did not call on labor organizations to participate. Leading oil magnates in the industry served on the drafting committee, including J. Howard Pew, Harry Sinclair, C. B. Ames, A. L. Beaty, and W. R. Kingsbury of Standard Oil Company of California. Soon after the delegates had gathered, the API took the initiative by offering a proposed draft code to the assembled representatives. Axtell J. Byles, president of API, warned them that unless they took immediate action, Congress might very well nationalize the whole industry.[16]

The Chicago meeting revealed much disunity among petroleum producers. Under the code suggested by the API, the federal government would issue permits to allow drilling and would fix production quotas and minimum prices. This last provision gave rise to violent debate, for many of the independents, and also some of the larger companies, opposed it. C. B. Ames of Texaco, J. Howard Pew of Sun Oil, and Van Derwoude of Shell Oil criticized the suggestion; Amos Beaty, L. P. St. Clair of Union Oil, and Wirt Franklin, president of the Independent Oil Producer's Association, favored it. But the proponents of the API code

15. Quoted in *ibid.*, 95–96; *NYT*, May 28, 29, 1933; 73 Cong., 1 sess., Senate Committee on Finance, *Hearings on National Industrial Recovery* (Washington, 1933), 2, 6, 35, 38, 61.

16. *NYT*, June 9, 1933; for Ickes' views see *ibid.*, June 11, 1933, Section VIII; *ibid.*, June 18, 21, 23, 24, 25, 1933; *O&G Jl.* (June 8, 15, 22, 1933).

had their way. Before adjournment, the delegates approved the draft of a code that was close to the API model in most of its provisions.[17]

Just a week after the producers had deliberated on a proposed charter, the oil marketers came to Chicago for the same purpose. Sixty-two associations sent delegates, and each had a representative on the committee that was to draft a marketing code. A. J. Byles warned the assembled group to display unity lest they face a revolution. Despite the fact that independents were dominant on the drafting committee, their proposed code followed API suggestions, with one exception. This was a rule to change the retail distributing system for gasoline. All of the delegates agreed on the need for price-fixing, however, and included such a stipulation in the draft, despite Hugh Johnson's known opposition to it.[18] Thus, by July 1, 1933, both oil producers and distributors had agreed on a preliminary code, which they presented to Johnson. But even then not all segments of the industry were united. Although the directors of the API gave their formal approval to the "Chicago Code," some independent producers feared the provisions for price-fixing. Labor leaders were also suspicious of it, since provisions concerning wages and hours of labor were conspicuously missing. Consequently, on July 5, 1933, Johnson returned it to the API for revision.[19]

During July, while the oil industry representatives were reworking the Chicago Code, Roosevelt took stop-gap action to prevent further demoralization of the industry. On July 12 he issued an executive order under the National Industrial Recovery Act to prohibit the shipment of hot oil, to be enforced by the Interior Department. Ickes estimated that at least 500,000 barrels daily were being shipped illegally in violation of state laws, especially in Texas and Oklahoma. Representative Marland had earlier introduced legislation to provide Congressional sanction for Roosevelt's action.[20]

---

17. *NYT,* June 18, 21, 1933; "Washington Oil Well: Progress of Oil Control," *Business Week* (June 17, 1933), 8–9.

18. *NYT,* June 22, 23, 25, 1933; *O&G Jl.* (June 29, 1933); an interesting foreign view of FDR's efforts of this period is in "The Roosevelt Government and America's Petroleum Problem," *Rotterdamsche Bank Vereeniging Monthly Review,* XIV (June –July, 1933), 147–153, 171–177.

19. *NYT,* July 2, 4, 6, 7, 11, 1933; *O&G Jl.* (July 6, 13, 1933); Hugh S. Johnson, *The Blue Eagle, From Egg to Earth* (Garden City, 1935), 216, 235.

20. *NYT,* July 12, 13, 1933; Ickes, *Secret Diary,* I, 49–50, 65; *Congressional Record* [hereafter cited as *CR*], 73 Cong., 1 sess. (May 19, 1933), 3776, (May 20, 1933), 3843; E. W. Marland to Louis M. Howe, April 22, 1933, in FDR Mss.

In mid-July, the API resubmitted a revised petroleum code to Johnson. The proposal included authority for the President to control production through allocation of quotas and price fixing. At Johnson's insistence the draft now included safeguards for labor, including a minimum wage of 40 to 47 cents an hour, and a maximum 40-hour week. Administration of the code was to be entrusted to a general planning and coordinating committee composed of twenty-six producers and twenty-eight refiners—and no representatives of labor. The group was chosen by the API from representatives at the Chicago conference with President Roosevelt's approval. In many ways, it was similar to the industry committee that had advised the United States Fuel Administration during World War I. On July 21 the API called members of this committee to Washington to prepare for hearings before the NRA.[21]

Despite an apparent show of unity by the industry, a battle for control was shaping up between representatives of some major oil companies and independents over the issue of price-fixing, favored by the latter. Nor could the smaller operators take much comfort in the appointment of Walter C. Teagle, president of Standard Oil of New Jersey, as advisor to the NRA during the forthcoming code hearings. The independents also favored a shorter working week to cut their labor costs. Harry Sinclair, chairman of the labor subcommittee that had helped draft the code, came out for a 40-hour week, while the Independent Petroleum Association favored 30 hours. Labor leaders themselves also advocated the shorter week. Harvey Fremming, president of the International Association of Oil Field, Gas Well, and Refinery Workers, criticized the API code sharply. He thought that it would lead to a decline of income for his men. He urged a 30-hour week with a guaranteed wage of $4.75 daily for a 6-hour day. This dispute over wage provisions led Johnson on July 25 to appoint a committee of five, representing the API, the independents, and two labor representatives, to work out a compromise.[22]

NRA hearings on the proposed oil code in late July, 1933, revealed further rifts. Indeed, Johnson warned the various factions that unless they could work out a quick compromise he would have to write the code himself.[23] One area of disagreement concerned proposed federal

---

21. *NYT,* July 16, 17, 18, 1933; *O&G Jl.* (July 13, 20, 1933).

22. *NYT,* July 16, 18, 23, 1933.

23. *NYT,* July 24, 25, 26, 27, 1933; National Recovery Administration, *Hearings on Proposed Oil Code* (No. 10), National Archives (Microfilm), 3–7.

price-fixing. Among the advocates of strong federal price regulation was J. A. Moffett, vice-president of Standard Oil of New Jersey and a son of one of John D. Rockefeller's early partners. A Democrat and a personal friend of Roosevelt, Moffett clashed with Walter Teagle and W. S. Farish, who opposed price controls. In fact, Teagle forced Moffett to resign at Standard in late July. Similar conflicts prevailed in other companies. K. R. Kingsbury of Standard Oil of California and Harry Sinclair of Consolidated Oil agreed with Moffett, but Standard Oil Company of Indiana, Standard Oil of New Jersey, Dutch Shell, the Texas Company, and Gulf were against federal price regulation. This bitter disagreement broke up preliminary hearings on the code after three days and left the fate of the industry uncertain. Since the Oil Code was the first to be drawn up under the NRA the controversy augured ill for the success of the entire experiment in industrial self-regulation.[24]

With the industry seemingly hopelessly divided, Johnson himself drafted a model code for consideration. With Moffett's help he outlined a plan to conciliate some of the big oil producers. Johnson proposed a 40-hour work week for producers in the industry, and 36 hours for marketers. Although both the API and Wirt Franklin of the Independent Petroleum Association favored price-fixing, Johnson opposed it, thus siding with Teagle.[25]

Unfortunately, Hugh Johnson seemed unable to bring the divergent oil interests together, for other issues were dividing them as well. Their dispute over oil imports was a good example. Major producers favored limitations, independents desired the exclusion of all foreign oil. Another source of friction was the separation of pipelines and refineries, an ardent demand of independents eager to break up major integrated companies. Large companies also favored adoption of unit operations, to which independents objected. In the realm of marketing arrangements, major companies desired recognition of their lease and agency agreements with gasoline stations, a demand to which independent companies objected. Finally, while the major companies desired administra-

24. *NYT*, July 29, 30, 1933; Ickes, *Secret Diary*, I, 72–73, 85–86.

25. National Recovery Administration, *Hearings on Proposed Oil Code*, 8–12; *O&G Jl.* (July 27, August 3, 1933); *NYT*, July 23, 25, 27, 29, August 1, 2, 1933.

tion of industry codes by the NRA, the independents favored the Department of Commerce.[26]

Ickes opposed Johnson's draft, however, and was eager to become administrator of the code himself. Since Johnson seemed unable to bring divergent oil interests together in early August, Ickes found a sympathetic ear in the White House. Unlike Johnson, he favored the inclusion of rigid price regulations in the code, a stand for which he found support from oil magnates like Sinclair and Kingsbury, and from Wirt Franklin. Roosevelt himself was characteristically coy and did not reveal his own preference, if any, to either side. Johnson, naively thinking he had the confidence of the President, conferred with him on August 17 and presented his draft code, which made no provision for price regulation.[27] No sooner had he left the White House than Ickes and his aides trooped in to see the President on a similar mission. Ickes, too, had the draft of a code for the petroleum industry, but his version placed great emphasis on rigid price-fixing and production controls. Seeking to attract wider support, Johnson lost no time, and within a day met with prominent oilmen to secure their backing for his code. But, alas, they still could not agree to his proposal, and unwittingly perhaps, strengthened Ickes' hand. On the next day, August 19, 1933, Roosevelt, as he was wont to do when his aides disagreed, ordered Johnson and Ickes to work out a compromise. The final product of their deliberations reflected the view of many major producers. It granted the federal government powers only to recommend production quotas and not to impose them. As a sop to Ickes, the President was to be given discretionary authority to fix prices for 90 days.[28]

But Ickes won a decisive victory by persuading Roosevelt to appoint him as Administrator of the Oil Code, rather than Johnson, as had been widely expected. On August 30 Roosevelt named Ickes to direct execu-

26. *NYT*, August 3, 4, 5, 6, 1933; FDR at Press Conference, August 8, 1933, in *Transcript of FDR Press Conferences*, II, 219–220, FDR Mss.
27. *NYT*, August 18, 19, 1933; Ickes, *Secret Diary*, I, 81–82; *O&G Jl.* (August 24, 1933); FDR to Harold Ickes, August 19, 1933, NRA Records, National Archives, Washington, D.C., Microfilm Document Series of National Recovery Administration, Petroleum; Henry L. Doherty to FDR, August 14, 1933, in FDR Mss.
28. *NYT*, August 19, 20, 1933; FDR to Hugh Johnson, August 19, 1933, in FDR Mss.

tion of the Code, thus withdrawing jurisdiction from the National Recovery Administration. To aid Ickes in the administration of controls, Roosevelt also appointed an industry advisory group, the Production and Coordination Committee, composed of fifteen individuals nominated by the API, independents, and trade associations. At the same time he appointed a majority of men to the committee who favored price-fixing. Most of these individuals represented smaller companies. In order not to alienate those who, like Ames of Texaco, Sinclair, and Van Eck of Shell, supported the code but opposed price-fixing, the committee took no immediate action on this controversial issue but left it to the President.[29]

Thus, the petroleum code was finally promulgated on the basis of a tenuous consensus in industry and government. It granted the Petroleum Administrator power to determine monthly production quotas upon recommendations made by the Production and Coordination (P&C) Committee. He also received authority to restrict oil imports to an amount equal to that of the last six months of 1932. At the same time the administrator could issue regulations for the marketing of refined products, and if necessary, for price regulation. Also under his jurisdiction was the administration of labor provisions, including Section 7(a) of the National Industrial Recovery Act as it applied to the oil industry.[30] In functions and in structure, the Oil Administration greatly resembled the old Oil Division of the United States Fuel Administration in World War I. But 1933 was not 1917, and many oilmen wondered: What would the future bring?

During the first month of operation, the prime concern of Ickes was to limit production. In addition to the P&C Committee, Ickes also created a Petroleum Administrative Board to provide expert advice on technical aspects of this problem. Working on the basis of recommendations made by the P&C committee, he set monthly oil quotas for each state, seeking a reduction of about 300,000 barrels daily on a national scale. Ickes also issued an order limiting oil imports to the amount brought into the country during the last months of 1932. As for price-

29. *NYT*, August 22, 24, 27, 30, 31, September 2, 1933; Ickes, *Secret Diary*, I, 82–84.
30. National Recovery Administration, *Codes of Fair Competition* (Petroleum) (Washington, 1933); successive drafts can be found in Microfilm Document Series of NRA, Petroleum.

fixing, after consulting with Roosevelt, Ickes reported that it would be utilized only when necessary—as it never was.[31] Roosevelt himself feigned ignorance on the issue, and referred all questioners to Ickes. The President's political acumen accurately gauged the disruptive nature of the question.

By the end of 1933, many oilmen considered the Oil Code a great success, especially in reducing production. At their annual meeting on October 24–25, 1933, the API directors gave their warm approval to the Code, despite a tongue-lashing from Ickes. In his address Ickes warned the convention that unless Code violations stopped, the industry faced more rigid regulation. For the moment, however, he did not advocate price-fixing as a panacea.[32]

Yet, during the last three months of 1933 Ickes continued to press for price-fixing. In October he again conferred with Roosevelt on this matter and seemed to have won him over. But the President was unwilling to commit himself without a clear mandate from the industry.[33] On October 16 Ickes did indeed announce that he would soon issue a price fixing order with the President's approval, and that the P&C Committee would work out a detailed schedule. As the flow of "hot oil" continued to depress the industry that month, a few days later Ickes actually prepared maximum quotas for refined oil production, and issued projected price schedules.[34]

Some independent producers opposed his plan, however, since they believed that it would put them out of business. By early November their protests were becoming so loud and vociferous that they led Ickes to postpone his order, scheduled to take effect on December 1, until he had held further hearings.[35] These hearings before the Petroleum Administrative Board were scheduled to begin on November 20 and prom-

31. FDR at Press Conference, September 16, 1933, and October 13, 1933, in *Transcript of FDR Press Conferences*, II, FDR Mss.; *NYT*, September 3, 6, 8, 10, 12, October 4, 8, 1933.

32. API, *Proceedings of 14th Annual Meeting* 1933, 20–26; *NYT*, October 27, 28, 1933; *O&G Jl.* (October 26, November 2, 1933).

33. *NYT*, October 4, 8, 13, 1933; Ickes, *Secret Diary*, I, 97–99, 106–107.

34. *NYT*, October 16, 20, 22, 25, 26, 1933. Basil O'Connor also expressed his opposition to price-fixing in the oil industry; Basil O'Connor to FDR, November 13, 1933, in FDR Mss. Similar views are found in E. L. Doherty to FDR, August 14, 1933, and Mary Rumsey [NRA Consumers Advisory Board] to FDR, November 8, 1933, in FDR Mss.

35. *NYT*, November 1, 3, 5, 14, 15, 1933; *O&G Jl.* (November 16, 23, 1933).

ised to reveal a deep split among the various oil producers. Large oil companies had as many variant attitudes on price-fixing as the independents. Fear of this disunity led Ickes again to postpone the investigation until December 5, and to announce that he would abandon his price-fixing plan if the industry could demonstrate that it was competent to settle its own problems.[36]

By December Ickes' ardor for price-fixing had cooled. After conferring with divergent factions in the industry he urged that they agree among themselves on maintaining price levels so that no action on his part would be required. Under this pressure the groups agreed to the creation of a money pool to buy up distress stocks of gasoline and so to stabilize prices. Created largely by big corporations, this fund was established with about $10 million in contributions. Ickes was so encouraged by this action that he deferred his price-fixing order further until February 1, 1934. As a matter of fact, he never implemented it.[37]

At the end of the year oilmen generally expressed satisfaction with the operation of the Code. C. B. Ames, chairman of Texaco, considered it a major step in achieving many of the oil industry's objectives. Similar views were expressed by Teagle, who noted that his company's position had improved greatly as a result of federal efforts to prevent shipment of hot oil. A. J. Byles of the API heartily agreed.[38] But at the same time labor groups in the oil industry were becoming discontent, largely because they had not been allowed any substantial participation in the work of administering the Code.

As a matter of fact, both Ickes and oil industry leaders virtually ignored the oil workers' unions during the first months of Code enforcement. They assumed that the provisions of Section 7(a) of the NIRA would eventually encourage collective bargaining and so allow labor a voice. One of the draftsmen of the NRA, Donald Richberg, clearly expressed the view in June, 1933, that Code authorities were to be primarily spokesmen for management. This attitude was openly challenged by Harvey Fremming, head of the oil worker's union, who urged establishment of a joint Standing Committee of the industry with equal representation for labor unions and trade associations. After pondering

36. *NYT,* November 20, 21, 22, 26, 1933; *O&G Jl.* (November 30, 1933).
37. *NYT,* December 5, 8, 31, 1933.
38. *NYT,* December 9, 15, 1933, January 2, 3, 1934; *O&G Jl.* (December 22, 29, 1933).

testimony presented at the hearings on the Oil Code during the summer of 1933 both Roosevelt and Ickes rejected this suggestion. Instead, they created the Production and Coordination Committee to represent industry alone. The question of allowing representation for labor was left for the future.[39]

But Fremming and other officials of the oil worker's union continued to protest. Thus, on October 10, 1933, the P&C Committee recommended creation of a Petroleum Labor Policy Board. This was to be composed of three members from industry, three from labor, and one individual as an impartial member. Ickes wholeheartedly approved of this plan. In the inimitable, benign manner of an enlightened despot he made appointments. His slighting of labor leaders brought an immediate outcry, however, because Harvey Fremming, one of the appointees, refused to serve with his two supposed "labor" colleagues. One of these was Charles C. Jones, a company union man from Bayonne, New Jersey. The other was a well-known economist, Professor George W. Stocking, who, while respected, certainly was not a labor leader. Fremming's bitter opposition led Ickes to revamp the board by selecting three impartial members. This new board was still not a representative body like the P&C Committee but a paternal creature of the Oil Administrator. Its task was to watch over labor interests in the administration of the Code. Ickes remained steadfast in his refusal to appoint a committee that represented labor organizations as the P&C Committee represented industry.[40]

The functions of the board were never made explicit. During 1934 its work came to center on the accreditation of authorized labor bargaining groups for workers and the conduct of elections. Once an oil worker's union was recognized by management, the Petroleum Labor Policies Board also acted as a conciliation agency to settle strikes and other disputes over working conditions.

In the spring of 1934, the Petroleum Labor Policies Board became involved in an acrimonious controversy over wages, which had been a

39. *NYT*, June 23, August 31, 1933; Richberg in 73 Cong., 1 sess., Senate, Committee on Finance, *Hearings on National Industrial Recovery*, 26; Fremming in National Recovery Administration, *Hearings on Proposed Oil Code*, 97.

40. *NYT*, November 24, 1933; Petroleum Administrative Board, *Press Release* No. 8398 in National Archives, Washington, D.C.; Renee de Visme Williamson, *The Politics of Planning in the Oil Industry Under the Code* (New York, 1936), 54–57.

controversial issue from the very start of the Code. In October, 1933, Roosevelt and Ickes left wage differentials between skilled and less skilled workers to future settlement. Nothing was done regarding this problem until April, 1934, when the P&C Committee recommended a specific schedule of minimum wage levels to Ickes. Ickes referred it to the Petroleum Labor Policies Board for advice. In an effort to get the union view the board held public hearings in May, 1934. Almost all union representatives declared the suggested wage schedule to be unsatisfactory. As a result, the board revised the schedule upward. With his characteristic paternalism Ickes approved this recommendation and made it retroactive to September, 1933, when the Oil Code had first become effective. A storm of protest arose from industry as well as labor leaders, both of whom were becoming disenchanted with Ickes' rule by fist. Nevertheless, Ickes ultimately had his way.[41]

During 1934 Ickes continued the campaign to centralize his powers over production and distribution of petroleum. In the spring of that year he promoted Congressional legislation designed to make him the virtual arbiter of the industry. He also enlisted the support of the Petroleum Administrative Board, which was disturbed by decisions in the federal district courts of Texas. Increasingly, they were issuing injunctions to curb federal orders curtailing the flow of hot oil. Thus, the Petroleum Administrative Board also lobbied in Congress for the expansion of federal authority. President Axtell J. Byles of the API at this time gave his cordial endorsement to a proposed expansion of the Oil Administrator's powers.[42] Consequently, on May 1, 1934, Senator Thomas introduced a bill bestowing new authority over the oil industry on the Secretary of the Interior. In the House, Representative W. M. Disney introduced a measure to allow the Administrator of the Oil Code to enforce hot oil quotas directly in the states. But Congressional hearings revealed bitter opposition to the bill, much of it centered in Texas.[43] And in Senator Tom Connally and Congressman Sam Ray-

41. *NYT*, April 14, 15, 20, August 30, 1934; U.S. Petroleum Labor Policies Board, *Report* (Washington, 1935, mimeo.), 3–37, summarizes work of Board. Extensive records of the agency are in the National Archives, Washington, D.C.

42. FDR to Harold Ickes, March 26, 1934, in FDR Mss.; *NYT* February 21, 23, April 29, 1934.

43. *NYT*, April 29, May 1, 6, 18, 1934; FDR to Sam Rayburn, May 22, 1934, FDR to Clarence Dill (June 4, 1934), Elbert Thomas to FDR, (June 20, 1934), in FDR Mss.; FDR at Press Conference, May 23, 1934 in *Transcript of FDR Press Conferences,* III, 365, FDR Mss.

burn, Texas had two powerful representatives in Washington who successfully blocked extension of direct federal authority over petroleum production and, with it, the ambitions of Harold Ickes.

Failing to secure desired powers, Ickes acted unilaterally in October, 1934, to improve the enforcement of his monthly production quotas under Section 9(c) of the National Industrial Recovery Act. Since violations were most flagrant in the important East Texas field, by executive order he created a Federal Tender Board there to issue permits (tenders) to producers for transporting oil out of the state. This ad hoc agency proved quite effective in curbing the flow of hot oil from Texas, and for the moment helped to create a greater measure of stability in the industry.[44]

But Congress seemed unwilling to grant Ickes the desired broad powers. Instead, the House undertook a thorough investigation of federal and state regulation of the petroleum industry. Under the direction of Representative William P. Cole (Pa.) a subcommittee traveled extensively for several months through the oil regions and heard testimony from scores of witnesses. Although this proved to be the most exhaustive Congressional investigation of the oil industry ever undertaken by Congress, the results were inconclusive. In its report, the majority rejected the Thomas-Disney Bill or any other measure conferring extensive regulatory powers on the federal government. Rather, Cole and his colleagues urged an interstate compact to control production.[45]

Just as federal enforcement of the hot oil ban was becoming increasingly effective in East Texas, the United States Supreme Court in the "Panama" decision declared Section 9(c) of the National Industrial Recovery Act invalid. In its Panama decision on January 7, 1935, the Court decided that federal officials lacked the power to enforce production quotas determined by state agencies. Thus, the program that Ickes had carefully wrought to restrict production and the flow of hot oil seemed in imminent danger of collapse.[46]

44. Ickes, *Secret Diary,* I, 218; *NYT,* October 12, 18, 20, 25, 26, 27, 28, November 11, 1934; FDR to Sam Rayburn, May 22, 1934, in FDR Mss.

45. 73 Cong., 1 sess., House Committee on Interstate and Foreign Commerce, Subcommittee on Petroleum Investigation, *Hearings on House Resolution 441* (5 parts, Washington, 1935) [hereafter cited as Cole Committee, *Hearings*]; 74 Cong., 1 sess., *House Report* No. 2 (Washington, 1935), 3–12.

46. *Panama Refining Co.* vs. *Ryan,* 293 U.S. 388 (1935); the opinion is also found in 74 Cong., 1 sess., *Senate Document* No. 10; *NYT,* January 8, 9, 10, 11, 12, 1935, Ickes, *Secret Diary,* I, 273.

In direct response to the Panama decision Secretary Ickes immediately sought legislation that would continue to outlaw the interstate shipment of oil produced in violation of state quotas. Just a day after the Court handed down its verdict, on January 8, 1935, Ickes readied a hot oil bill, which Senators Thomas Gore and Tom Connally introduced in the Senate. Within a month these measures were consolidated and rushed through both houses. Considerably more detailed than the now defunct Section 9(c) of the National Industrial Recovery Act, the Connally measure prohibited the interstate shipment of contraband oil. Whenever the President had cause to believe that the act resulted in an imbalance in supply and demand he could suspend its operation. Roosevelt also issued an executive order reestablishing the Federal Tender Board, whose task it was to impede the flow of hot oil from East Texas. At first enacted for two-year periods, in 1942 Congress extended the Connally Act indefinitely. After 1937 its administration was vested in a Petroleum Conservation Division in the Interior Department as was supervision of the Federal Tender Board. The Connally Act proved its worth almost immediately. It drastically curtailed the flow of illegal oil between states, and buttressed the work of state agencies engaged in limiting production.[47]

A few months after the Panama decision the United States Supreme Court in June, 1935, again placed the oil industry's fate in doubt when it declared the entire National Industrial Recovery Act unconstitutional. Roosevelt thereupon cautiously endorsed the Thomas Bill in Congress, designed to confer power to control oil production on the Secretary of Interior. But in June and July, 1935, Roosevelt was coy. Amid jockeying behind the scenes, he withheld his wholehearted support, and adopted a "wait and see" attitude.[48]

The API sought to adjust to the Panama decision by making arrangements for the continuation of some provisions contained in the NRA Code. In the first of three resolutions the directors advocated

47. CR, 74 Cong., 1 sess. (January 10, 18, 1935), 635, 2521; NYT, January 10, February 10, 23, 24, 1935; Samuel I. Rosenman (ed.), The Public Papers and Addresses of Franklin Delano Roosevelt (13 vols., New York 1938–1950), IV, 88–89; Harold Ickes to FDR, February 27, 1935, in FDR Mss.

48. Ickes, Secret Diary, I, 372–374, 415–416; NYT, May 28, 1935; William P. Cole to FDR, May 24, 1935, FDR to E. W. Marland, May 17, 1935, FDR to William P. Cole, June 20, 1935, William P. Cole to FDR, July 12, August 15, 1935, FDR to William P. Cole, August 23, 1935, in FDR Mss.

restoration of the 1931 voluntary marketing rules for the oil industry, developed under the aegis of the Federal Trade Commission. Roosevelt felt, however, that such voluntary codes were not permitted under the antitrust laws. A second step of the API was to incorporate regional, state, and local committees of the NRA's Production and Coordination Committee in its own organization. These now became organs of the API's Division of Marketing. In a third resolution the directors asked for continuation of the wage-and-hour provisions of the NRA's Oil Code. Their actions received Secretary Ickes' endorsement.[49]

The NRA phase of federal oil regulation thus came to an end. Certainly it was not a complete failure, for the experiment revealed both the strengths and the weaknesses of national regulation. On the basis of this experience Roosevelt fashioned a consensus as he capitalized on the NRA with a political astuteness that had been largely lacking in Herbert Hoover. In an industry characterized by great diversity, federal control of production and distribution was a herculean task, difficult to accomplish. Moreover, it was clear by 1935 that there was strong opposition to the centralization of federal regulatory powers among many segments of the oil industry, especially in Texas. Thus, neither Congress nor the President gave Ickes the required backing for such control.

On the other hand, the NRA era had been fruitful for the industry. The experiment in self-regulation had revealed that cooperation among the states to restrict oil production could be reasonably effective, especially if supplemented by federal prohibitions over oil transported across state boundaries. Also, state or federal laws to enforce conservation measures—unit agreements, drilling and pressure laws—were generally welcomed by responsible producers. The NRA Code Administration acted as a sieve that selected the most workable elements of public oil policies from the plethora of proposals initially attempted.

With the NRA defunct, the big question facing both the oil industry and the federal government was: "What next?" A variety of alternative proposals were made in the spring of 1935. State governors, including Alfalfa Bill Murray of Oklahoma, were urging an interstate oil compact to limit production. Such a proposal was also endorsed by the Cole

49. *O&G Jl.* (June 6, 13, 27, 1935); API, *Proceedings of 16th Annual Meeting 1935* (New York, 1935), 14 ff.

Committee, then engaged in its comprehensive Congressional inquiry about conditions in the petroleum industry. Ickes, sulking somewhat because of lack of support from the White House, still hoped for enactment of federal legislation that would grant him absolute powers over the production and distribution of oil products. It would, in effect, have declared the industry a public utility. And a small group of Brandeisians were urging Roosevelt to revitalize federal antitrust actions as a means of solving problems of oligopolist industries. To all of these suggestions Roosevelt listened carefully while moving warily and slowly in determining a course of public policy. Although the oil industry was still plagued by the Depression, the exigencies of the 1933 crisis had abated. Roosevelt expressed greater interest in long-range reform of federal oil policies, perhaps distilled from the NRA experience.

Even before the United States Supreme Court's invalidation of the NRA, sentiment for an interstate oil compact had been gathering momentum among oilmen. When Congress failed to enact legislation authorizing federal control over oil production in 1934 many industry leaders turned to support more rigorous state regulation, an alternative widely discussed during the Coolidge era. Thus, the P&C Committee adopted a resolution on October 12, 1934, urging the formation of an interstate compact, a plan that President Hoover also had encouraged several years earlier. Just a month later, on November 15, 1934, the directors of the API voted to support a compact if it was accompanied by federal regulation of imports to balance production with demand. In addition, they thought it should be reinforced by an effective hot oil law. Their program reflected fears aroused by a recent speech of Harold Ickes. Addressing the API meeting in Dallas in November, 1934, Ickes told the assembled members he favored legislation declaring the oil industry a public utility, to be subjected to rigid federal controls. This address so upset the API's directors that they reversed their previous support of federal regulation in favor of an interstate compact.[50]

As this sentiment crystallized in the fall of 1934 it was carried forward by Governor-elect E. W. Marland of Oklahoma. A former Congressman who had sponsored many oil regulation bills in Congress, Marland invited the governors of oil-producing states to meet at his

50. API, *Proceedings of 15th Annual Meeting* 1934 (New York, 1934), 27–30; *O&G Jl.* (January 3, 1935) has an important analysis of compact by Mark L. Requa; *NYT,* November 14, 16, 1934.

home in Ponca City, Oklahoma, on December 3, 1934, to discuss the possibilities of a compact and to gauge their general attitudes toward federal oil legislation. He hoped that the governors could appoint a committee to study supply and demand, to allocate production for each state, and to foster uniform state conservation laws. Only Governors Alfred Landon of Kansas and James Allred of Texas appeared at the first meeting, and at a similar one at Marland's home a month later.[51]

At these gatherings, the governors revealed at least two divergent views on state policies. Marland and a majority of delegates believed that their prime aim should be an agreement for the economic stabilization of the industry. This would include manipulation of prices by regulating production in relation to market demand. At the same time this policy would lead to conservation. Administration of such a program, Marland proposed, should be in the hands of a joint state-federal committee.

Governor James Allred of Texas advocated a somewhat different plan. Allred believed that state conservation laws should prevent physical waste only, and should not seek economic stabilization as a primary aim. Interested mainly in curbing inefficient production practices, he opposed regulation of the amount of oil produced and regulation of prices. And the prevention of physical waste, Allred believed, was the exclusive business of the State of Texas, its legislature and executive agencies, and no one else. Although he favored some federal regulation in the form of a hot oil law, and the restriction of foreign oil imports, otherwise he opposed any federal participation in the enforcement of conservation statutes in Texas. Instead, he proposed that standardization of state conservation laws could best be accomplished through the formation of an interstate compact.[52]

On February 15, 1935, both Marland and Allred presented drafts of their proposals to a meeting of governors of oil-producing states in

51. 73 Cong., 1 sess., Cole Committee, *Hearings,* 2884 ff., for discussion of conference by participants; Interstate Oil Compact Commission, *The Compact's Formative Years, 1931–1935* (Oklahoma City, 1954), 1–3; *O&G Jl.* (December 7, 1934); see also *Second Report of the Attorney-General Pursuant to Section 2 of the Joint Resolution of July 28, 1955, Consenting to an Interstate Compact to Conserve Oil and Gas* (Washington, 1958), 36–42.

52. *NYT,* January 2, 4, 1935; *O&G Jl.* (January 10, 1935) discusses conference in detail; see also *O&G Jl.* (January 24, 1935); minutes of this meeting can be found in 73 Cong., 1 sess., Cole Committee, *Hearings,* 2886 ff.

Dallas. The assemblage then appointed a committee under former United States Senator Warwick Downing to work out a compromise. For several weeks the delegates were hard at work, but with the knowledge that the Texas delegation was unyielding and adamant. And, without Texas, no agreement on curtailment of oil production and conservation would be very meaningful, for the state accounted for almost half of the nation's oil supply. Thus, the final draft that the committee presented largely followed the outlines of Allred's plan. But the Texans made a concession by agreeing to the creation of a permanent interstate compact board to oversee the execution of future interstate agreements. They also dropped objections to a provision that encouraged states to coordinate policies for the attainment of maximum ultimate recovery from oil reserves. In practice, this allowed the Compact Commission to recommend allowable production quotas to those states that desired them, as most did in later years.[53]

President Roosevelt encouraged the formulation of the Compact, especially in the aftermath of the Panama decision. The delegates at Dallas unanimously adopted the Downing Committee's draft, which was to become the Interstate Compact to Conserve Oil and Gas. By March, 1935, three other states ratified the agreement, and in August of that year the President sent it to Congress, strongly urging its approval. There the Cole subcommittee of the House Committee on Interstate and Foreign Commerce considered the document, but without enthusiasm. The most immediate need, Cole felt, was to restrict production, and the proposed compact did not provide for effective controls to achieve this goal. Although the committee approved the document, at the same time it urged enactment of the Thomas-Disney bill, which provided for federal regulation of oil production. But the opposition to this bill in Congress, and Roosevelt's own reluctance to place the Administration's prestige behind it, persuaded many Congressmen to approve the compact. Late in August, therefore, Cole offered a simple House Joint Resolution (No. 407) to ratify the compact. After short debate Congress gave its approval but limited it to two years, in the expectation that it would be supplemented by later federal legislation.

53. *NYT*, February 5, 16, 17, 1935; *O&G Jl.* (February 14, 21, 1935); *Transcript of Proceedings, Oil States Compact* (Dallas, 1935), 1–8; Blakely M. Murphy (ed.), *Conservation of Oil and Gas: A Legal History, 1948* (Chicago, 1949), 556–570.

Thus, on August 27, 1935, the Interstate Oil Compact became a reality. Congress renewed it at two-year intervals till 1943, and at four-year intervals thereafter.[54]

Nevertheless, Ickes continued to press for centralized federal controls over the oil industry. Accordingly, in June, 1935, he opposed alternative policies, such as an interstate oil compact. He was even against a federal law to prohibit interstate shipment of hot oil then being sponsored by Senator Tom Connally. If for no other reason, this earned him the enmity of the Texan. Ickes argued that efforts by the states were bound to fail, and that only federal control of production was feasible. When he opposed the Connally Act, at the same time he endorsed the Thomas Bill, which proposed to declare the oil industry a public utility. The President was known to be wary of this measure, however.[55]

Characteristically, Roosevelt led the various factions in the dispute over oil policies to believe that he supported their particular positions. Speaker Rayburn's opposition to a federal oil control bill was a major factor in turning the President away from Ickes' plan. But Roosevelt—in his Machiavellian political style—encouraged each to believe that he had White House support behind him. With exasperation the sponsor of the federal oil bill, Representative W. M. Disney, wrote Roosevelt that unless the President clearly voiced his support, Congress would not enact it. While carefully refraining from just such an endorsement during the first half of 1935, Roosevelt egged Ickes on to promote the Disney Bill. Concurrently, the President asked Rayburn for his suggestions concerning desirable oil legislation. And in November, 1935, Roosevelt sent a message to the Independent Petroleum Association of America in which he urged cooperation and self-regulation in the oil industry to obviate federal action.[56]

During the late summer of 1935 President Roosevelt made his decision concerning the immediate course of federal oil policies. He clearly

54. *CR,* 74 Cong., 1 sess. (August 24, 1935), 14583–14593, *ibid.* (August 26, 1935), 14768; *O&G Jl.* (August 29, 1935); 74 Cong., 1 sess., *Senate Document No.* 118 (Washington, 1935).

55. *O&G Jl.* (February 14, 28, June 20 [text of Thomas Bill], July 4, 1935).

56. Andrew Fahy to Harold Ickes, May 15, 1935, FDR to Sam Rayburn, May 23, 1935, Harold Ickes to FDR, May 21, 1935, in FDR Mss.; FDR at Press Conference, January 9, 1935, in *Transcript of FDR Press Conferences,* V, 42–46, FDR Mss.; FDR at Press Conference, June 4, 1935, *ibid.,* 344, 349; *O&G Jl.* (January 10, November 7, 1935).

sided with Connally and Rayburn against Ickes. At a White House conference of August 6, which included Ickes, Rayburn, Cole, Disney, and Charles Fahy (PAB), the group drafted a new bill to provide for continuation of the temporary Connally Hot Oil Act. And a week later the President enthusiastically endorsed the Interstate Oil Compact and also approved continued import restrictions on foreign oil. These actions were regarded as a bitter blow to Ickes.[57]

As relations between oil industry leaders and Harold Ickes cooled in 1935 the Roosevelt Administration shifted to a revival of more intensive antitrust activity policies. Such a move was motivated by political rather than economic considerations, for the problems of stabilization and overproduction in the oil industry were not necessarily directly related to collusion among the nation's oil producers. Indeed, on many occasions the opposite was true. Consequently, the flurry of intensive antitrust activities from 1936 to 1941 contributed little toward solving the industry's major problems. Much sound and fury accompanied new antitrust suits against oil companies during these years, but in the end little was accomplished. Even the extensive and exhaustive investigations of the industry by the Temporary National Economic Committee (TNEC), and the Federal Trade Commission bore virtually no fruit.

The Administration's antitrust crusade against the oil industry began soon after the demise of the NRA. Its origins were to be found in intraindustry conflict. At the behest of Ickes in 1934, the large oil companies agreed to buy a portion of "distress" gasoline of small refiners in each major refining area rather than have them dump it on the already depressed market. Hopefully this would stabilize the price of gasoline. Each large company was usually assigned one independent producer whom it was to bolster through this scheme. When the Supreme Court declared the NRA unconstitutional in May, 1935, Secretary Ickes approved the continuation of the arrangement, however. But in mid-June a group of disgruntled oil jobbers, including representatives of the National Association of Petroleum Retailers, went to Washington and complained to the United States Attorney General concerning the collusion among large companies in fixing jobber margins.[58]

---

57. *NYT*, August 7, 1935; *O&G Jl.* (August 15, 1935); FDR at Press Conference, August 9, 1935, in *Transcript of FDR Press Conferences,* VI, 91, FDR Mss.

58. Ellis W. Hawley, *The New Deal and the Problem of Monopoly* (Princeton, 1966), 374–375, emphasizes the ambiguity of this antitrust crusade; *NYT*, October 31, 1935.

In Attorney General Robert H. Jackson they found a sympathetic listener. On August 1, 1935, he announced initiation of an antitrust investigation of the oil companies. According to Ickes, he himself knew nothing of the action until he read about it in the newspapers. For the next nine months FBI agents helped to collect information concerning the relationship of major companies and jobbers, and in April, 1936, the Justice Department announced the impaneling of a grand jury in Madison, Wisconsin, to conduct the investigation.[59]

Why Madison? To be sure, it was the home of Progressive antimonopoly sentiment. But the federal court dockets there were less crowded than elsewhere. The grand jury met for two months and in July, 1936, issued a criminal rather than a civil indictment against 23 oil companies and 58 individuals who allegedly conspired to fix prices. The trial on the first indictment began in October, 1937. Oil executives poured into Madison, where their luxurious mode of living soon raised eyebrows among many simple and frugal midwesterners. They rented the leading hotel in town, occupied the country club and the largest private homes, and utilized the building of a bank that had failed, thus arousing much hostility in the locality. Most frustrating to the oil companies' case was their inability to secure testimony from Harold Ickes concerning his sanctioning of their arrangement. Ickes did not wish to appear as a voluntary witness lest he embarrass the Roosevelt Administration. On the other hand, the oil companies were reluctant to force him to testify by subpoena, for there was no assurance as to just what Honest Harold might feel inclined to say. Thus, the court adjudged the defendants guilty of a misdemeanor under the Sherman Act in September, 1938, a decision the United States Supreme Court upheld two years later. With considerable justice, executives of the integrated companies claimed that they had been betrayed, for they had only embarked on the pricing program at the direct behest of Ickes.[60]

The Madison suit also spurred Congressional antitrust legislation. In

---

59. U.S. Attorney-General, *Annual Report* 1935 (Washington, 1938), 41–48, 307–310; Homer Cummings to FDR, September 19, 1936, in FDR Mss.; *NYT*, April 10, 16, October 28, 1936; "Mamma Spank; 18 Major Oil Companies Indicted," *Time*, XXX (October 18, 1937), 63.

60. *O&G Jl.* (November 18, 25, December 2, 9, 1937); Ickes, *Secret Diary*, II, 341, 347, III, 337; John F. O'Ryan to Marvin McIntire, August 13, 1937, and John F. O'Ryan to Robert Jackson, June 23, 1937, in FDR Mss.; "Oil Trial Tremors," *Business Week* (October 16, 1937), 18; Murphy (ed.), *Conservation of Oil and Gas*, 630–636.

April, 1938, Senator Guy Gillette (Iowa) introduced a bill to compel separation of marketing from other lines of the petroleum business. This proposed legislation was designed to break up integrated companies. In another move, Senator Borah urged that pipelines be divorced from oil-producing companies.[61]

The next salvo in the Administration's antitrust campaign came in June, 1938, with the creation of the Temporary National Economic Committee, headed by Senator Joseph C. O'Mahoney. It included representatives from the Justice Department, the Securities and Exchange Commission (SEC), the Federal Trade Commission (FTC), and the Departments of Labor, Commerce, and Treasury. Its hearings on a large number of industries began on December 1, 1938, and continued until April, 1941. Testimony alone filled 37 volumes. Oil industry representatives appeared on September 25 and October 20, 1939, and discussed virtually every phase of their operations.[62]

In addition, the TNEC sponsored 43 monographs that traced the extent of monopoly and economic concentration in various spheres of American enterprise. Partly on the basis of testimony presented at the TNEC hearings, Roy Cook, a member of Thurman Arnold's staff, prepared a monograph about the oil industry. He highlighted a well-known fact—the important position of major integrated companies. In his survey of production, refining, transportation, and marketing of petroleum, Cook emphasized the dominant role of large corporations. Stressing the importance of oil to the economy and to national defense, he concluded that the industry bore all the earmarks of a public utility and thus should be subject to strict federal and state controls.[63] In essence, this conclusion was a distillation of Ickes' view on the oil problem.

The climax to the New Deal's antitrust policies in the oil industry came with the Mother Hubbard Case. This was an all-embracing antitrust suit against 22 major oil companies and also some independents, charging them with 69 violations of the Sherman Act. Since the action

61. CR, 75 Cong., 3 sess. (March 30, 1938), 4344; CR, 76 Cong., 1 sess. (April 17, 1939), 4282.

62. Temporary National Economic Committee, Hearings before TNEC [September 25, 30, 1939], Part 14, Sect. I, 7097–10, 213, Part 16, Sect. III, [October 9–13, 16, 1939], Part 17 [October 17–24, 25, 1939] (Washington, 1940).

63. Roy Cook, Control of the Petroleum Industry by Major Oil Companies, TNEC Monograph No. 39, (Washington, 1941).

was so broad in scope, it was dubbed as a Mother Hubbard suit. Before the Attorney General carried it very far, however, he suspended it in the face of World War II. As Wilson had in 1917, so Roosevelt dropped antitrust activities against the oil industry during wartime. The Justice Department briefly revived the case in 1946, but federal lawyers asked for its dismissal in 1951. It seemed to have accomplished not much more than harassment.[64] Indeed, the New Deal's antitrust actions against the oil industry between 1937 and 1941 had little relation to the major problems of stabilization and conservation. Consequently, even after World War II, the antitrust campaign against integrated oil companies was allowed to lapse, except for a few isolated cases.

The years between 1935 and 1941 marked the reform era in the New Deal's program for the oil industry. This was a period of consolidation, of sifting from available proposals those that had been widely discussed in the preceding decade and that seemed feasible to Roosevelt. This reform phase came to include reliance on an interstate compact to regulate production within the states, a hot oil (Connally) law to prevent interstate shipment of oil produced in violation of state quotas, and maintenance of a tariff on foreign oil imports to prevent undue disruption of domestic producers. Roosevelt had been unable to discern a consensus in favor of direct federal control of production or for the dissolution of large integrated companies. As a consequence, his finely attuned political ear led him to drop his support for these proposals, to the great dismay of Ickes.

Was there a New Deal for oil? If Roosevelt made few substantive innovations in the realm of policy, he made important contributions to its administrative implementation. Certainly the Roosevelt Administration offered little that was new to U.S. oil policies. Virtually every one of the measures affecting the oil industry promoted between 1933 and 1940 had crystallized from experience in the preceding decade. But the great contribution of Roosevelt was his political skill. He not only fostered a consensus between industry and government concerning goals of national oil policy upon which there was wide agreement—stabilization and conservation—but he also fashioned the administrative means to implement them. His contribution was of no small consequence.

64. Murphy (ed.), *Conservation of Oil and Gas,* 633; *U.S.* vs. *Socony-Vacuum Oil Co.,* 310 U.S. 150 (1940).

Viewed in its entirety, the New Deal for oil was a moderate success. Certainly the NRA experiment cannot be dubbed a failure. Not only did it help to curb oil production between 1933 and 1935, it also led to the crystallization of an area of agreement concerning the course of public policy. After its demise leaders in business and government were intent on maintaining its most workable features. These included the continuation of monthly production forecasts by the United States Bureau of Mines, the Interstate Oil Compact and the Connally Hot Oil Act, an oil tariff, and emphasis on voluntary cooperation. They came to constitute the gist of the New Deal for oil. As for the antitrust phase after 1935, it was an aberration from the mainstream of national business regulation in the twentieth century. In emphasizing the dissolution —rather than regulation—of large integrated corporations. Roosevelt was experimenting with Brandeisian principles that were unrealistic in light of the petroleum problems confronting both government and industry during this period. Roosevelt abandoned this course as quickly as he had embarked upon it. By 1939, therefore, the New Deal embodied a loose consensus on national oil policies, a consensus that was to be rudely disrupted by the outbreak of World War II.

8 / World War II

THE NEW DEAL'S efforts to develop a satisfactory national
oil policy were suspended in 1939 by gathering war clouds in Europe.
Indeed, from the German invasion of Poland to VJ Day the federal
government's prime aim was to divert the American oil industry to
wartime status. Considerations of national defense now took precedence
over all other goals of the nation's resource policies. And, as in World
War I, new federal agencies were needed to guide the industry through
the transition period from peace to war. As in 1917 the major aim of
public policy now became maximum production—a goal to which both
industry and government adhered over the next six years. By close cooperation with federal officials the industry met unprecedented production quotas. In turn the federal government was able to supply its own
domestic and military supply requirements as well as those of its allies.
The experience of World War II further crystallized the goals of national
resource policy and their implementation through a complex network of
federal and state controls of business.

For the oil industry wartime requirements presented problems without precedent. Maximum production was the most pressing one, for to a
far greater extent than in World War I the conflict, from beginning to
end, was a war of oil. Between December, 1941, and August, 1945,
Allied requirements totaled 7 billion barrels of crude petroleum, of

which the United States supplied 80 percent. If the Allies floated to victory on a sea of oil during World War I it was equally true that in World War II they flew to victory on oil. Charles E. Wilson, vice-chairman of the War Production Board, accurately phrased it in 1943: "The responsibility which rests upon the petroleum industry . . . is nothing less than the responsibility for victory."[1] In addition to problems of production, there were others involving transportation of oil and its equitable distribution, of concern to both industry and government. Domestic issues were complicated enough in themselves, but in addition the apportionment of available supplies among the Allies and various battlefronts often presented puzzles to confound a Solomon.

The major challenge for the federal government was to shift its policies from curtailment to promotion of oil production. From 1924 to 1939 all of its efforts had been geared largely to restrict production and to maintain a semblance of stability in the industry. Now the war required new efficiencies in drilling and in the exploitation of new wells. By grants of subsidies and favorable tax provisions, and by shrewd allocation of scarce machinery and drilling supplies, federal and state authorities were able to boost the nation's total oil output. The achievement was possible only because of a cooperative relationship of government and industry, which constituted a wartime version of what Theodore Roosevelt had envisaged as the New Nationalism.

Within a few months the European war resulted in fuel oil and gasoline shortages in the United States. As German submarines increasingly cut down the flow of Allied tanker traffic in the Atlantic, crude oil shipments from California and the Gulf of Mexico region to the Northeast were seriously disrupted. Available rail and truck facilities to provide overland transportation were insufficient to move oil products needed in the large eastern cities; pipelines connecting the Atlantic Coast with the midcontinent and Gulf oil regions were too few to take on the added load. Thus, the Atlantic Coast, which received 95 percent of its oil supply by sea, faced serious fuel oil and gasoline shortages during the fall of 1940 and again in the winter of 1941.[2]

1. General surveys of World War II problems can be found in Harold F. Williamson *et al., The American Petroleum Industry* (2 vols., Evanston, 1959–1963), II, *The Age of Energy,* 747–794; John W. Frey and H. Chandler Ide, *A History of the Petroleum Administration for War* (Washington, 1946), 1–7.

2. FDR to William P. Cole, March 4, 1940, March 26, 1940, November 29, 1940, William P. Cole to FDR, March 7, 1945, Harold Ickes to FDR, August 1,

ORGANIZATIONAL PROBLEMS

The Administration's response to such problems was slow and haphazard. Soon after the outbreak of the European war the widow of Mark Requa wrote to President Roosevelt to remind him of her husband's experiences in mobilizing the United States Fuel Administration during World War I. The President was not unaware of the need and throughout 1939 and 1940 urged Congress to enact legislation that would empower the Secretary of the Interior to allocate oil production and distribution. In 1940 the House Committee on Commerce headed by William P. Cole once again held lengthy and extensive hearings on the Thomas Bill, designed to confer broad powers on the Secretary of the Interior to control production and distribution of oil. But Congress continued to reflect its distrust of Ickes by refusing to enact the measure. In the meantime, the loan of fifty American tankers to the British further aggravated the supply situation.[3]

When Congress revealed increasing reluctance after 1939 to expand federal controls over the petroleum industry, growing shortages led President Roosevelt to use his executive powers. Soon after the outbreak of the European war in September, 1939, Roosevelt delegated his authority to deal with many of the oil problems it created for the United States to Secretary of the Interior Ickes. These included the establishment of voluntary rationing programs for fuel oil and gasoline in the Northeast and the development of makeshift arrangements for transport facilities. It was Ickes who frequently located rail and motor transport for oil products when tankers were unavailable. And it was Ickes also who protested loudly and vehemently against the State Department's policy in 1939 and 1940 of issuing export licenses for oil shipments to Japan.[4]

As these wartime problems became more numerous in the spring of 1941, Roosevelt conferred formal advisory powers on Ickes when on

---

1940, FDR to Mrs. Mark Requa, June 6, 1941, in Franklin D. Roosevelt Papers, Franklin D. Roosevelt Library [hereafter cited as FDR Mss.], Hyde Park, N.Y.; FDR to William P. Cole, March 22, 1941, Secretary of the Interior, Administrative Files, National Archives [hereafter cited as DI Records], Washington, D.C.

3. 76 Congress, 1 sess., House, Committee on Interstate and Foreign Commerce, *Hearings Before Subcommittee on H.R. 7372 and H. Resolution 290* (5 parts, Washington, 1939–1940), *passim; NYT,* January 18, 19, April 3, May 3, December 6, 7, 1940.

4. *NYT,* May 14, 15, June 15, June 19, July 13, 1941.

May 28, 1941, he designated him as Petroleum Coordinator for National Defense (PCND). Roosevelt was vague, however, about the jurisdiction of this new agency. Its powers were to be largely advisory in promoting greater cooperation within the oil industry. The coordinator was to make an inventory of available oil reserves, and to facilitate pooling of scarce resources and equipment. He was also to organize advisory committees composed of industry representatives and to coordinate petroleum policies of various federal agencies.[5]

Like Mark Requa in World War I, Ickes developed plans for closer cooperation within the oil industry, based in part on suspension of the antitrust laws. Obviously, close cooperation in the oil industry was difficult if the Justice Department discouraged such "collusion," especially the formation of regional industry committees. Thus, shortly after assuming his responsibilities as Petroleum Coordinator in early June, 1941, Ickes approached Attorney General Biddle about the possibility of suspending antitrust suits during the defense emergency. A lively correspondence ensued between the two men on this subject. Biddle was loath to halt various pending cases. He acquiesced very reluctantly and only under White House pressure. Ickes won his point, which was to allow oil companies to enter upon voluntary agreements, including pooling, as enforcement of the Sherman and Federal Trade Commission Acts ended. The Department of Justice also agreed temporarily to suspend its antitrust suits against oil companies pending on appeal, although Biddle promised to keep the activities of the various petroleum corporations under close surveillance.[6] Meanwhile, *The Nation* and other liberal critics charged that Ickes was staffing his new office almost exclusively with executives of the large integrated companies. To this Ickes replied that he chose the best men available for his openings, irrespective of their business backgrounds.[7]

5. *Ibid.*, May 29, June 1, 3, 1941; FDR to Ickes, May 28, 1941, in DI Records.
6. Robert H. Jackson to Ickes, June 3, 1941, Ickes to Attorney General Robert H. Jackson, June 16, 1941, Francis Biddle to Ickes, June 18, 1941, in DI Records; Rosenman Memo for FDR, March 14, 1942, in FDR Mss. outlines the President's position in giving priority to the war effort before antitrust prosecutions.
7. *NYT*, June 10, 15, 1941; FDR to H.D. Collier, June 4, 1941, in DI Records; Ickes to FDR June 4, 1941, in FDR Mss.; Ickes vigorously defended his policy of utilizing the services of oil industry leaders against bitter criticisms of liberals. See Ickes to editors of *The Nation*, October 11, 1941, in DI Records; *NYT*, November 30, 1941; *O&G Jl.* (December 18, 1941).

With his customary energy, Ickes at once sought to rally the leading representatives of the oil industry to his support. In view of the eight years of hostility and suspicion between himself and the oil company executives this was no easy task. In 1941 he was still greatly feared and distrusted in oil industry circles. Had he not tried—albeit unsuccessfully —to nationalize the industry just a year before, with himself as its arbiter?

Throughout the fall of 1941, and during the tense months thereafter, Ickes tried various means to stimulate the war petroleum program. He sought to aid oil companies in coordinating facilities of transportation. He also encouraged their pooling programs as a means of relieving shortages in particular areas. On many occasions he intervened on their behalf with the War Production Board to aid them in securing priorities for scarce materials. He also expanded production of 100-octane avia tion gasoline by offering special incentives for refiners, by encouraging refinery conversions, and by stimulating federal construction of 100-octane facilities through loans from the Reconstruction Finance Corporation. His responsibilities also embraced procurement of necessary oil supplies for the Lend-Lease program, the purchase of which, he assured an anxious Congressman, Lyndon B. Johnson, would be made in American dollars.[8]

OIL EXPORTS

Another means of increasing available petroleum supplies for domestic use, Ickes thought, was to curb oil exports. His excessive zeal in this sphere led him into a head-on clash with Secretary of State Cordell Hull and earned him an ultimate reprimand from the President himself. Ickes particularly wanted to stop oil deliveries to Japan. In his customary brusque—and tactless—manner, on June 11, 1941, he ordered Secretary Cordell Hull as well as the Administrator of Export Controls, Russell Maxwell, to stop American oil exports to Japan. Ickes had no authority for such action and Hull apparently was furious. Within a week President Roosevelt himself wrote to Ickes pointing out that only he himself and the Secretary of State had the power to suspend exports, and that this was primarily a matter of foreign policy over which the

8. *N.Y.T,* August 15, 1941. Harold Ickes to Lyndon B. Johnson, January 8, 1942, in DI Records.

Interior Department had no jurisdiction.[9] Ickes was hurt, but castigated what he termed the ostrichlike attitude of the State Department. But his strictures were to no avail. Roosevelt reiterated his complete agreement with Hull on the export policy, which was based on considerations of diplomacy not in the domain of Ickes.[10]

OIL TRANSPORTATION

Ickes also found himself faced with a knotty array of transportation problems. The tanker shortage first became serious in the early months of 1941, when President Roosevelt ordered the equivalent of fifty oil-carrying ships removed from their regular runs to transport vital petroleum to England. This led to an immediate reduction in the East Coast's oil supply by about 250,000 barrels daily. Thus, Ickes urged the major oil companies to embark on a publicity campaign to urge the public to reduce consumption. Although the companies followed his advice, oil consumers ignored it. Consequently, in June, 1941, Ickes asked oil companies to eliminate wasteful tanker runs, to increase their average tanker load, and to step up their scheduled sailings.[11]

More controversial was the Petroleum Coordinator's directive to oil companies to make greater use of tank cars. Movement of petroleum by rail was about ten times as expensive as by water. Moreover, virtually all of the loading and terminal facilities of petroleum distributors large and small were geared to water transport and not to railroads. The suggested reliance on rail carriers required construction of new and expensive facilities. To ease this financial burden, Ickes personally appealed to Joseph B. Eastman, chairman of the Interstate Commerce Commission, to support lower freight rates for petroleum. At the same time, he received permission from the Department of Justice to encourage the major oil companies to pool their reserves and shipments and to share their increased transportation costs. Most of the technical details

9. Ickes to Cordell Hull, June 11, 1941, Ickes to General Russell Maxwell, June 11, 1941, FDR to Ickes, June 18, 1941, in FDR Mss.

10. Ickes to FDR, June 20, 1941, Sumner Welles to FDR, June 24, 1941, FDR to Ickes, June 25, 1941, in FDR Mss.

11. *NYT,* January 30, July 31, 1942; Harold L. Ickes, *Fightin' Oil* (New York, 1943), *passim;* Ickes, *Secret Diary,* III, 529–531; Ickes to Sinclair Oil Company, June 24, 1941, Records of the Petroleum Administration for War, National Archives [hereafter cited as PAW Records], Washington, D.C.; Ickes sent similar letters to other oil companies.

of the operation were worked out by the Petroleum Industry War Council (PIWC) and the Association of American Railroads. Voluntary acceptance of Ickes' plan resulted in a thirtyfold increase of oil shipments by rail to the East Coast in 1941, adding 142,000 barrels daily.[12]

By mid-1941, however, as the number of Allied tanker sinkings in the Atlantic increased, Ickes felt compelled to seek long-range methods for overland transportation of petroleum to the East Coast. Little did he realize then that he was promoting a revolution in oil transportation. From primary reliance on seagoing tankers, characteristic of the pre-World-War-II era, petroleum during the war and in succeeding decades came to be moved largely by rail, trucks, and pipelines. Since new railroad cars and tanker trucks were scarce during the wartime years, Ickes placed great emphasis on the immediate need for construction of new pipelines.[13]

In fact, the campaign for building of new pipelines became almost a passion with Ickes. And possibly the federal government's greatest achievement in solving wartime oil transportation problems was the eventual construction of the Big Inch and the Little Inch Pipelines. At a time when railroad opposition to new pipelines was still strong, Ickes was urging federal aid to hasten their construction. As early as December, 1940, Ickes warned President Roosevelt that the East Coast must have pipelines to assure fulfillment of its petroleum needs in time of war, and that these could be met only with a government-sponsored pipeline-building program. This statement aroused considerable fears among private pipeline operators. Indeed, early in 1941 eleven major oil companies announced a plan to form a National Defense Pipelines and Emergency Pipelines Corporation to finance a privately owned system. President Roosevelt meanwhile asked the House Committee on Interstate and Foreign Commerce to make a study of the entire southeastern oil transportation system.[14]

12. J. S. Grover, "15 Hours Ahead of Schedule: How Railroads Rush Oil Across the Continent," *Nation's Business,* XXX (November 1942), 30–32; "Wartime Revolution in Oil Transportation," *Business Week* (April 17, 1943), 57.

13. Ickes to Smith W. Brookhart, June 27, 1941, in DI Records; *NYT,* July 23, 1941; Williamson *et al., American Petroleum Industry,* II, 763–766.

14. FDR to H. C. Lea [Chairman, House Committee on Interstate and Foreign Commerce] January 23, 1941, FDR to William P. Cole, March 22, 1941, FDR to Dawson Kea, May 12, 1941, in DI Records; *NYT,* January 12, February 7, March 20, 28, May 21, June 1, 6, 1941.

But the building of private pipelines soon encountered local obstacles, as the stubbornness of the Georgia legislature indicated. Although President Roosevelt himself endorsed a bill in the Georgia Senate to grant rights of way to private pipeline companies engaged in construction vital to defense, the legislators refused to enact it, largely because of strong dissent from affected railways and railroad unions. Instead, they offered to pass a bill granting such privileges to the federal government. Such obstruction led the President to write to Speaker Sam Rayburn in May, 1941, advocating federal legislation to grant rights of way to interstate pipeline companies. By the end of July, Congress enacted the Cole bill, which contained the required authority. Not until American entrance into the war was there much effort to implement it, however. Ickes continued to take the initiative by calling a conference of leading pipeline operators in Tulsa, Oklahoma, on March 23, 1942. They worked out a detailed plan of construction to be undertaken by private capital, but this still did not meet the oil requirements of the Northeast.[15]

Ickes continued to press for direct federal ownership and operation. In particular, he urged the building of what would be the largest pipeline in the world, linking East Texas with New York. Dubbed as the Big Inch, this project had strong support of the Petroleum War Industries Committee. But elsewhere the proposal engendered opposition, especially with Donald Nelson and the War Production Board (WPB) and the Supply Priorities and Allocations Board. Ickes first appealed to them for necessary building materials in September, 1941, but the WPB rejected his application. Deputy Administrator Davies made a similar request in November, 1941, which was also turned down. His renewed appeal in February, 1942, was also fruitless. Meanwhile, in June, 1942, Ickes went before the House Committee on Interstate and Foreign Commerce to plead for steel allocations necessary for his project.[16]

Worsening petroleum shortages strengthened the arguments of Ickes and in October, 1942, Nelson and the WPB reluctantly issued the nec-

15. *NYT*, July 13, 14, 15, 16, 18, 1941; *Congressional Record* [hereafter cited as *CR*], 77 Cong., 1 sess. (May 20, 1941), 4301 (June 5, 1941), 4781–4799 (July 15, 1941), 6027–6044, 6047–6055 (July 31, 1944), 6520.

16. Ickes to Donald M. Nelson, February 20, 1942, Ickes to Carl Vinson, April 20, 1942, Ickes to FDR, April 21, 1942, Ickes to Donald M. Nelson, May 25, 1942, and September 29, 1942, in DI Records; *NYT*, February 18, March 6, May 11, June 12, 1942; *O&G Jl.* (January 28, 1943).

essary priorities for the needed steel. The entire cost of construction was paid by the Defense Plant Corporation, a subsidiary of the Reconstruction Finance Corporation. In 1943 this government agency also built a shorter line, the Little Inch, from Illinois to the East Coast. Together, both pipelines delivered about 379,207,208 barrels of crude oil from the Texas fields to the East between 1943 and 1945 and saved the Atlantic Coast from a fuel famine.[17] The construction of these pipelines was one of the federal government's greatest achievements in solving domestic oil shortage problems in the East.

Throughout the war Ickes continued the attempt to encourage maximum oil production through extension of tax benefits. The 27½ percent depletion allowance of 1926 was maintained. Although Ickes refrained from specifically endorsing it, he withheld criticism with equal care. On the other hand, in 1944 he embarked on a heated campaign against a new Treasury ruling that prohibited oil prospectors from deducting drilling costs as intangible expenses. To a remarkable extent Ickes came to be a spokesman for many views held by leaders of the industry.[18]

But as the wartime mobilization program gathered increasing momentum by the middle of 1942 Ickes found himself hampered by insufficient powers. President Roosevelt's letter of May 28, 1941, contained many ambiguities concerning the coordinator's jurisdiction. More seriously, he lacked effective powers to enforce directives, and thus could not do much more than to issue recommendations. Initially, the President had given little thought to petroleum problems other than a threatened oil shortage. Ickes, however, was anxious to embark on a comprehensive program that would affect all phases of production and distribution. Moreover, he also hoped for greater coordination of federal policies, as by December, 1941, about 40 separate federal agencies were concerned with some phase of oil policies, creating much overlapping and confusion. In Congress, meanwhile, demands for mandatory rationing controls were crystallizing. One man to reflect such

17. The literature on these pipelines is immense. For a good summary, with bibliography, see F. B. Dow, "The Role of Petroleum Pipelines in the War," *Annals of the American Academy of Political and Social Science,* CCXXX (November 1943), 93–100; "Oil Rechanneled: Vast New Pipeline Pattern Evolved by Industry," *Business Week* (May 9, 1942), 17–18; *NYT,* June 12, July 19, October 29, 1942.

18. Ickes to John J. McCloy, May 4, 1942, Ickes to Henry Morgenthau, December 22, 1943, in DI Records.

sentiment was Senator Henry Cabot Lodge, who introduced a bill on August 13, 1942, to create a National Petroleum Administrator. Deputy Administrator Davies was also greatly distressed over the public's apathy in practicing voluntary conservation. In fact, Senator Harry Byrd (Va.) urged national gasoline rationing.[19] The increasing shortage of petroleum products and the various difficulties of distribution led to a developing and serious crisis.

Throughout the spring of 1942 Ickes continued to press the President for expansion of his authority over oil. Finally, in July, 1942, Roosevelt agreed to let him draw up a tentative proposal, which was passed around to Cabinet members, industry leaders, and others. In August, 1942, Ickes actually made public his broad program for a new federal agency to mobilize the industry more effectively.[20]

Within the Administration, a bitter conflict ensued over the Ickes proposal. The draft for the proposed petroleum war agency that Ickes prepared was designed to grant him far-reaching powers. He hoped to secure centralized controls not only over the production of oil, but also over its domestic and foreign distribution, and over prices. Moreover, he also planned to exercise authority over scarce war materials needed for drilling and manufacturing equipment. When this draft was circulated among members of Roosevelt's Cabinet it evoked strong and unanimous opposition. Stimson, Hull, and Knox were particularly disturbed over the constant effort of Ickes to interfere in their departments, and their concern was shared by the Director of the War Production Board, Donald Nelson. Between August and December, 1942, in a series of conferences with Nelson and his Cabinet colleagues, Ickes was forced to work out an acceptable compromise with them and with representatives of the industry.[21]

PETROLEUM ADMINISTRATOR FOR WAR

The result was President Roosevelt's executive order of December 2, 1942, in which he created the Petroleum Administration for War (PAW). As Administrator, Ickes was authorized to issue necessary

19. *NYT,* August 9, 14, 16, 1942.
20. Ickes to Donald M. Nelson, July 2, 1942, Ickes to FDR, August 4, 1942, Ickes to FDR, August 19, 1942, in DI Records; Ickes to FDR, September 19, 1942, Harold Smith memo for FDR, October 1, 1942, in FDR Mss.
21. Harold D. Smith to FDR, October 22, 1942, Ickes to FDR, November 18, 1942, in FDR Mss.

rules governing the production, transportation, and distribution of petroleum. His agency was instructed to develop necessary policies to increase production by fostering improved conservation practices, by encouragement of drilling, or by changing consumption patterns. But control over allocation of scarce materials—such as steel—needed to increase oil production, was vested in the War Production Board, to the great discomfiture of Ickes. And even more to his dismay, regulation of prices for petroleum products was left with the Office of Price Administration (OPA).[22]

Ickes' immediate task was to secure an increase of petroleum production. One means to solve this problem was to procure priorities from the War Production Board for scarce oil exploration tools and machinery. Unfortunately, in 1942 producers had discovered only four new big producing wells despite a 25 percent increase in their drilling. A more intensive search for oil was therefore a necessity. The PAW also encouraged discovery of wildcat and stripper wells by publicizing potential locations and by offering financial incentives for their exploitation.[23]

In another effort to spur crude-oil production the PAW attempted to stimulate scientific research to increase the amount and variety of products extracted from crude petroleum. This was especially true of its herculean effort to secure large-scale production of 100-octane aviation gasoline, special fuels for the Navy, and the production of synthetic rubber. During 1940 and 1941 Ickes had his staff make a survey of potential needs and available facilities for 100-octane gasoline. Ickes also appointed an industry committee for each of the five districts into which the PAW divided the United States to plan the construction of new facilities. At the urging of the PAW in November, 1942, the RFC stimulated the program by awarding long-term contracts for aviation gasoline. In addition, improved blending techniques boosted production. Similar encouragement resulted in the development of a major new synthetic rubber industry by a subsidiary of the RFC, the Rubber Reserve Corporation.[24]

22. *NYT*, December 3, 6, 1942; *O&G Jl.* (September 17, 1942).

23. Frey and Ide, *History of Petroleum Administration for War*, 177–187.

24. Scientific work is well described in Frey and Ide, *History of Petroleum Administration for War*, 191–226; on the 100 octane gasoline program see Ickes to FDR, January 19, 1942, Ickes to Donald M. Nelson, March 6, 1942, Ickes to FDR, June 2, 1942, in DI Records; FDR to Ickes, January 18, 1942, in FDR Mss.

The PAW also sought to increase the supply of available oil by promoting approved conservation practices such as proper well-spacing. In 1943 the PAW issued an order to compel producers to drill no more than one well for every forty acres. Although it had no formal enforcement powers, the PAW did have means of coercion. Those who refused to follow its conservation guidelines, for example, were denied priorities for necessary drilling or refining machinery. This persuaded many producers to follow the PAW's rulings on a great number of practices, such as the maintenance of proper reservoir pressures. Other PAW orders stimulated unitization agreements, secondary recovery methods, and repressuring to assure maximum yields from crude petroleum.[25]

Many of the conservation rules of the PAW were formulated and supported by state oil conservation agencies. In fact, the PAW urged state legislators to improve their own oil conservation statutes. It was a result of such persuasion, for example, that the Oklahoma legislature in 1943 amended its well-spacing and unitization laws.[26]

Of course, a prime means of stimulating production was to offer direct monetary incentives. The PAW itself lacked the explicit authority to determine prices for petroleum products, for this power lay in the province of the Office of Price Administration (OPA). Nevertheless, Ickes, Davies, and the PAW's officers placed continual pressure on the OPA to increase oil price ceilings in the hope that this would stimulate more intensive exploration by private producers. Unfortunately, the ceilings that the OPA authorized in January, 1942, were based on October, 1941, price levels, and did not encourage the wildcatting which the PAW sought to promote. Both Ickes and Davies became convinced in 1942 that some increases for oil products were necessary, especially to encourage new drilling in Wyoming and California. After a series of long verbal battles between Ickes and the OPA in March, 1943, the OPA reluctantly allowed selected price increments in those states.[27]

But Ickes was not satisfied. Reflecting the concern of the Petroleum Industry War Council (PIWC) and of Davies, late in 1942 he came

25. Frey and Ide, *History of Petroleum Administration for War,* 162–168, 178–189.

26. Ickes to Oklahoma Corporation Commission, February 27, 1942, in DI Records; *O&G Jl.* (December 11, 1941).

27. *NYT,* January 7, 21, 1942; *O&G Jl.* (December 17, 1942).

out strongly for a general rise in crude oil ceilings to stimulate production. His action resulted partly from the PIWC's Cost and Price Adjustment Committee report early in 1943, which urged the PAW to advocate higher price levels. Its view was supported by the officials in the PAW's Production Division, whose main responsibility was to further new oil exploration. Texans were particularly anxious for higher crude oil prices. In 1943 the Texas legislature enacted a resolution urging the OPA to revise its oil ceilings, and E. O. Thompson of the Texas Railroad Commission wrote to the President to secure his support. Consequently, on April 7, 1943, Ickes made a formal recommendation to the OPA for the raising of price ceilings on crude oil by 35 cents a barrel. His recommendation was not appreciated by OPA Administrator Brown, who rejected it, seeking to abide by a recent "hold the line" executive order in regard to prices issued by the President. Instead, Brown urged federal subsidies as the best means for opening new wells and for increasing production.[28]

For over a year this disagreement gave rise to a bitter and drawn-out dispute between Ickes and the OPA over the most desirable methods of increasing oil production. Both Ickes and Davies were vehemently opposed to the payment of subsidies to private producers, and in June, 1943, they renewed their plea for higher ceilings. But OPA Administrator Brown again turned down their suggestion. Meanwhile, Representative Disney introduced a bill to raise oil price ceilings. Ickes in August, 1943, then made a direct appeal to Fred Vinson, head of the Office of Economic Stabilization. After due consideration, Vinson also denied Ickes' proposal. Instead, he directed him to elaborate a subsidy program to encourage stripper wells and to foster repressuring operations.[29]

Yet Ickes' stubbornness was not spent. After devoting some time to studying the feasibility of a subsidy plan during the fall of 1943, he concluded, with full backing from the API and the PIWC's production

28. E. O. Thompson to FDR, February 16, 1943, M. H. McIntire to E. O. Thompson, February 22, 1943, Ickes to FDR, April 7, 1943, FDR Memo for Prentice Brown, April 8, 1943, FDR to Ickes, April 15, 1943, Prentice Brown to Ickes, April 15, 1943, in FDR Mss.
29. Ickes to Prentice M. Brown, June 10, 1943, Ickes to Prentice Brown, August 16, 1943, Ickes to James F. Byrnes, August 14, 1943, Ickes to Fred Vinson, August 9, 1943, in DI Records; *O&G Jl.* (July 1, 1943); *NYT,* March 4, 6, August 6, 13, 23, 28, 1943; *CR,* 78 Cong., 1 sess. (June 7, 1943), 5455, *ibid.,* (July 7, 1943), 7412–13 (November 15, 1943), 9527.

committee as well, that it would not be desirable for the PAW to embark on such a program. But Fred Vinson, now Director of the Office of Production Management, was equally unyielding.[30] Throughout the spring of 1944 Ickes doggedly refused to initiate subsidy payments. Ironically, in view of his past background, Ickes now received the enthusiastic support of the Standard (N.J.) Oil Company, while the C.I.O. opposed his stand.[31] He bowed only as a last resort when on June 28, 1944, James F. Byrnes, Director of Economic Stabilization, himself authorized the PAW to pay subsidies to oil producers.[32]

This long, drawn-out battle was only one aspect of the PAW's herculean effort to increase the nation's wartime stock of petroleum. In addition to his attempts to boost domestic production Ickes also sought to stimulate foreign sources of supply. The most available areas for additional supplies appeared to be Mexico, Venezuela, Colombia, and other Latin American nations, West Africa, and Saudi Arabia.

EXPLOITATION OF FOREIGN SOURCES

Quite early in the war, therefore, Ickes created special agencies to investigate the feasibility of foreign oil imports. In December, 1941, he appointed a Foreign Oil Committee composed of nine executives from major oil companies having foreign interests. In addition, Ickes and Davies maintained contacts with the petroleum representatives of Great Britain and the Netherlands stationed in the nation's capital. They also secured the appointment of a Petroleum Attaché in the United States Embassy in London.[33] Ickes himself was very optimistic about American exploitation of Mexican oil reserves. Between 1941 and 1943 he continually urged Roosevelt to establish U.S. government-owned pro-

30. *NYT,* October 24, 30, 1943; Ickes to Fred Vinson, November 4, 1943, Ickes to James F. Byrnes, October 25, 1943, Ickes to Fred Vinson, March 18, 1944, in DI Records; Fred Vinson to FDR, October 29, 1943, and a copy of his decision, in FDR Mss.; *O&G Jl.* (November 4, 1943, December 9, 1943).

31. Ickes to Fred Vinson, May 25, 1944, in DI Records; Jesse Jones to Fred Vinson, June 22, 1944, Jesse Jones to H. A. Mulligan, June 29, 1944, FDR Memo for James F. Byrnes [June 30, 1944], in FDR Mss.; FDR noted that he would not recognize a stripper well if he saw one on the stage; *NYT,* August 23, 28, 1943.

32. *NYT,* July 6, 1944.

33. Frey and Ide, *History of Petroleum Administration for War,* 250–274.

ducing and refining facilities there. But Cordell Hull, Donald Nelson, and others successfully fought this scheme, which could have embroiled the United States in the nationalization program of the Mexican petroleum industry.[34] Instead, the attention of Roosevelt and his key planners after 1943 shifted to the Middle East. As E. L. De Golyer, Assistant Deputy Administrator of the PAW, noted in a report early in 1944, the center of the world oil industry was shifting from the Gulf area to that region.[35]

In the Middle East, Cal-Tex, a joint corporation formed by the Texas Company and by the Standard Oil Company of California, had for some years exploited the rich oil fields of Saudi Arabia. By late 1942, however, company officials as well as U.S. military men feared that the British were seeking to have Americans expelled. Early in 1943 Harry D. Collier, president of Standard Oil Company of California, and W. S. S. Rodgers, chairman of the Texas (Oil) Company visited Ickes to voice their fears that the British were seeking to edge them out of their Saudi Arabian oil concessions. They hoped that Ickes could persuade the President to intercede with King Ibn Saud on behalf of U.S. oil interests.[36] Rodgers also urged Ickes to prevail upon Roosevelt to include the Arabian monarch in the Lend-Lease program. Rodgers and Collier then visited Hull, Stimson, and Knox to secure additional support in Administration circles. Ickes kept his word. On February 18, 1943, Roosevelt ordered the extension of Lend-Lease aid to Ibn Saud's government.[37] Meanwhile, as by mid-1943 many oil industry leaders as well as government officials feared an imminent oil shortage, on July

---

34. Ickes to FDR, December 3, 1941, Ickes to FDR, February 20, 1942, FDR to Ickes, February 28, 1942, Ickes to FDR, April 17, 1942, FDR to Ickes, May 4, 1942, Ickes to Cordell Hull, August 4, 1942, in DI Records; James F. Byrnes Memo for FDR [on foreign oil situation], October 4, 1943, Ickes to FDR, February 4, 1944, in FDR Mss.

35. Ickes to FDR, July 9, 1941, in FDR Mss.; Ickes to Cordell Hull, June 24, 1941, Ickes to H. D. Collier [President, Standard Oil Company of California], June 27, 1941, Ickes to Frank Knox, June 30, 1941, in DI Records.

36. *NYT*, February 7, 1943.

37. 80 Cong., 1 sess., Senate, Special Committee Investigating the National Defense Program, *Hearings, Petroleum Arrangements with Saudi Arabia* [hereafter cited as *Saudi Hearings*] (Washington, 1948), Part 41, 25232; Benjamin Shwadran, *The Middle East, Oil and the Great Powers* (New York, 1955), 308–312; *O&G Jl.* (October 14, 1943).

14, 1943, President Roosevelt called a Cabinet conference to plan U.S. oil strategy on a global scale.[38]

In this pressing oil crisis Ickes saw another opportunity to establish direct federal control over petroleum resources. He now became an advocate of American exploitation of Saudi oil reserves, not by private companies, however, but by the federal government itself. Many oilmen believed that under the guise of wartime necessity, Ickes was seeking to accomplish what he had failed to do during the New Deal: the nationalization of the business of oil production. As recently as 1935, and again in 1940, Ickes had formulated specific proposals toward that end and he had given little indication about a change of mind on this matter.

Amid such fears Ickes plowed ahead, perhaps with the example of Josephus Daniels during World War I before him. He saw his opportunity during the spring of 1943, when widespread fears of an imminent oil shortage were especially rife among military and diplomatic circles in the nation's capital. In June, 1943, Ickes wrote to President Roosevelt urging him to take immediate action in acquiring foreign oil reserves. He warned of an impending oil shortage for the armed forces in 1944, which could also affect essential industries at home. He urged Roosevelt to create a Petroleum Reserves Corporation—under the RFC —which would acquire and develop new foreign oil reserves. In his detailed proposal he outlined the functions of such a government corporation. Its first venture would be to exploit Saudi Arabian oil, not only to conserve petroleum at home, but to counteract British influence.

At the same time, on June 8, 1943, the Joint Chiefs of Staff made a report to the President in which they expressed their alarm over the dangerous depletion of domestic reserves in the United States. They, too, hoped for exploitation of overseas supplies. Four days later James F. Byrnes, Director of the Office of War Mobilization, presided over a White House meeting attended by Stimson, Knox, Ickes, and Herbert Feis at which they agreed that the federal government itself must search out new oil reserves. For that purpose they recommended the organization of a U.S. government corporation to produce oil in Saudi Arabia.

---

38. *Saudi Hearings,* 24, 861; *CR,* 80 Cong., 1 sess. (April 28, 1948), 4948; Shwadran, *The Middle East,* 310; Cordell Hull to FDR, March 30, 1943, in FDR Mss.; Cordell Hull, *The Memoirs of Cordell Hull* (2 vols., New York, 1948), II, 1511–12; *NYT,* July 11, 15, 29, 1943.

During the next ten days an interdepartmental committee representing the Departments of War, State, Navy, and Interior further discussed the question and worked out detailed plans for the proposed Petroleum Reserves Corporation (PRC). Hull, Stimson, Ickes, and Acting Secretary of the Navy James Forrestal approved this report on June 26, 1943, and four days later the RFC created the new corporation.[39]

Under Ickes' guidance, the PRC now made an effort to purchase all of the lucrative Saudi Arabian properties of the California-Arabian oil companies. In August, 1943, Ickes approached Collier and Rodgers of Cal-Tex with this proposal. Both men were furious at the suggestion. Ickes then suggested that the U.S. government acquire shares, perhaps 70 percent or 51 percent, or maybe only 33⅓ percent in the California-Arabian Oil Company. Until October, 1943, the negotiations continued, but by then General Rommel's threat to North Africa and the Middle East oil supply routes was removed and the oil situation became less critical; the bargaining then broke off.[40]

Many factions of the oil industry strongly opposed joint private and government exploitation of Arabian oil reserves as envisioned by the PRC. Indeed, bitter opposition developed. In November of that year the Foreign Oil Committee of PAW presented its own plan for a foreign oil policy, which contained no mention of any direct federal involvement. Although Ickes spoke at the annual meeting of the API to defend the PRC, the institute formally adopted a resolution to condemn it. In December, 1943, the PIWC itself placed itself on record with a declaration protesting proposed federal oil operations in Arabia. At the same time it appointed a special committee to outline a plan for American oil policies abroad. This group specifically condemned the Petroleum Reserves Corporation. At the same time the directors of the Independent Petroleum Association of America, representing smaller operators, also

---

39. *Saudi Hearings,* 25, 237–238; *CR,* 80 Cong., 1 sess. (April 28, 1948), 4961–4962; Ickes had hoped that the PRC would be in the Department of the Interior; FDR to Ickes, July 30, 1943, in FDR Mss.; PRC charter in Records of the Petroleum Reserves Corporation in National Archives, Washington, D.C.; *Federal Register,* July 2, 1943, 9044; *NYT,* July 2, 1943; Shwadran, *The Middle East,* 311–314; *O&G Jl.* (August 26, 1943).

40. *Saudi Hearings,* 25, 220–25, 242; James F. Byrnes to FDR, January 17, 1944, in FDR Mss.; Herbert Feis, *Petroleum and American Foreign Policy* (Stanford, 1944), 36–39; Shwadran, *The Middle East,* 314–315.

enacted a resolution vigorously protesting government-controlled oil production overseas.[41]

With his usual stubbornness, however, Ickes continued to give backing to the project. Under auspices of the PRC he sent out an exploratory mission to Saudi Arabia in November, 1943, composed of E. L. De Golyer, a well-known oil geologist, and W. E. Wrather, director of the United States Geological Survey, and C. S. Snodgrass, director of Foreign Refining Division of the PAW. In their report of January, 1944, these experts stated their belief that the center of world oil production had definitely shifted to the Middle East. Meanwhile the Petroleum Administrator of the United States Navy, Admiral Andrew Carter, decided after a trip to Saudi Arabia, that it would be well for the United States to build a pipeline from the Saudi oilfields to the coast of the Eastern Mediterranean.

Ickes enthusiastically embraced this plan. On February 6, 1944, the PRC announced that it had made an agreement with the Gulf Oil Company and with Aramco to build and operate a government-owned pipeline from Saudi Arabia to the Mediterranean. Under it, the Arabian-American Oil Company was to build a privately owned and financed refinery at Bahrein, Saudi Arabia, to produce oil for the United Nations. The companies were to repay the cost of the pipeline ($160 million) to the federal government, which would retain ownership. The United States would be entitled to receive one billion barrels of crude oil from Gulf's and Aramco's reserves at a discount of 25 percent of the market price in the United States. Both Ickes and representatives of the oil companies signed the agreement, but it aroused a further storm of protest. The PIWC on February 2, 1944, passed a resolution advocating the abolition of the PRC, and in the next month voted to urge abandonment of the new agreement. Similar pressures from Congressmen, from leaders in the oil industry, and from the British government forced Ickes to defer his Arabian agreement as well as operation of the PRC, lest the industry withhold its cooperation in other phases of the vital wartime effort.[42]

41. Petroleum Industry War Council, *United States Foreign Policy and the Petroleum Reserves Corporation* (Washington, 1944), and *A Foreign Oil Policy for the United States* (Washington, 1944); *NYT*, November 12, 1943; Memo for FDR, February 5, 1944, in FDR Mss.

42. *NYT*, February 4, 6, 1944; *Saudi Hearings*, 25387–25388; *CR*, 78 Cong., 2 sess. (February 9, 1944), 1466–1471; *ibid.*, 80 Cong., 2 sess. (April 28, 1948), 4962; Feis, *Petroleum*, 40–50; Shwadran, *The Middle East*, 318–322.

A heated debate over this project broke out during the first few months of 1944. On the floor of the United States Senate it gave rise to considerable acrimony. Elsewhere the President, Ickes, Knox, and the Joint Chiefs of Staff defended it on familiar grounds. They argued about the necessity to conserve rapidly depleting domestic oil reserves; they underscored the vital importance of oil to the war effort and to needs of national security in the future; they stressed the potential profitability of the enterprise; and they emphasized the importance of U.S. government support for private American investments abroad.[43]

Opponents were no less vociferous. Senator E. H. Moore (Okla.) called the pipeline an imperialist venture and urged an investigation of U.S. oil policy. The PIWC condemned it again, as did President Ralph T. Zook of the Independent Petroleum Association, who feared the collapse of domestic operators because of cheap foreign competition. Herbert Feis, Economic Advisor of the State Department, warned against the foreign embroilments the project would bring. And in its report on petroleum, the Truman Committee urged a U.S. policy stressing private enterprise.[44]

Nevertheless, the merits of the Ickes plan continued to be widely discussed throughout 1944. It became evident that the Administration could not implement the joint venture without causing serious rifts in the U.S.-British alliance. It would also endanger prevailing harmony in its relations with many major oil producers. Thus, when the private companies decided to embark on the project entirely on their own, the Administration maintained a discreet silence. In March, 1945, Aramco began construction of the pipeline, a major enterprise that required five years for completion.[45]

Yet many oil industry leaders, especially those who served on the PIWC, desired an international agreement to guarantee the rights of American oil companies in various portions of the world. They had not forgotten French and British efforts to exclude American oil interests after World War I. They also hoped that they could secure some kind of formal commitment on the part of their own government to extend

---

43. *NYT,* February 10, 11, 14, 1944.

44. *Ibid.,* February 17, March 3, 4, 5, 7, 1944; *CR,* 78 Cong., 1 sess. (February 3, 1944), 1135–1138, *ibid.,* (February 9, 1944), 1466–1471; Shwadran, *The Middle East,* 322–324.

45. U.S. Federal Trade Commission, *The International Petroleum Cartel,* 82 Cong., 2 sess. (Washington, 1952), 125; Shwadran, *The Middle East,* 331–337; *NYT,* March 12, 14, 17, 22, 1944.

diplomatic support to them wherever it was needed. President Roosevelt was sympathetic to their pleas, and as he shelved the PRC in May, 1944, he took the first steps toward the negotiation of an Anglo-American oil treaty to delimit the respective rights of British and American oil companies in various nations. On March 7, 1944, Under-Secretary of State Edward R. Stettinius announced that the President had appointed Hull and Ickes chairman and vice-chairman respectively of an Anglo-American Conference on world oil supplies to be held in Washington. The Department of State appointed ten important oil executives as advisers, and on April 10, 1944, this group began holding technical discussions with British representatives in Washington. By July, 1944, they had worked out a draft treaty, which was submitted to the President's Cabinet, and thereafter negotiations were conducted in greater earnest.[46]

The British government now became increasingly concerned over the aggressive attitude of the United States toward Middle Eastern oil reserves. Both Roosevelt and Ickes sought to exert pressure on the British to recognize U.S. interests in the Middle East by urging a high-level policy conference. As early as February 20, 1944, Prime Minister Churchill cabled Roosevelt that Great Britain was worried over American attempts to force the British out of Saudi Arabia. Roosevelt noted then that Anglo-American oil relations needed clarification. Both leaders agreed to a compromise announced on March 4, 1944, under which initial discussions were to be developed first on a technical level, and only thereafter by Cabinet officials. In Parliament there were bitter criticisms of the proposal, since most members had not been consulted and felt that the United States was seeking to force the hand of the British government. Even in early April, 1944, Foreign Minister Anthony Eden had to confess that he had received no official notice of the meetings.

The first deliberations took place in Washington during the spring of 1944. Sir William Brown led the British delegation while Charles Rayner, the State Department's Petroleum Adviser, represented the American point of view in the discussions held between April 13 and May 3, 1944. It seemed that the British were stalling, and their reluc-

46. Hull, *Memoirs,* II, 1522–1523; *NYT*, March 8, 1944; Great Britain, Parliament, *Parliamentary Debates,* House of Commons, February 9, 1944, 396, col 1744, 399, col 786 (April 26 1944); *O&G Jl.* (June 3 1944).

tance to engage in Cabinet-level discussions was attributed to their opposition to the pipeline project. For when the State Department deferred action on the Bahrein pipeline, the British government in July, 1944, sent a delegation to Washington headed by Lord Beaverbrook. Hull and Ickes led the U.S. representatives. On August 8, 1944, they published an agreement, which President Roosevelt sent to the Senate several weeks later.[47]

The Anglo-American Oil Agreement was designed to allow an orderly development of Middle Eastern oil reserves. It defined mutual American and British interests in the area and provided for future collaboration on the construction of new pipelines. But the treaty aroused great resentment in the United States. Many leading oil executives, including J. Howard Pew of the Sun Oil Company, were angered by the Administration's neglect in not consulting them in preparation of the treaty. Others feared the creation of a cartel. In January, 1945, the Senate returned the pact to the President for revision. Business leaders, such as J. Howard Pew and James Moffett feared that the treaty would be a first step toward nationalization of the oil industry in the United States. Senator Tom Connally of Texas, chairman of the Senate Committee on Foreign Relations, spoke for many independent producers opposed to ratification. Their main fear was that large-scale imports of foreign petroleum would seriously depress the domestic industry.[48]

In view of such strong negative reactions to the treaty, Senator Tom Connally predicted its defeat. Therefore, on January 10, 1945, Roosevelt asked the Senate to return the draft for revisions to be made with the help of industry representatives, State Department officials, and members of the Senate Foreign Relations Committee.[49] In September, 1945, Ickes headed an American delegation to England to renegotiate the agreement with the British.[50] Two months later President Truman

47. *Saudi Hearings,* 25, 243–44; Hull, *Memoirs,* II, 1517–1527; Edward R. Stettinius Memo for FDR, February 12, 1944, FDR to Cordell Hull, April 5, 1944, Cordell Hull to FDR, April 7, 1944, in FDR Mss.; Ickes to FDR, August 7, 1944, DI Records; Schwadran, *The Middle East,* 327–329; *O&G Jl.* (March 9, 1944); *NYT,* August 9, 25, 1944.

48. *NYT,* December 3, 1944, March 20, May 18, 22, 1945; *O&G Jl.* (November 25, 1944, December 23, 30, 1944).

49. *CR,* 79 Cong., 1 sess. (January 10, 1945), 179–180; text in *O&G Jl.* (December 16, 1944); *NYT,* January 11, 12, 16, February 23, 27, 1945.

50. *NYT,* September 17, 18, November 2, 1945; text is reproduced in *CR,* 79 Cong., 1 sess. (November 2, 1945), 10,323–324, and in *NYT,* September 25, 1945.

submitted this revised version to the Senate. This time many industry representatives, such as the PIWC and the powerful API, gave their approval to the measure.[51]

But Southwestern opposition had not abated. The Senate did not begin hearings until June, 1947. Domestic producers, especially powerful Texans such as Senator Tom Connally and Speaker Sam Rayburn, were still reluctant. Despite a favorable report from the Senate Foreign Relations Committee on July 1, 1947, the Senate itself took no action on the treaty, and it was not ratified.[52] It had aroused the hostility of the most important domestic producers, who did not feel inclined to compromise. As after World War I, therefore, American oil interests overseas were not defined by international agreement.

In retrospect, it is clear that the myriad of decisions that comprised U.S. oil diplomacy during World War II were based on a few well-established principles. As during the earlier period, the President and the State Department continued to uphold the principle of the Open Door and to support the economic enterprises of American nationals abroad. Such a policy was directed with consummate skill by President Roosevelt between 1941 and 1945, in stark contrast to the fumbling that had characterized similar efforts by Wilson and Harding. But Roosevelt's endeavors to bring the federal government directly into foreign oil production evoked strong protests from influential sectors of the American oil industry, determined to maintain this sphere entirely under the aegis of private enterprise. The prevailing consensus between government and the industry was more tenuous than Roosevelt thought; it did not reach beyond mutual concerns. Industry leaders were eager to secure access to cheap foreign oil, and to conserve their more expensive reserves at home. The federal government, on the other hand, was anxious to safeguard a stable oil supply for the military forces. Thus, their common interests did not extend much beyond implementing the Open Door principle overseas.

Altogether, both businessmen and government officials could take great pride in the achievements of U.S. oil policy during World War II.

51. *NYT,* November 2, 4, 15, 1945.

52. 80 Cong., 1 sess., Senate, Committee on Foreign Relations, *Hearings on Petroleum Agreement with Great Britain and Northern Ireland* [June 2–25, 1947] (Washington, 1947); 79 Cong., 1 sess., Senate, Committee on Foreign Relations, *Report on Anglo-American Oil Agreement* (Washington, 1947).

Much of the credit for accomplishment was due to Harold Ickes and his deputy, Ralph Davies. Despite Ickes' cantankerousness and lust for power, he handled the multifold problems of mobilization with great skill. The imagination of the two men in devising new forms of petroleum transportation averted serious shortages at home and abroad. Their discriminating encouragement of scientific research to boost existing yields and to develop new products greatly augmented available supplies. And their encouragement of domestic producers—while insisting on approved conservation practices—succeeded in meeting most petroleum requirements of the United States and its Allies.

World War II firmly crystallized government's role as arbiter of the American economy, and proved that such a relationship was both practical and efficient. By the standards of pragmatism, the arrangement worked. On the basis of the consensus fashioned during the New Deal, government and business leaders further developed a complicated network of administrative relationships to facilitate their cooperation in the solution of common problems. These included the maintenance of economic stability in the petroleum industry and the conservation of oil. By 1945 the responsibilities of state and federal governments in regulating a wide array of industry practices to achieve these ends was rarely questioned. Rather, the degree of type of regulation occasioned conflict. Slowly, in the course of a generation, the once new relationships had won wide acceptance. And in 1945 there was little reason to believe that they would be seriously disrupted in the postwar decades.

9/ Forging Consensus: Oil Policies Under Truman and Eisenhower

THE DECADE and a half after World War II witnessed few significant changes in American oil policy. These were years of consolidation rather than of innovation and experiment. Both industry and government continued to embrace the twin goals of conservation and economic stabilization. In executing this consensus, in the postwar period they agreed implicitly on the need for federal encouragement through tax benefits and research and for regulation of production by both federal and state authorities. Proposals for direct government ownership and manufacture of petroleum were temporarily laid to rest as production and distribution of petroleum products was left largely to private enterprise. Nor was Harold Ickes' plan to have Congress declare the oil industry a public utility revived. In form and substance, then, the pattern of American oil policy between 1945 and 1960 embraced regulated competition very much as Theodore Roosevelt had envisaged it in his New Nationalism.

THE TRUMAN YEARS

The viability of this consensus was particularly evident through Harry Truman's presidency. Although the new Chief Executive sought numerous changes in U.S. oil policy in order to give the federal government a more direct role in the industry, he found himself thwarted by

Congress in almost every instance. His greatest success, perhaps, came in his gradual dismantlement of wartime controls over oil. Truman's demobilization program allowed for a relatively smooth transition from war to peace that contrasted most favorably with Woodrow Wilson's handling of similar problems in 1918–1919. But his efforts to extend national authority over off-shore tidelands, to reduce the depletion allowance for oil, or to prosecute a vigorous antitrust policy came to naught. Such frustrations were offset only by his Administration's efficient mobilization of the petroleum industry during the Korean War. But both in failure and success his aggressive leadership differed markedly from that of Dwight Eisenhower, who made few recommendations concerning the ends or means of natural resource policies during the ensuing seven years, but who was content, instead, to watch over the execution of existing laws.

Harry Truman was not a complete stranger to oil policy. He had been introduced to the industry's problems in 1943 and 1944 as chairman of the Special Senate Committee to Investigate Defense Expenditures. This group had examined both domestic and foreign aspects of petroleum in considerable depth, so that he was equipped to deal with some of the issues that confronted him in the White House.[1] Most immediate was the dismantlement of the PAW, the alleviation of oil shortages, and the control of prices.

As expected, the end of the war brought a strong Republican demand for the abolition of most wartime agencies, including the PAW. By December, 1945, this body was in the last stages of dissolution as its various division heads presented their final reports to Congress before Senator Joseph O'Mahoney's Special Senate Committee. Meanwhile, the Petroleum Industry War Council voted to dissolve by December 31, 1945, and wound up its meetings before the year was out. Many of its members voted against continuation of a peacetime counterpart because they feared violation of the antitrust laws now that wartime exemptions were no longer in effect. Late in 1945, they felt much uncertainty about

1. 78 Cong., 2 sess., Senate, Special Committee Investigating the National Defense Program, *Senate Report* No. 10 (Washington, 1944); *NYT*, November 6, 1943, February 10, 17, April 18, 1944; *Congressional Record* [hereafter cited as *CR*], 77 Cong., 2 sess. (May 26, 1942), 4544, 4552, *ibid.* (June 15, 1942) 5192–5194, *ibid.*, 78 Cong., 1 sess., (February 15, 1943), 927; Harry S. Truman, *Memoirs* (2 vols., Garden City, 1955–1956), I (*Year of Decisions*), 97, 126–127, 187.

their status in this matter, while the President hesitated about formal abrogation of the wartime program until the following May.[2]

But demobilization of the federal oil program was made without Harold Ickes. The Old Curmudgeon, with an appropriate sense of timing, brought his long (1933–1945) career as Secretary of the Interior to a dramatic close with two bursts of furor. The first led to his resignation from the Cabinet; the second created embarrassment for his deputy in the PAW, Ralph Davies.

The Pauley Incident

The immediate cause for Ickes' departure was Harry Truman's nomination of Edwin Pauley to be Undersecretary of the Navy in January, 1946. Pauley was a prominent California oil operator and also a power in the Democratic Party. In 1945 he served as treasurer of the Democratic National Committee, combining business and politics as he frequently did in his long career. His special interest at the end of the war was to secure the grant of federal tidelands to the states. Since a bill to accomplish this objective was just then being heatedly discussed in Congress during late 1945, his nomination only added to the controversy.[3]

As usual, the Senate Naval Affairs Committee held hearings on Pauley's appointment. Among the parade of witnesses Harold Ickes captured the largest headlines. Ickes charged that while he and Pauley were returning from Franklin D. Roosevelt's funeral on President Truman's train, the California oilman offered him a contribution of several hundred thousand dollars for the Democratic Party campaign fund if the Justice Department would drop a pending federal suit against California, Texas, and several other states to secure title to the offshore tidelands. This accusation Pauley heatedly denied, although Abe Fortas, Ickes' Undersecretary of Interior, confirmed the details of the alleged conversation.[4]

The controversy aroused by Ickes' charges made it doubtful whether the Senate would confirm the nomination. Although President Truman

2. *O&G Jl.* (December 1, 8, 15, 29, 1945, January 5, May 11, 1946); *NYT,* November 28, 1945; Truman, *Memoirs,* I, 487.

3. On Pauley's background, see *NYT,* January 19, 1946, *Current Biography* (June 1945), 457–460; Truman, *Memoirs,* I, 553–555.

4. *NYT,* February 1, 2, 6, 8, 15, 21, 1946; *CR,* 79 Cong., 2 sess. (March 5, 1946), 1893, *ibid.* (March 8, 1946), 2090; *O&G Jl.* (February 16, 23, 1946).

noted publicly that his Secretary of the Interior had a right to his opinions, he was furious, and expressed determination to back Pauley. Consequently he reiterated his support of the California oilman. Some leaders of the oil industry shuddered at the prospect of having an oilman like Pauley in charge of naval oil reserves. Indeed, the editors of the *Oil and Gas Journal* noted that the President's action brought back memories of Teapot Dome. They feared that the publicity engendered by the proposed appointment would do the industry no good. Also, if Pauley's name were not withdrawn, he might damage possible appointments of responsible oil industry leaders to important federal posts in the future. In short, serious oilmen generally opposed the nomination.[5]

Understandably, President Truman could not tolerate Ickes' opposition and even refused to see him. But before he had a chance to act, Ickes announced his intention to leave the Cabinet. At a carefully staged and melodramatic press conference—with more than 300 newsmen present—Ickes proudly announced his resignation. He was leaving the Cabinet, he said, because: "I don't care to stay in an administration where I'm expected to commit perjury for the sake of the party." The President was so incensed that he refused the request of Ickes to remain in office until March 31, 1946, to complete unfinished business, especially pertaining to the tidelands. Instead, Truman insisted that Ickes vacate his office within seventy-two hours, by February 15.[6] Thus did the Old Curmudgeon end twelve years of honest and iron rule of the Department of Interior. Characteristically, he lost the battle, but won the war. A few weeks later, on March 18, 1946, Truman felt compelled to withdraw Pauley's nomination since Senate confirmation seemed unlikely.[7] In view of the developing tidelands issue and Pauley's political connections, the propriety of his nomination was open to question.

5. *NYT*, February 8, 17, 1946; *O&G Jl.* (February 9, 1946), 61; Harold Ickes, *Secret Diary of Harold Ickes* (3 vols., New York, 1953), III, 58, 392, 624–625, relates his early relationships with Pauley.

6. Harold Ickes, "Why I Chose to Resign," *Vital Speeches*, XII (March 15, 1946), 351–352; *NYT*, February 14, 15, 19, 1946; *O&G Jl.* (February 16, 23, March 2, 1946); Harold Ickes to Harry Truman, February 12, 1946, Truman to Ickes, February 13, 1946, Truman Papers, Harry S. Truman Library [hereafter cited as Truman Mss.], Independence, Mo. The two men later patched up their differences at least superficially. See Truman to Ickes, August 29, December 17, 1949, and Ickes to Truman, December 12, 1949, in Truman Mss.

7. *NYT*, March 4, 7, 8, 14, 15, 19, 1946; *O&G Jl.* (March 23, 1946).

Soon thereafter Ickes created another minor furor when he sought to intervene in the management of the Standard Oil Company of California. Seeking a key position for Ralph Davies, his deputy administrator in the PAW, who was just returning to private life, Ickes bought ten shares of Standard Oil Company (Calif.) stock so that he could make an appearance at the annual stockholder's meeting in San Francisco. There, in May, 1945, amid the glare of newspaper publicity, he demanded the immediate reinstatement of Davies as senior vice-president. The latter was mortified, and telegraphed from New York that he would rather resign his present position with the company than to cause it further public embarrassment.[8]

With the departure of Ickes from the Cabinet, President Truman was free to carry out his policies with more tractable subordinates. As his successor he appointed J. A. Krug, who soon inaugurated a businesslike management of the department. Krug, a protégé of David Lilienthal and Donald Nelson, had been chief power engineer of the Tennessee Valley Authority before the war and chairman of the War Production Board after the Nelson-Wilson rift in 1944.[9] For some time Ickes must have viewed him as a competitor.

One of Krug's first actions was to complete the dissolution of the PAW. Its formal demise came on May 8, 1946, when the President issued an executive order declaring it abolished. But the order carefully refrained from mentioning any future federal controls over the oil industry, for Krug feared that this would arouse opposition from the industry and would disrupt their prevailing consensus.[10]

Yet Krug urged that the wartime experiences concerning government cooperation with the oil industry could be incorporated in postwar policies. He revived the old Ickes proposal for establishment of a federal bureau with far-reaching powers over oil production and distribution as in wartime. Its functions were to include close liaison with the industry, coordination and unification of oil policies made by several dozen federal agencies, and collaboration with various organs of state govern-

8. *NYT*, May 2, 3, 1946.
9. *Ibid.*, February 27, March 6, 1946; *The Nation*, CLXII (March 9, 1946), 273.
10. *O&G Jl.* (March 23, May 11, 1946); Truman to Henry Wallace, September 3, 1946, in Truman Mss.; Secretary of the Interior, *Annual Report* 1946 (Washington, 1946), 231–232.

ment. This plan would not, it was hoped, arouse fears of federal centralization among important oil leaders.[11]

Postwar Federal Oil Policy

The abolition of the PAW thus necessitated an immediate decision on a successor peacetime agency and also an assessment of the federal government's postwar oil policies. Throughout the spring of 1946 both leaders of the oil industry and federal officials were making plans for continuing some of the most fruitful relationships that had been developed during the war years. At the same time, therefore, that he was contemplating the final abandonment of the PAW, President Truman instructed Krug to create some other agency to coordinate the petroleum policies of more than thirty federal agencies. As Truman explained: "We have just ended a war in which petroleum and petroleum products played a very important role. It is clear that the war effort was supported to a high degree by the coordinative mechanism that was established in the Government to obtain maximum availability and utilization of petroleum and petroleum products. To embark upon the peacetime era without attempting to discover whether the war experience has applications that would appear to me to be a very real mistake."[12]

In carrying out these instructions, Krug created the Oil and Gas Division in the Department of the Interior. The prime purpose of this agency was not to control, but to coordinate federal policies affecting the petroleum industry. It was designed to serve as a communications link between the federal government and the industry and with state regulatory boards. Its other responsibilities were to act as a clearinghouse for oil and gas statistical and technical data.[13] The Truman Administration thus abandoned the Ickes plan for strong federal control of oil production and distribution, but followed Franklin Roosevelt's policy of loose control.

The reaction of the industry was what Truman hoped it would be. Although the *Oil and Gas Journal* still expressed fears that centralization might be an aim of the Truman Administration, it noted with

11. *O&G Jl.* (May 11, 18, 1946); Harold Smith [Director, Bureau of the Budget], Memo for HST, April 29, 1946, in Truman Mss.
12. Text of Truman's letter in *O&G Jl.* (May 11, 1946), 68.
13. *O&G Jl.* (May 18, June 1, 15, 1946).

satisfaction that neither Congress nor the President had granted any new or additional powers to the Oil and Gas Division, and that the existing détente between government and the industry would not be disturbed.[14]

At the same time Krug took the initiative in revitalizing the Petroleum Industry War Council. A few weeks after he had established the Oil and Gas Division, Krug wrote to Attorney General Tom Clark inquiring about the status of an industry advisory board under the antitrust laws. Clark noted that such consultation would not be considered a conspiracy, although mere membership on the committee would not automatically endow its members with immunity from prosecution under the Sherman Act. Moreover, proposals for investigation of the industry should emanate from the Oil and Gas Division rather than from business representatives.[15]

With these assurances in June, 1946, Krug created a National Petroleum Council. This advisory committee of 85 members included the chief executives of most major oil companies and also representatives from trade associations, producers, and refiners. In fact, small independent companies had a majority of members on the council. The first chairman was Walter Hallahan, president of the Plymouth Oil Company of Charleston, West Virginia. Establishment of such a consulting body represented the realization of a long-standing demand by the industry, which as early as 1929 had contended for some advance exemption from antitrust legislation to carry out consultation. A major function of the council was to serve as the main avenue of communication between the oil industry and the federal government. In addition, it was to undertake studies and investigations concerning problems of oil policy as these arose.[16]

The Truman Administration, therefore, did not inaugurate centralized federal control over oil production. Rather, it continued policies of loose coordination as inaugurated in earlier years by the FOCB in the

14. See, for example, *O&G Jl.* (June 22, 29, 1946).

15. For text of the Krug-Clark Correspondence see *O&G Jl.* (June 29, 1946), 57; see also *ibid.* (June 1, 22, 1946), and *ibid.* (April 27, 1946).

16. Ms. Minutes of National Petroleum Council 1946–1951 are in the National Archives, Washington, D.C., and for later years in Office of Oil and Gas, Department of the Interior, Washington, D.C.; *O&G Jl.* (June 29, 1946), 56; U.S. Dept. of Interior, *Annual Report* 1946.

1920's and the Petroleum Administrative Board in the 1930's. The Oil and Gas Division made investigations of matters such as secondary recovery practices, and drafted needed legislation. Most of its energies were devoted to the gathering of data for federal officials in different agencies. Meanwhile, the National Petroleum Council engaged in studies of the petroleum shortage of 1946 and recommended the lifting of price controls. It also urged the industry to take advantage of the Anti-Inflation Act of 1947, which provided immunity from antitrust prosecution for firms engaging in voluntary allocation and control programs.[17]

The abolition of the PAW did not result in the decontrol of oil prices, however. That authority rested in the hands of the OPA, which was loath to lift its control over the industry during the first half of 1946, especially in view of a severe postwar fuel-oil shortage. Whether there was a cause and effect was widely disputed. In fact, Harold Ickes —long jealous of the power of the OPA—blamed price control for the shortage. Producers diverted crude oil to gasoline rather than fuel oil, he felt. But the OPA was unwilling to lift its ceilings before its authority expired on June 30, 1946. During April and May, officers of the API held conferences with John W. Snyder, director of the Office of War Mobilization and Conversion, but failed to persuade him to order an immediate end to controls over oil. Various moves in Congress to achieve this objective were also to no avail.[18]

While President Truman was dismantling the PAW, Congress was concerned with the formulation of a workable long-range oil policy for peacetime. Already in 1944 the Senate had created a Special Committee Investigating Petroleum Resources, headed by Senator Joseph C. O'Mahoney (Wyo.). The eleven members of this group first investigated the proposed joint wartime project between the government-owned Petroleum Reserves Corporation and the Arabian-American Oil Company to build a Saudi Arabia pipeline. In June, 1945, the Senate instructed the committee also to investigate American oil investments

17. In addition to Minutes of NPC, see Secretary of the Interior, *Annual Report* 1947 (Washington, 1947), 269; *ibid.* 1948 (Washington, 1948), 249–252; *ibid.,* 1949 (Washington, 1949), 212–213.

18. *O&G Jl.* (January 5, April 20, 27, May 4, 25, June 22, 29, 1946); *NYT,* March 10, 14, 22, 23, April 2, May 30, June 14, 23, July 8, 11, 1946; *CR,* 79 Cong., 2 sess., Appendix (March 8, 1946), 1295–1297 (March 13, 1946), 1327– 1328 (March 25, 1946), 1618–1620 (May 9, 1946), 2569–2571.

overseas, the extent of domestic oil resources and requirements, and, in addition, the disposal of war petroleum manufacturing properties. On the basis of its findings the committee formulated recommendations for a national oil policy.[19]

After extensive hearings during the latter half of 1945 the committee presented its conclusions. To everyone's surprise the testimony revealed that there was much satisfaction with existing policies, and very little sentiment for change. Consequently, the committee did not advocate any great alterations in U.S. oil policy.[20]

In following many of the Petroleum Industry War Council's guidelines, the senators agreed with industry leaders that U.S. oil policy should continue to reflect at least four characteristics. First, it was agreed that the petroleum industry should remain primarily in the hands of private enterprise. Secondly, federal policy should encourage petroleum production by granting tax relief, either through depletion allowances or for intangible drilling. Third, the federal government was to encourage conservation. Since the states controlled most of the details concerning regulation of conservation practices, the prime effort of the national government in this sphere would be through enforcement of the Connally Act to supplement state regulatory efforts. Finally, federal policy was to encourage overseas development of foreign oil sources by U.S. companies. This would not only conserve the domestic supply at home, but would also prepare for unforeseen military needs. Such a program required a delicate balance between foreign oil imports and domestic U.S. production. Duties on imported crude oils must be high enough to encourage American producers, yet not so high as to keep out foreign oil that supplemented U.S. resources. An effort to draw on foreign oil also required American diplomatic support for U.S. oil com-

19. 79 Cong., 1 sess., Senate, Special Committee Investigating Petroleum Resources Pursuant to Senate Resolution 36, *Senate Report* No. 179 (Washington, 1945).

20. *O&G Jl.* (March 30, 1946); 79 Cong., 2 sess., Senate, Special Committee Investigating Petroleum Resources (O'Mahoney Committee), *Hearings, 1945–1946* (6 parts, Washington, 1945–1946), including *American Petroleum Interests in Foreign Countries,* June 27, 28, 1945; *The Independent Petroleum Company,* March 19, 20, 21, 22, 27, 28, 1946; *Investigation of Petroleum Resources,* June 19, 20, 21, 22, 25, 1945; *Petroleum Requirements—Post-War,* October 3, 4, 1945; *War Emergency Pipeline Systems and Other Petroleum Facilities,* November 15, 16, 17, 1945; *Wartime Petroleum Policy Under the Petroleum Administration for War,* November 28, 29, 30, 1945.

panies engaged in overseas oil exploitation, in a manner, it was hoped, more effective than in the years after World War I.[21]

Four years later the National Petroleum Council issued its own report on guidelines for a national oil policy. In their appraisal of desirable goals and means of public policy, the representatives from the industry differed very little from Senator O'Mahoney and his senatorial colleagues. Government sought conservation to meet domestic and military needs. Industry desired conservation as a method of stabilizing production and increasing its efficiency. The existing network of relationships between them had succeeded in the attainment of their common goals. Thus, the report urged retention of the depletion allowance and scientific aid by the United States Geological Survey and the United States Bureau of Mines. The council strongly favored state conservation laws, implemented by the Connally Hot Oil Act. And they strongly urged U.S. diplomatic support for American oil companies in foreign lands.[22]

An additional dimension to this consensus was added by a special committee that President Truman appointed in 1949 to make a comprehensive study of all of the nation's energy requirements. This group of distinguished citizens undertook an exhaustive study of the nation's present and future needs. Headed by William S. Paley of the Columbia Broadcasting System, it revealed great breadth in its outlook. But the committee left most of the labor required to make an extensive five-volume report to its large research staff. Among members of these working groups bitter conflicts broke out over the nature of recommendations concerning future policies. As a result, the final proposals were broad, bland, and general, apparently designed to avoid controversy. In regard to petroleum the committee urged no important changes in federal or state policies, and especially recommended continuation of depletion allowances.[23]

The prime task of the Truman Administration, then, was not so much to innovate in the formulation of new lines of public policy as to

21. 80 Cong., 1 sess., Senate, Special Committee Investigating Petroleum Resources, *Final Report,* in *Senate Report* No. 9 (Washington, 1947), 5–59; see also *O&G Jl.* (April 6, 1946).

22. National Petroleum Council, *A National Oil Policy for the United States: A Report* (Washington, 1949), 3 ff.

23. U.S., President's Materials Policy Commission, *Resources for Freedom* (5 parts, Washington, 1952), I, 25–36, II, 129–131, 167–169.

implement programs that were first crystallized by the New Deal and that were now firmly embedded in public policy in the half dozen years after World War II. In this period leaders in government and industry worked out a consensus governing oil policies, as reflected in the 1949 Report of the National Petroleum Council. Even the President, with his great powers and prestige, was unable to make significant modification of this consensus, for he was dependent on the industry for maintaining adequate petroleum supplies to serve national defense, whether by conservation at home or by development of foreign sources.

The Tidelands Issue

Despite some efforts at change, President Truman envisaged no drastic modification of existing policies. He did not tinker with depletion allowances and other tax benefits or the tariff during his first term in office (1945–1948). Nor was Thurman Arnold's antitrust policy revived. Since the Interstate Oil Compact was unexpectedly successful in coordinating state conservation legislation, Washington left this sphere largely untouched. Truman's concern with national security, however, led him to take a strong stand against the grant of offshore tidelands to the states. He hoped to secure direct access to petroleum resources for the federal government but in this stand he was eventually overruled by Congress. The Fair Deal for oil, therefore, largely consolidated the New Deal. Its program was one of attending to business left unfinished by wartime interruptions rather than one of bold departures.

The disposition of the offshore tidelands along the East Coast, the Gulf, and the Pacific slope had simmered as an issue in Congress since the second Roosevelt Administration. It became controversial at that time largely because of the development of new technological processes which made it possible to tap oil resources under the ocean floor.[24]

Consequently, in 1937, Secretary Ickes persuaded Senator Gerald P. Nye to introduce a bill declaring that lands under the marginal seas of the coastal states were part of the federal domain. In the course of debate the Senate transformed it into a resolution, which was passed on August 19, 1937. This directed Attorney General Biddle to assert federal title over the tidelands in view of the increasing number of private individuals who were extracting oil there. A year later, in February,

24. The best discussion of background is in Ernest R. Bartley, *The Tidelands Oil Controversy* (Austin, 1953), 27–94.

1938, Chairman Hatton Summers (Tex.) of the House Judiciary Committee held hearings on the resolution, but the House failed to take any action.[25] In 1939 Senator Nye revived the issue, encouraged as he was by the report of the National Resources Committee (headed by Ickes), which urged a strengthening of federal claims in the interests of petroleum conservation. This plea was reinforced by military planners. The Secretary of the Navy wrote a letter to the Chairman of the Senate Public Lands Committee in 1940 urging adoption of a law declaring submerged tidelands as a portion of the public domain. Occupied with problems of national defense, Congress neglected to consider the proposal, however. And during the next two years, the war made the dispute academic.[26]

Throughout these years Harold Ickes persisted in seeking formal recognition of federal ownership of the offshore tidelands. When he first broached the matter to Roosevelt at a White House luncheon in 1937 the President told him to get a legal opinion on the matter. Whether Roosevelt ever authorized Ickes to press a federal suit, however, is questionable. Nevertheless, Ickes persisted and did not forget this problem amid his wartime duties. Soon after the end of hostilities he approached Harry Truman with respect to the issue.[27]

President Truman was sympathetic to extending national jurisdiction over the tidelands. Prompted by the postwar revival of conservation sentiment, on September 28, 1945, he issued a proclamation announcing that the U.S. government regarded natural resources of the subsoil and sea bed of the continental shelf as federal property. Although this statement was designed to clarify the federal government's position in international law, its implications for domestic policy were clear, for it constituted a barrier to possible state claims of areas beyond the three-

---

25. Ickes, *Secret Diary,* II, 127, 330–331, 426; Bartley, *Tidelands,* 101–102; 75 Cong., 3 sess., House, Judiciary Committee, *Hearings on Senate Joint Resolution 208* (Washington, 1938), 5.

26. *CR,* 76 Cong., 1 sess. (March 14, 1938), 2689; 75 Cong., 3 sess., *House Report No. 2378* (Washington, 1938); National Resources Committee, *Energy Resources and National Policy* (Washington, 1939), 230–231; FDR at Press Conference, April 18, 1940, *Transcript of FDR Press Conferences,* XI, 260, FDR Mss.

27. 75 Cong., 3 sess., House, Judiciary Committee, *Hearings on Senate Joint Resolution 208,* 31; Ickes, *Secret Diary,* III, 127; Bartley, *Tidelands,* 137; 80 Cong., 2 sess., Judiciary Committees, House and Senate, *Joint Hearings on S. 1988* (Washington, 1948), 1119, 1124–1131.

mile limit. Truman further showed his intent to extend federal authority over the offshore lands by successfully vetoing a Congressional resolution that would have surrendered them to the states. And he was persuaded by Harold Ickes to institute direct legal action to secure explicit recognition of national control. Accordingly, he authorized Attorney General Tom Clark to file an original suit against California in the United States Supreme Court. This was three months after the previous Attorney General, Biddle, had filed an action against the Pacific Western Oil Company in the Federal District Court for Southern California to the great dismay of Ickes, who hoped to bring the matter immediately before the United States Supreme Court.[28]

While these cases were pending in 1945, the tidelands issue unexpectedly became front-page news. When the President submitted Edwin Pauley's name to the Senate for confirmation as Under-Secretary of the Navy, it provided Harold Ickes with an opportunity to make a grand play for federal ownership of the tidelands. Ickes charged that Pauley had offered a bribe in the form of a $300,000 contribution to the Democratic Party campaign fund if he held up the federal tidelands suit. Suddenly the whole nation learned of the looming struggle for the tidelands.[29]

Although two legal actions regarding the tidelands were pending in the courts between 1945 and 1947, interest centered largely on the original suit filed by the federal government against California in the United States Supreme Court. The state compiled a voluminous brief (weighing 3 lbs. 9 ounces) and made a strong case for its claims. But in *United States* vs. *California,* in June, 1947, a majority of a divided court decided in favor of federal jurisdiction. Justice Hugo Black wrote the 5-5 opinion, which denied California jurisdiction over the offshore areas. But he refrained from any discussion of actual ownership by either the state or the federal government.[30]

Yet the issue was hardly settled. The advocates of states' rights now shifted the struggle from the courts to Congress. Spurred by fears that similar federal suits would be filed against Louisiana and Texas, they had scores of bills introduced in Congress during 1948 to quiet federal

28. Bartley, *Tidelands,* 137–138, 161.

29. See *supra,* p. 182 ff.; *NYT,* February 6, 7, 8, 1946; *O&G Jl.,* February 9, 1946.

30. 332 U.S. 19; Bartley, *Tidelands,* 159–181, discusses the issues in detail.

claims. At the same time, proponents of national control also sponsored appropriate legislation. The struggle between them was to continue for five years. While the advocates of state ownership had a majority in Congress they knew that they did not have sufficient strength to override a probable presidential veto. Each year during this period Congressional committees held hearings on the issue while Senate and House members argued its merits.[31] Finally, in April and May, 1952, the Senate and the House by substantial majorities approved a compromise bill allowing state claims. But on May 29, 1952, the President sent the measure back with a relatively conciliatory veto message in which he reasserted national preeminence. He invited Congress to develop another bill, one in which 37.5 percent of royalties from tideland oil produced under federal authority would be returned to the states. Since Congress could not muster the necessary two-thirds majority to override the veto, it stood, and the tidelands issue entered the presidential campaign of 1952.[32]

The major parties in 1952 offered the voters a clear choice on the tidelands issue. Adlai Stevenson and the Democrats decidedly opposed any surrender of federal claims to the continental shelf. On the other hand, the Republican candidate, Dwight Eisenhower, took an unequivocal position in favor of deeding the offshore properties to the states. The two viewpoints were discussed widely in the press and the ensuing election virtually settled the controversy.[33]

The Eisenhower Administration lost little time in implementing the Republican position. With the knowledge that the new occupant of the

31. *CR,* 81 Cong., 1 sess. (H.R. 180); *CR,* 81 Cong., 1 sess. (S. 155); *CR,* 81 Cong., 2 sess. (H.R. 8137); *CR,* 80 Cong., 2 sess. (S. 2165, H.R. 5528); *CR,* 81 Cong., 1 sess. (S. 923). The 80th Congress witnessed 33 bills to confirm state titles, and the 81st Congress, 32 bills. (*CR,* 80 Cong., 2 sess., *Index,* 458; *CR,* 81 Cong., 1 sess., *Index,* 624). Bartley, Tidelands, 213–246, discusses some of this legislation and the Congressional hearings. For a listing of 16 Congressional hearings on the tidelands between 1937 and 1953 see Bartley, *Tidelands,* 285–286.

32. *CR,* 82 Cong., 2 sess., Senate Joint Resolution 20, (May 16, 1952); 5335 (May 19, 1952); 5391–5393; Truman's veto message is in 82 Cong., 2 sess., *Senate Document* No. 139 (Washington, 1952); *NYT,* April 3, 4, 6, May 7, 16, 17, 18, text of veto, May 30, 1952.

33. Kirk Porter and Donald B. Johnson (eds.), *American Party Platforms, 1840–1960* (New York, 1961), 502; Eisenhower's speech advocating state ownership is in *NYT,* October 14, 1952; see *NYT,* July 1, 1952, concerning Stevenson, and for text of his plea for federal ownership see *NYT,* August 24, 1952.

White House favored the formal surrender of federal claims to the continental shelf, Congress passed two important measures. The first of these was the Submerged Lands Act of May 22, 1953, which President Eisenhower approved with enthusiasm. It deeded title and ownership of the tidelands (within the three-mile continental limit) to the states. This included all natural resources under navigable tidal waters seaward to a state's historical boundaries upon entering the Union, to a distance of not more than three geographical miles from the coastline to the Atlantic or Pacific, or more than three marine leagues into the Gulf of Mexico.[34] A few months later, on August 7, 1953, Congress enacted the Outer Continental Shelf Act, which designated the area outside state limits as the Outer Continental Shelf, under exclusive federal jurisdiction. The Secretary of the Interior could lease such areas in lots not to exceed 5,760 acres through competitive bidding. By 1958 a total of 1,586,709 acres had been so leased.[35] Thus the struggle over ownership of these valuable lands culminated in a victory for advocates of state and private ownership.

The disposition of the tideland issue reflected divergent assumptions about the fundamental aims of national resource policy, much as after World War I. That the national government required large potential petroleum reserves to serve the needs of national defense was clear. But what were the best means to achieve this aim? The Democratic position was one that placed primary reliance on direct federal control over exploitation of the potentially oil-rich tidelands in the future. Many Republican partisans claimed that state ownership would lead to more rapid exploitation by private individuals, and hence result in the availability of more and cheaper oil to meet governmental needs. Certainly these were not the only motivations of those who took a stand in this debate. It was a stand, basically, over the best means of exploitation, with arguments similar to those used between 1917 and 1924 by Josephus Daniels and Franklin K. Lane in the debate over the naval oil reserves.

34. *CR*, 83 Cong., 1 sess., *Senate Joint Resolution* 13 (May 5, 1953), 4488, 4905, *ibid.* (May 14, 1943), 4953, *ibid.* (June 1, 1953), 5842; *NYT*, April 1, 2, 5, 6, May 6, 23, 1953.

35. *CR*, 83 Cong., 1 sess. (July 30, 1953), 10500 (H.R. 5134), *ibid.* (August 1, 1953), 10955; *NYT*, May 14, 15, July 30, August 8, 1953; Secretary of the Interior, *Annual Report* 1958 (Washington, 1958), 273.

The Korean War

If long-range oil policies such as the dispute over the offshore tide-lands progressively tended to take on a less urgent aspect, this was due to the outbreak of the Korean War, which created new resource problems for the Truman Administration. To supply more than a quarter of a million men in the United Nation forces in the Far East presented problems of supply and transportation not dissimilar to those of the recently concluded World War.

Congress responded to the challenge by conferring sweeping emergency powers on the President. The Defense Production Act of 1950 was as broad in scope as the Lever Act had been in 1917, and endowed Truman with wide authority over the mobilization of natural resources. Acting under this mandate, the Chief Executive on October 3, 1950, created the Petroleum Administration for Defense (PAD). Established largely in the image of the PAW, the task of this emergency agency was to allocate petroleum products, to arrange transportation, and to make forecasts for anticipating future needs. Nominally under the Secretary of the Interior, the PAD was under the actual supervision of Bruce K. Brown, the Deputy Administrator. Brown, a former vice-president of Standard Oil (Indiana), infused the PAD with much energy and recalled many former executives of the PAW to join his staff during the Korean crisis.[36]

One of the most immediate problems of the PAD was the shortage of high-octane aviation gasoline. Brown met this difficulty by coordinating the efforts of the industry with various organs of government. He selected individuals from the Military Petroleum Advisory Board to work with representatives from industry and from the Defense Department. Such cooperation made it possible to meet the war requirements. Another bottleneck was the shortage of necessary equipment to increase oil production. For this purpose the PAD created a Materials Division, which allotted equipment needed by the oil industry. It also worked out

---

36. Brown discusses his Korean War experiences in detail in *Oil Men in Washington; an informal account of the organization and activities of the Petroleum Administration for Defense during the Korean War, 1950–1952* (no publ., 1965); see also Bruce K. Brown Memo for Oscar Chapman, February 5, 1951, Oscar Chapman to George A. Wilson, May 16, 1951, Oscar Chapman to Lyndon B. Johnson, July 11, 1951, Secretary of the Interior, Administrative Files, National Archives [hereafter cited as DI Records], Washington, D.C.

cooperative procurement programs with other federal agencies. During the first months of operation, therefore, the PAD provided administrative machinery for coordination of federal activities, which facilitated the flow of oil to the armed forces in the Far East.[37]

The PAD's efforts at home were rendered more difficult by the oil crisis in Iran, which caused serious dislocations in the American petroleum supply. As the Iranian government prepared to nationalize the country's petroleum resources it temporarily disrupted the regular flow of oil to the West. For the United States this could not have come at a more inopportune time. The PAD was forced to seek other sources of crude oil supplies to make up for the amounts usually imported from Iran. Pressed at home and abroad, the PAD utilized Section 708 of the Defense Production act of 1950. This allowed private oil companies exemption from the antitrust laws and from Federal Trade Commission rulings, so that they could enter upon voluntary agreements and supply pools to provide oil in periods of emergency. Under the guidance of the PAD, nineteen U.S. oil firms formulated such a voluntary scheme, administered by a Foreign Petroleum Supply Committee appointed by the PAD Administrator and composed of representatives of participating companies. This pooling of available oil resources alleviated the shortage caused by the cessation of the Iranian supply and quickly tapped alternate sources.[38]

The PAD also encouraged oil production through special financial inducements. Under the Defense Production Act it was authorized to offer accelerated mortage loans to companies seeking to expand their output. Slightly more than half of the companies undertaking such expansion programs took advantage of this privilege.[39]

37. Secretary of the Interior, *Annual Report* 1951 (Washington, 1952), 437–438, *ibid.*, 1952 (Washington, 1953), 475–477; *NYT*, February 1, April 1, May 27, June 23, 1951, February 19, 1952.

38. Secretary of the Interior, *Annual Report* 1951, 440, *ibid.* 1954 (Washington, 1954), 209; *O&G Jl.* (March 8, 15, 22, 1951); A. P. Frame to Oscar Chapman, April 25, 1951, in DI Records, reveals initial PAD program in response to the Iranian crisis; Bruce K. Brown to Oscar Chapman, June 25, 1952, in DI Records, reviews PAD work in voluntary import program; Oscar Chapman to Henry Fowler, September 26, 1952, in DI Records, discusses termination of program.

39. Oscar Chapman to Bruce K. Brown, April 6, 1951, Bruce K. Brown to Ellis Arnall, February 29, 1952, in DI Records; S. L. Digby to Dean Acheson, September 18, 1952, in Truman Mss.

As the Korean War drew to a close, the PAD, having successfully accomplished the job of supplying the fuel requirements of American forces in the Far East, dissolved. By March, 1953, it lifted most controls on strategic materials and withdrew the authorization allowing large companies to pool oil supplies. Nevertheless, the Defense Department felt that the production forecasts of the Foreign Petroleum Supply Committee were still so essential to national security that the committee functioned for another year. On April 30, 1954, President Eisenhower finally abolished the PAD by executive order.[40] Some of its activities were continued by the Military Petroleum Advisory Board—composed of experts from the industry—and the Military Fuels General Advisory Committee—composed of technical experts. Both of these groups worked on forecasts of oil requirements for the military forces.

The Depletion Allowance

During the war President Truman also failed to secure a reduction in the depletion allowance for oil producers. To be sure, they were not the only group to benefit from this privilege. Miners of coal, sulfur, uranium, and other minerals were also permitted to deduct varying amounts. But oilmen were allowed the largest percentage deduction and were thus peculiarly vulnerable. And to a larger extent than in earlier years, percentage depletion aroused controversy during the Truman and Eisenhower eras.

President Truman (and his Secretary of the Treasury, John W. Snyder) urged a reduction of the oil percentage depletion allowance in the midst of his second term. As an old New Dealer, perhaps Truman remembered that in 1933 Roosevelt had made a similar proposal. He was aided by a small but vociferous bipartisan minority of senators who without much success labored to secure a revision of the tax structure in Congress. The coalition included Senators Paul Douglas (Ill.), Hubert Humphrey (Minn.), William Proxmire (Wis.), and John Williams (Del.), who for a decade after 1949 kept the matter continually before the lawmakers.

President Truman broached the issue in his annual tax message of January, 1950. There he pleaded not for the abolition of depletion credits, but for their reduction. Meanwhile, his arguments before the

40. Secretary of the Interior, *Annual Report* 1954, 207–210.

House Ways and Means Committee were amplified by Secretary of the Treasury John W. Snyder. The President did not wish to do away with the allowance, Snyder said, but merely sought a reduction of the 27½ percent allowance to 15 percent of gross income. The original level had been determined by Congress as a rather arbitrary compromise in 1926 when oil exploration was a more risky enterprise than it was thirty years later. A related tax loophole was the intangible drilling allowance for producers, Snyder felt, which he wished abolished. But Congress was not persuaded by his plea. Later in the year the House Ways and Means Committee voted to retain the 27½ percent rate, and the ensuing Revenue Act of 1950 made no changes.[41]

Despite this setback, in the following year Truman renewed his request. Once again he used his annual tax message to Congress to advocate a reduction in the depletion allowance for oil producers. On the floor of the Senate the freshman senator from Minnesota, Hubert Humphrey, took up the battle before an empty chamber. In an elaborate argument, Humphrey cogently presented many of the general points advocated by those who favored a somewhat lower tax exemption. Humphrey noted first that the amount of percentage depletion bore no relation to the capital cost of property, but only to income. Unlike other corporations, therefore, oil producers and refiners escaped a large share of taxation. In a memorandum prepared by the United States Treasury on the subject, its statisticians estimated that in 1947 this amounted to about $400 million annually. In the second place, Humphrey argued, depletion was of prime benefit to large producers with capital investment of $100 millions or more, and not to small producers, as was so often claimed. The Treasury report estimated that 80 percent of the depletion benefits went to these giant enterprises. Third, he pointed out that although depletion was granted to other mineral producers, it constituted a special privilege for the oilmen, since 85 percent of all federal depletion deductions were allowed for petroleum. Moreover, two-thirds of these enterprises were engaged in manufacture rather than in the production of oil products. Finally, he felt that conditions in the petroleum industry had changed greatly since

41. *NYT,* January 24, 1950; also 81 Cong., 2 sess., *Senate Document* No. 451 (Washington, 1950).

Congress had established the 27 ½ percent allowance in 1926, and that risks were no longer as great as they had once been.[42]

The advocates of the depletion allowance were quick to respond with counterarguments. They included not only spokesmen for the large integrated oil companies and the API, but also the representatives of the smaller, independent oil producers, and Congressional and state representatives from large oil-producing states. Senator Lyndon B. Johnson (Texas) was one of their most vocal spokesmen, along with John Carlson (Kansas) and Matthew Neely (W. Va.). They were supported by petitions from the Texas legislature and the governors of Kansas and Oklahoma. Senator Lyndon B. Johnson in particular emphasized the needs of national security. These required encouragement of domestic production, he felt, so as to provide an excess capacity of petroleum for unforeseen emergencies equal to 15 percent of annual production. Secondly, he argued that dividend payments of oil companies would decline by about $500 million in the depletion allowance were reduced. Companies would then have to rely more on outside capital for financing. This would not only reduce production, Johnson and Neely argued, but would diminish the tax payments of the companies to the federal government, not to speak of the diminished tax payments of their stockholders. A reduction could undermine the economic stability of the entire nation.[43]

The group also adduced other reasons. They challenged the proposition that federal tax revenues would be increased by a reduction of the depletion allowance. Rather, it would force oil companies to raise prices. Such a step could lead to a decline of consumption, and a possible slowdown of the national rate of economic growth. Moreover, expenses of drilling were increasing, since producers found it necessary to bore deeper than in previous years. In 1958 only thirteen barrels of oil were secured for every foot drilled, compared to twenty-seven barrels in 1946. Capital requirements for production were also increasing

42. *NYT,* February 3, 1951; 81 Cong., 2 sess., House Committee on Ways and Means, *House Report* No. 2319 (Washington, 1950); see also 81 Cong., 2 sess., *Senate Report* No. 2375 (Washington, 1950), 66, 91; *CR,* 82 Cong., 1 sess. (September 28, 1951), 12306–12312, 12318; for a selection of opinions see *CR,* 82 Cong., 1 sess., *Appendix,* A900, A1188, A1196.
43. *CR,* 82 Cong., 1 sess. (September 28, 1951), 12,320–12,334.

rapidly, rising to about 50 percent of gross sales after royalties between 1946 and 1956, compared to an increase of only 10 percent in general manufacturing. Thus, the depletion allowance was an important incentive to new exploration and production.[44]

These various arguments helped to clarify a complex issue. In effect, the depletion allowance amounted to a federal subsidy for oil producers. Whether or not this was desirable—or necessary—was certainly debatable. Conclusions concerning the question depended not only on one's basic assumptions about natural resource policy, however. Increasingly, considerations of national defense complicated the formulation of federal action in this sphere as a growing military establishment became dependent on the industry for its multifaceted needs. A majority in Congress thus seemed to be concerned not with the economic arguments for and against the depletion allowance. They were more impressed by the fact that since 1926 it apparently had acted as an incentive for oil producers who had amply served the nation's needs during the automobile revolution and in two world wars, and in lesser crises. Rightly or wrongly, they believed, it worked. And this pragmatic view found wide acceptance among legislators who were apprehensive about tampering with an established policy device. The Senate defeated the Humphrey amendment by the overwhelming vote of seventy-one to nine.[45]

The dismantling of the PAD coincided with the departure of Harry Truman from the White House. During his tenure he had shown an active interest in the formulation of a national oil program. But the vigor of his efforts was matched only by his inability to secure acceptance of most of his proposals. His conception of policy aims was clear. The goals of federal resource policy still included conservation—to meet not only the rising domestic needs but also the burgeoning requirements of a rapidly growing military establishment. The economic stability of the industry continued to be a matter of national concern. But as markets expanded proportionately more rapidly than production in the years after World War II, depression problems of underconsumption did not become an issue. These goals could be accomplished best,

44. *Ibid.*, 85 Cong., 1 sess. (March 27, 1957), 4492–4498; *ibid.*, 85 Cong., 2 sess. (August 11, 1958), 16895–16900, 16918–16944.
45. *Ibid.*, 82 Cong., 1 sess. (September 28, 1951), 12334.

Truman believed, by strengthening federal powers over operations in the industry.

In his approach to resource policies Harry Truman showed himself to be not only a follower of the New Deal but of the New Nationalism as well. Perhaps his emphasis on direct federal action to safeguard the nation's petroleum supply was too blunt for Congress. His most successful achievement was his insistence on gradual, rather than immediate, abolishment of wartime controls over the oil industry during 1945 and 1946. His role during this period contrasted favorably with the abrupt abolition of the Fuel Administration by Woodrow Wilson in 1919, and allowed producers and marketers to make a much smoother readjustment.

Otherwise, Truman's efforts to shape national oil policies did not bear fruit. His attempt to secure title to the offshore tidelands as a means of allowing for direct federal control of new oil resources was eventually overridden by Congress. His campaign to secure a reduction of the depletion allowance failed to gather widespread support. The Paley Commission's findings were pallid. And, ironically, the President's effort to appoint Edwin Pauley as Under-Secretary of the Navy tainted him—in the public eye—with seeming political corruption. The Truman Administration thus had relatively little impact on national oil policies—in contributing either new goals or new methods—despite strenuous efforts by the Chief Executive. But it consolidated many New Deal measures.

THE EISENHOWER YEARS

In marked contrast to the vigor with which Harry Truman approached natural resource policies, his successor, Dwight Eisenhower, played a passive role and eschewed strong leadership. Between 1953 and 1960 he tried—whenever possible—to refrain from taking action. When this seemed unavoidable he preferred to delegate his responsibility to committees. Even then he sought to refrain from decisive measures except where crises virtually forced his hand. Since he showed little awareness of the problems involved in a national oil program during his two terms, it would be difficult to ascribe a positive course of policy to the President. Indeed, he seemed content to leave well enough alone. When called upon to exercise his executive authority he responded with great reluctance. That was shown in the dispute over oil imports and in the battle over reduction of the depletion allowance for oil producers. The Eisenhower era, even more than the Truman era, was a period of consolidation in federal oil policies, noted for lack of innovation.

Oil Imports

Perhaps the major problem of oil policy that Eisenhower could not shake off was the increasingly controversial issue of oil imports. It was a matter that stemmed from the Depression, when the glut of foreign oil—much of it produced by the major integrated companies in the Middle East and South America—depressed domestic markets. Largely as a result of agitation by midcontinent producers who feared this competition, Congress, in 1932, imposed a tariff on imported oil. In succeeding years both Congress and the Presidents maintained this levy. From 1932 to 1945 there was little discussion of the issue, since yearly foreign oil imports usually amounted to less than 5 percent of total annual production in the United States. These imports really did not become an acute problem until the immediate post-World-War-II era, when the amount of such crude petroleum shipments increased sharply, doubling between 1945 and 1950. Along with this rise came a strong outcry from Texas and Oklahoma producers, fearful of cheap competition and the power of the giants of the American oil industry. Oil imports, then, pitted independent producers against the mighty integrated corporations with their far-flung producing wells in virtually every corner of the globe.

At a time when the United States was a major world power the controversy transcended the mere interests of the disputants, however. Imports of oil raised numerous important considerations. First, foreign supplies directly affected the output of domestic producers, particularly those in the Southwest. The decade after 1954 saw an increasing awareness of depressed areas within the United States, such as Appalachia. And a growing unemployment rate focused attention on maintenance of a rapid rate of economic growth at home. In addition, such concern for economic stability was compounded by diplomatic problems. American purchase of petroleum from various foreign nations—such as Venezuela, Saudi Arabia, and others—constituted the main prop of their economies. If the United States was to retain their good will in the midst of the Cold War with Russia, it was essential to keep American petroleum markets open to them on a limited scale. Political considerations were therefore as important as strictly economic factors. In addition, the lower price of oil production outside the United States—with resultant benefits for the American consumer—merited some consideration. Finally, the President and the National Security Council could hardly ignore their military needs, which made it desirable to keep excess foreign oil sources open. Defense requirements in the 1950's demanded maintenance of a potential stored oil reserve equal to about 20 percent of annual domestic production. Emergencies such as the Korean War showed the wisdom of keeping such available stockpiles in readiness.[46]

With his characteristic penchant for delegation, President Eisenhower in 1954 appointed a Cabinet Committee on Energy Supplies to consider the oil import problem. Composed of the Director of Defense Mobilization, and the Secretaries of the Treasury, Interior, Commerce, and State, this group was similar to the FOCB that Coolidge had created. They were to undertake a comprehensive study of the nation's available supply of energy resources and particularly to make recommendations concerning the oil supply problem.[47]

Although slated to make its report before the end of 1954, the committee did not present its conclusions until February 26, 1955. It noted that national security would best be served by allowing oil imports into the United States if the quantity was kept in the same ratio to domestic production as during 1954. Since supply conditions were likely to change, the report noted the desirability of maintaining flexible ratios between domestic production and foreign imports in response to fluctuating demand. This could be done, the committee hoped, by Hooverian techniques, such as voluntary cooperation. Consequently, it urged the large oil importers to make voluntary restriction plans. Although all of the members of this committee were close associates of the President, he himself declined to express any opinion concerning their suggestions. Uncommitted, he neither approved nor rejected their proposals.[48]

---

46. *Supra*, p. 195 ff.; *CR*, 84 Cong., 2 sess. (July 27, 1956), 15022–15023, *ibid.* (March 8, 1956), 4345, *ibid.* (June 11, 1956), 10086–10087, *ibid.* (June 12, 1956), 10125, 10130, *ibid.* (June 18, 1956), 13333–13334; *O&G Jl.* (March 14, 1955).

47. *NYT*, July 31, 1954; *O&G Jl.* (August 9, 1954).

48. President's Cabinet Committee on Energy Supplies [Minerals Policy], *Report 1954* (processed); *O&G Jl.* (March 7, 1955) has text of *Report*; see also *O&G Jl.* (March 14, 1955), *NYT*, February 27, 28, 1955.

Many oil producers were unhappy with the committee's report. They wondered, too, about the unwillingness of the President to commit himself or his Administration to a clear course of action on the question. Independent oilmen desired the imposition of stricter import curbs, and they gleaned little comfort from the Administration's straddling.[49]

Unable to secure direction from the White House, the advocates of import restrictions turned their attention to Congress. Their intense lobbying was reflected in the heated debate over the Reciprocal Trades Agreement Act of 1955. On the floor of the House and in the Senate the advocates of restriction made impassioned pleas for curtailing the growing volume of foreign oil imported into the United States. It was averaging about 12 percent of total annual domestic production in the 1950's. But perhaps because of larger considerations of military and foreign policy, the Administration made no effort to support the demands of the domestic producers, and the Reciprocal Trades Agreement Act of 1955 passed both houses by large majorities. In the House even the Louisiana delegation was unanimously for the act, while Representatives from Texas split their vote. They were obviously swayed by considerations of foreign policy. The *Oil and Gas Journal* noted bitterly that most of the representatives from oil states had voted for the Act. The only solace for the independents was a compromise clause in the bill authorizing the President to impose import quotas whenever the imports of any article were so large as to constitute a threat to the national economy or to security.[50]

The Eisenhower Administration sought to placate the dissidents by urging the major companies to adopt a voluntary program of restricted oil imports. This proposal was reminiscent of the Hoover program of 1931 and 1932, which had broken down during its first three months of operation. A quarter of a century later this experience was to be repeated. To be sure, during most of 1955 the major oil companies did make a sincere effort to cooperate in curbing crude imports from their foreign producing properties. But fluctuations in the oil trade, and blatant violations as well, soon resulted in the breakdown of the voluntary

49. *O&G Jl.* (March 7, 1955).
50. *CR,* 85 Cong., 1 sess. (July 31, 1957), 13141–13142, *ibid.,* 86 Cong., 1 sess. (March 26, 1959), 5313–5325; *O&G Jl.* (March 7, 14, May 9, June 6, 13, November 7, 1955).

program in the early months of 1956. By that time many importers were planning large-scale expansion far exceeding the recommended ratios of the Presidential committee. Although the Office of Defense Mobilization was holding hearings on the issue in the spring of 1956 it was powerless to take immediate and effective action.[51]

The outbreak of the Suez crisis in 1956 temporarily obscured the problem of oil imports as a threatened oil shortage now brought considerations of national security to the fore. Oil from any source came to be in great demand.[52]

But after Suez, like war and pestilence, the oil import problem remained. It simply could not be wished away. During 1957 the large-scale import of oil into the United States was affecting domestic producers to such an extent that the Director of Defense Mobilization, Arthur S. Flemming, urged the President to use his authority under the Reciprocal Trades Agreement Act of 1955 to impose import curbs.[53]

Eisenhower was reluctant to act, however. Instead, he appointed a committee, the Special Committee to Investigate Crude Oil Imports. This group made another investigation of the problem. In its report of July, 1957, it recommended that the President use his powers under Section 7 of the Reciprocal Trades Agreement Act of 1955 to restore a balance between domestic oil production and foreign imports to 10 percent below the 1954 and 1955 levels.[54]

Much like Hoover, however, Eisenhower preferred to rely mainly on voluntary efforts. Reluctantly he agreed to impose oil import quotas on areas east of the Rocky Mountains. He did not include markets in the West because the population boom increased consumption there so greatly that it created petroleum supply shortages. In the West large oil importers were to agree to voluntary curtailment of imports in accordance with their own local conditions. Secretary of the Interior Douglas

51. *NYT,* January 18, 20, 28, May 3, 15, July 1 (Sect. III), September 7, 21, October 18, 1956.

52. Herman Finer, *Dulles over Suez: The Theory and Practice of His Diplomacy* (Chicago, 1964), discusses this crisis in detail.

53. *NYT,* February 6, 9, 15, 20, 1957; *O&G Jl.* (April 22, May 13, 27, July 1, 22, August 5, 1957).

54. *O&G Jl.* (August 12, 19, 1957); the President's Committee to Investigate Crude Oil Imports *Report* is in *NYT,* July 30, 1957; see also *ibid.,* June 27, July 30, 31, August 1, 2, 3, 1957.

McKay was instructed to create an Oil Imports Administration in his department to supervise this voluntary effort.[55] Congress approved this action by including a section in the Trades Agreement Act of 1958 that gave the President power to modify import quotas after investigations by the Director of Civil Defense. Throughout 1958–1959 this official modified the quotas. But to the dismay of the Administration, the voluntary effort broke down again. In February, 1959, Director of Civil Defense Flemming noted in a masterful understatement that "increased imports suggest circumvention of the limitation program." In other words, there was still much cheating.[56] Consequently, in that same month the President's special committee urged that the voluntary program be replaced immediately by a mandatory one. In March, 1959, President Eisenhower very reluctantly issued a proclamation authorizing such curbs. He instructed the Secretary of the Interior to license oil imports and to establish a schedule of quotas for the purpose. The special committee, having done its work, was now abolished.[57]

Despite more than four years of hesitation, therefore, the Eisenhower Administration was ultimately forced to resort to the use of federal powers to curb the flow of foreign oil into the United States. Its record was one of hesitation, straggling, and indecisiveness. Yet, without doubt, Administration leaders were loath to touch the problem, because it involved questions of national security and diplomacy. Nevertheless, the Eisenhower policies were prone to criticism because they seemed to neglect prior experiences with voluntary oil import restrictions during the Hoover era. A clear recognition of the advantages and defects of such programs might have provided a quicker solution to what came to be a chronic problem for some segments of the oil industry during the 1950's.

The Depletion Allowance

President Eisenhower was similarly passive in regard to the federal depletion allowance for oil producers. In his characteristic vein, he

55. *O&G Jl.* (November 11, 18, December 2, 9, 1957); *NYT,* October 25, 29, December 25, 1957, March 28, 1958; Secretary of the Interior, *Annual Report* 1959 (Washington, 1959), 445–446.

56. *NYT,* January 29, February 1, 3, 14, March 1, 1959; *O&G Jl.* (February 2, 16, 1959).

57. *NYT,* March 11, 12, 14, 1959; *O&G Jl.* (February 23, March 9, 16, 1959).

refused either to approve or condemn the existing depletion allowance. His Secretary of the Treasury, George Humphrey, was somewhat more explicit and thought the matter worthy of investigation. Congress, meanwhile, showed little inclination to make any change.[58]

The struggle during the Eisenhower years was reopened in 1954 when Senator Williams reintroduced the Humphrey amendment to lower the allowance to 15 percent. Again the Senate Finance Committee held hearings on the question, and Williams then brought his bill up in the Senate, which defeated it by a voice vote. Thereupon Senator Paul Douglas introduced a measure of his own, providing for a graduated depletion rate. He proposed 27½ percent for producers with a maximum gross income of one million dollars and a gradual reduction to 21 percent for those with five million dollars or more. Douglas argued brilliantly and persuasively for his bill, but it, too, was defeated in the Senate. The defeat of the bill may have been due to Secretary of the Treasury George Humphrey, who declared himself opposed to any change in prevailing tax privileges for mineral producers. He argued that the matter was extremely complicated and suggested a comprehensive investigation to determine whether modifications were desirable.[59]

The drama of 1954 was to be repeated four years later. Senator Williams reintroduced his bill to reduce the depletion allowance to 15 percent. This was defeated by a vote of sixty-three to twenty-six. Thereupon Senator William Proxmire (Wisc.) revived the Douglas scheme. The ensuing debate brought up many of the same arguments on both sides that had been offered in earlier battles. When the Senate finally voted on the measure in June, 1958, it again defeated the bill by a substantial margin (fifty-eight to thirty-one). Senator Douglas persisted, however, and in 1959 made his final unsuccessful effort to reduce the depletion allowance during the Eisenhower Administration.[60]

The Eisenhower years, thus, were generally barren of accomplishment in the field of national oil policies. The President made no contributions, in thought or action, to the formulation of new goals or administrative means to improve the execution of resource programs.

---

58. *CR,* 83 Cong., 2 sess. (June 10, 1954), 8001, *ibid.,* (June 30, 1954), 9301, 9308, 9319.

59. *Ibid.,* 83 Cong., 2 sess. (June 30, 1954), 9310–9319.

60. *Ibid.,* 85 Cong., 2 sess. (August 11, 1958), 16944; see also *O&G Jl.* (January 5, 19, 1959).

At the same time, the President did not alter significantly the complicated network of business-government relations that had been developed by his predecessors. In every respect, he preferred to preside over the administration of existing programs without making appreciable changes.

Perhaps more important than the static concept of public policy during the Eisenhower Administration was the broad consensus on national oil policies between business and government in the two decades after World War II. Bred in the critical years of the industry's development during the 1920's, crystallized and institutionalized during the New Deal, and consolidated during World War II, this consensus frustrated a strong and vigorous President seeking change, like Truman, while allowing a more restrained Chief Executive like Eisenhower to play a passive role. Such a consensus reflected many of the principles outlined by the National Petroleum Council in 1949 in its effort to identify outstanding characteristics of a national oil policy. It included conservation and economic stabilization as prime goals for both industry and government. These were to be achieved largely through private enterprise, albeit with government assistance in the form of depletion allowances, United States Bureau of Mines production forecasts, research aid from the United States Geological survey, and prohibition of hot oil shipments in violation of state conservation laws. If the Twenties and Thirties had viewed the painful formulation of basic elements of American oil policies, the Forties and Fifties were far less dramatic as they witnessed consolidation and refinement.

10 / Natural Gas: The Struggle Over Public Control, 1945–1964

THE POST-WORLD-WAR-II period witnessed a tremendous boom in the production and consumption of natural gas. For many years merely an unwanted byproduct of petroleum, natural gas suddenly emerged as a major new source of energy. Growing importance of this rapidly growing industry was unfortunately accompanied by a host of new problems that seemed to invite both federal and state regulation. In the two decades after 1945, therefore, spokesmen for the industry, Congress, the courts, and the Federal Power Commission all emerged as major architects in the formulation of public policies for the industry. Yet, the differences between gas and oil as commodities, and their variant uses, resulted in different patterns of federal and state policies. Instead of an emphasis on cooperation, the imposition of regulatory controls by the FPC came to be characteristic in the Truman and Eisenhower eras.

Why did the use of natural gas increase so greatly between 1945 and 1960? In the first place, the requirements of a rapidly growing population led to the increasing utilization of gas, since it was one of the most accessible and least exploited forms of energy. The continued high rate of urbanization and suburbanization in the United States, combined with the construction boom and the growth of gas heating and air conditioning in postwar America, created vast new markets for heating fuels and a multiplicity of new industrial uses. Certainly gasoline and fuel-oil shortages between 1945 and 1950 also stimulated the search for substitutes. Improved technology also made gas production cheaper and for the first time made distribution on a national scale feasible.[1]

Particularly essential to the growth of the natural gas industry were revolutionary improvements in pipeline technology. It was only after 1930 that engineers perfected electric welding processes for the manufacture of pipes adequate for long-range distances. Moreover, the transmission of gas over thousands of miles required high-pressure equipment, which necessitated solutions of multiple complex engineering problems. Until the construction of big pipelines from the Southwest, the major gas producer, to the most lucrative markets on the East and West coasts was completed, the industry could not develop on a large scale.[2]

These new needs were reflected in a tremendous increase in demands for natural gas. In 1940 total U.S. production was 2,660.2 billion cubic feet; in 1955, 9,405.4 billion cubic feet. The major producing states of the Southwest (Texas, Louisiana, Oklahoma, New Mexico, and Kansas) accounted for only 1,818.3 billion cubic feet in 1940, but in 1955 produced 8,037.5 billion cubic feet. Between 1930 and 1960, residential as well as industrial consumption increased more than tenfold.[3]

Before 1945 the relative unimportance of natural gas as an energy fuel created few problems requiring regulation. But the great increase of consumption in the following two decades aroused fears of monopoliza-

1. A brief historical account is in Temporary National Economic Committee (TNEC), *Reports of the Federal Trade Commission on Natural Gas, and Natural Gas Pipelines in the U.S.A.*, Monograph No. 36 (Washington, 1940), 85–89; Federal Trade Commission, *Report on Public Utility Corporations*, 70 Cong., 1 sess., *Senate Document* No. 92, Vol. 84A; Leslie J. Cookenboo, *Competition in the Field Market for Natural Gas*, in Rice Institute *Pamphlets*, Vol. 44, No. 4 (Houston, 1958).

2. A good summary of problems is Federal Power Commission, *Natural Gas Investigation* (Docket G-580), *Report of Commissioner Nelson Lee Smith and Commissioner Harrington Wimberley* [hereafter cited as *Smith-Wimberley Report*] (Washington, 1948), 65–120, 355–412; Ralph K. Huitt, "National Regulation of the Natural Gas Industry," in Emmette S. Redford (ed.), *Public Administration and Policy Formation* (Austin, 1956), 55–58; TNEC Monograph No. 36, 11–33; Richard L. Huntington, *Natural Gas and Natural Gasoline* '(New York, 1950), provides a technical survey.

3. Department of the Interior, *Minerals Yearbook* 1961 (3 vols., Washington, 1962), II, 327–331; Cookenboo, *Competition*, 13–39, 64–81.

tion of production and manipulation of prices. These prompted the imposition of restrictions by the FPC, just as the era between 1890 and 1911 had witnessed judicial actions against the alleged monopoly of Standard Oil.

The emergence of natural gas as a major energy resource also created new problems of public policy. In the first place, from its beginning the industry was highly integrated and characterized by concentration of capital. The cost of pipelines and other technical equipment was usually so great that economy of operation frequently dictated cooperation rather than competition among rival companies. Especially before 1950 gas production was accompanied by a great deal of physical waste. Perhaps only one-half of the gas produced was actually utilized. Since gas is a nonreplaceable energy resource the problem of exhaustion became increasingly acute with the rapid growth of consumption.[4] The sudden importance of the industry also made federal officials concerned with economic stability more sensitive to its national impact. Natural gas frequently displaced coal and had a disruptive effect on the older industry. The rise of this new source of energy worsened the crisis of the coal industry, which lost additional markets. One observer in 1947 estimated that natural gas would soon displace 50 million tons of coal each year, or about one-twelfth of total annual production.[5] And since natural gas entered the homes of millions of consumers, prices in this industry were very closely related to the cost of living. Although these problems first reached major proportions after 1945, they had accompanied the growth of the industry from the beginning.

The first efforts to deal with issues created by the production and distribution of natural gas were made by the states. Early laws were of limited scope, usually requiring plugging of abandoned wells or capping. Such restrictive measures—usually without administrative implementation—were adopted by Oklahoma in 1915 and Louisiana in 1918. But at the suggestion of engineers and producers, legislators gradually provided more comprehensive laws, as in Arkansas (1923) and New

---

4. An excellent study is Paul W. MacAvoy, *Price Formation in Natural Gas Fields* (New Haven, 1962); Frederick F. Blachly and Miriam E. Oatman, *Natural Gas and the Public Interest* (Washington, 1947), 2, 3.

5. For interfuel competition see *Smith-Wimberley Report*, 295–354; TNEC Monograph No. 36, 15–17; Blachly and Oatman, *Natural Gas and the Public Interest*, 3–5.

Mexico (1925). When great new gas wells were uncovered in the ensuing decade other states followed this legislative pattern, including California and Michigan in 1929, Mississippi in 1932, and Texas and Kansas in 1935. By the time of World War II at least 28 states had adopted gas conservation statutes to halt excessive waste. These included a wide array of rules concerning the maintenance of official production records, establishment of oil-gas ratios, repressuring, and well prices of gas. But as pipelines stretched across state boundaries after 1925 the limited jurisdiction of the states became an increasing problem in vitiating their regulatory efforts.[6]

By the time of the New Deal these weaknesses of state regulation led affected interests to demand some form of federal controls. Their pleas were closely related to a broad national resource program. As early as 1934 President Roosevelt appointed a National Power Policies Committee to study the need for new legislation. The recommendations of this group resulted in two bills. One became the Federal Power Act of 1935; the other, its more controversial twin, took form as the Holding Company Act of that same year. Neither the President nor Congress, however, requested similar laws to regulate the natural gas industry.[7]

Nevertheless, the Federal Trade Commission, at the same time that undertook an exhaustive investigation of power utilities, also made a thorough inquiry into the production and transmission of natural gas. The testimony that the commissioners heard from officials of state power commissions revealed that most were extremely desirous of having federal regulations govern natural gas problems that lay outside their own jurisdiction. Various Congressional committees heard similar appeals. Representatives of gas companies were not at all unfriendly to the idea of federal regulation. For them, it promised uniformity and

6. G. Lloyd Wilson, James M. Herring, and Roland B. Eutsler, *Public Utility Regulation* (New York, 1938), 43–66, 363–370; C. Emery Troxel, "Long Distance Natural Gas Pipe Lines," *Journal of Land and Public Utility Economics,* XII (November 1936), 344–354, "Regulation of Interstate Movements of Natural Gas," *ibid.,* XIII (February 1937), 20–30, and "Some Problems in State Regulation of Natural Gas Utilities," *ibid.,* XIII (May 1937), 188–203; Clyde O. Ruggles, *Aspects of the Organization, Functions, and Financing of State Public Utility Commissions* (Cambridge, Mass., 1937), *passim.*

7. National Power Policy Committee, *Report,* in 74 Cong., 1 sess., *Senate Report* No. 621 (Washington, 1935), Appendix; *NYT,* April 30, July 16, 17, 19, 1934; Samuel I. Rosenman (ed.), *Public Papers and Addresses of Franklin Delano Roosevelt* (13 vols., New York, 1938–1950), III, 98–103; 49 Stats. at Large 803.

standardization in the interstate transmission of gas; this would reduce cutthroat competition and promote stabilization of the industry. At the same time, national regulation promised an escape from what they often considered onerous stipulations of state agencies.[8]

Early in January, 1935, the testimony of various witnesses persuaded Sam Rayburn, chairman of the House Committee on Interstate and Foreign Commerce, to prepare specific legislation. He gave a copy of the Federal Power Bill to the legislative draftsmen of the House and asked them to revise it with specific application to natural gas. The fruit of their labors was a bill that he introduced on February 3, 1935. Originally Title III of an early draft of the Federal Power Act, it was offered by the House managers as a separate measure. Rayburn then appointed a subcommittee of the House Commerce Committee, headed by Clarence Lea, to elaborate the gas bill further.[9]

During the winter of that year Lea worked hard to improve his gas control measure. He called not only upon various staff members of the Federal Power Commission to help frame a final version; he also relied heavily on Federal Power Commissioner Clyde Seavey, who had supervised the actual drafting of the Federal Power Act and who had had experience with natural gas in his earlier days as a member of the public utility commission of California. Lea introduced this new bill in the House on March 6, 1936. At the same time he sent copies to all state public service commissions as well as to a special legislative com-

8. Dozier A. DeVane, "Highlights of Legislative History of the Federal Power Act of 1935 and the Natural Gas Act of 1938," *George Washington Law Review,* XIV (1946), 38–41; Judge DeVane was Solicitor of the Federal Power Commission in 1937–1938 and played a prominent role in the drafting of the Natural Gas Act of 1938; *Congressional Record* [hereafter cited as *CR*], 74 Cong., 1 sess. (February 6, 1935), 1624; 74 Cong., 1 sess., House, Committee on Interstate and Foreign Commerce, *Hearings on Public Utility Holding Companies* (H.R. 5423); 74 Cong., 2 sess., House, *Hearings Before a Sub-Committee of the Committee on Interstate and Foreign Commerce on H.R. 11662* [Gas Act] (Washington, 1936); 75 Cong., 1 sess., House, Committee on Interstate and Foreign Commerce, *Hearings on H.R. 4008;* Federal Trade Commission, *Report on Public Utility Corporations,* 70 Cong., 1 sess., *Senate Document* No. 92, Vol. 84A (Washington, 1928).

9. DeVane, "Highlights of Legislative History," 38–41; *CR,* 74 Cong., 1 sess., 1624 (H.R. 5423); *NYT,* February 4, 1935; National Association of Railroad and Utilities Commissioners, *Proceedings,* 47th annual convention, 1935 (New York, 1936), 82, 417; see also the letter of John Benton [Solicitor of the Association] to Congressman Clarence F. Lea, March 29, 1937, in *CR,* 75 Cong., 1 sess. (August 19, 1937), 9312.

mittee of the American Gas Association for suggestions. They raised no serious criticisms, but did ask for a few minor changes. Largely because of a lack of interest among Congressmen, however, during 1936 they took no action on the bill. Few came from districts in which natural gas was used and so the majority was singularly unconcerned. Nevertheless, Lea persisted, and reintroduced his bill in the next session, early in 1937. During the spring of that year the House Committee on Interstate and Foreign Commerce held extensive hearings on it, and closely questioned many of the individuals who had played a role in its preparation. Finally, after some delays, the measure received approval by both houses and on June 21, 1938, President Roosevelt signed it into law.[10]

The Natural Gas Act of 1938 was designed largely to supplement state regulation. It granted authority to the FPC to regulate interstate transportation and sales of natural gas for resale. In addition, the FPC could determine prices for gas flowing in interstate commerce. As the solicitor of the FPC and one of the draftsmen of the law, Dozier De-Vane, explained at the time, it was not designed to regulate intrastate producers.

Prime responsibility for enforcement of the act was placed in the hands of the Federal Power Commission. In the half dozen years after passage of the Natural Gas Act, the commissioners included Clyde Seavey as chairman, and Claude Draper, Basil Manly, Leland Olds, and John W. Scott. They generally agreed on the broad goals of national gas policy. These included conservation and prevention of overly rapid depletion of natural gas reserves. They were also alert to the requirements of national defense. Still under the impress of the Depression, the commissioners were also keenly conscious of their responsibility to supervise economic stability in the energy industries as a whole (particularly the ailing coal industry). But their prime obligation they felt was to natural gas consumers in maintaining reasonable rates.[11]

To achieve these ends, the FPC between 1939 and 1942 sought to clarify the scope of its jurisdiction over diverse segments of the natural

10. *NYT*, March 7, 1936; *O&G Jl.* (March 12, 1936); DeVane, "Highlights," 39–41; *CR*, 75 Cong., 1 sess. (April 22, 1937), 3771, *ibid.* (April 28, 1937), 3922, *ibid.* (July 1, 1937), 6720, 6733, *ibid.* (July 2, 1937), 6740, *ibid.* (August 11, 1937), 8670; for debate see *ibid.* (August 19, 1937), 9312–9317. Many mayors and urban officials representing consumers urged passage of the measure; for text, see 52 Stats. at Large 821; *NYT*, June 22, 1938.

11. These basic principles of federal gas policy are discussed in Federal Power Commission, *Annual Report* 1940 (Washington, 1941), 9–10.

gas industry. A key issue in this effort was the question whether the FPC's powers extended only over distributors of natural gas, and not to producers. Section 1(b) of the Act had declared: "The provisions of this chapter shall apply to the transportation of natural gas in interstate commerce . . . but shall not apply . . . to the production or gathering of natural gas." The intent of Congress seemed clear, yet it increasingly became the focal point in the dispute over the extent of federal powers during the next two decades.

The legislative history of the Natural Gas Act as well as its specific provisions seemed clearly to exclude the FPC's authority over independent gas producers. In 1938 the solicitor of the FPC, Dozier De-Vane, testified that the act was not intended to regulate field rates or prices charged by independents. Its sole purpose, he reiterated, was to fill the vacuum created by the limitations of state jurisdiction. Partly in response to his clear expression of purpose, the drafters of the act included the exemption clause, Section 1(b).[12] During the first years of the Natural Gas Act, the FPC clung to this interpretation. The United States Supreme Court noted in 1949: "For over ten years the Commission has never claimed the right to regulate dealings in gas acreage. Failure to use such an important power for so long a time indicates to us that the Commission did not believe the power existed." In the Columbia Gas decision of 1940, and in eight succeeding cases as well, the commissioners openly declared that they had no jurisdiction over gathering of gas.[13] But as the burden of actions coming before them increased, and with it the difficult task of clearly separating intra- and interstate jurisdiction, the FPC slowly extended its authority over prices charged by gatherers or producers of gas. This became evident as early as 1942, in the Colorado Interstate Gas Company Case, and in an action involving the Peoples Natural Gas Company.[14] Such extension of federal authority aroused considerable resentment in the industry and ultimately led to renewed contests in the courts.

To explore the necessity of federal regulation further, the FPC in

12. 74 Cong., 2 sess., House, Sub-Committee of Committee on Interstate and Foreign Commerce, *Hearings on H.R. 11662,* 28, 34, 42–43.

13. 2 F.P.C. 200; other similar cases are listed in Charles E. Crenshaw, "The Regulation of Natural Gas," *Law and Contemporary Problems,* XIX (1954), 336, n. 62.

14. Federal Power Commission, *The First Five Years Under the Natural Gas Act* (Washington, 1944), 3 ff.; 3 F.P.C. 32; 324 U.S. 581 (1945); 2 F.P.C. 704 and 127 F. 2d 153 (1942) for Peoples Natural Gas Co. Case.

1945 inaugurated a far-ranging and comprehensive inquiry into the natural gas industry. This was designed to investigate gas production and distribution practices, and state conservation policies as well. Some industry spokesmen and state officials reacted to the probe with "frank and alarmed apprehension," and all efforts by the FPC to quiet their fears were to little avail.[15]

Just a year later the United States Supreme Court further enlarged the FPC's scope by authorizing it to extend its control over gas producers. The problem it considered was whether any one portion of the process of manufacturing and transmission of natural gas could be separated from another, and so be intrastate, or whether each was so closely related as to constitute interstate commerce. The wording of the Natural Gas Act of 1938 as well as the debate at the time of its passage clearly assumed the former. But in 1945, the court moved to a broad interpretation of the commerce clause in regard to gas. The particular case concerned only one producer, the Colorado Interstate Gas Company, but the Natural Gas Association of America participated in this vital test case, hoping it would result in a clarification of the FPC's powers over the entire industry. Once again Justice Douglas asserted the right of the FPC to make rates based on a consideration of all of the multifold processes involved in the production and distribution of natural gas—until it reached the housewife's kitchen.

Many existing tensions and fears in the gas industry concerning possible new federal controls were heightened by the United States Supreme Court in 1947 in its Interstate decision, which extended FPC jurisdiction over local natural gas producers. The Interstate Natural Gas Company of Louisiana produced gas solely within the state, sometimes purchasing additional gas from other Louisiana producers. Producing from its own and from other wells, sometimes it commingled gas and sold it to pipeline companies that transported it in interstate commerce. The company maintained that it was purely a producer and thus exempt from FPC jurisdiction under Section 1(b) of the Natural Gas Act of 1938. But Chief Justice Vinson of the United States Supreme Court noted that it was engaged in interstate commerce and subject to

15. Quote is from Federal Power Commission, *Natural Gas Investigation* [1947], Transcript, 20–21, as quoted in Huitt, "National Regulation," 91; *Smith-Wimberley Report*, 167–171.

FPC regulation. Although Vinson was careful not to make any sweeping declarations, his decision was widely interpreted as subjecting all interstate gas sales by producers to federal authority.[16]

Even while the Interstate case was still pending on appeal to the United States Supreme Court, gas producers began a campaign to secure exemption from FPC jurisdiction through legislative action. During the 1946–1947 session, several Congressmen introduced bills to achieve their objective.[17] The FPC, on the other hand, on April 10, 1947, formally asked Congress to defer consideration on these measures until its extensive investigation of the industry was concluded. But the final United States Supreme Court ruling in the Interstate case on June 16, 1947, heightened the desire of gas producers for legislation. In this endeavor they were supported by some of the FPC commissioners themselves, who hesitated before the implications of the far-flung authority ascribed to them by the United States Supreme Court.[18]

Nevertheless, the FPC commissioners unanimously sought to assuage the uncertainty of natural gas producers through administrative action. On August 7, 1947, the FPC promulgated Order No. 139, which assured "independent producers and gatherers of natural gas that they can sell at arm's length and deliver such gas to interstate pipelines . . . without apprehension that in so doing they may become subject to assertions of jurisdiction by the Commission under the Natural Gas Act."[19] Of course, unlike a law of Congress, this ruling was not bind-

16. 331 U.S. 682; *O&G Jl.* (June 21, 1947); *NYT*, June 17, 1947. The law journals carry dozens of articles concerning the case; see Robert E. Hardwicke, "Some Consequences of Fears by Independent Producers of Gas of Federal Regulation," *Law and Contemporary Problems,* XIX (1954), 342–360; Raoul Berger and Abe Krash, "The Status of Independent Producers Under the Natural Gas Act," *Texas Law Review,* XXX (1951), 29–61.

17. *CR*, 80 Cong., 1 sess. (February 24, 1947), 1410, *ibid.* (February 26, 1947), 1480, *ibid.* (February 27, 1947), 1518, *ibid.* (July 1, 1947), 8055, *ibid.* (July 11, 1947), 8733, *ibid.* (July 12, 1947), 8760, *ibid.* (July 17, 1947), 8394; *O&G Jl.* (August 3, 1946).

18. 80 Cong., 1 sess., House, *Hearings before Committee on Interstate and Foreign Commerce on H.R. 2185* (Washington, 1947), 10; *NYT*, April 26, May 5, 1947; *O&G Jl.* (June 21, 1947); *Public Utilities Fortnightly,* XXXIX (June 5, 1947), 780–781.

19. Cited in 81 Cong., 1 sess., House, Committee on Interstate and Foreign Commerce, *Report* No. 1140 (Washington, 1950), 3; see also Federal Power Commission, *Report* 1946 (Washington, 1947), 66–70, 96–99, *ibid., Report* 1947 (Washington, 1948), 102.

ing upon succeeding commissioners, and was subject to revocation at any time. Thus, its effect was less soothing than a formal statute and did not diminish the gas industry's desire for congressional legislation.

The FPC sought to allay industry fears and uncertainties by encouraging appropriate bills. Just a week after the United States Supreme Court's decision, the commissioners themselves on June 23, 1947 urged, the House Committee on Interstate and Foreign Commerce to frame a bill, "in accord with the Commission's interpretation that the Congress intended independent producers and gatherers to have a nonjurisdictional status under Section 1(b) of the Act, and is likewise in accord with previous rulings and determinations by the Commission regarding this matter." This suggestion was taken up by Representative J. Percy Priest, who on July 8, 1947, introduced a bill (H.R. 4099) to exempt local gas producers from FPC jurisdiction.[20]

All of the commissioners, in unanimous agreement, urged enactment of this measure. But the House did not act on the Priest bill. Instead, on July 11, 1947, it passed the Rizley bill, which the FPC opposed. In addition to exemption, it also attempted to impose a rate formula on the FPC that was expected to result in higher consumer prices. Since the Senate did not act on this proposal, the Eightieth Congress adjourned on July 26, 1947, without taking any action to exempt gas producers from FPC regulation. Representative Rizley was so furious by what he considered improper propaganda against the measure by the FPC that he threatened to begin impeachment proceedings against the commissioners.[21]

The near unanimity that the FPC had reflected in issuing Order No. 139 was to be rudely disrupted, however. By the middle of 1948 the commission was evenly split over recommendations growing out of the completion of the Natural Gas Investigation in 1947. This was starkly

20. For Priest see *CR,* 80 Cong., 1 sess. (July 7, 1947), 8394; for the FPC's endorsement see its letter to chairman of the House Committee on Interstate and Foreign Commerce, Charles A. Wolverton, July 10, 1947, 81 Cong., 1 sess., House, Sub-Committee of Committee on Interstate and Foreign Commerce, *Hearings on S. 1498* (Washington, 1949), 91; *CR,* 80 Cong., 1 sess., (July 12, 1947), 8760.

21. Federal Power Commission, *Report* 1947, 115–118; text is in 81 Cong., 1 sess., *Senate Report* No. 567 (Washington, 1949), *Appendix;* only Commissioner Draper opposed the order; Rizley's charges are in *CR,* 80 Cong., 1 sess. (July 26, 1947), 10497.

revealed in the reports issued at the close of the FPC's exhaustive investigation of the natural gas industry. Commissioners Wimberley and Smith filed their own reports. They believed in a strict interpretation of Section 1(b) of the Natural Gas Act of 1938, which exempted intrastate gas producers from their jurisdiction. In view of prevailing uncertainties they urged Congress to pass a law to make such exemption explicit. Hoping that Congress would provide policy guidelines for the FPC, Wimberley and Smith also urged legislation to establish criteria for rate-making and control over wholesale sales. At the same time they urged the states to strengthen their cooperative agreements for gas conservation, and pleaded with the industry to show a greater awareness of its public responsibilities.[22]

In strong disagreement, Commissioners Olds and Buchanan issued a separate document to sustain their own and sharply differing opinions. They felt that no amendments to the Natural Gas Act were required. Indeed, they castigated the "insistence by representatives of the industry . . . for a virtually unregulated market." They hoped for a strengthening of the FPC's authority over conservation practices and requested increased funds for broad investigations in this sphere. Perhaps their greatest concern was over possible monopolization in the industry and consequent administered pricing policies. Believing that without stringent federal controls the supply of natural gas would soon be exhausted, they were opposed to any diminution of the FPC's powers.[23]

Why had Olds and Buchanan changed their minds? Olds was said to have noted that the self-restriction that the FPC imposed on itself with Order No. 139 led him to alter his earlier position in favoring limitation of FPC jurisdiction. That the new great demands for natural gas were changing the market structure of the industry, shifting it from a buyer's to a seller's market, was another reason for Olds's revised views. Certainly there was also a personal element involved in the adamant stance of Olds, who came to view himself increasingly as the guardian of the consumers' interests arrayed against a dark and sinister conspiracy of producers. Thus, after 1948 he took a somewhat rigid and uncompromising role vis-à-vis the industry. Something of a dogmatist by nature

22. *Smith-Wimberley Report,* 1–30.
23. Federal Power Commission, *Natural Gas Investigation* (Docket No. G–580), *Report of Commissioner Leland Olds and Commissioner Claude L. Draper* [hereafter cited as *Olds-Draper Report*] (Washington, 1948), 1–13, quotation on 12.

throughout his career, Olds had tended to view public issues in terms of stark opposites of good and evil. The question of natural gas regulation only provided him with another opportunity to take an uncompromising and—in his eyes—virtuous position.[24]

At the same time, spokesmen for natural gas producers coordinated their efforts and closed ranks. Their most powerful advocates in the United States Senate were Robert S. Kerr (Okla.) and Lyndon B. Johnson of Texas. Upon entering the United States Senate in 1946 Kerr expressed unabashed admiration for Leland Olds and his work as a Federal Power commissioner. Their correspondence during this period revealed a seemingly genuine effort by Kerr to establish a harmonious relationship between himself, Olds, and other members of the commission. Until 1948 their views on federal regulation of the natural gas industry were similar and clashed on no important issue. But Kerr's position then—and in ensuing years—was consistent in the belief that the FPC should regulate neither production nor transportation of natural gas within a state, but that it was necessary for the agency to extend such controls over interstate pipelines.

In this stand he was not only expressing his position as an important natural gas producer himself, but also that of other colleagues from the Southwest. Some of the large oil companies that also had valuable gas properties saw Kerr as their spokesman. A good example was Alvin Richards, attorney for the Pure Oil Company, who was of considerable help to Kerr in drafting legislation to exempt independent natural gas producers from FPC jurisdiction.[25]

During the national elections of 1948 the natural gas problems did not receive much attention from either party. The reasons were obvious. To stress either the expansion or curbing of the FPC would have split Democrats as well as Republicans. Both parties contained elements upholding each point of view. This was not a political but a sectional issue, and even more, a contest between natural gas producers as opposed to consumers.

24. *CR,* 81 Cong., 2 sess. (March 21, 1950), 3717; Nelson L. Smith to Federal Power Commission, February 2, 1948, in Leland Olds Papers, Franklin D. Roosevelt Library, Hyde Park, N.Y.; Huitt, "National Regulation," 92.

25. Robert S. Kerr to Leland Olds, July 12, 1946, in Robert S. Kerr Papers, Manuscripts Division, University of Oklahoma Library, Norman, Oklahoma; Robert S. Kerr to Alvin Richards, April 7, 1950, Kerr to Luther Bohanon, April 3, 1950, in Kerr Papers.

After the Presidential elections, however, the producers' drive to secure legislative action continued. Much of the attention centered on the hotly contested Kerr Bill. On March 17, 1949, the Oklahoma Senate adopted a resolution urging Congress to exempt arm's length sales from the FPC.[26] To implement this request, Oklahoma's Senators Robert Kerr and Elbert Thomas on April 4, 1949, introduced what became commonly known as the Kerr bill. It received strong support in the Senate from Lyndon B. Johnson and Russell Long. In substance, the Kerr bill was almost identical in scope with the Priest bill, which the FPC had supported in 1947. Its purpose was to amend Section 1(b) of the Natural Gas Act of 1938 by exempting independent natural gas producers from FPC regulation. It was vehemently opposed by representatives from states with large concentrations of natural gas consumers, lead by Senators Paul Douglas (Ill.) and Wayne Morse (Ore.).[27]

In addition, Senator Lyndon B. Johnson introduced an amendment of his own. Perhaps to placate the opposition, this amendment was designed to subject the issuance of securities by natural gas companies in interstate commerce to regulation by the FPC. Johnson hoped thereby to improve the regulatory process by enabling the FPC to scrutinize financing of natural gas companies, even though this was not a serious problem in 1949.[28]

Congress began work on the Kerr bill during the spring of 1949. The Commerce Committees in the House and Senate held lengthy hearings during May and June. The Senate Sub-Committee on Interstate and Foreign Commerce, headed by Lyndon B. Johnson, was strongly in favor of the Kerr bill, and on June 24, 1949, reported it unanimously. Throughout these deliberations the chairman of the Senate Committee on Interstate and Foreign Commerce, Senator Edwin Johnson (Colo.), assumed that President Truman approved of the measure, since the Chief Executive had supported the Priest bill of 1947. Thus, he was

26. For text of Resolution, see 81 Cong., 1 sess., Senate, *Hearings before a Sub-Committee of the Committee on Interstate and Foreign Commerce on S.1498*, 75; arm's-length sales are defined as sales "by any individual, partnership, association, or corporation not standing in such relation to the buyer by reason of voting-stock, common officers or directors . . . that there is liable to be such an absence of independent bargaining in transactions between them as to be contrary to the public interest."

27. *CR,* 81 Cong., 2 sess. (March 20, 24, 1950), 3618–4012; *ibid.,* (March 28, 1950), 4189–4200, contains the diverse viewpoints.

28. *CR,* 81 Cong., 1 sess. (October 19, 1949), 14968.

visibly surprised—and annoyed—when he learned on August 1, 1949, that Truman opposed the Kerr bill, and instead favored less restrictive proposals.[29]

Behind the scenes, however, the opponents of the Kerr bill were pressuring the President to join their ranks. As early as March, 1949, as the battlelines were forming, the Bureau of the Budget—especially Assistant Director Elmer Staats—severely criticized the Kerr bill, and advised Truman to oppose any relaxation of federal controls. He was urged to follow the advice of the FPC concerning necessary legislation. In late July, 1949, Commissioner Olds requested an appointment to see the President about the gas bill. The nature of his errand was obvious. At the same time, in early August, Frank Pace of the Bureau of the Budget sent another memorandum to the President urging him to oppose the Kerr bill, a course also recommended by Truman's politically suave administrative assistant, Charles Murphy.[30] By August, 1949, therefore, Truman decided not to support the measure. He made his views known officially through Elmer Staats. In a letter to Senator Edwin Johnson (Colo.), chairman of the Senate Committee on Interstate and Foreign Commerce, Staats noted that the President did not favor the pending bill, and instead approved a more innocuous proposal sponsored by the FPC (H.R. 1758).[31] This surprised Senator Johnson, since Truman had favored the Priest bill of 1947. Senator Johnson was greatly incensed by the President's position, particularly because the Chief Executive had not made his views known earlier. When he received the letter outlining Truman's position, Johnson was just about to send the Kerr bill to the Senate floor. Consequently, he sent a hostile and biting reply to Staats.[32]

The Kerr bill of 1949 also further widened the rift within the Federal Power Commission. During August, 1949, the subcommittee of the Senate Committee on Interstate and Foreign Commerce held additional hearings on the bill, to which the members of the FPC were invited. In

29. *Ibid.*, 81 Cong., 2 sess. (March 28, 1950), 4191–4195.

30. Charles Murphy Memo for Harry S. Truman, July 25, 1949, in Truman Papers, Harry S. Truman Library [hereafter cited as Truman Mss.], Independence, Mo.

31. *CR*, 81 Cong., 1 sess. (August 4, 1949), 10736; 81 Cong., 1 sess., *House Report* No. 1140 (Washington, 1949), 1–3.

32. *CR*, 81 Cong., 1 sess. (August 4, 1949), 10736.

their testimony, Commissioners Olds, Buchanan, and Draper revealed openly that they had changed their minds since supporting the Priest bill of 1947 and that they now opposed any legislative curtailment of FPC functions, including the pending Kerr bill. Rumors had it that Olds had persuaded Commissioners Buchanan and Draper to side with him. After ten years of service on the commission, part of the time as chairman, Olds had the prestige to enable him to win his colleagues over to his views. And he swung the majority of the FPC to a position of opposing any kind of legislative restrictions on its powers. From the viewpoint of producers, therefore, Olds stood out as the bête-noire of the FPC and as a serious obstacle to limitation of its jurisdiction.[33]

Yet throughout the spring of 1949, spokesmen for the gas producers felt that they must win the FPC to their side. They had experienced little success in influencing Congress, in shaping the views of the President, or in determining the attitude of the courts. But the Senate's power to confirm Presidential appointments did promise to give the lawmakers a measure of control in shaping the attitude of commission members. Thus, senators from gas-producing states had been able to delay confirmation of Federal Power Commissioner Thomas C. Buchanan's term for almost a year. His tenure expired in 1948, but the Senate did not confirm his reappointment until June, 1949. By one of those ironies of history, while the Kerr bill was pending in June, 1949, the term of Leland Olds himself expired. What would be the fate of Leland Olds, the strongest opponent of Congressional limitation of the FPC's powers?[34]

A furious battle ensued over the renomination of Olds to the FPC. President Truman, in a message of June, 1949, requested Senate approval of Olds to a third term on the FPC. The subcommittee of the Senate Committee on Interstate and Foreign Commerce that was to hear testimony on the nomination was headed by Senator Lyndon B. Johnson of Texas, who seemed inclined to postpone the matter for a

---

33. 81 Cong., 1 sess., Senate, Committee on Interstate and Foreign Commerce, Sub-Committee, *Hearings on H.R. 1498* (Washington, 1949); 81 Cong., 1 sess., *Senate Report* No. 567 (Washington, 1949); *CR,* 81 Cong., 2 sess. (March 21, 1950), 3717.

34. 81 Cong., 1 sess., Senate, Sub-Committee of Committee on Interstate and Foreign Commerce, *Hearings on Reappointment of Leland Olds to Federal Power Commission* [hereafter cited as *Olds Hearings*] (Washington, 1949).

year, as in the case of Buchanan. But considerable agitation for action occurred in the press and in Administration quarters, and so Senator Johnson agreed to begin hearings in September, 1949.[35]

The circumstances of the proceedings were not favorable to Olds. All of the members of the subcommittee later voted for the Kerr bill in April, 1950. Besides Senator Johnson, the committee included Democratic Senators McFarland, O'Conor, and Edwin Johnson, and Republicans Bricker, Capehart (Ind.), and Reed. In the midst of the McCarthy era, these men were inclined to be suspicious of self-styled or accused liberals or left-wingers. Moreover, the witnesses appearing before the subcommittee were generally favorable to proposals of natural gas producers, and included executives of oil and gas companies and Congressmen from gas-producing states.[36]

Olds's chief questioners were Senators Johnson (Texas), Robert S. Kerr, and Representative Lyle of Texas. The latter, in particular, steered the discussion away from issues of natural gas regulation to Olds's former left-wing or Communist affiliations. His questions brought out many facts about the early days of Olds's career. Between 1920 and 1929 Olds had evinced socialist leanings and had written widely as a journalist. Many of his articles had been distributed by the Federated Press, a news service sold to labor unions, and on occasion to *The Daily Worker*. As the hearings progressed they came to revolve less about Olds's fitness to be a member of the FPC than about his alleged pro-Communist sympathies in the decade after World War I. Olds's lack of tact at the hearings and his stubborn inflexibility did not help to alleviate the unfavorable impression that he made upon members of the subcommittee. He only enticed Representative Lyle, who was anxious to demonstrate that he was seeking to purge the FPC of its supposed Communist taint.[37]

Olds was not wholly blameless and did not help his own cause. There was at least a grain of truth in the charge that he desired to dominate the FPC and to determine its policies. Like many idealists, he tended to view issues in absolute terms, in blacks and whites, rather than in grays. Members of the subcommittee and other senators thus resented charges

35. *NYT,* August 25, September 28, 1949.
36. *Olds Hearings,* 3 ff.
37. *Ibid.,* 43–50.

made in many newspapers to the effect that many lawmakers were tools or dupes of natural gas interests. These accusations were made by newspapers prompted by—or so it was widely believed—Olds himself.

Late in September, 1949, Senator Johnson concluded the hearings and his subcommittee voted unanimously not to recommend confirmation of the Olds's nomination. Senator Johnson summarized the feelings of members of his group when he said that he believed Olds's policies to be harmful to the natural gas industry, that Olds had reflected pro-Communist leanings, and that he found Olds personally unfit for the post. It seemed unlikely, therefore, that Olds could receive approval by the full Senate.[38]

President Truman sought to salvage an unpromising situation by exerting political pressures. Despite the rebuke of Senator Johnson, on October 3, 1949, he wrote to Senator Edwin Johnson (Colo.), chairman of the full Senate Committee on Interstate and Foreign Commerce, urging him to use his personal influence for securing confirmation of Olds. Johnson answered him with a scathing and negative reply, while his committee voted ten to two against Olds. Frustrated, the President instructed the chairman of the National Democratic Committee, William Boyle, to telegraph all state Democratic chairmen, asking them to urge their senators to vote for Olds's confirmation. But even this maneuver failed to coerce the dissidents.[39]

The chief attack against Olds on the Senate floor came from Senator Lyndon B. Johnson of Texas. His record, Johnson noted, was "an uninterrupted tale of bias, prejudice, and hostility directed against the industry over which he seeks now to assume the power of life and death. Never once in his long career has Leland Olds experienced, first hand, the industry's side of the regulatory picture." He pointed to Olds's support of the Natural Gas Act before 1948, which clearly exempted producers from FPC jurisdiction, and wondered aloud about the reasons for his sudden switch thereafter.

He spoke first of the record of Leland Olds, then of the myth. The

38. See *CR*, 81 Cong., 1 sess. (October 11, 1949), 14219–14226; representative newspaper editorials in *Appendix*, 6125, 6129–6130, 6320. Eleanor Roosevelt also came to Olds's defense; see Washington *Daily News*, October 4, 1949.

39. For Truman's letter and Johnson's reply see *CR*, 81 Cong., 1 sess. (October 4, 1949), 13759–13760; text of Boyle's telegram in *ibid.* (October 7, 1949), 14121–14122.

myth, he noted, was of the white knight battling special privilege, of a humble, helpless man fighting sinister political power. Johnson challenged the charge of Olds's supporters that opposition came from a monopoly-seeking power lobby. Rather, he claimed that Olds had acted as a zealot, and not as a judicial-minded man. Let it not be forgotten, warned Johnson, that the power to determine natural gas policy resided in Congress, not in the FPC, or in the hands of a single man.[40]

The defenders of Olds fought a losing battle. Senator Hubert Humphrey was among those who reviewed his outstanding public service and strongly backed him. But his most eloquent supporter was Senator Paul Douglas, who had been intimately acquainted with Olds's father and the Olds family. Senator Douglas recalled his own early teaching days at Amherst College when George Olds, the commissioner's father, had been president. To consider Leland Olds a Communist was inconceivable to Douglas, who had known him well since his youth.[41] Eleanor Roosevelt, a special friend of Olds, also came to his aid publicly, denouncing those who sought to label him a Communist.

Neither side focused on the major issues underlying the dispute. Who was to be the prime architect of federal policy in the natural gas industry? Clearly this was a responsibility that belonged to Congress. Yet, both the House and Senate repeatedly showed themselves to be reluctant to take a position on this highly sensitive political issue, which affected millions of voters. By default, then, Congress left the problem of policy formulation to the FPC. But the commissioners themselves were bitterly divided over the extension of federal controls. Split two to two between 1947 and 1950, their division meant that their fifth colleague would, in effect, determine the direction of natural gas policy. Since Olds had had more than a decade of experience with the agency, and now took a rigid, uncompromising position in favor of the extension of strict federal controls, it was apparent in 1949 that his influence would most likely sway the commission. And while many members of Congress were willing to straddle on the issue, they were not quite as ready to assent to a clear and unalterable course of action.

Much on the minds of both critics and defenders was the possibility

40. Senator Lyndon B. Johnson's speech in *ibid.* (October 12, 1949), 14379–14385.
41. Humphrey in *ibid.,* 14373–14375; Senator Paul H. Douglas in *ibid.,* 14385–14386.

of higher natural gas prices. Certainly more comprehensive federal controls would constitute a barrier to large or sudden increases. Producers naturally sought to follow up their favorable position at a time of booming and expanding markets. Just as understandably, consumer groups hoped to prevent appreciable increases in the cost of natural gas. Thus, the Olds affair was not merely a struggle over the appointment of a public servant, but one involving pressure groups with conflicting economic interests.

Unfortunately, in this era of McCarthyism the battle over Olds was beclouded by efforts to taint him as a Communist. Dogmatic, self-righteous, and unyielding Olds was; in his youth, he had expressed sympathies for various kinds of reform movements, including some left-wing causes. But, a devout Christian Scientist, he was perhaps more of a latter-day Puritan than a Communist.

The Senate needed little time for deliberating about him, however. On October 19, 1949, it voted fifty-three to fifteen to reject the nomination. Many members from non-gas-producing states such as Harry F. Byrd (Va.), were angered by charges of Olds's supporters that they were merely tools—if not paid hirelings—of natural gas interests.[42] Without doubt, the specter of Communist accusations against Olds—although not clearly relevant—also had their effect. The Senate's decision now seemed to set the stage for eventual passage of Kerr's bill.

Elated by this victory, Kerr and his supporters redoubled their efforts during the spring of 1950. In March, 1950, the Senate spent almost an entire month on deliberation of the Kerr bill to the exclusion of virtually all other business. The whole problem was submitted to the most searching scrutiny.

The chief defender of the Kerr bill was the junior Senator from Texas, Lyndon B. Johnson. As a member of the Senate Sub-Committee of the Committee on Interstate and Foreign Commerce he steered the group to make a favorable report on the Kerr bill. Altogether, he had spent a year in its preparation.

Johnson presented at least three arguments for the bill. In the first place, he believed that it would clarify prevailing confusion concerning the jurisdiction of the FPC, particularly over independent natural gas producers. Congress should carry out its responsibility of determining

42. *Ibid.*, 14387.

policy. He pointed out that between 1938 and 1948 the FPC members did not feel that their authority extended to operators who were clearly not engaged in interstate commerce. In fact, during 1947 the FPC had unanimously supported the Priest bill in Congress, designed to exempt intrastate producers from federal jurisdiction. But then the Interstate decision in that same year created an even split in the commission (two to two) on the problem. With the appointment of Mon Walgren of Washington as the fifth member of the FPC in 1949 virtually the entire burden of determining natural gas policy fell on him. But should one individual be placed in a position to exert such great power, Johnson asked, when Congress had a duty to extend its mandate?

In addition, Johnson felt that the Kerr bill would dampen the efforts of the FPC to impose a cost formula on the natural gas industry, perhaps allowing it annual profits of no more than 6 percent. In view of the low levels of natural gas prices he considered such restrictions unnecessary. But he warned that if the FPC placed such limitations on producers they would stifle their incentive. This, in turn, could lead to a decline of production, and ultimately to higher costs for the consumer.

Finally, Johnson raised the problem of competing energy resources. Coal interests, in particular, were desirous of diminishing natural gas consumption, which cut into their markets. The National Coal Association had appealed to the FPC to consider the social and economic effects of its natural gas decisions upon competing fuel industries. Likewise the United Mine Workers advocated gas "conservation" as a means of promoting coal. Olds sympathized with these efforts, Johnson charged, and was seeking to restrict expansion of the natural gas industry through federal controls under which no other industry had to labor.[43]

Leading the opposition to the measure were Senators Paul Douglas (Ill.) and Hubert Humphrey (Minn.). Douglas, it appeared, had coached Humphrey in many of the intricacies of natural gas regulation. Both men emphasized the monopolistic nature of natural gas sources, which required federal controls. Even if once a commodity in a buyer's market, by 1950 it had become a commodity in a seller's market. Before 1945 most pipeline owners also produced gas, which they trans-

43. See his major speech in CR, 81 Cong., 2 sess. (March 28, 1950), 4189–4198; ibid. (March 29, 1950), 4298–4300, contains remarks of Edwin C. Johnson.

mitted and so came under federal controls over interstate transmission. But thereafter an increasing number of independents were drawn into the industry as the great demands of urban centers had to be met. These individuals and corporations should not be exempted from FPC jurisdiction. While Douglas made an elegant exposition of economic arguments against the bill, Humphrey saw the issue in simple terms. "Shall the large producers of natural gas be allowed freedom from regulation of their sales for ultimate resale to consumers?" he asked. This would be one effect of the Kerr bill, he argued. Moreover, he believed it would result in an appreciable increase of natural gas rates. Rising prices were already upsetting consumers as scores of telegrams and protests from new urban users in Minnesota, New York, and elsewhere indicated.[44]

Throughout March, 1950, Congress was preoccupied with lengthy debates on Kerr's measure. In the Senate the Kerr bill passed by a comfortable margin. In the House the battlelines were drawn much more closely, however. Speaker Sam Rayburn so feared for its passage that he himself took to the floor to argue for approval. He recalled his own opposition to power and gas monopolies on other occasions and his desire to defend consumer interests. He emphasized that it was he who had been the prime mover in the drafting and passage of the Public Utility Act of 1935 as well as the Holding Company Act of 1935 and the Natural Gas Act of 1938.[45] His apprehension was well grounded. When the votes were counted on March 29, 1949, it was found that the Kerr bill had passed by the narrowest of margins, 176 to 174.[46] When Johnson heard of the result he turned to Kerr, so the latter reported, to utter: "Landslide Johnson rides again."[47]

Both supporters and opponents of the Kerr bill looked hopefully to Harry Truman. Senator Kerr himself was quite confident that the President would sign the measure. Texas Governor Allan Shivers and Colonel E. O. Thompson of the Texas Railroad Commission also urged Truman to give his approval. Many Congressmen and petroleum trade

44. Douglas in *ibid.* (March 22, 1950), 3770–3784, and Humphrey in *ibid.* (March 22, 1950), 3790–3797.
45. *Ibid.* (March 31, 1950), 4565–4566.
46. *Ibid.* (March 31, 1950), 4567.
47. Robert S. Kerr to Luther Bohanon, April 3, 1950, in Kerr Papers.

associations echoed these requests.[48] But opponents also exerted strong pressures. Among the key men to discourage the President from signing the bill was a close associate of Olds, Thomas Buchanan of the FPC. Believing that it would result in higher rates and might have unfortunate political repercussions, he kept in close touch with White House Counsel Charles Murphy to urge a Presidential veto of the Kerr bill.[49]

Apparently political considerations weighed heavily in Truman's mind as he pondered his decision. In a memo that White House Assistant David Bell prepared for Charles Murphy he reported on an informal check of Truman Democrats on the House Ways and Means Committee. A veto of the Kerr bill would be advantageous for them, Bell noted, particularly in helping Stephen Young (Ohio) overcome Republican George H. Bender in the fall elections.[50]

On April 15, 1950, President Truman returned the Kerr bill with a veto. In a message characterized by moderation, he said that he did not think the measure to be fully in the national interest, for it promised to preclude the FPC from regulating sales of natural gas to interstate pipelines. Unlike coal and petroleum, consumers of natural gas did not have a wide choice of competing companies, since they were bound by the physical location of pipelines. In short, the natural gas industry was characterized by limited competition, and thus warranted federal controls. Thus, the President embraced one of the major arguments made by Senator Paul Douglas—who had gone to special pains to send Truman copies of his speeches on the subject.

A second reservation that he had about the Kerr bill was the concentration of ownership of natural gas reserves, a point also frequently stressed by Senator Paul Douglas. This, Mr. Truman felt, imposed further limitations on effective competition in the industry, particularly at a time when the consumption of natural gas was increasing. He felt that

48. Robert S. Kerr to Harry Truman, July 22, August 12, 1949, Ernest O. Thompson to Harry S. Truman, April 7, 1950, in Truman Mss., Allan Shivers to Robert S. Kerr, April 3, 1950, in Kerr Papers.

49. Ray Madden to Matt Connelly, April 4, 1950, Harry S. Truman to Ray Madden, April 11, 1950, Charles Murphy Memo for Harry S. Truman, July 25, 1949, Thomas C. Buchanan to Charles Murphy [March 7, April 7, 1950] in Truman Mss.

50. Charles Murphy Memo for Harry S. Truman, April 7, 1950, in Truman Mss.; see also Council of Economic Advisers [John D. Clark] to Harry S. Truman, April 7, 1950, in Truman Mss.

even with price regulation, the expanding demand would encourage gas producers to explore for new wells. With considerable moderation, he indicated that he would have no objection to amendments to the Natural Gas Act as experience indicated their necessity. Truman's veto stuck. The closeness of the vote in the House had indicated that it could not be overridden. Consequently the supporters of the Kerr bill made no effort to salvage their victory in Congress.[51]

During a post mortem on the struggle Senator Kerr sought to assess the blame. He noted: "Olds and Douglass [sic] are responsible." In an interview with journalist Marquis Childs he explained: "If Mr. Olds was right in the nine years of service on the Commission I was right in opposing his confirmation for another term because he repudiated his own unbroken record and threatened to pursue an entirely different course unless stopped by the Congress. If I was wrong in opposing his confirmation then he was wrong in that nine year record because I opposed him only after he had repudiated his own record."[52] Yet many of the letters in President Truman's correspondence seem to indicate that not Olds but Commissioner Thomas C. Buchanan exerted the most direct influence in prevailing upon him to impede enactment of Kerr's measure.[53]

There was some justice to the charge made by supporters of the Kerr bill that their opponents frequently distorted their purpose. The issue was not simply one between advocates and opponents of federal gas regulation. It was far more complex. Senator Douglas' view of the natural gas industry as a monopoly was relevant to its structure until World War II. But in the fifteen years thereafter numerous discoveries of new gas wells made the industry more genuinely competitive. At the same time, no great appreciable price rise took place during this period. Whether this was due to increasing competition or to restrictions of the FPC can be argued, of course. But at least one serious student of the industry concluded that natural gas prices would have been lower if the FPC had removed its artificial controls and allowed supply and demand to run a less fettered course. Finally, the burden of administrative detail

51. *NYT,* April 16, 1950, has text; see also *ibid.,* April 17, 19, 28, 1950.

52. Newspaper clipping in Kerr Papers has Childs's interview. See also "Personal Notes of Senator Kerr" (n.d.), in Kerr Papers, in which Kerr blames Olds and Douglas.

53. For examples, see *supra,* n. 49.

that control over intrastate gas producers imposed upon the FPC was staggering. By 1960 it was about three years behind in processing permits and applications, raising questions about the wisdom of too intricate regulation.[54]

With the failure of Congressional legislation to clarify national gas policy the prime burden was again left with the FPC. Yet the rejection of Leland Olds and the battle over the Kerr bill had a chastening effect upon it. Between 1947 and 1950 Commissioners Smith and Wimberley had been inclined to construe the FPC's authority narrowly, according to legislative intent, and were sympathetic to the pleas of producers. As long as Olds was on the commission, however, they were in a minority. His influence led Draper and Buchanan to assume a "broad construction" view concerning FPC powers, and to evince prime solicitude for consumers. With Olds removed in 1949, the FPC was again beset by an even split over policy. Within a year, however, Commissioner Draper came to vote with Smith and Wimberley on crucial issues and to assume an outlook more similar to theirs. This stood him in good stead in May, 1951, when the Senate promptly—and with despatch—confirmed his renomination as a Federal Power Commissioner.[55]

But Commissioner Buchanan's fate was to be different. The Senate subcommittee considering his reappointment voted nine to four against his nomination. President Truman continued his tenure with a recess appointment, but in 1953 the new Chief Executive, Dwight D. Eisenhower, withdrew Buchanan's name from consideration by the Senate for a regular appointment. Instead, he nominated Jerome Kuykendall, a former member of the Washington State Public Utility Commission, who was promptly confirmed. Gas producers thus secured some satisfaction in the changed complexion of the FPC, which was now disposed to favor limitations upon its own authority and jurisdiction.[56]

54. MacAvoy, *Price Formation,* 149 ff.

55. See particularly the Phillips Petroleum Company Case, 10 F.P.C. 283, and 10 F.P.C. 35, 105, 152, 225, 391, 425, for decisions in which Draper concurred; *CR,* 82 Cong., 1 sess. (May 16, 1951), 5419, *ibid.* (June 20, 1951), 6807, *ibid.* (June 21, 1951), 6888.

56. 82 Cong., 2 sess., Senate, Sub-Committee of Committee on Interstate and Foreign Commerce, *Hearings on Nomination of Thomas C. Buchanan to the Federal Power Commission* (Washington, 1952); *NYT,* July 9, 1952; *CR,* 82 Cong., 2 sess. (July 2, 1952), 8809–8810, *ibid.* (July 5, 1952), 9493; *NYT,* April 23, 1953; *CR,* 83 Cong., 1 sess. (April 22, 1953), 3523, *ibid.* (April 23, 1953), 3693, *ibid.* (April 17, 1953), 3279.

Who could foretell in 1953, however, that the new and more flexible attitude of the FPC only represented a Pyrrhic victory for the advocates of the natural gas industry? In 1954 the United States Supreme Court upset most of their hopes with its decision in the Phillips case. This was perhaps the most important step in expanding the FPC's powers over the natural gas industry. Proceedings in this action began before the FPC in 1951 to determine whether the Phillips Corporation came under federal jurisdiction. The company gathered gas entirely within Louisiana, but sold it to distributors in various states. Although a large integrated oil and gas company, Phillips claimed exemption of its gas-gathering operations from FPC rules under Section l(b) of the Natural Gas Act of 1938. Did Phillips come under FPC jurisdiction?

The FPC was divided on the question. Three of the Commissioners (Smith, Wimberley, and Draper) thought it did not. They were joined by representatives of ten state utility commissions and several natural gas trade associations, who entered the Phillips case as interveners. On the other hand, Commissioner Buchanan agreed with the plaintiffs that the interstate commerce clause clearly subjected the Phillips Company to FPC control. The FPC thus refused to assume jurisdiction. But the United States Circuit Court of Appeals reversed the FPC ruling in 1953 and instructed the commission to exercise its authority over Phillips.[57] All parties to the dispute thus looked expectantly to the United States Supreme Court for guidance.

In 1954 the United States Supreme Court affirmed the lower court's decision. In strong language Justice Sherman Minton held that the Natural Gas Act of 1938 did not bar the FPC from regulating the wholesale rates of the Phillips Company for gas sold to pipelines that were clearly participating in the flow of interstate commerce.[58] This ruling brought about a minor revolution in the FPC by greatly increasing its administrative burden. In compliance with the court's will the FPC now had to assume jurisdiction over approximately 40,000 additional gas producers previously not included under its authority.[59]

The Phillips decision also evoked a loud outcry of protest from the

57. 10 F.P.C. 283; 90 P.U.R. (NS) 325–329; 205 F 2d 706 (1953).
58. 374 U.S. 672; *NYT,* June 8, October 15, 1954; *O&G Jl.* (June 14, 1954).
59. Federal Power Commission, *Annual Report 1955* (Washington, 1955), 176–179, 183–187; *CR,* 83 Cong., 2 sess. (August 16, 1954), 14580; *O&G Jl.* (June 21, 1954).

natural gas industry. The hopes for less detailed federal regulations that had been raised by the events of 1950 were now rudely shattered by judicial action.[60]

In their alarm, the gas industry forces once more turned to Congress in their struggle to curb the jurisdiction of the FPC. In fact, during October, 1954, they formed a Natural Gas and Oil Resources Committee for the specific purpose of securing federal legislation to revise the Phillips ruling. Senator Fulbright (Ark.) and Representative Harris introduced bills in the 1954–1955 session of Congress specifically to exempt independent gas producers from FPC jurisdiction. Congress did not approve these, however.[61] But it sought to assuage the wounded feelings of the gas producers by adopting the Hinshaw amendment, which modified an earlier decision of the United States Supreme Court that had placed intrastate gas companies under federal jurisdiction. The amendment now specifically exempted them from federal control.[62]

Further encouragement came from President Eisenhower and his Cabinet. Unlike Harry Truman, the President was quite sympathetic to the pleas of the natural gas industry. This view was reflected in the report of the President's Advisory Committee on Energy Supplies, composed of Cabinet members, during February, 1955. It is true that the members of the task force that aided in the preparation of the report was drawn largely from men associated with the oil and gas industries. In fact, Senator Paul Douglas became so concerned with what he considered to be the absence of representation for consumer interests that he wrote a strong protest letter to Arthur S. Flemming, Director of Defense Mobilization and chairman of the study group. Although most of its recommendations concerned the petroleum industry, the group also touched upon gas policies and recommended that Congress exempt independent natural gas producers from federal regulation. This, of course, evoked a loud chorus of approval from natural gas interests.[63]

Once more the natural gas bill aroused a lengthy and protracted

60. See, for example, *O&G Jl.* (June 28, 1954); "Federal Control of Natural Gas: The Battle Warms Up," *Business Week* (January 15, 1955), 76–78.

61. *CR,* 84 Cong., 1 sess. (June 6, 1955), 7675, *ibid.* (June 28, 1955), 9417, *ibid.* (July 28, 1955), 11752, 11855, *ibid.* (July 29, 1955), 11952.

62. *Ibid.* (March 7, 1955), 2455, *ibid.* (June 6, 1955), 7675.

63. *Report of the President's Cabinet Committee on Energy Supplies* (Washington, 1954), 3–18; *O&G Jl.* (February 13, 1956); *CR,* 84 Cong., 2 sess. (February 3, 1956), 1971–1972, for Douglas-Flemming exchange; see also *ibid.* (January 18, 1956), 763.

debate. Most of the same arguments that had been considered pro and con in 1950 were now revived.[64] Newcomers to the Senate reiterated many of the familiar themes. Thus, Senator John F. Kennedy, representing a natural-gas-consuming state, explained his reasons for opposition to the bill. The problem was not whether the United States Supreme Court's decision in the Phillips case was right or wrong, he said, but whether the Fulbright-Harris Bill was in the public interest. In his estimation, it pitted 29 million consumers against eight thousand producers. Yet, this time the proponents of the bill were hopeful of gathering sufficient votes in both houses to secure its passage.[65]

The favorable outlook in 1955 led them to intensify their efforts. Indeed, Senator Aiken, one of the bill's opponents, complained about the frenzied activity of what he termed the "power lobby." Senator Hennings (Mo.) in turn urged a Senate investigation of the oil lobby. But not only did the President and his chief advisors favor the Fulbright-Harris Bill. The chairman of the FPC, Ralph Kuykendall, appointed by Eisenhower in 1953, also strongly urged such action.[66]

Thus, the supporters of the old Kerr bill, including Senators Lyndon B. Johnson and William F. Fulbright, revived it in the 85th Congress, in which it became known as the Fulbright-Harris Bill. Although very similar in its provisions to the earlier Kerr measure, it did empower the FPC to determine reasonable market prices for natural gas. On New Year's day of 1956 the chances for its passage seemed bright, indeed. Senator Lyndon Johnson's heart attack at this juncture, however, prevented him from taking a leading role in its advocacy.[67]

Once again, however, the seeming bad luck that had plagued natural gas producers for over a decade, that had snatched victory from them time after time, struck again, and in an unexpected quarter. On February 3, 1956, just three days before the Senate passed the bill, Senator Case, a Republican from South Dakota, dramatically announced on the Senate floor that he had rejected a $2,500 campaign contribution from

64. *CR*, 84 Cong., 2 sess. (January 31, 1956), 1688–1702, *ibid.* (February 3, 1956), 1972; New York *Post*, February 2, 1956.

65. *CR*, 84 Cong., 2 sess. (January 25, 1956), 1261–1264, *ibid.* (February 7, 1956), 2269.

66. *Ibid.* (January 18, 1956), 764–766, for Kuykendall's letter; Commissioner Draper dissented from support of the Fulbright-Harris Bill, *ibid.* (January 17, 1956), 644–646.

67. *NYT*, July 3, 4, 7, 10, December 13, 15, 29, 30, 1955, January 1, February 20, 1956.

a Nebraska lawyer representing the Superior Oil Company of Texas, which desired approval of the measure. Although an isolated instance, to many newspapers it appeared as if the natural gas lobby was resorting to wholesale bribery in its efforts to secure enactment of the Fulbright-Harris Bill.[68] Sincerely shocked, at Lyndon Johnson's behest the Senate appointed a special investigating committee to look into the matter. Its report, not rendered until late 1956, examined the details of the affair and concluded that the offer was the result of misguided judgment rather than any conscious effort to practice bribery.[69]

Yet the damage has been done. Apparently President Eisenhower was sufficiently impressed by the publicity that the press gave to the bribery accusations surrounding the passage of the bill that he was ready to impede it. When the Fulbright-Harris Bill reached his desk, President Eisenhower returned it with a veto. He noted that his sympathies lay with the objectives of the legislation, but he denounced the irresponsible lobbying that had accompanied its enactment. The methods used to secure its passage, he wrote, were "so much in defiance of acceptable standards of propriety as to risk creating doubt . . . concerning the integrity of governmental processes." As if to confound his supporters, however, he said that he did feel that such legislation was needed since the Natural Gas Act of 1938 "will discourage individual initiative and incentive to explore for and develop new sources of supply. In the long run this will limit supplies of gas which is contrary not only to the national interest, but especially to the interest of consumers."[70] The inconsistency of the President's arguments aroused considerable speculation in Congress concerning his real stand on the issue. But whatever his reasoning, he did exercise his veto. One of his political opponents, Senator William Ellender of Louisiana, charged that the President made his decision primarily in order to curry favor with consumers, since he was contemplating his upcoming renomination for a second term.[71]

68. *Ibid.*, February 4, 1956; *CR,* 84 Cong., 2 sess. (February 3, 1956), 1963, 1994, 1995, *ibid.* (February 6, 1956), 2001, 2009–2020, *ibid.* (July 26, 1956), 14654–14656.

69. Text of report of Special Committee to Investigate Charges of Senator Case of South Dakota in *CR,* 84 Cong., 2 sess. (February 7, 1956), 2167–2168, *ibid.* (July 26, 1956), 14651; also in 84 Cong., 2 sess., *Senate Report* No. 1724 (Washington, 1956).

70. Veto in *CR,* 84 Cong., 2 sess. (February 17, 1956), 2793, 2796.

71. *Ibid.,* 2793.

Although the big battles between representatives of gas producers and consumers had been fought by 1956, the struggle continued. The Harris bill was introduced again in 1958 but did not come before the Senate for a vote. In 1959 it was also submitted, only to be defeated by a formal vote.[72] President Kennedy in 1962 urged a bill to publicize natural gas prices and encouraged the FPC to inaugurate a program designed to assure consumers of an adequate supply of gas at reasonable rates. At the same time the FPC established a Natural Gas Advisory council to allow industry representatives and consumers an advisory voice in policy formulation.[73] And the United States Supreme Court continued to extend federal jurisdiction over the natural gas industry. In a major case, the Texas Eastern Transmission Corporation case in June, 1965, it approved FPC control over the production and price of gas even if it was still in the ground. Underlying this extension of the FPC's powers was the Justices' belief that the manufacture of natural gas was a monopoly.[74]

Thus, in the period between the New Deal and the Great Society, the relation of the federal government to natural gas diverged from that in the oil industry. Instead of focusing on cooperation, public policies emphasized regulation and control. Yet these differences were more apparent than real. Federal gas policies were at a stage of development during this period comparable to those affecting the oil industry at the beginning of the twentieth century. Then, too, an overriding fear of monopoly and economic concentration had led Congress, the courts, Presidents, and members of administrative agencies to support a federal antitrust program. As technological changes and expanding markets created increasing competition in the oil industry, the relation between it and state and federal officials became increasingly cooperative. By 1960, some economists believed natural gas production and distribution had become increasingly characterized by competition and had made obsolete many detailed federal regulations designed to prevent monopoly. But changes in the industry occurred so rapidly that they were not always quickly grasped. Rightly or wrongly, therefore, the belief that the natural gas industry was, in fact, monopolistic, guided public policy in the two decades after World War II.

72. *Ibid.*, 85 Cong., 2 sess. (March 14, 1958), 4394–4395, *ibid.*, 86 Cong., 2 sess. (March 7, 1960), 4728.
73. *NYT*, March 16, 22, 1962.
74. *NYT*, June 2, 1965.

11 / Conclusion: Cooperation in American Economic Policy

THE FIRST six decades of the twentieth century witnessed the development of a consensus by business and government concerning the ends and means of public policy. In 1900 some segments of American industry were characterized by monopoly, by corporations that were symbolized by Standard Oil. Government's response was embodied in the antitrust crusade, in regulation to prevent abuses emanating from bigness and the concentration of economic power. Over the course of the next half century, however, technological innovations, depressions, wars, and other factors fostered great changes in the structure of American industry. Federal policy reflected these transformations. By 1960 many major industries were characterized by oligopoly. Highly integrated large corporations whose ownership was diffused among millions of stock-owning individuals dominated important spheres of the economy. In the face of this economic transformation, which witnessed the rise of the publicly owned giant corporation as one of the dominant institutions in American society, state and federal governments reappraised their functions. Slowly and imperceptibly they assumed the role of arbiters in industries that, in one way or another, affected the lives of large numbers of Americans. If monopoly gave rise to the antitrust movement in the United States, therefore, oligopoly resulted in making government an arbiter.

How did this consensus develop? To a considerable degree it was the child of a century of crisis. Was it any wonder that a century torn by two world wars·within a generation and by chronic international tensions bred a sense of unity? And was not such a feeling strengthened by economic depressions so severe that they threatened to rend asunder the basic fabric of society? This is not to say that severe policy conflicts ceased to arise during this era. But many crucial issues in public affairs elicited a common ground of agreement where in previous years there had been bitter strife. Such consensus became perceptible during World War I as the wartime mobilization effort induced a large measure of cooperation between industry and government. Indeed, that conflict heralded a new era in business-government relations, one that became well established later in the twentieth century. After 1920 a succession of international crises tended further to foster a consensus among businessmen and government officials on the course of oil policies. The efforts of the British between 1919 and 1945 to keep American petroleum interests out of the Middle East created a close liaison between the State and Commerce Departments and large U.S. oil corporations. The menace of Nazism and Japanese expansion in the 1930's caused a further rapprochement between government and the industry, whatever their differences. And the Cold War with Russia after 1945 created a decided sublimation of major policy disputes, as men in business and in government sought to reduce their differences in the face of foreign pressures.

ECONOMIC CRISES

Economic crises had an important tendency to create an area of agreement between industry and government. Already in World War I the Wilson Administration evinced concern about inflation in the midst of a domestic mobilization program so far-reaching that it had few precedents in prior American experience. During the postwar decade President Coolidge often voiced his feelings about federal responsibilities for maintaining a stable economy, but he did little to quiet his worries. With the Great Depression, federal and state governments consciously assumed responsibility for maintaining the economy—and major industries—on an even keel, a responsibility that was laid upon them largely by businessmen themselves. The Employment Act of 1946 formally announced the incorporation of this function in public policy. In the twenty years thereafter neither industry nor government seriously challenged the proposition that assurance of economic stability was one of the prime duties of federal and state governments.

Throughout the twentieth century the changes generated by crises created at least two major problems for the petroleum industry and for state and federal officials. These included the attainment of economic stability and the promotion of conservation. The industry itself became increasingly concerned with the stabilization of competition and the regulation of production as a means to minimize the shock of violent business fluctuations. The federal government, too, came to have an abiding interest in softening the impact of economic cycles to avert disasters such as the Great Depression. In addition, many oilmen came to espouse the cause of conservation as they realized that restrictions on production could be an important method of limiting their surplus. For rather different reasons, including a growing apprehension over the availability of adequate oil supplies for national defense, the national government also developed a keen interest in conservation of oil by private industry and on the public domain. Thus, throughout the twentieth century the issues faced by government and industry came to be increasingly similar although their attitudes were often shaped by different motives.

In the face of common problems, leaders in industry and government came to support at least two major goals of public oil policy. For different reasons, they both evinced increasing concern about economic stability, whether in the industry or in an increasingly interdependent economy. Industry spokesmen were occupied with stability largely because of the frequently disruptive nature of competition in petroleum production and perhaps even more because of the rapid development of new and competing energy sources. As ownership of large corporations became increasingly spread among millions of stockholders, the new breed of corporate managers sought in various ways to minimize investment risks. And the long-range investment programs of large integrated corporations—often involved in expending millions of dollars in new technological processes and machinery—induced caution among their executives who sought to eliminate as many future uncertainties as possible.

After 1890 federal and state governments came to support a similar goal, although prompted by other motives. In an interdependent, closely knit industrial complex an economic crisis in one major industry such as petroleum could easily affect other important sectors of the economy. Moreover, the broader social goals of the administrations after 1933 led them to strive for the attainment of a greater measure of security for the common man. Government leaders were no less cautious than corporate managers in seeking to avoid violent economic fluctuations. And their increasing preoccupation with problems of foreign affairs made them especially anxious to maintain stability in domestic affairs, a stability not too different from that envisaged by the leaders of giant corporations.

For different reasons, then, executives in the oil industry and in government became aware of some commonly desired goals. They still had their differences over many issues, of course, but found themselves in agreement concerning the desirability of economic stability as a major goal of federal oil policy.

A second objective of both was petroleum conservation. Industry leaders had first grasped its advantages in the mid-1920's. Conservation promised greater technical efficiency in production and refining, the elimination of waste, and ultimately greater profits. In addition, conservation promised to be an effective means of restricting production. In times of great surpluses, the cry of conservation could be raised without incurring the wrath of the advocates of antitrust measures. Conservation thus became almost synonymous with efficiency and attracted the support of large segments of the industry.

For very different motives, federal and state officials also became strong advocates of conservation. Above all, the military requirements of the armed forces came to be a dominant consideration in the minds of many men in the public service as the foreign commitments of the United States expanded with each decade of the twentieth century. If such motives were not sufficiently compelling in themselves, the need to conserve an exhaustible natural resource—one that played an increasingly important role as the automobile became a major component of the American transportation system—also impelled state and federal governments to espouse the cause.

How did individuals and groups representing industry and government work out this consensus? To a large extent, the interests that represented various segments of the industry operated through the existing framework of political institutions to lobby, to coerce, and to arrange compromises with state and federal authorities. The process of conflict and mutual accommodations through formal and informal institutional channels was continuous and provided the means for formulating agreement on the principal components of a national oil policy. But this policy was developed only slowly, guided not by ideological considerations but by three decades of pragmatic trial and error.

At the opening of the century the twin problems of economic stability and conservation already weighed on the minds of thinking men although their scope was still limited. Monopoly—and its purported consequences in creating high prices for consumers—appeared to be a major economic issue during the Progressive Era. Rightly or wrongly the Standard Oil Company symbolized this new phenomenon in American business. Few other problems aroused fears such as this one. Hardly less alarming were the scientific forecasts of the United States Geological Survey and the Bureau of Mines, which predicted that the nation's reserve of crude oil supplies might well be exhausted in less than a generation. The despair generated by the prospect of an early depletion of natural resources, in the light of a rapidly burgeoning population, was one major source of the conservation movement. It was also prompted by the advocates of efficiency, by the followers of Frederick W. Taylor and Scientific Management, and by professional engineers and influential scientific associations. Economic stability and conservation thus emerged as vital oil problems.

During the Progressive Era many leaders of the industry hoped for greater stability in the petroleum business. Competition was rapidly increasing, not only because of the emergence of new markets for petroleum products, but also because of the entry of at least a dozen strong competitors with Standard Oil. Moreover, competition of other fuels, such as coal, whetted a desire among many oilmen for a common front against competitors. Improvements in petroleum technology also required increasingly large—and long-term—investments, which further aroused a desire among many corporate leaders for stabilization rather than the uncertainties of cutthroat competition.

At the same time, many businessmen during the Progressive Era began to realize the advantages of conservation. Some were professional engineers themselves, and extremely anxious to apply principles of efficiency and rationalization to multifold processes of oil production and refining to secure greater profits. Moreover, they realized that the quickening rate at which crude oil resources were being exploited boded ill for future expansion of the industry at a time when neither technology nor new discoveries promised to augment existing reserves. Depending on their particular self-interest, then, many industry spokesmen threw their support behind campaigns for better conservation.

In government offices state and federal officials mulled over similar considerations. Much of the motivation behind antitrust advocates between 1904 and 1917 was grounded in the belief that monopoly—or any undue concentration of economic power—boded ill for the stability of the economy as a whole. Monopoly brought unjust discrimination, restricted the untrammelled processes of competition, and resulted in artificial, administered prices. And the power to allocate huge investment funds seemed to be becoming too important for the nation as a whole to reside in the hands of a powerful private corporation. In Congress, in the courts, in administrative agencies, and in the White House, public regulation of monopoly—and of the economy—came to be discussed more widely.

A genuine desire for oil conservation also prompted men in government. Engineers who worked for the United States Bureau of Mines and the United States Geological Survey were eager to apply scientific principles to oil production and to eliminate excessive waste. And they were seriously concerned about the inadequacy of the nation's potential oil reserve. Their doubts were shared by a small but growing group of naval officers primarily concerned with providing a sufficient fuel supply for the United States Navy. They, too, looked hopefully toward a policy of conservation.

The changing objectives of the oil industry—and the needs of government—were clearly grasped by Theodore Roosevelt. Indeed, perhaps better than any other Chief Executive of his era he recognized the dimensions of the new relationship between government and business in twentieth-century America. With remarkable perspicacity he sketched its outlines when in 1910 he proclaimed the New Nationalism and forecast major aspects of its development over the next sixty years. Trusts were not to be busted, but to be regulated, and such regulation required a closer cooperation between government and business than had been true in earlier years. To cement this policy he secured the creation of the Bureau of Corporations in 1903 and stimulated court campaigns against "evil" trusts. These forays were designed to curb corporations that, like Standard, appeared to abuse their powers to the detriment of consumers.

Both Roosevelt and Taft also became disciples of oil conservation. In part, they were motivated by the warnings from their Navy departments predicting dire results unless remaining known oil deposits be retained as reserves. Since some of the best of these were still on the public lands, their withdrawal from private exploitation promised at least a temporary halt to waste. And both men made constructive efforts to frame a new—and, it was hoped, improved—method of disposing of oil-bearing lands in the federal domain. The Mineral Lands Leasing Act of 1920 was their product. In short, the Progressive Era witnessed an understanding between important oilmen and the federal government that gave the latter an increasing voice in dealing with problems of common interest. The changing structure of the industry was leading government to assume the role of arbiter.

World War I greatly accelerated these trends in the joint relationship. As the goal of maximum wartime production transcended all other objectives, the function of the federal oil director as virtual dictator of the American petroleum industry stood out in bold relief. Optimum efficiency in production required a degree of cooperation within the industry that had not been possible under the restrictions of the anti-trust laws. These restrictions the Wilson Administration suspended as military requirements forced it to promote cooperation. The results in attaining production goals were so encouraging that in 1919 sentiment for maintaining key features of the wartime relationship was strong among business leaders. But political pressures from President Wilson for abandonment of emergency agencies could not be overcome, and within a year virtually all were abolished. Yet the new role of government as supervisor of a wide array of cooperative practices within the industry was not forgotten by those who had a part in the wartime mobilization program. In the following decade they tried to continue some of these techniques, if only on a limited scale.

The most crucial issue for oil producers in the years between 1919 and 1924 was the fear of an impending oil famine. This was uppermost in the minds of officials in both industry and government. That available resources were inadequate to meet the demands of a new generation of automobile users and home owners was a view commonly shared by most experts of the period. Consequently, top policy planners in large integrated oil companies turned to contemplate the possibilities of exploiting overseas oil resources. Their eyes were fixed on the Middle East, the Dutch East Indies, and Latin America. Since Americans were latecomers on the scene of international oil politics, however, they were at a decided disadvantage with the French, the British, and the Dutch who had preceded them. Under such circumstances it was only natural for them to turn to the federal government for support.

Technical experts in the State Department, the United States Bureau of Mines, and the United States Geological Survey in the Wilson and Harding Administrations shared these fears. They preferred to soft-pedal the antitrust activity of the Progressive Era and to focus instead on promoting efforts of American oil companies abroad. Their motivation was somewhat different from that of business groups. President Harding and his advisers were concerned about the impact of an impending shortage on rapidly expanding domestic needs. Moreover, in the throes of postwar economic readjustments a decline of the oil industry could seriously affect other aspects of the national economy. Nor did they lose sight of conservation. Teapot Dome notwithstanding, Harding and his Administration were acutely aware of military and naval requirements. Not only the Navy, but a fledgling air force was becoming increasingly dependent on petroleum products. Exploitation of foreign reserves would meet this need and at the same time preserve a domestic supply. The aims of the federal government thus coincided with some of the industry's desires, and so both found a common meeting ground.

That mutual interest resulted in a foreign policy in which the federal government provided diplomatic support for American oil companies engaged in overseas exploitation. Such a course was not entirely new, but represented an eclectic blend of the Open Door with Dollar Diplomacy of the pre-World-War-I era. Unfortunately, the State Department's goals were much clearer than its instruments of implementation. In the Middle East, between 1919 and 1924, Colby and Hughes failed miserably in securing equal opportunities for Americans. In the Far East their efforts against the stubborn Dutch were even more disheartening. Only in Latin America did U.S. diplomacy of this period experience a small measure of success in locating potentially accessible petroleum reserves. American oil diplomacy of these years suffered from amazing ineptitude, especially at the hands of Secretary of State

Charles Evans Hughes, who opened few doors for Americans. If American oil companies came to concentrate on Latin America in the 1920's this was largely a result of the effective road blocks placed in their path in other portions of the world.

U.S. interest in overseas oil exploration flagged after 1924 because the discovery of new fields at home transformed the industry's major problem from expected shortage to unexpected glut. Discovery of new oil fields in Texas, the midcontinent area, and California far outdistanced available market channels and created a new chronic problem of oil surplus. Overseas operations thus declined greatly in significance, as oil industry leaders now concentrated on serious difficulties emanating from the production spree that characterized the industry for the next decade. In one way or another, these difficulties concerned economic instability and conservation. The enormous surplus of oil produced led to violent price fluctuations in the industry, with a precipitous decline throughout the later 1920's. Cutthroat competition and unethical business practices rather than cooperation were frequent in the industry. At the same time the orgy of production was accompanied by much inefficiency and waste and by a decided neglect of the good conservation practices introduced in previous years.

In light of these changing conditions oilmen appealed to state and federal governments for aid. Hoping to stabilize competitive conditions in the industry, men like Doherty, or groups like the API, urged state and even federally enforced unit plans for drilling to restrict output. They also recommended modification of the antitrust laws to allow oil producers to cooperate in limiting their output. And they prevailed upon Congress in 1926 to grant them special tax benefits through the 27½ percent depletion allowance. Interest in federal support for foreign operations of U.S. oil companies waned rapidly as spokesmen for the industry urged government above all to stabilize competition and, at the same time, to enforce desirable conservation practices on an industry-wide basis, a task beyond the reach of voluntary efforts.

The Coolidge Administration showed only partial sympathy for these demands. Yet the President and his advisers made strenuous efforts to adjust public policies to reflect changing conditions in the oil industry. Coolidge, too, became greatly concerned with the economic imbalance between the supply of and demand for petroleum products and the consequent effects of depression in this industry on others. And the parsimonious Chief Executive was as chagrined by waste in oil production as he was by other kinds of waste. He was receptive, therefore, to the pleas of some of his technical advisers, such as Herbert Hoover and George Otis Smith of the Geological Survey, who urged him to take the lead in forcing the industry to adopt more efficient practices. Coolidge himself also revealed nagging fears of a shortage of petroleum that would endanger the country's defense program.

Thus, the Coolidge Administration, largely through the Federal Oil Conservation Board, consciously sought to work out a consensus between government and the industry. The President was unwilling to accept the industry's recommendation that Congress amend the antitrust laws to allow greater leeway for cooperative agreements to restrict production. But he did instruct the board to study various other proposals to attain this end. And to aid oilmen in weathering the crisis of declining prices between 1924 and 1929, he agreed to the enactment of federal tax benefits. As for conservation, he spoke a great deal about its necessity, although the actual work of implementing such proposals fell to Oklahoma and Texas, where state agencies began to limit production in the effort to eliminate waste.

The Great Depression after 1929 only intensified a problem of overproduction for the oil industry with which it had been grappling for half a decade. Producers large and small appealed to state and federal authorities to aid them in enforcing production curbs to achieve at least a measure of stabilization in the increasingly chaotic industry. Conservation practices were frequently thrown to the wind as cutthroat competition and rock-bottom prices encouraged production at any cost. Thus the API and other trade associations spoke for many segments when they advocated public policies to restrict production and to enforce conservation.

Despite near unanimity within the industry about the necessity for governmental action, the Hoover Administration refused to assume this responsibility. The President himself felt that the federal government should not concern itself with economic stabilization, a function to be left primarily to private efforts. Thus he refused even to explore possibilities of federal controls over production and marketing of oil despite strenuous pleas from business leaders. His prime concern was with conservation, but even in this sphere he accomplished little of significance. The major burden for the enforcement of conservation policies lay with the states, he believed, and lay outside the sphere of federal action. An interstate compact for conservation, he cautiously observed, would win his approval. Otherwise, he did little more than to encourage voluntary efforts for improved drilling practices, and withdrew selected public oil lands from private entry. His lack of leadership—and his insensitivity to the demands of the oil industry for government to assume the role of arbiter—aroused much consternation and dismay, and undoubtedly added to his growing unpopularity.

In marked contrast, Franklin D. Roosevelt in 1933 made special efforts to sound out diverse elements within the oil industry in an effort to secure a consensus on needed public policies. Certainly his various moves to deal with the industry's ills marked him as a great consensus-maker. His immediate reaction to the API's pleas for restriction of production and raising of price levels was favorable. The NRA's Oil Code authority under Harold Ickes between 1933 and 1935 concerned itself with primarily these problems and experienced a limited degree of success. Voluntary agreements to control the amount of oil produced were also legalized during this period as the antitrust laws were suspended. After 1935, production restrictions were worked out under joint auspices of state and national governments. State agencies bore prime responsibility for the enforcement of quotas, while federal officials curbed shipments of hot oil—oil produced in violation of state regulations. Other arrangements were worked out by the Interstate Oil Compact and by the United States Bureau of Mines and other federal agencies in regard to conservation practices. The New Deal very effectively encouraged the formulation of a *modus vivendi,* a consensus between governments and the industry, which incorporated proposals from virtually every important interest group affected by oil production.

As during an earlier generation, World War II rudely changed existing problems in the oil industry. Maximum production again became a major goal. Yet petroleum now played such an important function in the national economy that the task of supervising the industry fell not to one, but to several, agencies. Although Harold Ickes and the Petroleum Administration for War largely supervised production and consumption patterns, the difficult problem of price levels was left to the Office of Price Administration and a succession of economic czars. Certainly economic stabilization and conservation were not wholly ignored by the industry or the federal government during World War II, but they were subordinated both by the industry and public officials to broader war-time needs. More than ever, the war experience dramatized the increasingly important role of government as arbiter of the national economy.

The twenty years after 1945 witnessed few radical changes in the consensus on national oil policies that had been developed until then. In assuming broad national responsibility for the maintenance of economic stability with the Employment Act of 1946, the Truman Administration and a Republican Congress were expressing what had come to be a widely accepted view. In the oil industry, the network of relationships between the Federal Bureau of Mines, the Interstate Compact, and individual states served well in applying production limitations to prevent violent economic fluctuations. And at the same time these arrangements were designed to promote the cause of conservation. Further to prevent rapid depletion of domestic resources the federal government again threw its diplomatic support behind the efforts of American oil companies in foreign countries. In the Middle East they finally secured entry. The strong protests that such oil imports brought from domestic producers, however, led Congress not only to maintain a tariff on foreign oil, but in 1959 to impose special curbs on the amount that might be brought into the United States. By the 1960's, therefore, the multifold functions of governments in the petroleum industry made them the virtual arbiters of private enterprise.

In the related field of natural gas, conflict rather than consensus was characteristic. This was largely true because the industry was at a stage comparable to that of petroleum at the beginning of the century. Congressional battles between producing and consuming sections of the country over the imposition of controls over natural gas generated violent emotions between 1948 and 1964, and made the Federal Power Commission a pivotal agency. While the viewpoint of consumers won out during these years through decisions of the United States Supreme Court and the FPC, by the end of the period accommodation between these two major interest groups became discernible.

Consensus revealed at least four areas of agreement between industry and government in respect to national oil policies. In the first place, the oil industry was to be primarily in private hands but under public supervision. Second, government was to promote the industry, by tax favors, by research aid, or by direct money subsidy. Third, government had a responsibility to exercise its regulatory powers to aid the industry in coping with its multivaried problems. Finally, in the foreign sphere, it was the duty of government to provide support for American oil companies in foreign countries. Other issues of policy were in the realm of conflict, and elicited a much less unified response.

By 1964, then, government had assumed the function of an arbiter in the oil industry. For varying reasons, both government and industry worked in close collaboration. This they did frequently through agencies especially created to facilitate communication between government and company officials—who dealt with common problems. Of these issues, efforts to maintain stability in the industry loomed large. And as military and foreign commitments of the United States increased, conservation came to be almost equally important. The process by which government assumed the role of economic arbiter was not unique to the petroleum industry, however, but was also common in other sectors of the economy. It reflected accurately the changed face of American industry, from a monopolistic phase at the turn of the century to one characterized by oligopoly sixty years later.

What factors had wrought this great transformation that underlay the growth of a consensus in public policy? Certainly great technological advances that led to the creation of mass industries during the twentieth century were one important force. The increasing frequency of economic crises and depressions till 1941 further prompted agreement on selected aspects of government's role in the economy. Nor can the impact of wars and foreign involvements be ignored. The rapid growth of a large-scale military establishment in the United States also forced consensus on some issues under the guise of nationalism and patriotism, issues that a generation earlier would have generated active conflict. Increasing population pressures on the nation's natural resources underscored the need for conservation. In the oil industry, as in others, such considerations aided the formulation of a consensus between industry and government concerning their mutual relations.

Indeed, so widely accepted did this sphere of agreement appear to be in the 1960's that it ceased to be an object of heated public debate. Instead, it was increasingly superseded by other issues. Problems of racial integration and civil rights, urban life, and weighty problems of international relations came to dominate newspaper headlines and political debates. The proper role of government in the nation's economy no longer aroused the violent arguments that it had a generation earlier.

A peaceful revolution had taken place—in thought and in fact—about government's role in the American economy. As American industry came to be characterized by the giant corporation, federal action moved toward comprehensive cooperation and supervision. Theodore Roosevelt's vision of the New Nationalism in 1910 had been prophetic. Succeeding generations only worked out administrative details to implement the broad outlines that he had sketched. In so doing they demonstrated anew the great flexibility of American political and administrative institutions. These allowed the demands of political and economic interests to be channeled through a complicated network of policy-making agencies, which formulated compromises that ultimately found their way into public policy.

Appendix
Bibliographical Essay
Index

Appendix

DIFFICULTIES OF reproduction have prevented the inclusion of many statistical tables pertaining to the historical development of the petroleum industry. For the most readily available numerical data, see the annual volumes of the American Petroleum Institute, *Petroleum Facts and Figures*, particularly the Centennial edition (New York, 1959), and U.S. Bureau of the Census, *Historical Statistics of the United States, Colonial Times to 1957* (Washington, 1960).

The tables that have been included here have been numbered especially for this volume. The "A" tables (A1–A5) give data from the first part of the century to 1958; the "B" tables (B1, B3, B4, B5) update the same data to 1966, except that in Table A2, for which information was not available. The first group of tables appear in the 1959 API volume *(Petroleum Facts and Figures)* on pages 368, 104, 213, 374, and 174, respectively. The second group of tables appear in the 1967 API volume on pages 250, 155, 254, and 133, respectively. (Copyright © 1959, 1968, American Petroleum Institute; reproduced by permission.)

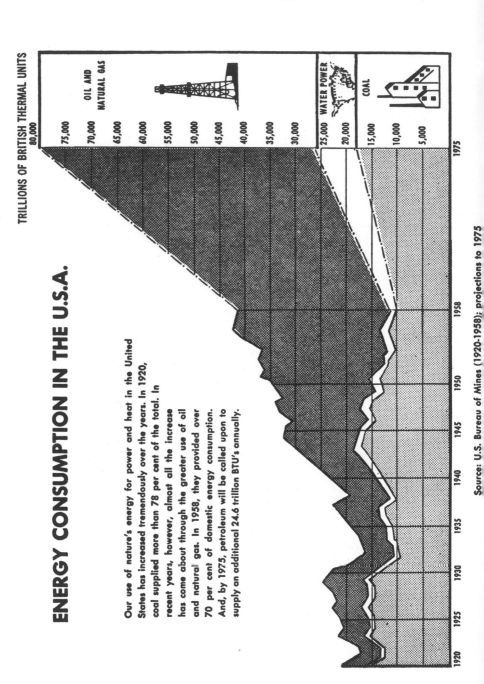

ENERGY CONSUMPTION IN THE U.S.A.

Our use of nature's energy for power and heat in the United States has increased tremendously over the years. In 1920, coal supplied more than 78 per cent of the total. In recent years, however, almost all the increase has come about through the greater use of oil and natural gas. In 1958, they provided over 70 per cent of domestic energy consumption. And, by 1975, petroleum will be called upon to supply an additional 24.6 trillion BTU's annually.

TRILLIONS OF BRITISH THERMAL UNITS

80,000
75,000
70,000
65,000
60,000
55,000
50,000
45,000
40,000
35,000
30,000
25,000
20,000
15,000
10,000
5,000

OIL AND NATURAL GAS

WATER POWER

COAL

1920 1925 1930 1935 1940 1945 1950 1958 1975

Source: U.S. Bureau of Mines (1920-1958); projections to 1975

256

PERCENTAGE OF U. S. ENERGY CONSUMPTION, BY TYPE OF FUEL CONSUMED, 1920-1958

Year	Anthracite Coal	Bituminous Coal and Lignite	Total Coal	Crude Oil	Petroleum Products Net[1]	Natural Gas Dry	Natural Gas Liquids	Total Petroleum	Total Mineral Fuels	Water Power	Total Mineral Fuels and Water Power	Year
1958[2]	1.2	23.2	24.4	39.6	2.7	26.5	3.0	71.8	96.2	3.8	100.0	1958[2]
1957	1.3	25.8	27.1	40.5	.9	24.8	3.0	69.2	96.3	3.7	100.0	1957
1956	1.4	27.0	28.4	40.5	1.0	23.4	2.9	67.8	96.2	3.8	100.0	1956
1955	1.5	27.8	29.3	39.9	.9	23.1	3.0	66.9	96.2	3.8	100.0	1955
1954	1.9	26.2	28.1	40.8	.7	23.5	2.8	67.8	95.9	4.1	100.0	1954
1953	1.9	29.7	31.6	39.5	.5	21.6	2.7	64.3	95.9	4.1	100.0	1953
1952	2.4	30.0	32.4	39.0	.4	21.2	2.6	63.2	95.6	4.4	100.0	1952
1951	2.5	33.3	35.8	37.6	.3	19.6	2.4	59.9	95.7	4.3	100.0	1951
1950	3.0	34.8	37.8	36.0	1.2	18.0	2.3	57.5	95.3	4.7	100.0	1950
1949	3.0	36.9	39.9	36.1	.2	16.7	2.1	55.1	95.0	5.0	100.0	1949
1948	3.8	40.1	43.9	35.5	-.4	14.8	1.8	51.7	95.6	4.4	100.0	1948
1947	3.7	43.5	47.2	33.7	-.8	13.8	1.7	48.4	95.6	4.4	100.0	1947
1946	4.5	43.0	47.5	33.7	-.9	13.4	1.6	47.8	95.3	4.7	100.0	1946
1945	4.2	46.5	50.7	32.3	-1.8	12.6	1.5	44.6	95.3	4.7	100.0	1945
1944	4.7	48.5	53.2	31.2	-2.1	11.9	1.4	42.4	95.6	4.4	100.0	1944
1943	4.8	51.1	55.9	28.1	-1.0	11.4	1.2	39.7	95.6	4.4	100.0	1943
1942	5.2	50.7	55.9	28.6	-1.1	11.1	1.3	39.9	95.8	4.2	100.0	1942
1941	5.0	48.4	53.4	31.3	-.5	10.7	1.4	42.9	96.3	3.7	100.0	1941
1940	5.2	47.2	52.4	31.1	-.7	11.4	1.0	43.8	96.2	3.8	100.0	1940
1939	5.9	45.6	51.5	33.9	-2.2	11.8	1.0	44.5	96.0	4.0	100.0	1939
1938	5.8	44.3	50.1	34.8	-2.3	11.8	1.1	45.4	95.5	4.5	100.0	1938
1937	5.6	49.6	55.2	30.8	-1.7	10.8	.9	40.8	96.0	4.0	100.0	1937
1936	6.3	49.9	56.2	30.0	-1.4	10.4	.9	39.9	96.1	3.9	100.0	1936
1935	6.8	48.9	55.7	30.4	-1.6	10.3	.9	40.0	95.7	4.3	100.0	1935
1934	7.9	50.2	58.1	28.6	-1.8	10.2	.9	37.9	96.0	4.0	100.0	1934
1933	7.5	49.2	56.7	30.4	-1.8	9.5	.9	39.0	95.7	4.3	100.0	1933
1932	7.8	49.1	56.9	29.5	-1.5	9.7	1.0	38.7	95.6	4.4	100.0	1932
1931	7.9	51.8	59.7	28.2	-1.8	9.1	1.1	36.6	96.3	3.7	100.0	1931
1930	7.7	53.5	61.2	27.6	-2.2	8.8	1.1	35.3	96.5	3.5	100.0	1930
1929	7.6	57.3	64.9	24.8	-2.5	8.2	1.0	31.5	96.4	3.6	100.0	1929
1928	8.4	58.4	66.8	24.4	-3.2	7.1	.9	29.2	96.0	4.0	100.0	1928
1927	8.7	60.0	68.7	23.0	-3.0	6.7	.8	27.5	96.2	3.8	100.0	1927
1926	8.7	62.0	70.7	21.7	-2.4	5.9	.7	25.9	96.6	3.4	100.0	1926
1925	7.8	62.6	70.4	22.2	-2.3	5.8	.5	26.3	96.7	3.3	100.0	1925
1924	10.0	62.0	72.0	20.7	-2.3	5.7	.5	24.6	96.6	3.4	100.0	1924
1923	10.2	62.7	72.9	20.4	-1.8	4.8	.4	23.8	96.7	3.3	100.0	1923
1922	8.4	65.0	73.4	19.7	-1.9	4.6	.3	22.7	96.1	3.9	100.0	1922
1921	12.7	62.6	75.3	18.4	-2.1	4.1	.2	20.7	96.0	4.0	100.0	1921
1920	11.0	67.4	78.4	15.3	-2.0	4.2	.2	17.7	96.1	3.9	100.0	1920

[1] Plus figures represent imports; minus figures represent exports.

[2] Preliminary.

Authority: Bureau of Mines.

U. S. ENERGY CONSUMPTION FROM MINERAL FUELS AND ELECTRICITY, 1958-1966[1]

(Trillions of British Thermal Units[2])

Year	Anthracite Coal	Bituminous Coal and Lignite	Total Coal	Crude Oil	Petroleum Products Net[3]	Natural Gas Dry	Natural Gas Liquids	Total Petroleum	Total Mineral Fuels	Electricity		Total Mineral Fuels and Electricity
										Water Power	Nuclear	
1966[4]	290	12,746	13,036	20,041	2,610	16,770	1,967	41,388	54,424	2,062	56	56,542
1965	328	12,030	12,358	19,194	2,372	16,097	1,853	39,516	51,874	2,050	38	53,962
1964	365	11,295	11,660	18,742	1,958	15,821	1,774	38,295	49,955	1,873	34	51,862
1963	361	10,722	11,083	18,434	1,797	14,843	1,668	36,742	47,825	1,740	33	49,598
1962	363	10,160	10,523	17,853	1,809	14,027	1,605	35,294	45,817	1,780	23	47,620
1961	404	9,809	10,213	17,372	1,617	13,228	1,498	33,715	43,928	1,628	17	45,573
1960	447	9,967	10,414	17,172	1,436	12,736	1,427	32,771	43,185	1,626	5	44,816
1959	478	9,596	10,074	16,994	1,405	11,991	1,348	31,738	41,812	1,695	0	43,507
1958	483	9,607	10,090	16,308	1,120	10,995	1,240	29,663	39,753	1,740	0	41,493

[1] Beginning in 1959, data for Alaska and Hawaii are included.

[2] The unit heat values employed are: anthracite, 24,400,000 Btu per short ton; bituminous coal and lignite, 26,200,000 Btu per short ton; crude oil, 5,800,000 Btu per barrel, weighted average Btu on petroleum products, 5,248,000 gasoline; 5,670,000 kerosine; 5,825,000 distillate; 6,287,000 residual; 6,064,800 lubricants; 5,537,280 wax; 6,636,000 asphalt; and 5,796,000 miscellaneous; natural gas dry, 1,035 Btu per cubic foot; natural gas liquids weighted average Btu based on production; natural gasoline 110,000 Btu per gallon and LPG 95,500 Btu per gallon. Hydro and nuclear power are converted to coal equivalent at the prevailing rate of pound of coal per kwh each year at central electric stations.

[3] Represents imports.

[4] Preliminary. Data for other years are final.

Authority: Bureau of Mines, *Mineral Industry Surveys,* "Petroleum Statements," Annual and December.

Table A2

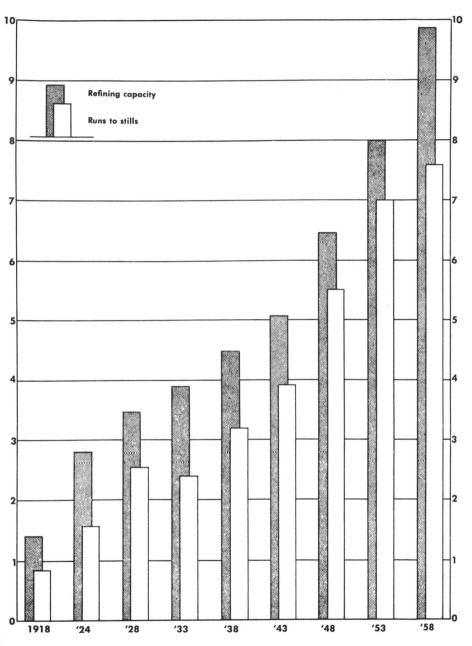

Refining capacity

Runs to stills

GROWTH OF U.S. REFINING CAPACITY, 1918 – 1958

259

U. S. CRUDE OIL SUPPLY AND DEMAND, 1919-1958

(Thousands of Barrels)

Year	Production	Imports	Total New Supply	Change in Stocks	Indicated Total Demand	Exports	Indicated Domestic Demand	Crude Oil Run to Stills	To Distillate Fuel Oil	To Residual Fuel Oil	Total Transfers	Crude Oil Used as Fuel and Losses[1]	Year
1958[2]	2,448,837	348,007	2,796,844	− 19,083	2,815,927	4,329	2,811,598	2,776,094	950	10,965	11,915	23,589	1958[2]
1957	2,616,901	373,255	2,990,156	++ 15,799	2,974,357	50,243	2,924,114	2,890,436	1,305	13,884	15,189	18,489	1957
1956	2,617,283	341,833	2,959,116	++ 404	2,958,712	28,624	2,930,088	2,905,106	1,375	6,439	7,814	17,168	1956
1955	2,484,428	285,421	2,769,849	++ 7,225	2,762,624	11,571	2,751,053	2,730,218	1,347	5,559	6,906	13,929	1955
1954	2,314,988	239,479	2,554,467	−16,060	2,570,527	13,599	2,556,928	2,539,564	1,500	5,924	7,424	9,940	1954
1953	2,357,082	236,455	2,593,537	++ 2,517	2,591,020	19,931	2,571,089	2,554,865	1,966	5,617	7,583	8,641	1953
1952	2,289,836	209,591	2,499,427	++16,145	2,483,282	26,696	2,456,586	2,441,259	2,705	6,343	9,048	6,279	1952
1951	2,247,711	179,073	2,426,784	++ 7,320	2,419,464	28,604	2,390,860	2,370,404	2,863	6,006	8,869	11,587	1951
1950	1,973,574	177,714	2,151,288	− 4,893	2,156,181	34,823	2,121,358	2,094,867	2,537	5,325	7,862	18,629	1950
1949	1,841,940	153,686	1,995,626	− 3,271	1,998,897	33,069	1,965,828	1,944,221	2,701	4,750	7,451	14,156	1949
1948	2,020,185	129,093	2,149,278	++25,973	2,123,305	39,736	2,083,569	2,048,349	3,543	6,699	10,242	24,978	1948
1947	1,856,987	97,532	1,954,519	++ 478	1,954,041	46,355	1,907,686	1,852,246	3,263	27,091	30,354	25,086	1947
1946	1,733,939	86,066	1,820,005	++ 6,917	1,813,088	42,436	1,770,652	1,730,197	3,123	23,142	26,265	14,190	1946
1945	1,713,655	74,337	1,787,992	− 3,511	1,791,503	32,998	1,758,505	1,719,534	3,047	20,727	23,774	15,197	1945
1944	1,677,904	44,805	1,722,709	−22,435	1,745,144	34,238	1,710,906	1,665,684	3,242	28,515	31,757	13,465	1944
1943	1,505,613	13,833	1,519,446	++ 6,041	1,513,405	41,342	1,472,063	1,429,738	3,070	24,087	27,157	15,168	1943
1942	1,386,645	12,297	1,398,942	− 11,924	1,410,866	33,834	1,377,032	1,334,103	2,496	19,283	21,779	21,150	1942
1941	1,402,228	50,606	1,452,834	−18,937	1,471,771	33,238	1,438,633	1,409,192	2,513	12,969	15,482	13,859	1941
1940	1,353,214	42,662	1,395,876	++23,307	1,372,569	51,496	1,321,073	1,294,162	2,576	7,699	10,275	16,636	1940
1939	1,264,962	33,095	1,298,057	−37,324	1,335,381	72,076	1,263,305	1,237,840	2,741[3]	9,668[3]	12,409	13,056	1939
1938	1,214,355	26,412	1,240,767	−28,913	1,269,680	77,254	1,192,426	1,165,015	623	10,037	10,660	16,751	1938
1937	1,279,160	27,464	1,306,644	++18,247	1,288,397	67,234	1,221,163	1,183,440	(')	17,423	17,423	20,300	1937
1936	1,099,687	32,327	1,132,014	−26,276	1,158,290	50,313	1,107,977	1,068,570		15,732	15,732	23,675	1936
1935	996,596	32,239	1,028,835	−22,399	1,051,234	51,430	999,804	965,790		13,067	13,067	20,947	1935
1934	908,065	35,558	943,623	−16,969	960,592	41,127	919,465	895,636		8,382	8,382	15,447	1934
1933	905,656	31,893	937,549	++15,437	922,112	36,584	885,528	861,254		7,361	7,361	16,913	1933
1932	785,159	44,682	829,841	−30,479	860,320	27,393	832,927	819,997		6,603	6,603	6,327	1932
1931	851,081	47,250	898,331	−40,963	939,294	25,535	913,759	894,608		(')	(')	19,151	1931
1930	898,011	62,179	960,140	−19,636	979,776	23,705	956,071	927,447				28,624	1930
1929	1,007,323	78,933	1,086,256	++35,816	1,050,440	26,401	1,024,039	987,708				36,331	1929
1928	901,474	79,767	981,241	++12,209	969,032	18,966	950,066	913,295				36,771	1928
1927	901,129	58,383	959,512	++64,631	894,881	15,844	879,037	828,835				50,202	1927
1926	770,874	60,382	831,256	−30,834	862,090	15,407	846,683	779,264				67,419	1926
1925	763,743	61,824	825,567	−16,655	842,222	13,337	828,885	739,920				88,965	1925
1924	713,940	77,775	791,715	++21,018	770,697	18,239	752,458	643,719				108,739	1924
1923	732,407	82,015	814,422	++80,907	733,515	17,534	715,981	581,238				134,743	1923
1922	557,531	127,308	684,839	++89,487	595,352	10,805	584,547	500,706				83,841	1922
1921	472,183	125,364	597,547	++67,876	529,671	9,627	520,044	443,363				76,681	1921
1920	442,929	106,175	549,104	++17,933	531,171	9,295	521,876	433,915				87,961	1920
1919	378,367	52,822	431,189	++ 2,101	429,088	6,348	422,740	361,520				61,220	1919

¹ Transfers included in "Losses" prior to 1932.
² Preliminary.
³ On wet basis.

U. S. CRUDE OIL SUPPLY AND DEMAND, 1958-1966

(Thousands of Barrels)

	1966[1]	1965	1964	1963	1962	1961	1960[2]	1959[2]	1958
Production	3,038,999	2,848,514	2,786,822	2,752,723	2,676,189	2,621,758	2,574,933	2,574,590	2,448,987
Imports	447,120	452,040	438,643	412,660	411,039	381,548	371,575	352,344	348,007
Total new supply	3,486,119	3,300,554	3,225,465	3,165,383	3,087,228	3,003,306	2,946,508	2,926,934	2,796,994
Change in stocks	+29,338	−9,768	−7,304	−14,650	+7,347	+4,864	−17,329	−5,613	−19,083
Indicated total demand	3,456,781	3,310,322	3,232,769	3,180,033	3,079,881	2,998,442	2,963,837	2,932,547	2,816,077
Exports	1,477	1,097	1,363	1,698	1,790	3,227	3,087	2,526	4,346
Indicated domestic demand	3,455,304	3,309,225	3,231,406	3,178,335	3,078,091	2,995,215	2,960,750	2,930,021	2,811,731
Crude oil runs to stills	3,447,193	3,300,842	3,223,329	3,170,652	3,069,631	2,987,158	2,952,534	2,917,661	2,789,404
Transfers:									
To distillate fuel oil	752	773	755	807	1,198	851	1,001	970	950
To residual fuel oil	3,551	3,950	3,720	3,305	3,797	3,854	3,948	7,386	10,965
Total transfers	4,303	4,723	4,475	4,112	4,995	4,705	4,949	8,356	11,915
Losses	3,808	3,660	3,602	3,571	3,465	3,352	3,267	4,004	10,412

[1] Preliminary. Data for other years are final.
[2] Includes Alaska beginning in 1959 and Hawaii beginning in 1960.

Authority: Bureau of Mines, *Mineral Industry Surveys,* "Petroleum Statements," Annual and December.

Table A4

CRUDE OIL PRICES AT SELECTED U. S. FIELDS, 1912-1958

(Dollars Per Barrel)

December (Lowest Price in Month)	Oklahoma-Kansas 36-Deg Gravity[1]	Bradford-Allegheny, Pa.	Illinois Basin	East Texas	Conroe, Texas	Gulf Coast 24-Deg Gravity[2]	Signal Hill, Calif. 27-Deg Gravity[3]	December (Lowest Price in Month)
1958	3.00[4]	3.90	3.00	3.25	3.53	3.28	3.06	1958
1957	3.07	4.65	3.15	3.25	3.53	3.38	3.17	1957
1956	2.82	4.68	2.90	2.90	3.13	2.98	2.92	1956
1955	2.82	3.85	3.00	2.90	3.13	2.98	2.76	1955
1954	2.83	3.35	2.95	2.90	3.13	2.98	2.76	1954
1953	2.82	4.05	3.02	2.90	3.13	2.98	2.76	1953
1952	2.57	4.25	2.77	2.65	2.83	2.68	2.41	1952
1951	2.57	4.25	2.77	2.65	2.83	2.68	2.41	1951
1950	2.57	4.10	2.77	2.65	2.83	2.68	2.37	1950
1949	2.57	3.40	2.77	2.65	2.83	2.68	2.37	1949
1948	2.57	4.50	2.77	2.65	2.83	2.68	2.45	1948
1947	2.07	4.50	2.27	2.15	2.33	2.68	1.95	1947
1946	1.62	3.55	1.82	1.70	1.88	1.81	1.50	1946
1945	1.17	3.00	1.37	1.25	1.43	1.36	1.15	1945
1944	1.17	3.00	1.37	1.25	1.43	1.36	1.15	1944
1943	1.17	3.00	1.37	1.25	1.43	1.36	1.15	1943
1942	1.17	3.00	1.37	1.25	1.43	1.36	1.15	1942
1941	1.17	2.75	1.37	1.25	1.43	1.36	1.15	1941
1940	1.02	2.15	1.15	1.10	1.27	1.16	1.03	1940
1939	1.02	2.50	1.05	1.10	1.27	1.16	1.10	1939
1938	1.02	1.68	1.15	1.10	1.27	1.16	1.10	1938
1937	1.22	2.20	1.35	1.35	1.39	1.29	1.10	1937
1936	1.10	2.57		1.15	1.30	1.22	1.10	1936
1935	1.00	2.30		1.00	1.15	1.12	.80	1935
1934	1.00	2.05		1.00		1.12	1.00	1934
1933	1.00	2.45		1.00		1.12	1.00	1933
1932	.69	1.72		.75		.88	1.00	1932
1931	.77	1.85		.75		.80	.75	1931
1930	.95	2.15				1.10	1.26	1930
1929	1.45	3.05				1.45	1.13	1929
1928	1.36	3.85				1.35	1.13	1928
1927	1.28	2.80				1.35	.94	1927
1926	1.90	3.15				1.40	1.52	1926
1925	1.79	3.40				1.50	1.34	1925
1924	1.25	2.85				1.50	1.16	1924
1923	1.00	2.60				1.00	.68	1923
1922	1.40	3.00				1.25	1.15	1922
1921	2.00	4.00				1.25		1921
1920	3.50	6.10				2.50		1920
1919	2.50	4.50				1.00		1919
1918	2.25	4.00				1.80		1918
1917	2.00	3.50				1.00		1917
1916	1.00	2.60				.65		1916
1915	1.00	2.00				.50		1915
1914	.55	1.45				.40		1914
1913	1.03	2.50				.80		1913
1912	.76	1.85				.75		1912

[1] Thirty-six degree gravity crude oil beginning with 1922; no gravity scale used in pricing prior to that year.

[2] Prices for 1912-1925 apply to the Batson, Saratoga, Spindletop, Humble, and Electra fields; Gulf Coast coverage revised in 1926 and in 1947 to include a more representative group of Gulf Coast fields.

[3] Prices for 1922-1924 apply to 27-degree gravity crude oil in fields in the Los Angeles Basin. Prices for 27-degree gravity crude oil at Signal Hill were not available

Table B4

(Dollars Per Barrel)

State and Area	1958	1959	1960	1961	1962	1963	1964	1965	1966
Alaska [2]	(3)	(3)	2.56	3.09	3.09	3.09	3.09	3.09	3.09
Arkansas	2.82	2.82	2.72	2.68	2.68	2.68	2.63	2.63	2.63
California Fields:									
Buena Vista, Elk Hills & Midway-Sunset	3.44 [4]	3.20 [4]	3.20 [4]	3.20 [4]	3.20 [4]	3.24	3.24	3.24	3.24
Elk Hills	3.37	3.07	3.07	3.07	3.07	3.07	3.07	3.07	3.07
Huntington Beach & Long Beach (Signal Hill)	3.52	3.02	3.27	3.27	3.27	3.27	3.27	3.27	3.27
Inglewood	3.38	2.91	3.11	3.11	3.11	3.11	3.11	3.11	3.11
Kettleman Hills & Coalinga	3.40	2.90	3.16	3.16	3.16	3.16	3.16	3.16	3.15
Torrance	2.94 [6]	2.98 [6]	2.75 [6]	2.92 [6]	2.92 [6]	2.92 [6]	2.92 [6]	2.92 [6]	2.92 [6]
Wheeler Ridge	3.50	3.20	3.20	3.20	3.20	3.20	3.20	3.20	3.20
Wilmington & Richfield [5]	3.43	2.98	2.98	2.98	2.98	2.98	2.98	2.98	2.93
Colorado	2.85	2.85	2.85	2.67	2.67	2.67	2.67	2.67	2.67
Illinois-Indiana [7]	2.67	2.67	2.67	2.67	2.67	2.67	2.67	2.67	2.67
Kansas	2.92	2.62	2.69	2.69	2.69	2.79	2.79	2.79	2.73
Kentucky [7]	2.47	2.87	2.65	2.80	2.80	2.73	2.73	2.73	2.73
Louisiana:									
East	(3)	(3)	(3)	3.02	3.02	3.02	3.02	3.02	3.02
North	2.77	2.77	2.77	2.77	2.67	2.67	2.67	2.67	2.67
South	3.17	3.02	3.02	3.02	3.11	3.11	3.11	3.11	3.11
Flat Price Crudes	3.00	3.00	3.00	2.90	2.90	2.90	2.90	2.90	2.93
Michigan [7]	2.73	2.73	2.73	2.73	2.58	2.58	2.58	2.58	2.58
Mississippi [7]	2.00	2.00	2.00	2.00	2.00	2.00	2.00	2.00	2.25
Montana	2.79	2.61	2.79	2.41	2.41	2.50	2.50	2.50	2.60
Nebraska	2.85	2.85	2.85	2.70	2.80	2.80	2.80	2.80	2.85
New Mexico	2.94	2.79	2.79	2.79	2.79	2.79	2.79	2.79	2.87
North Dakota	2.62	2.62	2.47	2.47	2.47	2.50	2.50	2.50	2.62
Ohio [7]	2.72	2.72	2.72	2.72	2.72	2.67	2.67	2.67	2.77
Oklahoma	2.83	2.62	2.69	2.83	2.83	2.78	2.78	2.78	2.83
Pennsylvania Grade [7]	3.40	3.77	4.17	4.00	3.91	3.76	3.61	3.61	3.76
Texas:									
East [7]	3.25	3.05	3.05	3.10	3.10	3.10	3.10	3.10	3.10
East Central	3.07	3.07	2.74	2.92	2.92	2.92	2.92	2.92	2.92
Gulf Coast [8]	3.60	3.60	3.60	3.22	3.22	3.22	3.22	3.13	3.13
North, North Central	2.93	2.93	2.93	2.93	2.93	2.93	2.93	2.93	2.87
Panhandle	2.94	2.83	2.83	2.83	2.83	2.83	2.83	2.83	3.12
Southwest [9]	3.12	3.12	3.12	3.12	3.12	3.12	3.12	3.12	2.93
West Central	3.00	2.93	2.93	2.93	2.93	2.83	2.83	2.93	
West:									
Sweet	2.94	2.83	2.83	2.87	2.87	2.93	2.93	2.93	3.00
Intermediate	3.00	2.93	2.93	2.93	2.93	2.93	2.93	2.93	2.93
Sour	2.94	2.79	2.79	2.79	2.79	2.83	2.83	2.83	2.87
Flat Price Crudes	2.11	2.11	2.11	2.21	2.21	2.21	2.21	2.21	2.21
Utah-New Mexico	2.69	2.52	2.67	2.67	2.67	2.50	2.50	2.50	2.67
Wyoming	2.79	2.79	2.79	2.70	2.80	2.80	2.80	2.80	2.85

1 Lowest price posted at the end of each year, exclusive of local port or other governmental charges, sales taxes, etc.
2 Kenai Peninsula.
3 Not available.
4 35-35.9° API.
5 31-31.9° API.
6 28-28.9° API.
7 Flat prices.
8 "Mixed sweet" crude oil.
9 "Sweden" crude oil in Lower Gulf Coast.

Authority: Platt's Oil Price Handbook and Oilmanac.

263

Table A5

U. S. TANK SHIP FLEET (ACTUAL AND T2-SE-A1 EQUIVALENTS) 1900-1958

(Ocean-going Vessels of 2,000 Gross Tons and Over)

Year		Actual Fleet			T2-SE-A1 Equivalents	
	Number	Gross Tons	Deadweight Tons	Average Speed (Knots)	Number	Per Cent of World Total
December 31, 1958	474	5,316,100	8,309,200	15.5	529.5	15.6
December 31, 1957	470	5,097,400	7,959,900	15.4	503.1	16.8
December 31, 1956	477	5,040,700	7,892,700	15.2	493.4	18.9
December 31, 1955	490	5,094,900	7,989,500	15.1	497.4	20.8
December 31, 1954	525	5,376,500	8,446,200	15.0	521.7	23.3
December 31, 1953	550	5,475,800	8,639,800	14.8	525.3	26.2
October 1, 1952	550	5,284,400	8,446,400	14.6	508.3	29.4
April 1, 1951	560	5,363,699	8,520,800	14.6	510.0	33.0
September 1, 1950	559	5,322,698	8,460,700	14.5	505.1	34.4
September 1, 1949	578	5,439,009	8,639,800	14.4	513.2	38.0
January 1, 1949	593	5,656,497	9,016,200	14.1	524.2	41.1
April 1, 1948	621	5,878,786	9,395,500	14.0	541.9	42.9
October 1, 1947	744	6,995,223	11,171,400	14.07	646.4	50.8
January 1, 1947	951	8,784,894	14,035,000	13.86	800.5	62.3
September 1, 1945	907	8,379,542	13,379,143	13.74	756.2	59.8
1945 [1]	780	7,084,022	11,283,652	13.59	630.9	55.9
1944	556	4,784,954	7,608,833	13.12	410.6	45.2
1943	366	2,901,748	4,640,027	12.23	233.5	31.2
1942	389	2,931,193	4,680,863	11.31	217.8	27.4
1941	379	2,824,128	4,498,684	11.13	205.9	25.8
1940	383	2,824,160	4,493,493	10.96	202.6	25.1
1939	393	2,862,119	4,559,148	10.70	200.7	26.7
1938	382	2,745,227	4,364,459	10.55	189.5	27.4
1937	370	2,632,031	4,179,667	10.43	179.4	28.0
1936	371	2,602,600	4,125,181	10.37	176.0	29.1
1935	374	2,612,791	4,139,658	10.36	176.4	30.2
1934	377	2,632,824	4,169,636	10.35	177.6	30.5
1933	380	2,642,378	4,180,246	10.35	178.0	30.7
1932	383	2,659,180	4,204,776	10.35	179.0	31.4
1931	379	2,607,079	4,116,594	10.32	174.7	33.8
1930	371	2,517,126	3,964,648	10.27	167.4	35.8
1929	373	2,509,047	3,948,967	10.26	166.6	37.6
1928	375	2,480,994	3,893,922	10.23	163.9	41.3
1927	381	2,469,530	3,872,237	10.21	162.7	43.8
1926	382	2,461,004	3,855,763	10.21	161.9	45.6
1925	394	2,522,105	3,940,937	10.23	165.9	48.7
1924	400	2,553,929	3,984,812	10.23	167.7	49.8
1923	401	2,556,291	3,988,413	10.22	167.7	51.9
1922	399	2,532,602	3,953,335	10.22	166.1	56.4
1921	314	1,878,026	2,939,758	10.14	122.6	54.4
1920	227	1,316,077	2,071,397	10.09	86.0	47.2
1919	176	983,627	1,556,632	10.02	64.1	42.5
1918	145	774,551	1,221,897	9.89	49.7	38.8
1917	123	606,903	945,024	9.63	37.4	34.8
1916	97	438,272	679,704	9.35	26.1	27.1
1915	61	242,030	367,115	9.81	14.8	15.6
1914	53	197,218	297,503	9.72	11.9	15.5
1913	43	155,122	233,247	9.67	9.3	15.9
1912	37	130,708	197,497	9.55	7.8	15.6
1911	33	118,514	178,642	9.56	7.0	14.1
1910	31	108,865	164,252	9.53	6.4	13.3
1909	31	108,865	164,252	9.53	6.4	14.5
1908	28	92,629	139,322	9.45	5.4	14.6
1907	26	82,359	123,898	9.50	4.8	13.4
1906	25	77,749	117,398	9.50	4.6	13.3
1905	25	77,749	117,398	9.50	4.6	13.5
1904	19	58,014	87,625	9.47	3.4	10.3
1903	12	34,851	52,692	9.42	2.0	7.3
1902	8	21,225	31,795	9.30	1.2	4.9
1901	5	12,434	18,275	9.62	0.7	3.2
1900	3	7,611	10,350	9.67	0.4	2.0

[1] As of January 1, in the years prior to September 1, 1945.

Authority: Statistical Research Department, Sun Oil Company.

U. S. TANK SHIP FLEET (ACTUAL AND T2-SE-A1 EQUIVALENTS), 1958-1966

(Ocean-going Vessels of 2,000 Gross Tons and Over)

Year	Actual Fleet				T2-SE-A1 Equivalents		Year
	Number	Gross Tons	Deadweight Tons	Average Speed (Knots)	Number	Per Cent of World Total	
1966	387	5,343,700	8,549,900	16.1	566.3	8.5	1966
1965	410	5,479,800	8,733,500	16.0	575.8	9.6	1965
1964	422	5,553,400	8,816,300	16.0	579.3	10.6	1964
1963	440	5,631,000	8,912,600	15.9	583.5	12.1	1963
1962	456	5,726,900	9,045,300	15.9	589.8	13.0	1962
1961	469	5,751,400	9,085,300	15.8	590.1	13.7	1961
1960	478	5,664,000	8,894,600	15.7	575.0	14.1	1960
1959	485	5,593,600	8,766,300	15.6	563.0	14.7	1959
1958	474	5,316,100	8,309,200	15.5	529.5	15.6	1958

Authority: Sun Oil Company, "Analysis of World Tank Ship Fleet."

Bibliographical
Essay

THE MAJOR PORTION of this study has been based on primary source materials. Although legal and technical literature about petroleum problems and policies is extensive, there are few historical treatments of the subject.

Manuscripts

Among primary sources, Presidential papers proved rewarding. The Warren G. Harding collection at the Ohio State Historical Society contains valuable letters that indicate that Harding frequently took a stand on public issues and exerted some leadership in public affairs, especially overseas oil diplomacy. On the other hand, the papers of Calvin Coolidge at the Library of Congress in Washington proved extremely disappointing. Relevant correspondence of Herbert Hoover was examined at the Hoover Institution at Stanford University before it was transferred to the Hoover Library at West Branch, Iowa, where a useful collection is being assembled. Much more voluminous were letters of Franklin D. Roosevelt in the Franklin D. Roosevelt Library at Hyde Park, New York. They reflected extreme frankness and were invaluable for many aspects of both domestic and foreign oil policy of the New Deal period. The struggles over oil policy in the Truman era may be followed in part in the Harry S. Truman Papers at the Harry S. Truman Library in Independence, Missouri. Especially valuable for understanding the struggle over the tidelands and the Natural Gas Act of 1950 is the file of Charles F. Murphy, then a Presidential Assistant. The Dwight D. Eisenhower Library in Abilene, Kansas, is processing the former President's papers there and eventually will make materials concerning oil policies available to qualified researchers.

Other individuals who played a part in the formulation of United States oil policy have left manuscript collections that illuminate their roles. A key figure in the formulation of federal conservation policy was George Otis Smith, Director of the United States Geological Survey, 1917–1929. His papers are being deposited in the Western History Center of the University of Wyoming, which is also acquiring the manuscripts of Mark Requa. It is difficult to understand Albert Fall's ideas concerning oil policy without an examination of his correspondence—selected as it may be—in the Library of the University of New Mexico in Albuquerque. An inside view of policy formulation in the Hoover Administration is afforded by an examination of the Ray Lyman Wilbur Papers in the Hoover Institution at Stanford, California, which also contain many of President Hoover's own letters. One might have hoped that oil policy during the Great Depression would be amplified by the papers of former Oklahoma Governor Alfalfa Bill Murray. These are in the Manuscripts Collection of the University of Oklahoma, but unfortunately they are largely worthless. In the same depository are the papers of Senator Elbert Thomas, which are useful in tracing Congressional sentiment on oil problems. Although the Leland Olds collection at the Franklin D. Roosevelt Library in Hyde Park, New York, contains many items of limited value, it does contribute to a fuller understanding of the personality of Olds.

Archival Records

In addition to manuscript collections relating to individuals, some of the most valuable primary sources for United States oil policy are to be found in archives. The executive correspondence of the Secretaries of the Interior, 1890–1964, which I examined at the National Archives in Washington is of most immediate interest. Especially pertinent are the letters of Ray Lyman Wilbur, Hoover's Secretary of the Interior, and the very extensive files that Harold Ickes kept between 1933 and 1945. Many of the materials in the United States Fuel Administration records are of a routine nature, and only a small portion appear to be significant. A more diversified and very rich group of records is that of the Federal Oil Conservation Board, 1924–1933. This agency was fortunate in having as its Secretary, Earl S. Rochester, who systematically collected and preserved the greater portion of its important papers throughout its years of operation. They provide one of the most extensive available groups of manuscript records for tracing the vagaries of United States oil policy during the period. Rochester also maintained an extensive newspaper clipping file concerning the Federal Oil Conservation Board's work, which he retained in nine volumes of scrapbooks.

American oil diplomacy in the 1920's can be traced from an imposing body of records in the National Archives. The Department of State decimal files, which contain diplomatic correspondence regarding Mesopotamia and the Dutch East Indies between 1919 and 1927, are useful as are the records concerning the United States delegation at the Lausanne Conference in 1922 and 1923. Since the Bureau of Foreign and Domestic Commerce in the Department of Commerce was extremely active during the 1920's in encouraging American capitalists to invest overseas, its correspondence with businessmen and government officials concerning oil opportunities in Mesopotamia and the Dutch East Indies is invaluable.

The National Archives are also rich in holdings relating to United States oil policy in the New Deal period. Records of the National Recovery Administration contain the hearings on the proposed oil code and related correspondence. In addition, materials of the Petroleum Administrative Board reflect on the administration of the Oil Code, as do records of the Petroleum Labor Policy Board and the Federal Tender Board.

To understand the mobilization of the oil industry during World War II, it is essential to examine the manuscripts of the Petroleum Coordinator for Defense, and the Petroleum Administrator for War, which are deposited in the National Archives, where they have not as yet been fully declassified. But available correspondence is helpful in conveying the immediacy of special oil problems created by the war. These records also reveal bitter policy conflicts within the Roosevelt Administration during the war, particularly between Harold Ickes and the Office of Price Administration. No account of United States oil diplomacy in World War II can ignore the Petroleum Reserves Corporation, but unfortunately in 1965 its records were still classified and not available to researchers. On the other hand, materials relating to the Petroleum Administration for Defense, which operated during the Korean war, are available at the National Archives in Washington, D.C.

The minutes of the National Petroleum Council clearly outline the interplay between industry and federal officials in the formulation of national oil policies. The National Archives contain the records for the five years after 1945; for the subsequent period they can be examined in the Office of Oil and Gas in the United States Department of the Interior.

Newspapers

The daily press illuminates most phases of United States oil policy. For general coverage the New York *Times,* the Washington *Post,* the *U. S. Daily, Christian Science Monitor,* New York *World,* and the *Wall Street Journal* provided excellent guidance. Newspapers in the oil regions often provide intensive coverage of particular problems. In the Southwest the Tulsa *World,* the Tulsa *Tribune,* the Oklahoma City *News,* and the Oklahoma City *Times* are thorough and detailed. The Dallas *Morning News,* and Fort Worth *Star Telegram* are less thorough in covering Texas problems. In the Far West the Los Angeles *Times* and the Denver *Post* displayed a consistent interest in petroleum problems and policies.

Periodicals

Trade periodicals are indispensable for an understanding of the growth of the cooperative spirit between the oil industry and government. They are also most revealing for attitudes of various segments of the industry. Perhaps the outstanding oil industry spokesman was the *Oil and Gas Journal*, consistently informative and thorough. The *National Petroleum News* was hardly less important in expressing industry views. On particular issues *Oildom, Oil Trade, Inland Oil Index* and *Petroleum World* were suggestive. The *Transactions* of the American Society of Mining and Metallurgical Engineers often give accurate expression to the views of scientists and technicians concerning oil problems and policies. General business sentiment as it affected oil policy can be gleaned in part through *The Nation's Business* and the *Literary Digest*.

Government Documents

Federal documents also trace the growing cooperation between government and business. The annual reports of the Departments of the Interior, Navy, Commerce, and Justice, the Federal Trade Commission, and the Federal Power Commission are particularly relevant to oil policy. Some publications of the United States Bureau of Corporations between 1903 and 1912 bear directly on the petroleum industry, including its *Report of the Commissioner of Corporations on the Transportation of Petroleum,* May 2, 1906 (Washington, 1906), and its *Report of the Commissioner of Corporations on the Petroleum Industry* (3 vols., Washington, 1907–1909). These are essential to examination of anti-monopoly sentiment during the Progressive period. The Federal Trade Commission made several investigations of the oil industry. See U. S. Federal Trade Commission, *Investigation of the Price of Gasoline,* April, 1916 (Washington, 1916). "Advance in the Price of Petroleum Products," in 66 Cong., 2 sess., *House Doc.* No. 801 (Washington, 1920); *Report of the Federal Trade Commission on Foreign Ownership in the Petroleum Industry,* February 12, 1923 (Washington, 1923); "Petroleum Industry, Prices, Profits, and Competition," in 70 Cong., 1 sess., *Senate Doc.* No. 61 (Washington, 1928); U. S. Federal Trade Commission, *The International Petroleum Cartel,* 82 Cong., 2 sess. (Washington, 1952). U.S. Interstate Commerce Commission, *Report of Investigation of Railroad Discriminations and Monopolies of Oil,* January 28, 1907, in 59 Cong., 2 sess., *House Doc.* No. 606 (Washington, 1907) is relevant to the Roosevelt-Taft era.

Congressional hearings often reveal motivation in formulation of national policy. Problems involving the depletion allowance are discussed in 69

Cong., 1 sess., Senate, Committee on Finance, *Hearings on Revenue Act of 1926* (Washington, 1927) and 69 Cong., 1 sess., Select Committee on Investigation of the Bureau of Internal Revenue, *Report,* Part II in *Senate Reports* No. 27 (Washington, 1926), based on its *Hearings on Senate Resolution 168,* 1924–1926 (Washington, 1926), Vols. II–VIII. Oil import problems during the Great Depression are aired in 71 Cong., 3 sess., Senate, Committee on Interstate and Foreign Commerce, "Hearings on Regulating the Importation of Petroleum and Related Products" (Washington, 1931).

The controversy surrounding Teapot Dome and the naval oil reserves is brought out in 68 Cong., 1 sess., "Leases Upon Naval Oil Reserves," *Senate Report* No. 794, 3 vols. (Washington, 1924). During the New Deal era, motivation for framing of an oil code is seen in 73 Cong., 1 sess., House, Committee on Ways and Means, *Hearings on National Industrial Recovery* (Washington, 1933) and 73 Cong., 1 sess., Senate, Committee on Finance, *Hearings on National Industrial Recovery* (Washington, 1933). The very extensive investigation of the Cole Committee is contained in 73 Cong., 1 sess., House, Committee on Interstate and Foreign Commerce, Subcommittee on Petroleum Investigation, *Hearings on House Resolution 441* (5 parts, Washington, 1935). See also U. S. National Recovery Administration, *Hearings on Proposed Oil Code* (No. 10), National Archives (microfilm), and U. S. National Recovery Administration, *Codes of Fair Competition* (Petroleum) (Washington, 1933). The antitrust phase of the New Deal is illuminated by the hearings of the Temporary National Economic Committee, U. S. Temporary National Economic Committee, *Hearings Before TNEC* (84 vols., Washington, 1941–1945). National defense and wartime conflicts are crystallized in 76 Cong., 1 sess., House, Committee on Interstate and Foreign Commerce, *Hearings Before Subcommittee on H.R. 7372 and H.R. 290,* 5 parts (Washington, 1939–1940), 78 Cong., 2 sess., Senate, Special Committee Investigating the National Defense Program, *Senate Report* No. 10 (Washington, 1944). For the O'Mahoney Committee's findings see 79 Cong., 2 sess., Senate, Special Committee Investigating Petroleum Resources (O'Mahoney Committee), *Hearings,* 1945–1946 (5 parts, Washington, 1945–1946); 79 Cong., 1 sess., Senate, Special Committee Investigating Petroleum Resources pursuant to Senate Resolution 36, *Senate Reports* No. 179 (Washington, 1945). In the post-war era U. S. President's Materials Policy Commission, *Resources for Freedom* (5 parts, Washington, 1952) and *Report of the President's Cabinet Committee on Minerals Policy* (Washington, 1954), reveal trends in national resource policy.

From 1917 on, diplomatic phases of U. S. oil policy are partly revealed in the compilation of State Department correspondence, U. S. Dept. of State, *Papers Relating to the Foreign Relations of the United States* (Washington, 1918–   ). Especially useful for World War II is 79 Cong., 1 sess., Senate, Committee on Foreign Relations, *Report on Anglo-American Oil Agreement* (Washington, 1947), 80 Cong., 1 sess., Senate, Special Committee Investigating the National Defense Program, *Hearings-Petroleum Arrangements with Saudi Arabia* (Washington, 1948), and 80 Cong., 1 sess., Senate, Committee on Foreign Relations, *Hearings on Petroleum Agreement with Great Britain and Northern Ireland* [June 2–25, 1947] (Washington, 1947).

State documents that are of use include Oklahoma Corporation Commission, *Report* 1907–   (Oklahoma City, 1907–   ), and *Transcript of Proceedings of Interstate Oil Compact* (Dallas, 1935) as well as the informative quarterly reports of the Interstate Oil Compact Commission since 1935. See also U. S. Attorney General, *Second Report of the* [U. S.] *Attorney-General Pursuant to Section 2 of the Joint Resolution of July 28, 1955, Consenting to an Interstate Compact to Conserve Oil and Gas* (4 parts, Washington, 1958).

Public policy in relation to the natural gas industry can be traced in 74 Cong., 1 sess., House, Committee on Interstate and Foreign Commerce, *Hearings on the Public Utility Act of 1935* (H. R. 5423), 74 Cong., 2 sess., House, Sub-Committee of Committee on Interstate and Foreign Commerce, *Hearings on H.R. 11662* (Washington, 1936) and 75 Cong., 3 sess., House, Judiciary Committee, *Hearings on Senate Joint Resolution 208* (Washington, 1938). The post-World War II struggles are touched upon in 80 Cong., 2 sess., Judiciary Committees, House and Senate, *Joint Hearings on S. 1988* (Washington, 1948), 81 Cong., 1 sess., Senate, Sub-Committee of Committee on Interstate and Foreign Commerce, *Hearings on Reappointment of Leland Olds to Federal Power Commission* (Washington, 1949), 81 Cong., 1 sess., House, Sub-Committee of Committee on Interstate and Foreign Commerce *Hearings on S. 1498* (Washington, 1949) and 82 Cong., 2 sess., Senate, Sub-Committee of Committee on Interstate and Foreign Commerce, *Hearings on Nomination of Thomas C. Buchanan to the Federal Power Commission* (Washington, 1952). The Federal Power Commission's *Natural Gas Investigation* (Docket G–580), *Report of Commissioner Nelson Lee Smith and Commissioner Harrington Wimberley* (Washington, 1948), and *Report of Commissioner Leland Olds and Commissioner Claude L. Draper* (Washington, 1948), are indispensible. See also the Federal Power Commission, *The First Five Years Under the Natural Gas Act* (Washington, 1944).

Secondary Works

General

Among works that provide general background about development of the American petroleum industry, Harold Williamson *et al.*, *The American Petroleum Industry* (2 vols., Evanston, 1959–63) is the most recent. One must use it with caution because of numerous errors of detail and a heavy dependence on business sources, to the exclusion of other materials. Important to an understanding of changes in the industry's problems is

John G. McLean and Robert W. Haig, *The Growth of Integrated Oil Companies* (Cambridge, 1954). Joe S. Bain, *The Economics of the Pacific Coast Petroleum Industry* (3 vols., Berkeley, 1944–45), although it is an economic analysis, has some relevant historical chapters. Carl Coke Rister, *Oil-Titan of the Southwest* (Norman, 1949) and J. S. Spratt, *The Road to Spindletop: Economic Change in Texas, 1875–1901* (Dallas, 1955) describe oil discoveries in the Southwest. The well researched volumes concerning the history of the Standard oil companies are indispensable. Pace-setters were Ralph and Muriel Hidy, *Pioneering in Big Business, 1882–1911* (New York, 1955), and George S. Gibb and Evelyn H. Knowlton, *The Resurgent Years, 1911–1927* (New York, 1956) [Standard Oil Company of New Jersey]. Also significant are Paul H. Giddens, *Standard Oil Company (Indiana)* (New York, 1955), Kendall Beaton, *Enterprise in Oil: A History of Shell* (New York, 1957), and Henrietta M. Larson and Kenneth W. Porter, *History of Humble Oil and Refining Company* (New York, 1959).

Most discussions of United States oil policy do not tend to be historical, or focus on a short time span. The most reliable standard work on the subject for many years has been John Ise, *The United States Oil Policy* (New Haven, 1926), and this book is an exception to the rule. Less incisive and primarily descriptive is Erich W. Zimmerman, *Conservation in the Production of Petroleum* (New Haven, 1957), which is largely a summary and paraphrasing of *Legal History of Gas and Oil* (Chicago, 1938). This book, plus its two successors, Blakely M. Murphy (ed.), *Conservation of Oil and Gas: A Legal History, 1948* (Chicago, 1949) and Blakely Murphy (ed.) *Conservation of Oil and Gas, 1948–58* (Chicago, 1958), are three very useful volumes focusing on legal issues. The lawyer's approach is reflected in Robert E. Hardwicke, *Antitrust Laws, et al. v. Unit Operation of Oil or Gas Pools* (rev. ed., Dallas, 1961). Many journalists and publicists have also been attracted to petroleum problems. *The Politics of Oil* (New York, 1961) by Robert Engler is among the more recent of this genre. Surprisingly, studies of oil problems and policies in the states are virtually nonexistent. Nor has this field attracted writers of theses or dissertations at universities in Oklahoma, Texas, California, Louisiana, or elsewhere. An excellent scholarly account of state policy is in Leonard M. Logan, *The Stabilization of the Petroleum Industry* (Norman, 1930), which emphasizes problems in Oklahoma; Gerald D. Nash, *State Government and Economic Development* (Berkeley, 1964), surveys California.

An unfortunate dearth of reminiscences and biographies hampers the serious student of United States oil policy. The literature in the field needs detailed biographies of men important in industry and government such as Henry L. Doherty, Mark Requa, George O. Smith, Harry Sinclair, J. Howard Pew, Ray Lyman Wilbur, E. O. Thompson, and others. The Western History Research Center at the University of Wyoming is now gathering the papers of Requa and Smith. Among the more useful published reminiscences is *The Cabinet Diaries of Josephus Daniels,* edited by E. David Cronon (Lincoln, 1963). These papers are important for the World War I era, as are Anne W. Lane and Louise H. Wall (eds.), *The Letters of Franklin K. Lane* (New York, 1922). William H. (Alfalfa Bill) Murray, *Memoirs of Governor Murray and True History of Oklahoma* (3 vols., Boston, 1945), touches on the plight of Oklahoma during the Great Depression. Samuel I. Rosenman (ed.), *The Public Papers and Addresses of Franklin Delano Roosevelt* (13 vols., New York, 1938–1950), is a standard source, and Harold Ickes, *The Secret Diary of Harold Ickes* (3 vols., New York, 1953–54), is essential for the New Deal era. His *Fightin' Oil* (New York, 1943), an account of his policies during World War II, is disappointing. Bruce K. Brown, *Oilmen in Washington: An Informal Account of the Organization and Activities of the Petroleum Administration for Defense During the Korean War, 1950–1952* (n. p., 1965), is informative. More ephemeral in respect to oil policy are Ray Lyman Wilbur, *Memoirs of Ray Lyman Wilbur 1875–1949*, edited by E. E. Robinson and Paul C. Edwards (Stanford, 1960), and Bernard Baruch, *The Public Years* (New York, 1960). J. Howard Smith, *And Then They Indicted Me* (New York, 1936), is a diatribe against the New Deal. Hugh S. Johnson, *The Blue Eagle, from Egg to Earth* (Garden City, 1935) is a defense of the NRA; Cordell Hull, *The Memoirs of Cordell Hull* (2 vols., New York, 1948) touches upon wartime policies. Harry S. Truman, *Memoirs* (2 vols., Garden City, 1955–56), gives scant attention to petroleum.

Progressive Era, 1890–1917

In addition to the general works cited, there is a particularly valuable study by Arthur M. Johnson, *The Development of American Petroleum Pipelines: A Study in Private Enterprise and Public Policy, 1862–1906* (Ithaca, 1956), and the essays in *Oil's First Century* (Cambridge, 1960). Ida Tarbell's *History of the Standard Oil Company* (New York, 1904) provides contemporary criticisms of monopoly. John A. DeNovo discusses the Navy's dilemma in "Petroleum and the United States Navy Before World War I," in *Mississippi Valley Historical Review*, XLI (March 1955), 641–49, and J. Leonard Bates traces the development of conservation sentiment in "Fulfilling American Democracy: The Conservation Movement, 1907 to 1921," in *Mississippi Valley Historical Review*, XLI (June 1955), 46–54.

World War I

A comprehensive account of the role of petroleum in America's war effort during 1917–1918 still needs to be written. The fullest account is a chapter in Williamson *et al.*, *The American Petroleum Industry*, II. Grosvenor Clarkson, *Industrial America and the World War* (Boston, 1923) largely neglects oil. Walker D. Hines, *War History of American Railroads* (New Haven, 1928) only touches lightly on problems of oil transportation. J.

Leonard Bates, "Josephus Daniels and the Naval Oil Reserves," *Proceedings of the United States Naval Institute,* LXXXIX (February 1953), 302–23 discusses the adamant stance of Daniels in advocating federal control over the Navy's oil reserves.

The Harding-Coolidge Years

Unfortunately, analysis of domestic oil policy in the post-World-War-I period has been largely ignored. On the other hand, the Teapot Dome episode has received much attention. J. Leonard Bates, *The Origins of Teapot Dome* (Urbana, 1963) is a thorough account of the legislative evolution of the Mineral Lands Leasing Act of 1920. Burl Noggle, *Teapot Dome: Oil and Politics in the 1920's* (Baton Rouge, 1962) incisively discusses the political aspects of the affair. A more popular work about the political scandal is M. R. Werner and John Starr, *Teapot Dome* (New York, 1959). The introduction by David H. Stratton (ed.) to *The Memoirs of Albert B. Fall,* University of Texas at El Paso Monograph No. 15 (El Paso, 1966) is suggestive. J. Leonard Bates, "The Teapot Dome Scandal and the Election of 1924," *American Historical Review,* XL (January 1955), 302–22 discusses the political effects of the scandal.

Many aspects of United States oil diplomacy in the decade after 1919 remain to be explored. Various contemporary journalists have written on the international aspects of the worldwide struggle for oil, the best of which include Ludwell Denny, *We Fight for Oil* (New York, 1928), and the very competent study by Benjamin Shwadran, *The Middle East, Oil, and the Great Powers* (New York, 1955). American-Dutch diplomatic relations have been virtually ignored, and the many facets of United States oil diplomacy in the Middle East between 1919 and 1929 have not been fully explored. The diplomacy of Charles Evans Hughes, which deserves to be examined in detail, is hardly mentioned by Merlo Pusey, *Charles Evans Hughes* (2 vols., New York, 1963). Betty Glad, *Diplomatic Policies of Charles Evans Hughes and the Illusions of Innocence: A Study in American Diplomacy* (Urbana, 1966), dwells on intellectual orientation. Samuel Flagg Bemis (ed.), *The American Secretaries of State and their Diplomacy* is useful for general orientation, but space limitations do not allow it to explore the Hughes policies in detail. Similarly, United States oil policy toward Latin America has not been investigated in depth. An informative work not specifically directed towards American policy is Edwin Lieuwen, *Petroleum in Venezuela* (Berkeley, 1953). Since the expropriation of American oil companies from Mexico occasioned a great deal of controversy and discussion, one could expect detailed studies of this event, but the literature concerning it is surprisingly fragmentary. Howard F. Cline, *The United States and Mexico* (Cambridge, 1953) only briefly touches on oil problems, and Roscoe B. Gaither, *Expropriation in Mexico: The Facts and the Law* (New York, 1940) is a short contemporary commentary.

Oil Policy in the Depression, 1929–1939

Intensive studies of most phases of the Hoover policies still need to be made. The extremely favorable impressions conveyed by Ray Lyman Wilbur and Arthur M. Hyde, *The Hoover Policies* (New York, 1937) are highly subjective estimates compiled by Hoover's close associates. Neither Harris G. Warren, *Herbert Hoover and the Great Depression* (New York, 1959), nor Albert Romasco, *Poverty of Abundance: Hoover, the Nation, the Depression* (New York, 1965), delve into Hoover's petroleum policies.

The most intensive study of one aspect of New Deal petroleum policies is by Renée de Visme Williamson, *The Politics of Planning in the Oil Industry Under the Code* (New York, 1936). An informative contemporary account is by Myron W. Watkins, *Oil-Stabilization or Conservation?* (New York, 1937). Less objective is William J. Kemnitzer, *The Rebirth of Monopoly* (New York, 1938). Most phases of New Deal petroleum policies still invite closer examination. It would be instructive to have econometric analyses of production and distribution trends, since these were affected by public policies, by Section 7(a), by the development of the Interstate Oil Compact, and by the antitrust phase after 1937. On the latter, Ellis W. Hawley, *The New Deal and the Problem of Monopoly* (Princeton, 1966) is informative. A brief account is in Blakely Murphy (ed.), *Legal History of Oil and Gas, 1948*. Otherwise, contemporary periodical literature must be consulted, of which "Mamma Spank: 18 Major Oil Companies Indicted," *Time* XXX (October 18, 1937), 63, is typical. The Interstate Oil Compact Commission published an interesting history of its origins, *The Compact's Formative Years, 1931–1935* (Oklahoma City, 1954), which deserves to be consulted.

World War II

The World-War-II period still beckons for innumerable historical studies of public economic policies. An effort to chronicle salient events pertaining to petroleum has been made by John W. Frey and H. Chandler Ide, *A History of the Petroleum Administration for War* (Washington, 1946), a compilation of reports by the staff of the Petroleum Administration for War. Harold Ickes in *Fightin' Oil* (New York, 1943) discusses some of his policies in the Petroleum Administration for War. The realm of United States oil diplomacy between 1941 and 1945 also requires closer attention. Broad general studies that are relevant include Leonard M. Fanning, *American Oil Operations Abroad* (New York, 1947), and a fine short contemporary account by Herbert Feis, *Petroleum and American Foreign Policy* (Stanford, 1944). Reference should again be made to informative Congressional hearings on the World-War-II oil program, including those of the Truman Committee, 78 Cong., 2 sess., Senate, Special Committee Investigating the National Defense Program, *Report* No. 10 (Washington, 1944) and those of the O'Mahoney Committee, 79 Cong., 2 sess., Senate, Special

Committee Investigating Petroleum Resources, *Hearings,* 1945–1946 (5 vols., Washington, 1945–1946).

Truman and Eisenhower Policies

Scholarly studies of the Truman and Eisenhower Administrations are just beginning to appear and thus the number of secondary works that can provide guidance to the study of federal oil policies during these years are still few. On the tidelands issue Ernest R. Bartley, *The Tidelands Oil Controversy* (Austin, 1953) is a good guide. The short analysis of John H. Lichtblau, *The Oil Depletion Issue* (New York, 1959) is the only effort to provide a historical account.

Natural Gas

Although the legal and technical literature on natural gas and its public regulation is large, little has been written concerning historical development. Some understanding can be gleaned from Ralph K. Huitt, "National Regulation of the Natural Gas Industry," in Emmette S. Redford (ed.), *Public Administration and Policy Formation* (Austin, 1956). Less historical are Leslie J. Cookenboo, *Competition in the Field Market for Natural Gas,* Rice Institute, *Pamphlets,* vol. XLIV (Houston, 1958), no. 4, and Paul W. McAvoy, *Price Formation in Natural Gas Fields* (New Haven, 1962).

Comprehensive historical analysis of state regulation of natural gas is lacking. Clyde O. Ruggles, *Aspects of the Organization, Functions, and Financing of State Public Utility Commissions* (Cambridge, Mass., 1937) presents a generalized discussion, and Charles E. Crenshaw, "The Regulation of Natural Gas," *Law and Contemporary Problems,* XIX (Fall 1954), 336–52 discusses contemporary issues involving state and federal jurisdiction. This issue of *Law and Contemporary Problems* was entirely devoted to examining public policy towards the natural gas industry. Background is provided by C. Emery Troxel, "Regulation of Interstate Movements of Natural Gas," *Journal of Land and Public Utility Economics,* XIII (February 1937), 20–30, and his "Some Problems in State Regulation of Natural Gas Utilities," *ibid.,* XIII (May 1937), 188–203.

Index